High Performance Memory Systems

Springer
New York
Berlin
Heidelberg
Hong Kong
London
Milan
Paris
Tokyo

Haldun Hadimioglu David Kaeli
Jeffrey Kuskin Ashwini Nanda
Josep Torrellas
Editors

High Performance Memory Systems

With 115 Figures

Springer

Haldun Hadimioglu
Dept. of Computer and Information Science
Polytechnic University
Brooklyn, NY
USA

David Kaeli
Dept. of Electrical and Computer Engineering
Northeastern University
Boston, MA
USA

Jeffrey Kuskin
Atheros Communications, Inc.
Sunnyvale, CA
USA

Ashwini Nanda
IBM TJ Watson Research Ctr.
Yorktown Heights, NY
USA

Josep Torrellas
Dept. of Computer Science
University of Illinois
Urbana, IL
USA

Library of Congress Cataloging-in-Publication Data
High performance memory systems / Haldun Hadimioglu . . . [et al.].
p. cm.
ISBN 0-387-00310-X (alk. paper)
1. Computer storage devices. I. Hadimioglu, Haldun.
TK7895.M4.H52 2003
004.5—dc21 2003050492

ISBN 0-387-00310-X Printed on acid-free paper.

Printed in the United States of America.

9 8 7 6 5 4 3 2 1 SPIN 10906170

www.springer-ny.com

Springer-Verlag New York Berlin Heidelberg
A member of BertelsmannSpringer Science+Business Media GmbH

Preface

The State of Memory Technology

Over the past decade there has been rapid growth in the speed of microprocessors. CPU speeds are approximately doubling every eighteen months, while main memory speed doubles about every ten years. The International Technology Roadmap for Semiconductors (ITRS) study suggests that memory will remain on its current growth path. The ITRS short- and long-term targets indicate continued *scaling* improvements at about the current rate by 2016. This translates to bit densities increasing at two times every two years until the introduction of 8 gigabit dynamic random access memory (DRAM) chips, after which densities will increase four times every five years.

A similar growth pattern is forecast for other high-density chip areas and high-performance logic (e.g., microprocessors and application specific integrated circuits (ASICs)). In the future, molecular devices, 64 gigabit DRAMs and 28 GHz clock signals are targeted. Although densities continue to grow, we still do not see significant advances that will improve memory speed. These trends have created a problem that has been labeled the *Memory Wall* or *Memory Gap.*

Book Overview

In 2000, a workshop was held at the International Symposium on Computer Architecture on the topic of Solving the Memory Wall. The workshop was continued in 2001 and 2002, combining with the Scalable Shared Memory Workshop to address a wider range of memory performance issues. Some of the ideas presented in these workshops have been included in this book. This book provides a range of different research approaches to address the growing disparity between CPU and memory speed. This book discusses the subject of high performance memory systems from five different perspectives:

1. Coherence, synchronization and allocation
2. Power-aware, reliable and reconfigurable memory
3. Software-based memory tuning
4. Architecture-based memory tuning
5. Workload considerations

Intended Audience

The target audience for this book includes readers from both industry and academia. This book could easily be used as the basis for an advanced course on High Performance Memory Systems. We also expect that a computer engineer or computer scientist would pick up this book to begin to understand the causes of the *Memory Wall*, and to propose some solutions. We expect this topic to grow in importance as the gap between memory and CPU continues to grow.

Because the editors of this book come from both academia and industry, we have included both practical and theoretical issues that reflect the range of approaches currently under study. We hope that you enjoy this book, and we welcome feedback from our readers.

Acknowledgements

We would like to thank the many chapter authors who spent many hours preparing their contributions. We would also like to acknowledge the help of Frank Ganz for his LaTeX editing advice, Antonio Orrantia for his copy editing and of course our Springer-Verlag editors, Wayne Wheeler and Wayne Yuhasz.

Haldun Hadimioglu Polytechnic University
David Kaeli Northeastern Universty
Jeffrey Kuskin Atheros Systems
Ashwini Nanda IBM T.J. Watson Research Center
Josep Torrellas University of Illinois

Contents

1

Introduction to High-Performance Memory Systems

Haldun Hadimioglu[1], David Kaeli[2], Jeffrey Kuskin[3], Ashwini Nanda[4], and Josep Torrellas[5]

[1] Department of Computer and Information Science, Polytechnic University, Brooklyn, NY, USA haldun@poly.photon.edu
[2] Department of Electrical and Computer Engineering Northeastern University, Boston, MA, USA kaeli@ece.neu.edu
[3] Atheros Communications, Sunnyvale, CA, USA jsk@atheros.com
[4] IBM T.J. Watson Research Center, Yorktown Heights, NY, USA ashwini@watson.ibm.com
[5] Computer Science Department, University of Illinois, Urbana, IL, USA torrellas@cs.uiuc.edu

Abstract. We begin this book by providing the reader with an overview of the five perspectives of High Performance Memory Systems that are presented in this book.

1.1 Coherence, Synchronization, and Allocation

Processor designers have long had to cope with the *CPU-memory gap* - the increasingly large disparity between the memory latency and bandwidth required to execute instructions efficiently versus the latency and bandwidth the external memory system can actually deliver. Cache memories have been used to help mitigate the impact of this growing performance gap. Caches can be effectively exploited in both uniprocessor and multiprocessor systems. Key issues that can dramatically affect the design and performance of cache-based memory hierarchies include memory consistency and cache coherency. These issues are critical to producing the correct execution of memory accesses in a multiprocessor environment.

Memory consistency provides a contract between hardware and software that describes how ordering of memory accesses will be enforced. When an access is made to a shared memory location, some form of synchronization is necessary to guarantee private access to a memory location. Once an ordering of accesses can be enforced, we can provide a specification that documents the requirements of a system that supports the consistency model.

Memory coherency enforces the notion that there can only be one valid version of a memory address at any point in time. While there may be replicas of a single address stored in local caches, the value stored should be the same (unless speculation is being used). Coherency protocols are used to manage access to shared memory across a number of processes. In the first two contributions in this section, we look at advances in synchronization and coherency mechanisms to help accelerate memory performance.

The first chapter shows how to exploit advances in the area of multithreading, developing a fine-grained threaded design to explore using speculative locking. If we can successfully obtain a lock speculatively most of the time, and no conflicting accesses have been detected, large performance gains can be realized.

The second chapter looks at adding an additional hardware context to support dynamic verification of the cache coherency protocol. This chapter looks at the overhead associated with developing a fault-tolerant coherence verification scheme. The authors suggest that a distributed implementation is needed to help alleviate the scaling issues related to a centralized implementation. The impact upon performance of the proposed distributed checker is negligible.

In the third contribution in this section we look at improving the uniprocessor performance by introducing a new cache allocation strategy. When memory addresses alias into common locations in a cache, an entry may need to be replaced to make room for new addresses. But the question is which entry should be replaced? This chapter presents the design of a buffering mechanism that sits in front of the level-1 cache. This mechanism utilizes a novel time-stamp-based allocation algorithm to decide which entries will be replaced in the cache. A number of different allocation strategies are discussed and evaluated.

1.2 Power-Aware, Reliable, and Reconfigurable Memory

There is presently a focus on improving memory performance while also considering cost, power and functionality. These tradeoffs have motivated new memory design approaches, such as logic-in-memory, reconfigurable memory, systems-on-a-chip (SoC), non-volatile systems and mixed-logic designs.

Memory power consumption is expected to increase in spite of reduced on-chip voltage levels. Higher clock frequencies are a major cause of increased power consumption. The dynamic power dissipation, as opposed to the static dissipation, has been the dominant component of the total power consumption. Dynamic power dissipation arises from switching. Dynamic power consumption is expected to gradually become less of an issue as voltage levels are lowered. However, the static power dissipation component due to higher static leakage current is expected to continue to increase and will eventually dominate the overall power consumption. A peculiar point about the static dissipation is that it is independent of the rate of the operation. Transistor device characteristics and the number of devices determine the amount of the dissipation. There is now increased pressure on DRAM and cache memory designers who are looking at higher bit densities while considering static leakage current.

The ability to mix memory and logic on the same chip is due to semiconductor advances. While this approach was earlier considered to be infeasible because of issues related to different process technologies, a mixed approach is now considered a possibility. Today, mixing implies the inclusion of logic structures in memory circuits. But increased usage of memory-based structures in logic circuits can also be considered mixing. The first class of mixed logic includes processor-in-memory (PIM) and embedded-DRAM (eDRAM) designs. These chips are attractive since they lead to single-chip solutions with better power, size, weight, and reliability. Logic circuitry in memory can be used to implement reconfigurability, which in turn enables us to tune memory for different applications. Adding logic to a memory circuit offers high bandwidth and low latency rates for processing on the chip, leading to high-performance, more flexible, cheaper, less power-consuming products.

The first two chapters in this section aim at reducing cache memory power consumption. The Power Efficient Cache Coherence chapter presents an analysis of reduced speculative snoopy cache coherence implementations. The work shows that serial snooping in the case of load misses is responsible for a significant portion of cache miss latency, though there are considerable power savings compared with using speculative and directory-based protocols. The second chapter Improving Power Efficiency with an Asymmetric Set-Associative Cache proposes a set-associative cache memory where cache ways are of different lengths. While the performance is similar, the power consumption is reduced significantly compared with traditional caches of equivalent size.

The last two chapters focus on new applications of memory and logic. Memory Issues in Hardware-Supported Software Safety explores run-time hardware pointer checking for increased reliability and security. A software-accessible Hardware Accelerated Hash Table monitors pointers and a Hardware Reduction Queue combines redundant pointer checks at runtime to provide considerable speedups. The fourth chapter in this section, titled Reconfigurable Memory Module in the RAMP System for Stream Processing, presents a logic-in-memory module solution called RAMP. This system targets applications such as image processing, digital filtering, and color conversion. By mixing RAM and logic in a cluster-based, multilayered-interconnection scheme, the memory module becomes reconfigurable.

1.3 Software-Based Memory Tuning

Instead of developing customized hardware for memory performance enhancing algorithms or caches, we can instead develop software-based mechanisms that can enable an application to better utilize the available memory system.

Software has the property of being able to adapt to the specifics of the underlying hardware. Hardware fixes functionality into logic, whereas software can be changed based on the needs of an application.

Software-based mechanisms can be applied during compilation or at runtime. There have been many compile-time techniques proposed that attempt to improve the spatial and temporal locality of code and data. Most of these techniques attempt to map code or data structures to the first-level cache. Many consider the internal organization of the cache (line size, associativity, and cache size).

Software-based tuning can also be applied to accelerate applications during execution. Typically this form of optimization involves interaction with or modification to the operating system. By working with an application at runtime, we can adapt to changes in behavior of the application. Applications may possess phased behavior, where an application may exhibit a range of characteristic patterns. Dynamic optimization techniques can dynamically detect and react to these changes.

Another area where software-based tuning can be utilizéd is to support parallel processing. Parallelism has been shown to be an effective mechanism to hide memory latency. We can provide software-based techniques for managing memory during speculation to further exploit the parallel resources available.

This section presents four chapters that utilize software-based mechanisms to improve memory latency. The first chapter presents a combined hardware/software approach to implement dynamic memory compression. Poff et al. describe the Memory Expansion Technology (MXT) that has been developed at IBM. The chapter discusses the changes to Linux- and Windows-based operating systems necessary to support MXT. Using this mechanism, a 2:1 compression ratio is achieved.

The second contribution presents a hardware/software approach to remedy cache aliasing of pointer-based data structures. Yardimci and Kaeli describe a technique that utilizes hardware profile guidance to guide a *smart* heap allocator. The mechanism described attempts to avoid cache collisions between temporally local heap-based data structures. The profiling system monitors the state of the program stack in order to identify the current program state. A new memory allocator is developed and the authors present actual program execution time improvements using their Profile-Tuned Heap Access algorithm.

Genius et al. present an alternative approach to avoiding cache collisions for array-based data structures. They propose a technique that *merges* arrays that exhibit temporal locality. The goal is to obtain better page placement, improving the effectiveness of the translation lookaside buffer. The authors describe a compiler-based implementation that obtains significant speedups, especially for stencil-based access patterns.

The last chapter in this section presents a technique to support speculative parallelization. Speculative parallel execution poses significant changes to the memory system design and especially the cache hierarchy. There can be multiple values of a single variable generated at any time that will be stored in different caches. Only the committed value should be written to memory, and the other versions need to be discarded. This chapter describes a software logging structure that manages multiple versions of a variable in a multiprocessor caching system.

1.4 Architecture-Based Memory Tuning

With current superscalar CPU core clock rates in the gigahertz range and external memory latencies of tens of nanoseconds, every external fetch leads to a loss of hundreds of instruction issue slots. Bandwidth, too, has become a problem. Even with just a single 32-bit load/store unit, a CPU potentially can require several tens of gigabytes per second of memory bandwidth to avoid stalls due to load data being unavailable when needed. Latency and bandwidth effects interact as well, with long latencies leading to multiple, concurrent outstanding memory requests and a corresponding burstiness in the memory system usage.

As CPU clock rates have continued to increase, the performance loss caused by these effects has increased as well, to the point at which it is often the primary governor of CPU and overall system performance. Previously, designers tended to address the CPU-memory gap by adding larger and deeper cache hierarchies, initially with just the first level on-chip, and now with several cache levels on-chip or very closely coupled to the CPU die. However, as the incremental performance benefit of larger and deeper cache hierarchies has decreased, researchers and designers have started to explore (and implement) other techniques to tolerate and ameliorate the CPU-memory gap.

In addition to the CPU-memory gap, processor power dissipation also has become a serious issue. At the high end, modern CPUs dissipate well over 100 watts, even as transistor geometries and supply voltages have been reduced, making CPU and overall system cooling a challenge. At the low end, power has become important, too, with more and more portable and embedded devices including processors. For these systems, the primary focus is not so much on absolute performance but on balancing the competing demands of lower power consumption and performance.

The chapters in this section explore architectural techniques, as opposed to circuit or fabrication techniques, for reducing the effects of the CPU-memory performance gap as well as for balancing power consumption and performance. The techniques include both those that focus on using the cache hierarchy more efficiently as well as those that explore other areas in which the impact of the CPU-memory gap can be reduced.

In An Analysis of Scalar Memory Accesses in Embedded and Multimedia Systems, Unsal et al. consider how to best manage scalar data references. They propose a combination hardware/software technique that combines compiler passes to identify and segregate scalar variable references from array references with a hardware addition of a small single-cycle scratchpad memory to which the compiler directs all scalar loads and stores. The authors find that by treating scalar references as a group and adding a small (few kB) scratchpad memory alongside the first-level data cache, application performance can be improved while at the same time achieving a moderate power consumption reduction. These results are gathered by a detailed evaluation of several applications in the Mediabench suite.

Performance improves because the scratchpad memory is small enough to permit single-cycle access and because it removes all scalar references from the cache hierarchy, thus preventing cache interference between scalar and array references. Power improves because the scalar reference stream is directed solely at the small, on-chip scratchpad memory and does not incur the energy dissipation associated with misses within the larger and more power-hungry on-chip cache hierarchy.

Whereas Unsal et al.'s chapter focuses on the handling of scalar references, Hobbs et al.'s Bandwidth-Based Prefetching for Constant-Stride Arrays focuses on the handling of array references. In particular, the authors develop a compiler and hardware technique for identifying constant-stride array references and determining the most appropriate strategy for prefetching the array elements. The proposed technique differs from previous work in that it considers the hardware prefetch capacity and latency when determining what elements to prefetch and how far ahead (in terms of loop iterations) the prefetches should be issued.

The authors conclude that their scheme offers several advantages over traditional prefetch insertion strategies. By taking into account the latency and outstanding reference capabilities of the underlying hardware, for example, the proposed scheme can avoid oversaturating the memory system by issuing too many prefetches and can help avoid cache interference between prefetched and non-prefetched data items by issuing prefetches so that the data arrives just before required.

Rather than focusing on the cache hierarchy, Ahuja et al.'s Performance Potential of Effective Address Prediction of Load Instructions investigates a different performance limiter: the calculation of the effective address for load instructions. The authors note that because of register forwarding and other pipeline-related delays, the true effective load address is unavailable until several cycles into the load instruction's execution. Coupled with a multicycle first-level cache, this means that the load result is not available for dependent instructions until many cycles after the load instruction begins execution.

The authors propose to predict a load instruction's effective address very early in the pipeline and then to use a bypass path to the cache to initiate a fetch from the predicted address. Dependent instructions then can use the predicted load result. Later in the pipeline, the predicted load address is compared to the computed load address and, should they differ, the pipeline undertakes appropriate fix-up operations much as in the case of a branch misprediction.

The discussion is structured as an *upper bound* analysis to investigate the performance potential of several variations of load address predictors without regard for some of the lower-level implementation details but based on a realistic model of a contemporary out-of-order CPU.

Finally, KleinOsowski and Lilja's contribution titled Evaluating Novel Memory System Alternatives for Speculative Multithreaded Computer Systems, considers cache organizations for a multithreaded CPU. A multithreaded CPU incorporates several thread execution units that attempt to speculatively execute loop iterations in parallel. Key to such speculation is carefully tracking stores since stores originating from speculative threads cannot be committed to memory until the thread becomes non-speculative.

The authors investigate the performance and power attributes of three cache organizations, all incorporating both a traditional data cache as well as a speculative memory buffer to track speculative stores. The organizations trade off die area, routing complexity, and access latency.

1.5 Workload Considerations

Performance of a computer system, especially the memory system, is heavily dependent on the nature of the workload running on the system and varies widely from workload to workload. Therefore, it is critical that the right benchmarks are chosen while evaluating the system such that the performance characteristics are representative of the actual application environment for which the system is targeted. Traditionally, computer architects use standardized benchmarks such as SPECint and SPECfp for evaluating new processor and memory architectures. Actually, a large percentage of today's computing systems are used for commercial purposes such as database transaction processing, decision support, data mining, Web serving, file serving, and similar applications. The market focus on commercial computing has prompted researchers and computer designers to begin to consider the characteristics of these workloads in recent years.

Evaluating systems for commercial applications is more difficult than for using SPECint and SPECfp benchmarks for a number of reasons. Commercial applications tend to use the services provided by the operating system much more intensively than SPECint and SPECfp. As an example, it is possible for an application such as a Web server to spend 70-80% of its time executing operating system code. In most cases, traditional trace-driven or simulation mechanisms do not instrument or simulate operating system behavior adequately. The Stanford SimOS simulator in the mid-1990's led the way in bringing a *full system simulation* focus to system evaluation that helped make characterization of commercial workloads more accurate.

Real-world applications such as database transaction processing or decision support use a huge amount of disk space to accommodate large databases ranging from several hundreds of gigabytes to several tens of terabytes. It is expensive to build such an evaluation infrastructure and it is also cumbersome to tune the database system to obtain good performance. Even when a realistic system such as this is available, it is impossible to simulate such a system using a full system simulator, as the simulator would literally take years to complete a simulation run. Passive emulation systems such as the IBM MemorIES tool provide a way to evaluate cache miss ratios for sophisticated real world commercial applications by listening to the system bus traffic and emulating cache behavior in real time. These kinds of tools still need to evolve to become active agents on the system bus and stall the processors during a memory miss or coherence action to measure the impact of cache misses on execution times. The two chapters in this section focus on a database decision-support benchmark from the Transaction Processing Council (i.e., the TPC-H benchmark). This benchmark executes queries of varying complexities to answer typical business-related questions using databases of different sizes. This benchmark is widely used by server vendors to showcase a system's ability to run business applications.

The first chapter, from IBM and USC, uses the MemorIES tool to study the accuracy of trace sampling techniques in evaluating caches of relatively large size. Even though the MemorIES tool emulates caches of different sizes for real-time results, it is also practical to collect traces with this tool for later use in situations when the emulation tool and system environment are not available to take real-time measurements. Since storing full traces would require an exorbitant amount of storage, trace sampling is preferable. The chapter discusses difficulties associated with trace sampling for the TPC-H benchmarks.

The second chapter, from the University of Cyprus and University of Illinois, explores ways to enhance the performance of decision-support workloads for the Illinois FlexRAM architecture using simulation of the TPC-H benchmarks. The authors propose and evaluate several query parallelization mechanisms that leverage the intelligent memory architecture of FlexRAM.

Although this chapter does not discuss other workloads, there is a significant amount of research activity in both academia and industry dealing with a variety of commercial benchmarks, including TPC-C, TPC-W, SPECWeb, and others. In the future, emerging workloads such as eBusiness computing, rich media content on demand, networked virtual environments, heterogeneous workloads running simultaneously on large systems, etc., will play key roles in the evaluation of computer systems. The research community will need to develop relevant benchmarks and appropriate evaluation tools to deal with these emerging workloads.

Part I

Coherence, Synchronization, and Allocation

Speculative Locks: Concurrent Execution of Critical Sections in Shared-Memory Multiprocessors*

José F. Martínez[1] and Josep Torrellas[2]

[1] Computer Systems Laboratory, Cornell University, Ithaca, NY, USA
martinez@csl.cornell.edu
[2] Department of Computer Science, University of Illinois at Urbana-Champaign, Urbana, IL, USA torrellas@cs.uiuc.edu

Abstract. Multithreaded applications typically use coarse- or fine-grain locks to enforce synchronization when needed. While fine-grain synchronization enables higher concurrency, it often involves significantly more programming effort than coarse-grain synchronization. To address this trade-off, this chapter proposes *speculative locks*. In speculative locks, threads access a critical section without synchronizing while the underlying hardware monitors for conflicting accesses. If a conflict is detected, threads are rolled back and restarted on the fly. Forward progress in an active lock is guaranteed by the presence of a nonspeculative lock owner at all times, and all in-order conflicts between owner and speculative threads are tolerated. Overall, speculative locks allow the programmability of coarse-grain synchronization, while enabling the concurrency of fine-grain synchronization.

2.1 Introduction

Proper synchronization between threads is crucial to the correct execution of parallel programs. The choice of grain size used to synchronize offers a trade-off between programmability and concurrency. While fine-grain synchronization allows greater thread concurrency, it often requires greater development effort and, therefore, results in a longer time to market. On the other hand, coarse-grain synchronization, while restricting concurrency, delivers simpler and more stable software.

Furthermore, in some extreme cases, both fine- and coarse-grain synchronization can fail to deliver the levels of performance expected from a program. For example, fine-grain synchronization may penalize threads with costly overhead, even though the data accessed by different threads rarely overlap.

* This work was developed while José Martínez was with the Department of Computer Science, University of Illinois at Urbana-Champaign.

Ideally, we would like to combine the higher concurrency enabled by fine-grain synchronization with the higher programmability and lower overhead of coarse-grain synchronization. As an example from the commercial workload domain, we would like to combine the concurrency of tuple-level locking with the programmability and low overhead of table-level locking.

Recent research in thread-level speculation (TLS) has proposed mechanisms for optimistically executing nonanalyzable serial codes in parallel (e.g. [1, 3, 4, 6, 7, 9]). Under TLS special support checks for cross-thread dependence violations at run time, and forces offending speculative threads to squash and restart on the fly. At all times, there is at least one safe or *non-speculative* thread. While speculative threads venture into unsafe program sections, the safe thread executes code nonspeculatively. As a result, even if all the speculative work is useless, forward progress is guaranteed by the safe thread.

This chapter proposes *speculative locks*, a new hardware mechanism inspired in TLS for concurrent execution of critical sections in shared-memory multiprocessors. In speculative locks, threads access a critical section without synchronizing, and the underlying hardware monitors for conflicting accesses. If a conflict is detected, threads are rolled back and restarted on the fly. Forward progress in an active lock is guaranteed by the presence of a non-speculative lock owner at all times, and all in-order conflicts between owner and speculative threads are tolerated. In some cases, threads successfully execute critical sections without ever owning the associated lock. Finally, the cost of state commit and squash operations is independent of the amount of speculative data or the number of processors.

2.2 Speculative Locks

The goal of speculative locks is to enable extra concurrency in the presence of conservatively placed synchronization—sometimes even when data access conflicts between threads do exist. Our scheme allows threads to execute code past a busy lock. In conventional locking, such threads would be waiting.

This section presents speculative locks. First, we give a high-level description, and then we propose an implementation using a device that we call a *Speculative Concurrency Unit* (SCU). We limit our discussion to deadlock-free parallel codes; codes that can deadlock at run time are out of our scope. Furthermore, in this chapter, we assume a release consistency model.

2.2.1 High-Level Overview

Among the threads competing for a speculative lock, there is always one safe thread—the lock owner. All other contenders venture into the critical section speculatively. Owner and speculative threads are free to execute memory operations inside and past the critical section. However, speculative threads

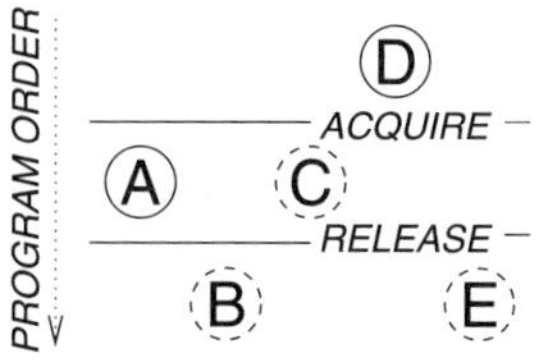

Fig. 2.1. Example of a speculative lock. Dashed and solid circles denote speculative and nonspeculative threads, respectively. Thread A is currently the lock owner.

may not *commit* their results to the system until they become safe. Figure 2.1 shows an example of a speculative lock with five threads. Thread A found the lock free and acquired it, becoming the owner. Thread A is therefore safe. Threads B, C, and E found the lock busy and proceeded into the critical section speculatively. Thread D has not yet reached the acquire point and is safe.

The existence of a lock owner has implications. The final outcome has to be consistent with that of a conventional lock in which the lock owner executes the critical section atomically *before* any of the speculative threads. (In a conventional lock, the speculative threads would be waiting at the acquire point.) On the one hand, this implies that it is correct for speculative threads to consume values produced by the lock owner. On the other hand, speculative threads cannot commit while the owner is in the critical section. In the figure, threads B and E have completed the critical section and are executing code past the release point,[3] and C is still inside the critical section. All three threads remain speculative as long as A owns the lock.

As the critical section is concurrently executed by safe and speculative threads, the hardware checks for cross-thread dependence violations. As long as dependences are not violated, threads are allowed to proceed. Access conflicts between safe and speculative threads are not violations if they happen *in order*, i.e., the access from the safe thread happens before the access from the speculative one. Any *out-of-order* conflict between a safe and a speculative thread causes the squashing of the speculative thread and its rollback to the acquire point. No ordering exists among speculative threads; thus, if two speculative threads issue conflicting accesses, one of them is squashed and rolled back to the synchronization point. Overall, since safe threads can make progress regardless of the success of speculative threads, performance in the worst case is still on the order of conventional locks.

Speculative threads keep their memory state in caches until they become safe. When a speculative thread becomes safe, it *commits* (i.e., makes visible) its memory state to the system. On the other hand, if the cache of a speculative thread is about to overflow, the thread stalls and waits to become safe.

[3] The fact that B and E have completed the critical section is remembered by the hardware. We describe the implementation in detail later.

Eventually, the lock owner (thread A) completes the critical section and releases the lock. At this point, the speculative threads that have also completed the critical section (threads B and E) can immediately become safe and commit their speculative memory state. They do so *without acquiring the lock*. This is race-free because these threads have completely executed the critical section and did not have conflicts with the owner or other threads. On the other hand, the speculative threads still inside the critical section (only thread C in our case) compete for ownership of the lock. One of them acquires the lock, also becoming safe and committing its speculative memory state. The losers remain speculative.

The action after the release is semantically equivalent to the following scenario under a conventional lock: after the release by the owner, all the speculative threads past the release point, one by one in some nondeterministic order, execute the critical section atomically; then, one of the threads competing for the lock acquires ownership and enters the critical section. In Figure 2.1, this corresponds to a conventional lock whose critical section is traversed in (A, B, E, C) or (A, E, B, C) order.

2.2.2 Implementation

Speculative locks are supported using simple hardware that we describe next. In the following, we start by describing the main hardware module. Then, we explain in detail how it works for single and multiple locks.

Speculative Concurrency Unit

The main module that we use to support speculative locks is the *Speculative Concurrency Unit* (SCU). The SCU consists of some storage and some control logic that we add to the cache hierarchy of each processor in a shared memory multiprocessor. The SCU physically resides in the on-chip controller of the local cache hierarchy, typically L1+L2 (Figure 2.2). Its function is to offload from the processor the operations on one lock variable, so that the processor can move ahead and execute code speculatively.

The SCU provides space for one extra cache line at the L1 level, which holds the lock variable under speculation. This extra cache line is accessible by local and remote requests. However, only the SCU can allocate it. The local cache hierarchy (L1+L2 in Figure 2.2) is used as the buffer for speculative data. To distinguish data accessed speculatively from the rest, the SCU keeps one *Speculative* bit per line in the local cache hierarchy. The Speculative bit for a line is set when the line is read or written speculatively. Lines whose Speculative bit is set cannot be displaced beyond the local cache hierarchy.

The SCU also has two state bits called *Acquire* and *Release*. The Acquire and Release bits are set if the SCU has a pending acquire and release operation, respectively, on the lock variable. Speculative, Acquire, and Release

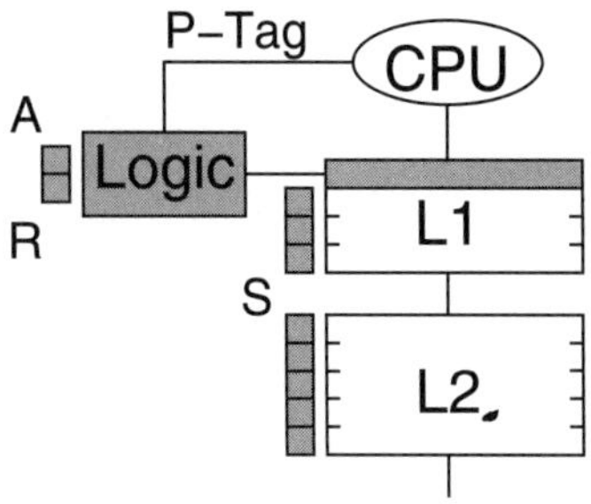

Fig. 2.2. The shaded areas show the Speculative Concurrency Unit (SCU) in a two-level cache hierarchy. The SCU consists of a Speculative (S) bit in each conventional line in the caches, Acquire (A) and Release (R) bits, an extra cache line, and some logic.

bits may only be set if the SCU is active; i.e., it is handling a synchronization variable. When the SCU is idle, all these bits remain at zero.

Overall, we can see that the SCU storage requirements are modest: For a 32 KB L1 cache and a 1 MB L2 cache with 64 B lines, the SCU needs about 2 KB of storage.

Lock Request

While we can use different primitives to implement a lock acquire operation, without loss of generality, in this work we use Test&Test&Set (T&T&S). Figure 2.3 shows a T&T&S loop on lock *lck*. In the example and in the rest of the chapter, a zero value means that the lock is free.

```
L: ld $1,lck    ; S1
   bnz $1,L     ; S2
   t&s $1,lck   ; S3
   bnz $1,L     ; S4
```

Fig. 2.3. Example of Test&Test&Set operation.

When a processor reaches an acquire, it invokes a library procedure that issues a request to the SCU with the address of the lock. At this point, SCU and processor proceed independently as follows:

SCU Side - The SCU sets its Acquire and Release bits, fetches the lock variable into its extra cache line, and initiates a T&T&S loop on it to obtain lock ownership (Figure 2.3). If the lock is busy, the SCU keeps spinning locally on it until the lock is updated externally and a coherence message is received. (In practice, the SCU need not actually "spin"—since it sits in the cache controller, it can simply wait for the coherence message before retrying.)

Processor Side - In order to allow quick rollback of squashed threads, we need to checkpoint the architectural register state at the beginning of the speculative section. We envision this to be done with a checkpoint mark or instruction that backs up the architectural register map [11], or the actual architectural register values.[4] The checkpoint instruction is included in the library procedure for acquire, right after the request to the SCU. No flushing of the pipeline is needed.

The processor continues execution into the critical section. Memory system accesses by the processor after the acquire in program order are deemed speculative by the SCU for as long as the Acquire bit is set. The SCU must be able to distinguish these accesses from those that precede the acquire in program order. To achieve this, we use processor hints similar to the way ASI address tags extend memory addresses issued by SPARC processors [10]. In our case, we only need a single bit, which we call the *Processor Tag*, or P-Tag bit. This bit is issued by the processor along with every memory address and is fed into the SCU (Figure 2.2). The processor reverses the P-Tag bit of all memory operations following the checkpoint *in program order*. This way, the processor can immediately proceed to the critical section and the SCU can still determine which memory accesses originate from instructions beyond the acquire point. This mechanism does not impose any restriction on the order in which the processor actually issues accesses to memory.

When a thread performs a first speculative access to a line that is dirty in any cache, including its own, the coherence protocol must write back the line to memory. This is necessary to keep a safe copy of the line in main memory. It also enables the conventional Dirty bit in the caches to be used in combination with the Speculative bit to mark cache lines that have been speculatively written.

At any time, if the thread is squashed, the processor completes any non-speculative work, flushes the pipeline, flash-invalidates all dirty cache lines with the Speculative bit set, flash-clears all Speculative bits, and restores the checkpointed register state. To perform the flash-invalidate and flash-clear operations, we need special hardware that does each of them in at most a few cycles. More details are given later.

Lock Acquire

The SCU keeps "spinning" on the lock variable until it reads a zero. At this point, it attempts a T&S operation (statement *S3* in Figure 2.3). If the operation fails, the SCU goes back to the spin-test. However, if the T&S succeeds, the local processor becomes the lock owner. This is the case for thread C in the example of Section 2.2.1 after thread A releases the lock. In this case, the SCU completes action: it resets the Acquire bit and flash-clears all Speculative bits, effectively turning the thread safe and committing all cached values. At this point, the SCU becomes idle. Other SCUs trying to acquire the lock will read that the lock is owned.

[4] Backing up architectural register values could be done in a handful of cycles and would free up potentially valuable renaming registers.

There is one exception to this mechanism when, at the time the lock is freed by the owner, the speculative thread has already completed its critical section. We address this case next.

Lock Release

The processor executes a release store to the lock variable when all the memory operations inside the critical section have completed. If the lock has already been acquired by the SCU and, therefore, the SCU is idle, the release store completes normally. If, instead, the SCU is still trying to acquire ownership for that lock, the SCU intercepts the release store and takes notice by clearing its Release bit. This enables the SCU to remember that the critical section has been fully executed by the speculative thread. We call this event *Release While Speculative*. Then, the SCU keeps spinning for ownership because the Acquire bit is still set. Note that the execution of the speculative thread is not disrupted.

In general, when the SCU reads that the lock has been freed externally, before attempting the T&S operation, it checks the Release bit. If the Release bit is still set, the SCU issues the T&S operation to compete for the lock, as described earlier. If, instead, the bit is clear, the SCU knows that the local thread has gone through a Release While Speculative operation and, therefore, has completed all memory operations prior to the release. As a result, the SCU can aggressively *pretend* that ownership is acquired and released instantly. Therefore, the Acquire bit is cleared, all the Speculative bits are flash-cleared, and the SCU becomes idle. In this case, the thread has become safe without ever performing the T&S operation. This is the action taken by threads B and E in the example of Section 2.2.1 after thread A releases the lock.

As indicated in Section 2.2.1, this optimization is race-free since: (1) the Release bit in the speculative thread is cleared only after *all* memory operations in the critical section have completed without conflict, and (2) a free lock value indicates that the previous lock owner has completed the critical section as well. If, at the time the speculative thread is about to become safe, an incoming invalidation is in flight from a third processor for a line marked speculative, two things can happen: If the invalidation arrives before the speculative thread has committed, the thread is squashed. This is suboptimal, but correct. Alternatively, if the thread has already committed, the invalidation is serviced conventionally.

Access Conflict

The underlying cache coherence protocol naturally detects access conflicts. Such conflicts manifest in a thread receiving an external invalidation to a cached line or an external read to a dirty cached line.

If such external messages are received by lines not marked speculative, they are serviced normally. In particular, messages to the lock owner or to any other safe thread never result in squashes since none of their cache lines is marked speculative. Note that the originator thread of such a message could be speculative; in this case, by normally servicing the request, we are effectively supporting *in-order* conflicts from a safe to a speculative thread without squashing.

On the other hand, if a speculative thread receives an external message for a line marked Speculative, the conflict is resolved by squashing the receiving thread. The originator thread may be safe or speculative. If the former, an *out-of-order* conflict has taken place, and thus the squash is warranted.[5] If the latter, we squash the receiving thread since our proposal does not define an order between speculative threads. In any case, the originator is never squashed. Once triggered, the squash mechanism proceeds as follows. The SCU flash-invalidates all dirty cache lines with the Speculative bit set, flash-clears all Speculative bits and, if the speculative thread has passed the release point, it sets the Release bit again. In addition, the SCU forces the processor to restore its checkpointed register state. In this way, the thread quickly rolls back to the acquire point. The flash invalidation is simply a flash clear of the Valid bit of all cache lines whose Speculative and Dirty bits are set (NAND gating). Finally, note that we do not invalidate cache lines that have been speculatively read but not modified since they are coherent with main memory.

If the squash was triggered by an external read to a dirty speculative line in the cache, the node replies without supplying any data. The coherence protocol then regards the state for that cache line as stale and supplies a clean copy from memory to the requester. This is similar to the case in conventional MESI protocols where a node is queried by the directory for a clean line in state Exclusive that was silently displaced from the cache.

Cache Overflow

Cache lines whose Speculative bit is set cannot be displaced beyond the local cache hierarchy because they record past speculative accesses. Moreover, if their Dirty bit is also set, their data are unsafe. If a replacement becomes necessary at the outermost level of the local cache hierarchy, the cache controller tries to select a cache line not marked speculative. If no evictable candidate is found, the node stalls until the thread is granted ownership of the lock or it is squashed. Stalling does not compromise forward progress, since there always exists a lock owner. The lock owner will eventually release the lock, and the node whose SCU then gains ownership (and any speculative thread that had gone through a Release While Speculative operation on that lock) will be able to handle cache conflicts without stalling. Safe threads do not have lines marked speculative and, therefore, replace cache lines on misses as usual.

[5] More sophisticated hardware could disambiguate out-of-order name dependences and potentially avoid the squash. For simplicity, we choose not to support it.

Supporting Multiple Locks

Speculative threads may meet a second acquire point. This can happen if there are nested locks or several consecutive critical sections. One approach for these two cases is to wait until a thread becomes nonspeculative prior to attempting the second acquire. However, a more aggressive approach can avoid unnecessary stalls.

Upon receiving a lock acquire request from the processor, the SCU checks its Acquire bit. If it is clear, the SCU is idle and can service the request as usual. If the SCU is busy, we first consider the more general case where the acquire request is for a lock variable different from the one currently being handled by the SCU. In this case, the SCU rejects the request, no checkpointing is done, and the speculative thread itself handles the second lock using ordinary T&T&S code. No additional support is required.

Handling the second lock using ordinary T&T&S code is correct because, since the thread is speculative, accesses to that lock variable are also considered speculative. Upon the thread reading the value of the lock, the line is marked speculative in the cache. If the lock is busy, the thread spins on it locally. If it is free, the thread takes it and proceeds to the critical section; however, the modification to the lock is contained in the local cache hierarchy since this is a speculative access. The lock is treated like any other speculative data.

There are two possible final outcomes to this situation. On the one hand, the thread could get squashed. This will occur if there is a conflict with another thread on any cached line marked speculative, including the one that contains the second lock variable itself. In this case, the squash procedure will roll back the thread to the acquire of the first lock (the one handled by the SCU). As usual, all updates to speculative data will be discarded. This includes any speculative update to the second lock variable.

On the other hand, the SCU may complete action on the first lock and render the thread safe. As always, this commits all speculatively accessed data—including the second lock itself. If the thread was originally spinning on this second lock, it will continue to do so safely. Otherwise, any action taken speculatively by the thread on the second lock (acquire and possibly release) will now commit to the rest of the system. This is correct because if any other thread had tried to manipulate the second lock, it would have triggered a squash.

Finally, there is a special case when the second acquire is to the same lock variable as the one already being handled by the SCU. In this case, the SCU holds the request until the thread becomes safe or until it completes execution of the first critical section (and the SCU clears the Release bit), whichever is first. If the former, the SCU completes action as usual and then accepts the new acquire request. If the latter (the case of Release While Speculative), the SCU simply sets the Release bit again and accepts the acquire request. This way, the SCU effectively merges the two critical sections into a single one. In this case, a second checkpoint is not performed. When the thread eventually commits, it will do so for both critical sections at once. On the other hand, if the thread gets squashed, it will roll back to the first (checkpointed) acquire.

Other Issues

There are a few other related issues that we briefly consider.

Support for Multiprogramming. In a multiprogrammed environment, the operating system may preempt some of the threads of an application. When a speculative thread is preempted, it is squashed and the local SCU is freed up. Any new thread that runs on that processor can use the SCU. When the first thread is finally rescheduled somewhere, it resumes from the synchronization point. On the other hand, safe threads are handled as in a conventional system; in particular, they are never squashed in a context switch. Finally, speculative locks may exhibit convoying under certain scheduling conditions. In general, preempting a lock owner would temporarily prevent speculative threads from committing. A number of techniques have been proposed to avoid preempting a lock owner [2, 5, 8].

Exception Handling. When a speculative thread suffers an exception, there is no easy way of knowing whether the cause was legitimate; it could be due to consuming incorrect values speculatively. Consequently, the speculative thread is rolled back in all cases.

False Sharing. Since our implementation uses the memory line as the unit of coherence, false sharing may cause thread squashes. However, our implementation will benefit from the many existing techniques that reduce false sharing. Any such technique that requires a per-word state in the caches will also require per-word Speculative bits.

Summary

The SCU is a simple hardware device that implements speculative locks at a modest cost and requires few modifications to the cache hierarchy and coherence protocol. The most salient features of our scheme are:

- Threads operate optimistically, assuming no conflicting accesses with other threads. Conflicting accesses are detected on the fly by the coherence protocol, and offending threads are squashed and eagerly restarted.
- The cost of commit and squash operations is independent of the amount of speculative data or the number of processors.
- Forward progress is guaranteed by forcing one lock owner to exist at all times. The owner can never be squashed due to conflicts, or stall due to cache overflow.
- All in-order conflicting accesses between the owner and a speculative thread are tolerated and thus do not cause squashes.
- Under the right conditions, speculative threads can commit the execution of a critical section without ever having to acquire the lock.

2.3 Evaluation

As a proof of concept, we evaluate the potential of speculative locks by simulating a simplified synthetic version of the TPC-B on-line transaction processing (OLTP) benchmark. The results show the advantages of a system featuring speculative locks over a conventional configuration.

2.3.1 Experimental Setup

We use a simplified synthetic model of TPC-B composed of five branches, five tellers per branch, and a number of accounts per teller that ranges from five to one thousand. Locks can be placed at any level: account, teller, branch, or even global. Figure 2.4 depicts such a system.

A 64-way multiprocessor hosting the OLTP system processes one million transactions. Each transaction is modeled as follows. First, it computes the branch, teller, and account to access using three random numbers. Then, it secures whatever lock is necessary. After some internal preprocessing, it reads the balance from the account, performs some internal manipulation, and writes the updated balance to the account. Finally, it does some internal postprocessing, and then it releases the lock. The duration of the preprocessing, balance manipulation, and post-processing is chosen randomly. We use a uniform distribution with a range of one to seven time units.

We model configurations with conventional and speculative locks. In the case of conventional locks, a transaction whose lock is already taken blocks. When the owner frees it, a new owner is chosen randomly among the contenders. In the case of speculative locks, a transaction starts processing whether its lock is available or not. The hardware monitors for conflicting accesses to the accounts and squashes and restarts offending transactions on the fly as needed.

A processor is assigned transactions dynamically, but it cannot initiate a new transaction until the resident one has graduated. Speculative transactions must wait for ownership of the lock before graduating. To the disadvantage of our scheme, transactions do nothing beyond the release point. This will stall the processor if the lock is still unavailable by the time its transaction hits the release point. If transactions had work to do past the release point, they could continue processing while ownership was pending.

2.3.2 Results

In our experiments we evaluate the performance of speculative locks at all grain levels: account, teller, branch, and global. In all four cases, we measure the execution time considering a different number of accounts per teller from five to one thousand. We compare the times obtained against those obtained for a conventional system that features locks at the account level, the finest possible grain. Figure 2.5 shows the results.

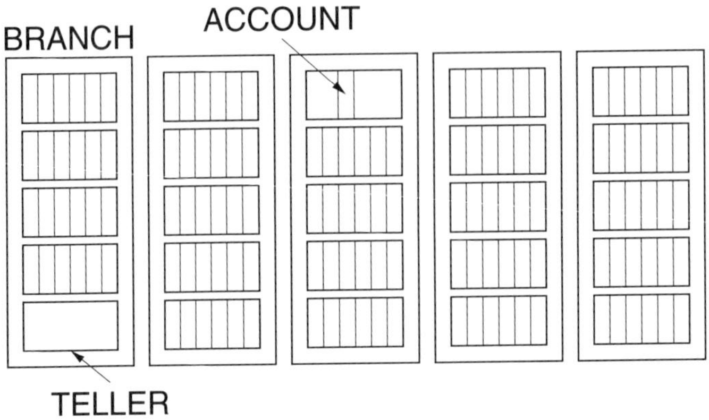

Fig. 2.4. Organization of the synthetic on-line transaction processing system used in the evaluation.

The results of this experiment show that systems using speculative locks coarser than the baseline quickly approach the performance of the latter, as the number of accounts per teller increases. This is because the larger number of accounts in the system makes the probability of conflict smaller, which the systems with speculative locks exploit. That conventional systems can be closely followed in performance by systems featuring speculative locks and much coarser grain locking is very good news. It means that we can reduce the programming complexity significantly with coarse-grain locks without compromising the code performance.

We also observe that systems using speculative locks perform better the finer the grain. This is because, with coarser-grain locks, the competition for ownership is fiercer, making speculative transactions wait longer to commit before they can be retired. The chances of conflict for each transaction increase with the time that it spends in a speculative state. Of course, this effect quickly loses relevance as the number of accounts increases.

Finally, we note that the system that uses speculative locks at the account level slightly (but consistently) outperforms the baseline system. This is despite the fact that, since transactions access a single account, all transactions using the same lock are guaranteed to conflict. Speculative locks outperform the baseline because they *tolerate conflicts* if they happen in order with the owner, something that the conventional system cannot exploit.

2.4 Conclusions

We have presented speculative locks, a hardware mechanism that allows the programmability of coarse-grain synchronization while enabling fine-grain concurrency. Threads access a critical section concurrently without synchronizing, and the system uses the underlying coherence protocol to continuously monitor for conflicting accesses on the fly, rolling back and eagerly restarting

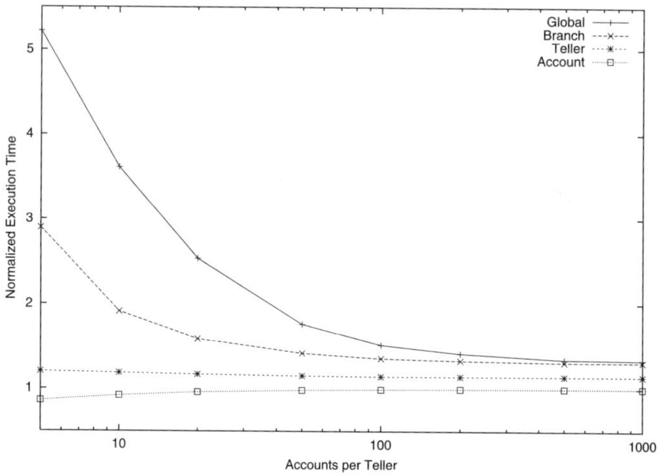

Fig. 2.5. Execution time of different systems featuring speculative locks normalized to that of a system that uses fine-grain (per account) conventional locks. Curves for speculative locks at all possible grain sizes (account, teller, branch, and global) are shown.

offending threads. Commit and squash operations take constant time, irrespective of the amount of speculative data or the number of processors.

We maintain a legitimate owner of the critical section at all times in order to guarantee forward progress. Owners can neither get squashed due to conflicts nor stall due to cache overflow, and all in-order conflicting accesses between owner and speculative thread are tolerated without squash.

In the absence of conflicts, the system allows multiple threads to execute the critical section concurrently. Furthermore, partial concurrency can be achieved in the presence of some conflicting accesses due to the eager restart mechanism. Under the right conditions, a system with speculative locks and coarse-grain synchronization performs about as well as one with conventional locks and fine-grain synchronization.

Acknowledgments

This work was supported in part by the NSF under grants CCR-9970488, EIA-0081307, EIA-0072102, and CHE-0121357; by DARPA under grant F30602-01-C-0078; and by gifts from IBM, Intel, and Hewlett-Packard.

References

1. M. Cintra, J. F. Martínez, and J. Torrellas. Architectural support for scalable speculative parallelization in shared-memory multiprocessors. In *International*

Symposium on Computer Architecture, pp. 13–24, Vancouver, Canada, June 2000.
2. J. Edler, J. Lipkis, and E. Schonberg. Process management for highly parallel UNIX systems. In *USENIX Workshop on Unix and Supercomputers*, San Francisco, CA, Sept. 1988.
3. S. Gopal, T. N. Vijaykumar, J. E. Smith, and G. S. Sohi. Speculative versioning cache. In *International Symposium on High-Performance Computer Architecture*, pp. 195–205, Las Vegas, NV, Jan.–Feb. 1998.
4. L. Hammond, M. Wiley, and K. Olukotun. Data speculation support for a chip multiprocessor. In *International Conference on Architectural Support for Programming Languages and Operating Systems*, pp. 58–69, San Jose, CA, Oct. 1998.
5. L. I. Kontothanassis, R. W. Wisniewski, and M. L. Scott. Schedule-conscious synchronization. *ACM Transactions on Computer Systems*, 15(1):3–40, Feb. 1997.
6. V. Krishnan and J. Torrellas. A chip-multiprocessor architecture with speculative multithreading. *IEEE Transactions on Computers*, 48(9):866–880, Sept. 1999.
7. P. Marcuello and A. González. Clustered speculative multithreaded processors. In *International Conference on Supercomputing*, pp. 365–372, Rhodes, Greece, June 1999.
8. B. D. Marsh, M. L. Scott, T. J. LeBlanc, and E. P. Markatos. First-class user-level threads. In *Symposium on Operating System Principles*, pp. 110–121, Pacific Grove, CA, Oct. 1991.
9. J. G. Steffan, C. B. Colohan, A. Zhai, and T. C. Mowry. A scalable approach to thread-level speculation. In *International Symposium on Computer Architecture*, pp. 1–12, Vancouver, Canada, June 2000.
10. D. L. Weaver and T. Germond, editors. *The SPARC Architecture Manual.* PTR Prentice Hall, Englewood Cliffs, NJ, 1994.
11. K. C. Yeager. The MIPS R10000 superscalar microprocessor. *IEEE Micro*, 6(2):28–40, Apr. 1996.
12. Y. Zhang, L. Rauchwerger and J. Torrellas. Hardware for speculative run-time parallelization in distributed shared-memory multiprocessors." In *International Symposium on High-Performance Computer Architecture*, pp. 162–173, Las Vegas, NV, Jan.–Feb. 1998.

3

Dynamic Verification of Cache Coherence Protocols

Jason F. Cantin, Mikko H. Lipasti, and James E. Smith

Department of Electrical and Computer Engineering University of Wisconsin-Madison, Madison, WI 53706
jcantin@ece.wisc.edu,lipasti@ece.wisc.edu,jes@ece.wisc.edu

Abstract. A method for improving the fault-tolerance of cache coherent multiprocessors is proposed. By dynamically verifying coherence operations in hardware, errors caused by manufacturing faults, soft errors, and design mistakes can be detected. Analogous to the DIVA concept for single-processor systems, a simple version of the protocol functions as a checker for the aggressive implementation. An example implementation is shown, and the overhead is estimated for a small SMP system.

3.1 Introduction

Cache coherence protocols are notoriously difficult to design and verify [1]. Though a protocol description may specify only a few states (e.g., MOESI), implementations quickly become very complicated as states are added to allow hardware optimizations and implement protocol optimizations [2]. The complexity increases the possibility of subtle errors in the specification and/or low-level implementation. Furthermore, transient failures caused by non-ideal operating environments, or cosmic rays and alpha particles interacting with very small devices, are likely to pose major reliability problems [3, 4]. Thus, tolerance against design errors and transient faults will be important for ensuring the reliability and scalability of cache coherent multiprocessor systems.

Recently, Rotenberg observed that the result of a complex computation may be checked for correctness more efficiently than it was first computed, provided the check is delayed in time [5]. Austin proposed a novel approach for runtime verification of complex superscalar processors based on this principle [6]. Because the verification hardware is simple and centralized, its correctness can be easily verified. We refer to this process as *dynamic verification.*

We propose using dynamic verification techniques to improve the fault-tolerance of cache coherent multiprocessor systems. However, a centralized check processor approach as used for single-processor systems exhibiting serial semantics [6] is probably inappropriate for distributed cache coherence hardware based on parallel multiprocessor semantics. Consequently, we propose a distributed version of dynamic verification for concurrently checking cache coherence protocols during execution. As an example, we illustrate how this concept might be applied to a symmetric multiprocessor system. In this chapter, we concentrate on the error detection and leave recovery techniques for future work.

3.1.1 Dynamic Verification

As mentioned above, a complex computation can be checked for correctness more efficiently than it was computed in the first place, provided the check is delayed in time [5]. The key is that the checker can exploit parallelism exposed by the original computation and need only verify results that update the architected machine state. This allows results to be recomputed in a simpler, more efficient way.

In the single-processor case, the primary execution core (e.g. a superscalar implementation) ultimately produces a sequence of state changes, <PC, reg, data> or <PC, mem address, data>, that capture the semantics of the computation. As proposed by Austin, this sequence is held in the reorder buffer (ROB) and can be passed to a check processor after any speculation has been resolved [6]. The check processor lags behind and re-executes the program. However, because of the time lag, the check processor does not need to predict branches, disambiguate addresses, or handle pipeline hazards. These dependences were identified and resolved by the execution core. Instead, the checker sees a filtered execution stream, with effectively perfect branch and value prediction. The check processor can then recompute the result of each instruction in a simpler way. After the check processor produces a result, that value is compared with the corresponding value produced by the execution processor. Hence, each instruction is dynamically verified.

As articulated in [6], the benefits of dynamic verification are the following:

- It detects hardware faults, assuming faults in the complex implementation and the checker are not correlated.
- It detects design errors in the complex implementation, assuming that the checker is correct. The check processor is simple, so verification should be straightforward.
- It can recover from faults, provided the checker maintains the architected state and can make forward progress when errors are detected.
- Going further, the technique may potentially be used to enhance performance. By intentionally letting the checker take care of rare cases, implementation for the common cases is simplified.

3.1.2 Cache Coherence

Modern multiprocessor systems are typically constructed from commodity processors with on-chip caches or cache hierarchies. Despite the replication of data in caches, it must appear to the programmer that there is one coherent memory. Cache coherence protocols are used to efficiently maintain this illusion.

Figure 3.1 shows a simple example of a coherence protocol, MOESI, where the states for a cache line are Modified, Owned, Exclusive, Shared, and Invalid. When a clean, read-only copy is present, the state is Shared (S). When a clean copy is present in only that cache, the state is Exclusive (E). If a dirty copy is present, the state is Modified (M). In this state, the data may be read or written by the processor. Finally, the Owned (O) state allows cache-to-cache transfers of dirty data without updating memory. More complete discussions of these states can be found in the literature [7].

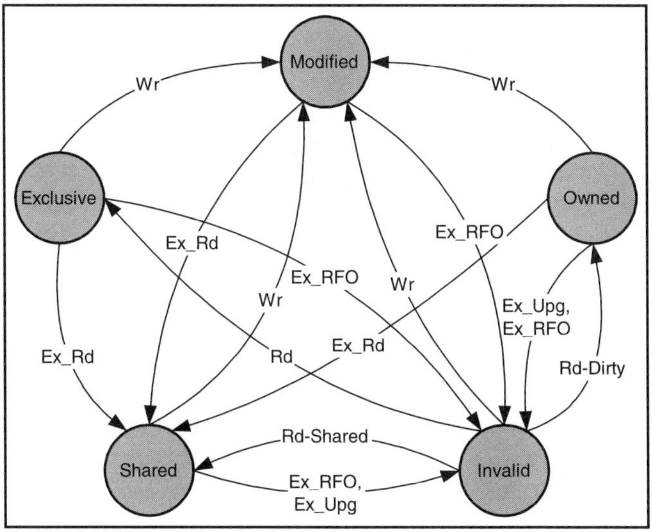

Fig. 3.1. State diagram of MOESI protocol

Note that not all combinations of cache states are allowed. For example, two processors with a modifiable copy of a cache line lead to an erroneous system state. For MOESI, the possible state combinations are shown in Figure 3.2.

The diagrams of Figures 3.1 and 3.2 provide a simple, high-level view of the protocol, with atomic transitions between states. Implementations require many additional states for concurrency and hardware optimizations [2]. For example, adding a split-transaction bus requires considerably more states (Figure 3.3). The complete protocol is even more complicated because in the interest of space we have omitted arcs for evictions and atomic memory instructions.

	Processor B:				
Processor A:	I	S	E	O	M
I	Ok	Ok	Ok	Ok	Ok
S	Ok	Ok	Error	Ok	Error
E	Ok	Error	Error	Error	Error
O	Ok	Ok	Error	Error	Error
M	Ok	Error	Error	Error	Error

Fig. 3.2. Allowed state combinations for MOESI with two processors. The general case is a straightforward extension.

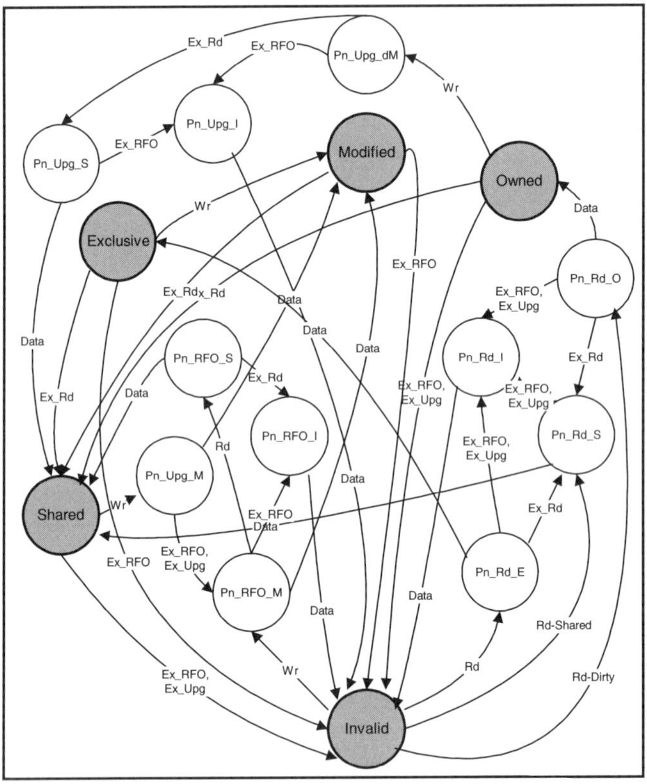

Fig. 3.3. MOESI with transient states (stable states shaded).

These additional transient states exponentially increase the state space for testing techniques and make formal verification cumbersome. For MOESI, the addition of transient states increased the verification time by orders of magnitude for our experiments with model checking [8]. Random testing would also take longer since more vectors would be necessary to achieve good coverage.

Before proceeding further, we define some useful terminology. We refer to the states used in Figure 3.1 as *stable states*. These states are defined in high-level descriptions of the protocol and used to reason about interactions between processors and memory. Given atomic execution of memory operations, the stable states are sufficient to correctly realize the protocol. The additional states added to implement the protocol with real hardware are referred to as *transient states*, following the convention in [2]. We refer to the state machine composed of stable states as the *simple protocol* and the combined state machine (stable and transient states) as the *implementation protocol*. The current state of the implementation protocol is the *implementation state*, and the current state in the simple protocol is referred to as the *architected state*. Finally, we use the term *coherence transaction* to refer to the tuple consisting of the initial state, final state, input request, action, and address of an event handled by the protocol.

We further explain dynamic verification for cache coherence in the next section and describe how it may be applied to a symmetric multiprocessor. In Section 3.3, we propose using model checking to determine if a checker meets correctness and coverage criteria. Section 3.4 presents data collected from simulations to estimate the performance impact. Sections 3.5 and 3.6 present related and future work in this area. We present conclusions in Section 3.7.

3.2 Dynamic Verification of Cache Coherence

Dynamic verification can be used for cache coherence. Unlike the centralized DIVA checker paradigm [6], a mechanism for dynamically verifying cache coherence should be logically distributed. Figure 3.4 shows a conceptual view. In the single-processor case, complex hardware does the computation initially, using some combination of implementation state (ROB, prediction tables, etc.) and architected state. The check processor maintains only the architected state and verifies the computations. For cache coherence, the implementation protocol initially computes the state, issues requests, and services external requests. The coherence checker maintains the architected tag state, recomputes the next state and actions of the protocol, and sends additional messages to other nodes to detect coherence violations. The additional messages may contain signatures that identify the data transferred, in order to detect loss or corruption of data.

Completed transitions between stable states are passed to the checker in completion order. More specifically, transitions are checked in the order in which they update the cache state. Depending on the memory model, the completion order may not be the program order since the replacement of conflicting cache blocks creates a structural dependence between memory operations such that re-execution in program order would yield different results. For example, a speculatively executed load operation may evict a block needed by an older store. If the resulting state transitions were sent to a checker in program order, an error would be falsely detected. Instead, coherence operations must (currently) be handled by the checker in the same order they were handled by the implementation protocol.

Implemented carefully in hardware, dynamic verification can detect subtle implementation mistakes and transient errors. Codesigned with the implementation protocol, dynamic verification can be used to flush out specification errors early in the design phase with simulations prior to implementation.

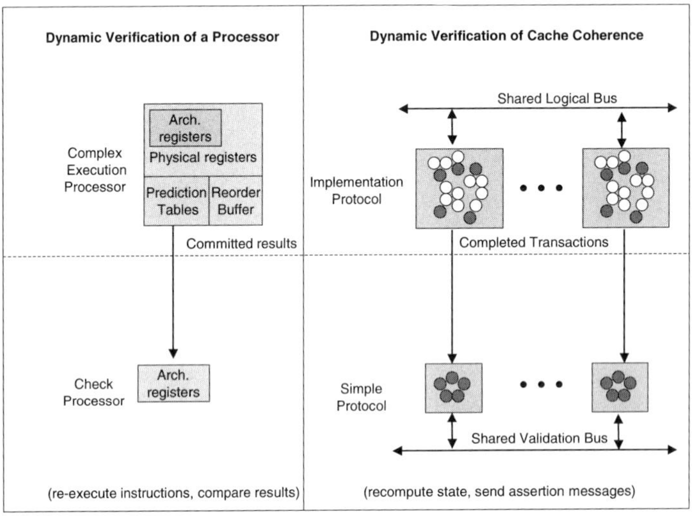

Fig. 3.4. A conceptual view of dynamic verification for cache coherence protocols

3.2.1 Symmetric Multiprocessor Example

To incorporate dynamic verification of coherence in a symmetric multiprocessor (SMP), a special checker circuit is placed in each node to verify the protocol actions locally (Figure 3.5). The checker implements a simplified version of the coherence protocol logic. In addition, it maintains its own copy of the tags for the architected state and a watchdog timer for omission failures [5].

A second logical network is used to check the protocol globally. We call this network the *validation network* to distinguish it from the main interconnection network. This network is used to broadcast final states in order to check for illegal combinations of states between nodes (e.g., caches with stale copies). We refer to these additional messages as *assertions*, since the node is declaring that it has or has had certain access rights to the block. For the SMP case, this is just a second bus for addresses, final states, and signatures.

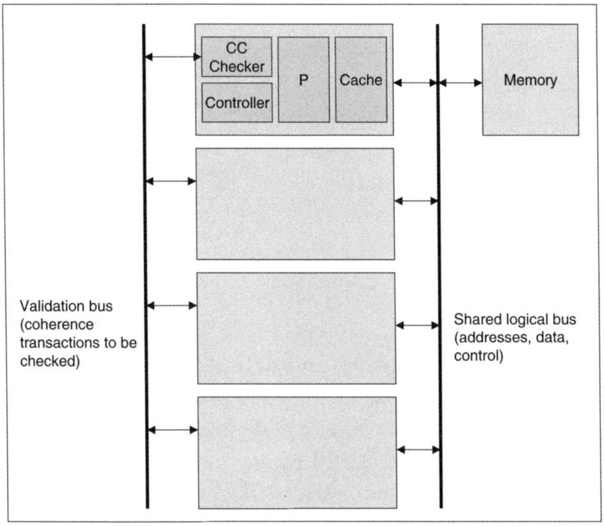

Fig. 3.5. SMP with support for dynamic verification

3.2.2 SMP Coherence Checker Operation

Following a network transaction in the implementation protocol, the address, input request, actions, and initial and final stable states are sent to the local checkers. Each checker recomputes the final state and actions for the cache line and compares them to the implementation protocol's result. If the final states or actions do not match, an error has occurred.

The checker also performs a tag lookup with the address to get the stable state of the cache line. The stable state stored in the checker must match the initial state reported by the implementation protocol. Disagreement signals an error, since the two protocols did not start with the same state. See Figures 3.6 and 3.7 for a simplified checker datapath.

Once the transaction has been verified locally, the cache states must be checked globally. The node that initiated the transaction (via request) broadcasts the final state and address of the cache block over the validation network.

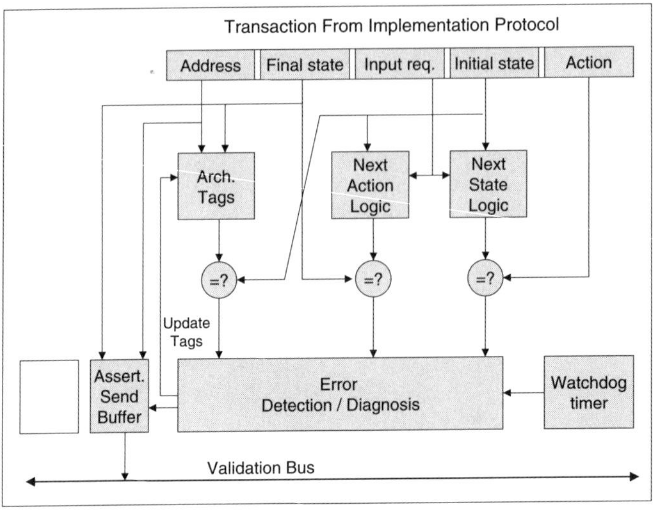

Fig. 3.6. Coherence checker logic (checking a transaction).

The other nodes snoop the network and determine if the cache state that was broadcast conflicts with the state of the cached copies they hold. For example, if a node acquires a modifiable copy of a memory block, it sends an assertion message indicating that it has the block in the *M state*. The other checkers must determine if they have any copies still in their caches. If an illegal com-

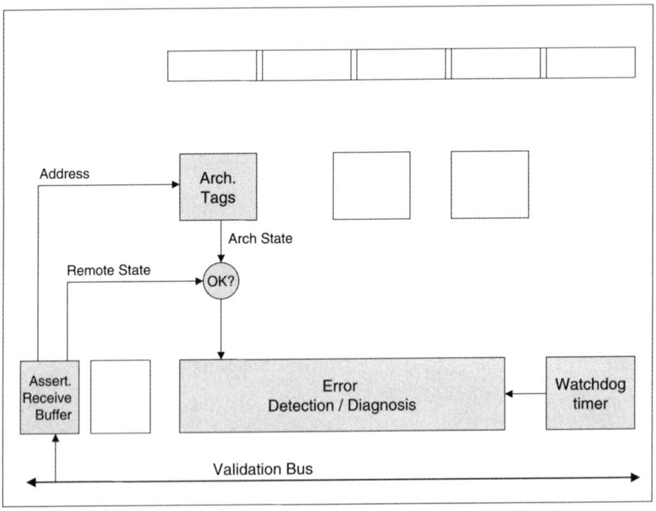

Fig. 3.7. Coherence checker logic (checking an assertion).

bination of cache states is detected for an address (Figure 3.2), an error is signaled.

Once the node that provided data for the transaction (the responder) sees the assertion, its checker knows that the transaction has completed. The transaction may then be retired and removed from any queues. Note that we do not allow further updates to the stable state of the receiving node until a corresponding check message is received. Depending on whether recoverability is desired, the initiator can retire the transaction after sending the assertion or buffer it long enough to make sure that no errors are signaled.

3.3 SMP Coherence Checker Correctness, Coverage, and Specificity

Ideally, a checker implementation should have full fault coverage. By full coverage, we mean complete detection of faults that have propagated to the point of being visible errors to the coherence checker. For example, a design error may cause the omission of a message in the implementation protocol; however, this will not be detected by our scheme until it results in an improper stable state transition.

In addition, the coherence checking hardware should not slow the system by introducing overhead or signaling false positives. For efficient recovery, it should not lag far behind the implementation.

3.3.1 Coherence Checker Coverage and Specificity

Symbolic model verification (model checking) is a powerful technique for verifying finite state machines and protocols [1, 8, 9, 10]. It has been successfully used to verify cache coherence protocols [9, 10]. Given a model of a system and a set of logical properties, a tool can automatically determine if the modeled system satisfies the properties in all cases. However, for model checking to be feasible, the modeled system must be a greatly simplified version of the implementation. With fewer states and transitions, it may be possible to use symbolic model checking techniques to verify the correctness of the simple protocol, determine the checker coverage, and find cases of false positives. Determining if the simple protocol is correct is straightforward. A model of the simplified state machine can be written in a language such as SMV (top part of Figure 3.8). A set of necessary conditions for maintaining coherence is then specified formally in temporal logic (e.g., CTL). The model checking software determines if the model always meets the conditions or produces a counter-example. Without the complexity of the full implementation, the state space will be relatively small and quickly searched by a model verifier such as NuSMV [8].

To determine if the coherence checker implementation detects errors, we write a detailed model for the checker implementation (middle part of Figure 3.8). Next, we formally define (in CTL) what sequences of events the coherence checker implementation should detect as errors. The checker implementation achieves full coverage if, for every defined error condition, the coherence checker signals an error.

To determine specificity, we can also use model checking (bottom part of Figure 3.8). We can combine the two models mentioned above such that the simple protocol is checked by the implementation of the coherence checker. Since the simple protocol has been proven correct, the coherence checker implementation should never detect an error in this configuration. Any errors signaled by the coherence checker in this configuration are considered false positives.

This is analogous to proving the correctness of a DIVA checker in the single-processor case; however, the burden of defining the necessary conditions for correctness is placed on the designer. It is also necessary for the designer to validate the model. This is true in general for verifying concurrent systems with model checking (a design may still be incorrect but satisfy the designer's specifications). Furthermore, model checking can only tell us if the checker implementation will detect errors specified by the designer, such as disagreement between the implementation protocol and the simple protocol.

3.4 Coherence Checker Overhead

Ideally, the coherence checker implementation proposed should not become a bottleneck for the base system or increase system cost. In this section, we present preliminary data collected to estimate performance overhead.

3.4.1 Preliminary Estimates

The absence of transient states keeps the checker logic simple and fast. Furthermore, the second bus proposed for the SMP configuration produces no more transactions than the main address bus, so duplicating the address and control portions of the bus may be sufficient to support the extra messages. However, if a second physical network is infeasible, the main network may be used to send extra messages (perhaps with low priority). If this is the case, bandwidth overhead is incurred by the extra messages used for dynamic verification.

To first estimate overhead, we collected data from a 4-processor SMP system with 1 MB 4-way set-associative L2 caches and 64-byte lines. From these data, we can determine how often the checker must verify a coherence transaction. Figure 3.9 shows (for five benchmarks) that between 0.5% and 7.2% of memory references (loads and stores) result in a change of stable state

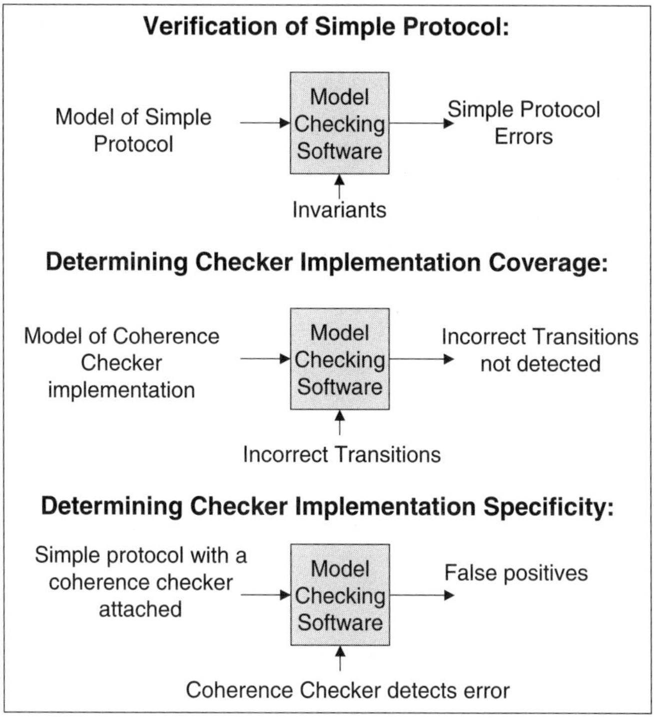

Fig. 3.8. Determining checker coverage and specificity.

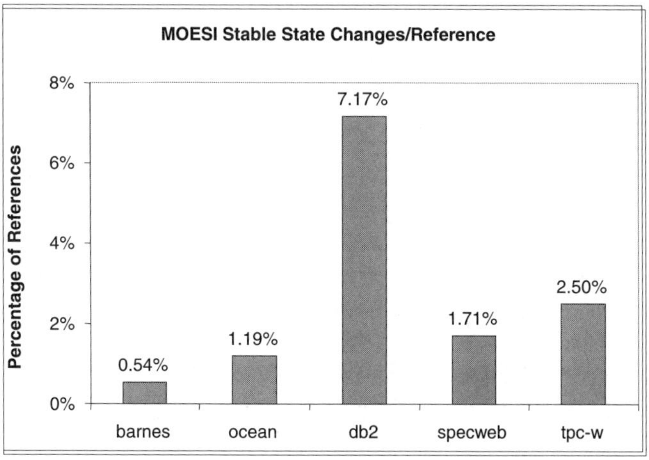

Fig. 3.9. Percentage of memory references that result in stable state transitions.

for a cache line. We infer from this that the checking of local state transitions is infrequent and need not be fast.

The estimated overhead incurred by extra messages is calculated for a few strategies in Figure 3.10.

The first approach is to have the node's checker send a message each time that a modifiable copy of a cache line is acquired. This ensures that no readable or writable copies exist. This simple approach requires 31% or fewer extra messages for the benchmarks simulated but cannot detect certain types of errors. Cache lines brought into a node in the shared state are not checked to see if modified copies still exist, and replacements are not checked.

A second approach is to have assertions sent for all transactions resulting in a data transfer. This checks that data are brought into a node in the correct state but does not check upgrades (S,O→M). This approach requires approximately 45% additional messages.

Third, assertions may be issued for all bus read or upgrade operations. This approach is a combination of the first two, with improved coverage. Each time a block is brought into the cache or upgraded, a message is sent by the initiator of the transaction. However, this is more costly than the previous methods (as much as 64%). Finally, an assertion message may be sent for all bus transactions. In addition to all cases checked by the third approach, write-backs resulting from replacements are also checked. In effect, the second bus proposed for checking purposes mirrors the main bus, ensuring that all transactions were completed correctly. This incurs 100% address bandwidth overhead (the same overhead as replicating the main address bus but with the ability to catch some design errors).

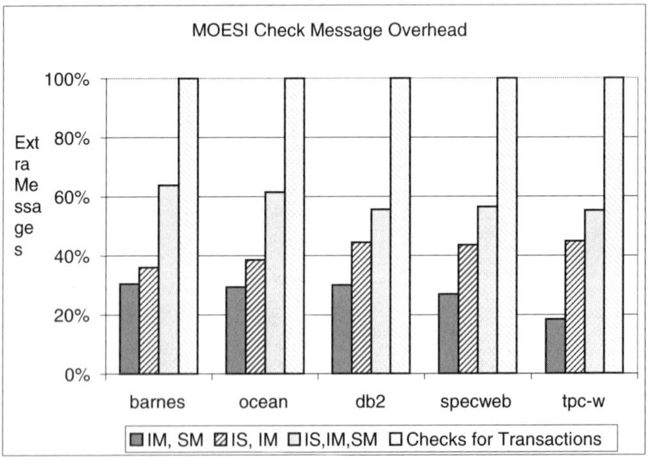

Fig. 3.10. Calculated message overhead for checker implementation strategies

None of the strategies mentioned checks the silent transitions (S→I, E→I, E→M). These transitions do not involve updating memory or sending data to other nodes. The data are simply discarded or modified, and we rely on the checker internal to the node to make sure that the correct activities are performed.

3.4.2 Simulation Results

For performance simulations, we used a modified version of SimpleMP, an execution-driven multiprocessor simulator developed at the University of Wisconsin-Madison [11]. Our simulation workload consisted of a combination of six SPLASH2 benchmarks.

The modeled system consisted of 16 processors connected by a 200 MHz split-transaction address bus and a 16 byte full crossbar for routing data. Each processor had a 1 GHz, 4-way superscalar out-of-order core with split 64 kB 2-way set-associative L1 caches. Main memory latency incurs a 60 ns access time, not including network and arbitration delays. The cache controllers implement an optimized MOESI protocol modeled after the Gigaplane [12]. In the interest of time, we removed the L2 caches and write-buffers from the simulated system. However, the additional memory traffic only increased the performance impact of dynamic verification. To check the protocol, we modeled a scalar checker for each cache with a 4-cycle latency. A small (4-entry) input queue was implemented to hold transactions while the checker is busy. This does not constrain the number of outstanding misses since only completed transactions enter the queue. For comparison, we modeled systems with and without a second bus for assertions and pipelined checkers. All data transfers were delayed until all state transitions for those data had been checked, and processors were not allowed to access fill data until assertions were complete.

For all benchmarks, the impact of the checking process was negligible. The impact of extra messages was significant when one bus was used and eliminated entirely with a second bus; see Figure 3.11.

	water	ocean	raytrace	barnes	fmm	volrend
Checking all transactions	167.6%	198.9%	197.1%	190.6%	148.8%	174.7%
All trans. + 2nd Bus	100.0%	99.9%	99.9%	98.5%	100.1%	100.0%

Fig. 3.11. Normalized execution time with dynamic verification.

The low overhead is the result of high miss latencies and a high level of concurrency. Despite an aggressive processor model and a high-speed bus, the number of processor cycles consumed by a cache miss is quite high. The added cycles for checking are relatively small and can usually be overlapped with other activities.

3.5 Related Work

Testing-based approaches are conventionally used for detecting both design errors and fabrication defects [13]. For design verification, the most commonly used technique is to develop a set of test vectors and use them to drive logic simulation [14, 15, 16]. The designer or a verification engineer may devise such test vectors. Parts of this process may be automated, but its effectiveness depends on the insight and skill of the engineers involved. This method is extremely time-consuming and typically miss some bugs.

For hardware failures, test patterns are generated to exercise the hardware, often using a fault model such as the stuck-at model [13]. The process can be largely automated [17, 18], and test coverage can be quantitatively estimated. The test patterns are then applied to verify correctness–up to the level of test coverage. In the field, this technique works better for permanent faults than for transient ones, as the fault must be present at the time the test is applied. Also, this method may require some downtime when the test is applied.

There have been a number of proposals for using a simplified *watchdog* processor [19] to check a main processor. Watchdog processors have many of the advantages we envision, but watchdog processors do not duplicate the entire computation. They check only certain aspects of the computation (e.g., the control flow [20], the memory access behavior [21], and *reasonableness* based on programmed-in assertions [22]). They do not check the entire computation, and therefore do not detect all faults, nor are they used for complete state recovery.

Rotenberg proposed a multithreaded processor that implements a form of time redundancy where a computation thread is re-executed later in time and the results of the two thread executions are compared [5]. His approach focused on transient hardware faults in the multithreaded processor's datapath and also built on previous approaches using time-shifted redundant execution [23, 24]. He referred to this new technique as Active-stream/Redundant-stream Simultaneous Multithreading (AR-SMT).

Reinhardt and Mukherjee further explored the use of multithreading for transient fault detection in [25]. They introduced an important abstraction for simultaneous and redundantly multithreaded (SRT) processors, identified some key implementation challenges, and suggested some microarchitectural solutions.

As described earlier, Austin proposed dynamic checking with a separate check processor for the second computation [6].

Conventional forms of dynamic checking have been proposed and implemented for many years. Probably the oldest is replication with comparison checking as protection against hardware failures [26, 27, 28, 29, 30]. This method can be effective against both permanent and transient hardware errors, but it does not catch design errors. Furthermore, it is likely to be more expensive than the dynamic checking method because the check processor is a complete replica and is not simplified. Many systems have used replication for failure protection. The IBM G5 [31] is a recent version where both processors are on the same chip.

For detecting design errors, formal methods [32, 33] provide an alternative to conventional simulation-based testing. Formal methods typically use an architecture specification and an implementation specification and then show that the two are equivalent. This equivalence is essentially proven for all possible computations, either via model checking [1, 9, 10], theorem proving [34], or a combination of the two [35, 36]. As high-performance implementations of coherence protocols become more complex, the computational complexity of formal methods becomes an issue.

3.6 Future Work

Currently, the burden is on the designers to identify the simple protocol. We intend to develop a framework for checker design, verification, and performance evaluation to facilitate the process of incorporating dynamic verification into parallel systems.

In the DIVA approach for single-processor systems, the check hardware had a well-defined sequence of operations to check via the reorder buffer. Unfortunately, such a serialization is not present for coherence operations in a multiprocessor that is not sequentially consistent since program loads can (correctly) become visible to the system before earlier stores. In future work, we will investigate dynamic verification for memory models and hopefully define what constraints must be placed on the implementation protocol in order to provide a simple interface to a checker.

Finally, we intend to combine dynamic verification with hardware and software recovery techniques. Once an error has been detected and diagnosed, it may be possible to restart from a checkpoint or use some form of forward error recovery.

3.7 Conclusions

With dynamic verification, errors in a cache coherence protocol caused by manufacturing faults, soft errors, and design mistakes can be detected at runtime. Since most memory operations do not cause a change in cache state, a simple checker can check the coherence protocol of an aggressive processor. Furthermore, with a second network for assertions, globally verifying cache coherence does not place pressure on the data network or memory. This approach can be combined with recovery techniques and methods of dynamically verifying program execution [6] to produce fault-tolerant multiprocessor systems.

Acknowledgments

We give special thanks to Ravi Rajwar for his detailed multiprocessor simulator. We thank Timothy Heil, Ashutosh Dhodapkar, and the anonymous reviewers for comments on drafts of this chapter. This work is supported by NSF grant CCR-0083126 and by IBM. Jason Cantin is supported by a Wisconsin Distinguished Graduate Fellowship.

References

1. D. L. Dill, A. J. Drexler, A. J. Hu, and C. H. Yang. Protocol Verification as a Hardware Design Aid. In *International Conference on Computer Design, VLSI in Computers and Processors*, pp. 522–525, Oct. 1992.
2. D. Culler and J. Singh, Parallel Computer Architecture: A Hardware / Software Approach, Morgan Kaufmann Publishers, San Francisco, CA, 1999.
3. T. C. May and M. H. Woods. Alpha-Particle-Induced Soft Errors in Dynamic Memories. *IEEE Transactions on Electronic Devices*, pp. 2–9, 26(2), 1979.
4. T. J. O'Gorman, J. M. Ross, A. H. Taber, J. F. Ziegler, H. P. Muhlfeld, C. J. Montrose, H. W. Curtis, J. L. Walsh, Field Testing for Cosmic Ray Soft Errors in Semiconductor Memories. *IBM Journal of Research and Development*, pp. 41–49, Jan. 1996.
5. E. Rotenberg, AR-SMT: A Microarchitectural Approach to Fault-Tolerance in Microprocessors. In *Proceedings of the 29th International Symposium on Fault-Tolerant Computing*, pp. 84–91, June 1999.
6. T. Austin. DIVA: A Reliable Substrate for Deep-Submicron Processor Design. In*Proceedings of the 32nd Annual ACM/IEEE International Symposium on Microarchitecture*, pp. 196–207, Dec. 1999.
7. P. Sweazy and A. J. Smith, A Class of Compatible Cache Consistency Protocols and their Support by the IEEE Futurebus. In *Proceedings of the 13th Annual International Symposium on Computer Architecture*, pp. 414-423, June 1986.
8. A. Cimatti, E. Clarke, F. Giunchiglia, and M. Roveri, NuSMV: A New Symbolic Model Verifier. N. Halbwachs and D. Peled, eds. In *Proceedings of the 11th International Conference on Computer-Aided Verification*, Lecture Notes in Computer Science 1633, Berlin: Springer-Verlag, pp. 495–499, 1999.
9. E. Clarke, O. Grumberg, H. Hiraishi, S. Jha, D. E. Long, K. L. McMillan, and A. L. Ness. Verification of the Futurebus+ Cache Coherence Protocol. In *Proceedings of the 11th International Symposium on Computer Hardware Description Languages and their Applications*, Apr. 1993.
10. E. Clarke, O. Grumberg, and D. Peled, Model Checking. Cambridge: MIT Press, 1999.
11. SimpleMP was obtained via personal correspondence with Ravi Rajwar.
12. A. Charlesworth, A. Phelps, R. Williams, and G. Gilbert, Gigaplane-XB: Extending the Ultra Enterprise Family. In *Hot Interconnects V*, pp. 97–112, Aug. 1997.
13. M. Abramovici, M. A. Breuer, and A. D. Friedman. Digital Systems Testing and Testable Design. IEEE Press, New York, 1992.

14. T. Sasaki, A. Yamada, and T. Aoyama. Hierarchical Design Verification for Large Digital Systems. In *Proceedings of the 18th Design Automation Conference*, pp. 105–112, June 1981.
15. M. Monachino. Design Verification System for Large-Scale LSI Designs, In *Proceedings of the 19th Design Automation Conference*, pp. 83–90, June 1982.
16. A. Aharon. Test Program Generation for Functional Verification of PowerPC Processors in IBM, In *Proceedings of the 32nd Design Automation Conference*, pp. 270-285, June 1995.
17. J. Roth, W. G. Bouricius, and P. Schneider. Programmed Algorithms to Compute Tests and Detect and Distinguish Between Failures in Logic Circuits, *IEEE Transactions on Electronic Computers*, EC-16(10), pp. 567–579, Oct. 1967.
18. P. Goel. An Implicit Enumeration Algorithm to Generate Tests for Combinational Logic Circuits, *IEEE Transactions on Computers*, C-30(3), pp. 215–222, Mar. 1981.
19. A. Mahmood and E. J. McCluskey. Concurrent Error Detection Using Watchdog Processors–A Survey. *IEEE Transactions on Computers*, C-37(2), pp. 160–173, Feb 1982.
20. D. J. Liu. Watchdog Processor and Structural Integrity Checking. *IEEE Transactions on Computers*, C-31, pp. 518–685, July 1982.
21. M. Namjoo and E. J. McCluskey. Watchdog Processors and Capability Checking. In *Proceedings of the 12th International Symposium on Fault-Tolerant Computing*, pp. 245-248, June 1982.
22. A. Mahmood, D. J. Liu, and E. J. McCluskey. Concurrent Detection Using a Watchdog Processor and Assertions. In *Proceedings of the 1983 International Test Conference*, pp. 622-628, Oct. 1983.
23. J. Patel and L. Fung. Concurrent Error Detection in ALUs by Recomputing with Shifted Operands. *IEEE Transactions on Computers*, C-31(7), pp. 589–595, July 1982.
24. G. Sohi, M. Franklin, and K. Saluja. A Study of Time-Redundant Fault-Tolerance Techniques in High-Performance Pipelined Computers. In *Proceedings of 19th Fault-Tolerant Computing Symposium*, pp. 436–443, June 1989.
25. S. Reinhardt and S. Mukherjee. Transient Fault Detection via Simultaneous Multithreading. In *Proceedings of the 27th International Symposium on Computer Architecture*, pp. 25–36, June 2000.
26. S. Webber. The Stratus Architecture. D. Siewiorek and R. Swarz, eds. Reliable Computer Systems: Design and Evaluation. Bedford, MA: Digital Press, 1992.
27. O. Serlin. Fault-Tolerant Systems in Commercial Applications. *IEEE Computer*, pp. 19–30, Aug. 1984.
28. J. A. Katzman, A Fault-Tolerant Computing System. Tandem Computers, Inc., Cupertino, CA, 1977.
29. J. P. Eckert Jr., J. R. Weiner, H. D. Welsh, and H. F. Mitchell. The UNIVAC System, In *Proceedings of the Joint AIEE-IRE Computer Conference*,pp. 6-16, Dec. 1951.
30. A. W. Burks, H. H. Goldstein, and J. von Neumann. Preliminary Discussion of the Logical Design of an Electronic Computing Instrument. *Papers of John von Neumann.* MIT Bridge, Cambridge, MA, pp. 97–146, 1987.
31. L. Spainhower and T. A. Gregg. IBM S/390 Parallel Enterprise Server G5 Fault-Tolerance: A Historical Perspective. *IBM Journal of Research and Development*, 43(5/6), pp. 863, May 1999.

32. E. M. Clarke and J. M. Wing. Formal Methods: State of the Art and Future Directions. *ACM Computing Surveys*, 28(4), pp. 626–643, Dec. 1996.
33. E. Clarke and R. Kurshian. Computer-Aided Verification. *IEEE Spectrum*, 33(6), pp. 61–67, June 1996.
34. A. Kuehlman, A. Srinivasan, and D. LaPotin, Verity–A Formal Program for Custom CMOS Circuits. *IBM Journal of Research and Development*, 39(1/2), pp. 149–165, 1995.
35. R. Kurshan and L. Lamport. Verification of a Multiplier, 64 Bits and Beyond. In *Proceedings of the 5th International Conference on Computer-Aided Verification*, Lecture Notes in Computer Science 697, Berlin: Springer-Verlag, pp. 166–179, 1993.
36. S. Rajan, N. Shankar, and M. Srivas. An Integration of Model Checking with Automated Proof Checking. In*Proceedings of the 7th International Conference on Computer-Aided Verification*, Lecture Notes in Computer Science 939,Berlin: Springer-Verlag, pp. 84-97, June 1995.

4

Timestamp-Based Selective Cache Allocation

Martin Karlsson and Erik Hagersten

Department of Information Technology, Uppsala University Uppsala, Sweden
martink@it.uu.se,eh@it.uu.se

Abstract. The behavior of the memory hierarchy is key to high performance in today's GHz microprocessors. The cache level closest to the processor is limited in size and associativity in order to match the short cycle time of the CPU. Even though only data objects soon reused again will benefit from the small cache, all accessed data objects are normally allocated in the cache.

In this chapter we demonstrate how an "optimal" selective allocation algorithm, based on knowledge about the future, can drastically increase the effectiveness of a cache. The effectiveness is further enhanced if the allocation candidates are temporarily held in a small staging cache before making the allocation decision. We also present an implementable selective allocation algorithm based on knowledge about the past (RASCAL) that measures reuse distance in the new time unit *cache allocation ticks*, (CAT). CAT is shown to be a fairly accurate and application-independent way of detecting good allocation candidates.

4.1 Introduction

Cache systems are designed to minimize the average access time for memory references. Uniprocessor cache misses can be classified into the three categories: conflict, compulsory, and capacity misses [Hil87]. The number of conflict misses can be reduced by a more associative cache or by the introduction of a victim cache [Jou90]. Larger cache lines and a number of prefetching algorithms have been proposed to reduce compulsory misses, while the conventional approach for reducing capacity misses is simply to increase the size of the cache – a brute force approach often enabled by a manufacturing process shrink. However, at the lower levels of the cache hierarchy, a larger cache may not be feasible, since the cache size can be limited by the speed requirements of the CPU. The access time of the L1 cache is often tied to the pipeline architecture such that a larger and slower L1 cache would effectively slow down the CPU pipeline.

The Virtually Indexed Physically Tagged (VIPT) scheme [WBL89] which can remove the TLB lookup from the critical path, also limits the cache size.

Aliasing problems arise if the L1 cache size is larger than the page size.[1] Sometimes this is circumvented by a more associative cache, but there is also a limit to the degree of associativity achievable in the fast L1. Agarwal et al. predict that due to advances in chip technology the CPU performance will be bound by communication constraints rather than by capacity limitations [AHKB00]. They predict the number of SRAM bits reachable in one CPU cycle will decrease over time – yet another negative impact for the L1 cache size. Chip Multiprocessors (CMP) with several CPUs, each with its own L1 cache, sharing the same die is another reason to keep the L1 caches small.

We conclude that the first-level caches are likely to remain small relative to the active working set of most applications and that selective cache allocation should be studied. By a more selective L1 allocation, the data objects well suited for the L1 cache will reside longer in the L1 cache. This will increase the *effective cache* size of the L1 cache and remove some of the *capacity misses.*

The contributions of this chapter are threefold:

- We suggest streaming the data through a small staging cache before deciding about the L1 allocation and demonstrate its effect on an optimal allocation algorithm.
- We suggest a new timestamp-based allocation algorithm based on the new time unit cache allocation ticks.
- We compare three different implementation options for selective cache allocation.

The rest of this chapter is outlined as follows. First, we discuss different selective allocation schemes and their advantages and drawbacks. Second, we evaluate the *optimal* allocation algorithm and show how a small staging cache can drastically improve its effectiveness. We then propose the new timestamp-based algorithm, RASCAL. Finally, we propose a feasible implementation of the algorithm and compare its performance to some of the other algorithms presented.

4.2 Related Work

The importance of cache allocation decisions has already been partly addressed in some CPU architectures by the introduction of dedicated load and store instructions hinting where in the memory hierarchy an accessed datum should be installed. One example is the UltraSPARC's VIS instruction set, which has *block load* and *block store* instructions that bypass the cache hierarchy. These instructions can, for example, be used in a bcopy loop to avoid polluting the caches with copy data, which are unlikely to be reused soon

[1] Some computer vendors employ restrictions on the virtual-to-physical mapping that relax this requirement somewhat.

again. The UltraSPARC III CPU also has a special *prefetch once* instruction that installs the data in a fully associative 2 kB prefetch cache accessed in parallel with the L1 cache. That way, the larger L1 will not get polluted from prefetched data that are likely to be used only once. The instruction *prefetch many* is used to prefetch data that should be installed in the normal L1 data cache. Another approach to selective caching has been taken in the implementation of the HP PA7200 CPU [KCZ+94], which has a small parallel *assist cache* in addition to a large, one-cycle latency off-chip cache. All cache lines are initially allocated in the assist cache and, upon replacement, allocated in the off-chip cache, unless a certain *spatial only* hint was specified in the instruction fetching the data. If so, the data will bypass the off-chip cache. While the allocation decision could be controlled by static compiler analysis, such analysis can sometimes be hard. We therefore believe that there is a need for a hardware algorithm, which dynamically can identify the data objects worthy of allocation in the L1 cache.

Several approaches for efficient dynamic management of the L1 data cache have been proposed lately. In the algorithms, allocation decisions are based either on the address of the instruction accessing the data or on the data address. Most of the schemes propose a statically partitioned cache consisting of several subcaches, where each subcache is tailored for a certain category of cache blocks [GAV95][MMT96][RD96] [RTT+98][SG99]. Cache blocks are allocated in different sub-caches based on their type of reuse in terms of spatial and temporal locality. Najjar et al. also proposed a statically partitioned cache [MT97] and allocate scalar and array data in different subcaches. Srinivasan et al. takes a different approach, where the cache is statically partitioned into critical/non-critical subcaches [SJLW01]. Critical loads are here defined as loads that must complete early in order not to degrade the pipeline performance. The drawback of using a statically partitioned cache for different categories of data is that it may perform worse than a conventional cache if the access pattern of a program doesn't suit the partitioning of the cache.

Several cache bypass schemes have also been proposed where some cache blocks are not allocated in the cache upon a cache miss [McF92]. The cache allocation algorithms introduced by Tyson et al. [TFMP95] and Johnson and Hwu [JH97] are based on access frequency and prevent frequently accessed cache blocks from being replaced by less frequently used cache blocks.

We present an address-based run-time algorithm, the RASCAL algorithm, in Section 4.5.3. The distinguishing feature of our proposal is that we stream cache blocks through a small staging cache before making the L1 allocation decision. The algorithm does not explicitly make any distinction between cache blocks of different reuse categories or access frequencies, nor does it statically divide the cache into different subcaches for different categories. Instead we monitor each allocation and adaptively make allocation decisions based on the duration between recent cache allocations. The model most similar to our proposal is the MAT model introduced by Johnson and Hwu [JH97][Joh98][JH99]. The MAT model is discussed in detail in Section 4.5.1.

4.3 Evaluation Methodology

All evaluations are performed using the Simics full-system simulator simulating a Sun SPARC machine running Solaris 7 [MDG+98]. Since SIMICS has a modest slowdown rate, we were able to study applications from SPLASH2 and SPEC CPU2000 with (close to) a realistic problem size. We have restricted our evaluation in this chapter to data references only. All caches are write-around and assume a perfect write buffer. A cache block size of 64 bytes is used unless otherwise stated. Since this paper focuses on reducing misses in small caches, we have opted to isolate our study to the cache performance of the first-level cache. The SPLASH-2 applications were run to completion using the problem sizes suggested by Woo et al. [WOT+95]. The SPEC CPU2000 benchmarks were run with the reduced input data sets suggested by KleinOsowski et al. [KFML00].

In order to get an upper bound for our allocation algorithm, we first studied an optimal exclusion/allocation algorithm [McF92] based on future knowledge. The basic idea is that, if the cache line singled out by the replacement algorithm will be referenced sooner than the new cache line, the new cache line will not get allocated in the cache. Note that we do not change the replacement algorithm and will only compare the new cache block with the victim that was singled out by the existing replacement algorithm; i.e., the optimal allocation algorithm we are using is not the same as the optimal replacement algorithm suggested by others [Bel66, SA93]. While the optimal allocation algorithm cannot feasibly be implemented, it represents the optimal allocation strategy and initially convinced us that this area is indeed worth exploring. This algorithm will be referred to as the *optimal* algorithm.

4.4 Staging Cache L0

We have observed that a large fraction, often a majority, of the objects allocated in an L1 cache have temporal properties ill-suited for the L1 cache. Some of these objects are never accessed before being replaced, while others have an intense, but short-lived, reuse pattern; e.g., objects with only spatial locality and read-modify-write objects with a load/store pair in a short time distance. These objects are reused shortly after the allocation but are not touched again before replacement and will spend most of their L1 tenure unused (which is later illustrated by Figure 4.8). Neither of these object types make efficient use of the L1 cache. It's the objects with a long-lived temporal locality, the ones reused over and over again during a long time interval, that make the best use of the L1 cache. We label these three classes of cache lines non-temporal (NT), short-lived temporal (ST), and long-lived temporal (LT) localities.

Figure 4.1 shows the performance of the *optimal* algorithm, OPT L1, using the metric *miss ratio reduction*, which is defined as

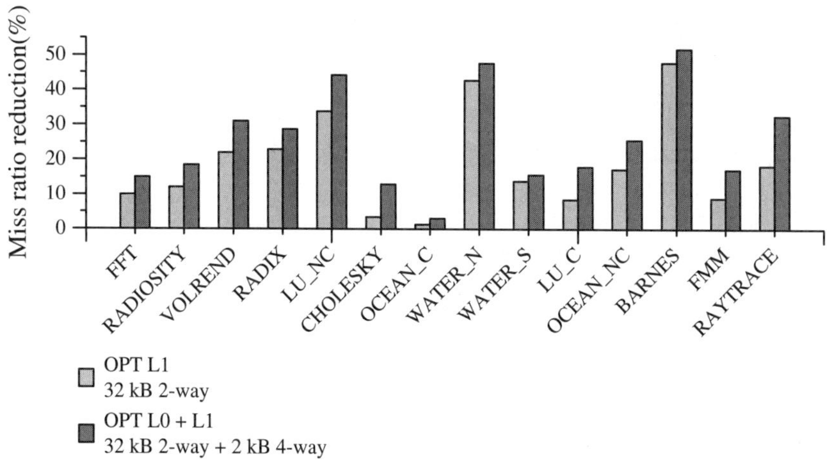

Fig. 4.1. Comparative miss ratio reduction data for the OPT L0+L1 and OPT L1 allocation algorithms compared to a conventional cache (2-way 32 kB). Here, the L0 is a 4-way associative 2 kB cache.

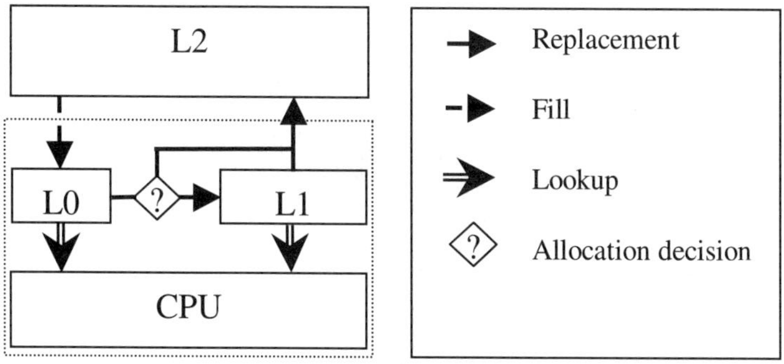

Fig. 4.2. The baseline architecture.

- $1 - MissRatioXCache/MissRatioConventionalCache$;

where the studied caches and the conventional cache are compared, assuming they have the same size and organization. The optimal algorithm will effectively avoid allocation of NT objects. However, it will happily allocate the ST objects.

In order to allocate neither the NT nor the ST objects in the L1 cache, all cache blocks can be streamed through a small staging cache, called L0, before the L1 allocation decision is made. On a cache lookup, the L0 is accessed in parallel with, and has the same access time as, the L1 cache. On a cache miss the cache block is allocated in L0. The L0 victims are, based on the selection algorithm, either allocated in the L1 or bypassed. Figure 4.2 shows the organization of the L0 and L1 caches. By delaying the allocation decision until after the L0 cache, most of the NT and ST objects have become inactive and will not get allocated in the L1 cache. The graph in Figure 4.1 shows that adding the L0 cache significantly improves the effect of the optimal algorithm.

The potential performance gain of selective allocation is further shown in Figure 4.3, comparing three options for improving a 2-way, 32 kB cache: doubling the cache size, doubling the associativity, and the optimal allocation decision in combination with small staging cache L0. For all of the applications, optimal allocation with L0 performs better than twice the associativity (a 4-way LRU cache of the same size), and for ten of the fourteen applications the optimal algorithm performs comparably with a cache twice the size while maintaining the same degree of associativity. We conclude that a selective allocation in combination with a small staging cache can have a huge impact on the miss rate of a small 2-way cache. Next, we will study different practical algorithms for implementing selective allocation.

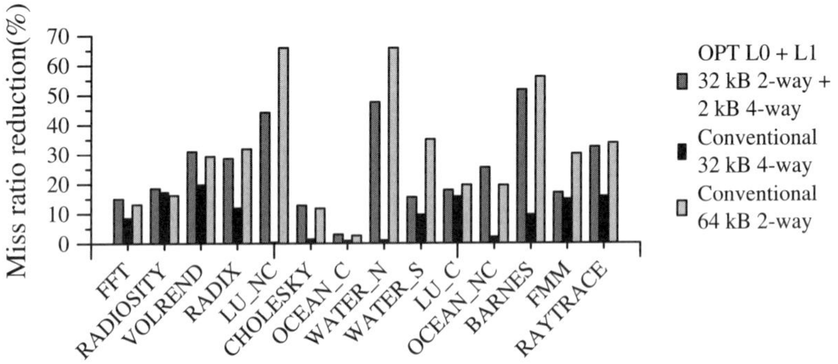

Fig. 4.3. Miss ratio reduction compared to a conventional cache (2-way 32 kB).

4.5 Selective Allocation

4.5.1 The MAT Model

The MAT model by Johnson and Hwu bases its allocation decision on access frequency [JH97][Joh98][JH99]. The MAT model monitors accesses per macro block, which is defined as a contiguous block of memory small enough that cache blocks belonging to the same macro block are likely to display the same usage pattern. Each macro block has a hit counter associated with it, which is incremented upon a hit to a cache block belonging to the macro block. The hit counters are stored in a cache structure called the Memory Address

Table (MAT), which stores access frequency information for some of the macro blocks. Upon a cache miss the macro block hit counter of the victim selected by the replacement algorithm is decremented and compared to the new cache block. If the victim has the highest macro block counter value, the cache block generating the miss will not be allocated in the main cache but instead in a separate smaller cache called the bypass buffer.

Since the first MAT publication[JH97], the MAT model has been enhanced by adding the notion of a decrementing counter, *decr_ctr*, for each macro block in the MAT [Joh98][JH99]. The decrementing counter of a macro block is incremented by one on every conflict for a cache location held by the macro block and cleared to zero upon a cache hit to the macro block. Upon a conflict, the access counter is decremented by the value of *decr_ctr* plus one instead of just decrementing by one as in the original MAT model. The MAT models require quite complex hardware circuitry since on every cache hit a counter must be incremented through a read-modify-write operation. It also requires, as previously mentioned, a separate cache structure holding the access and decrementing counters.

4.5.2 The AAA Algorithm

This algorithm is based on the existence of a staging cache L0, as shown in Figure 4.2. The algorithm audits each cache block during its tenure in the L1 cache. The audition result is kept in the L2 cache and will allow for allocation into L1 for as long as the cache block *performs well.* We call this the Audition-based Allocation Algorithm (AAA). The algorithm uses an *allocation history bit* for each cache block in the L1 cache. When a cache block is accessed in the L1 cache, the *allocation history bit* is set. The *allocation history bit* value of the last L1 tenure is stored in L2 as meta data and follows the cache line into the L0 cache, from the L2 cache. Cache blocks that are evicted from the L0 cache with their *allocation history bit* cleared are bypassed, while cache blocks with the bit set are allocated in the L2 cache with their *allocation history bit* set to zero. In this study we have assumed that storing metadata in memory is expensive and have opted to "forget" the last audition result upon L2 eviction. Cache blocks that are allocated directly from memory get their *allocation history bit* set in the L0 cache, which will allow for a new L1 audition.

While the advantage of the AAA algorithm is its simplicity and low implementation cost, an obvious problem with this scheme is that the algorithm has no way of detecting and changing its decision if a cache block was wrongfully classified as a bypass type. This may cause a severe performance penalty from repeated bypasses of cache blocks that would benefit from allocation in the L1 cache. This problem is somewhat eased since whenever a cache block generates an L2 miss the cache block is given a new audition.

4.5.3 RASCAL–Timestamp-Based Allocation

The Runtime Adaptive Cache ALlocation (RASCAL) algorithm is also based on the existence of a staging L0 cache and has some metadata stored together with the cache block. Each cache block has a timestamp storing its last *time of allocation decision*[2] together with the *allocation history bit* in the metadata. A cache block with a cleared *allocation history bit* will still be allocated in L1 if the elapsed time since the last L0 eviction is short enough. We call the elapsed time the *reuse distance.* If the reuse distance is shorter than the expected *survival time*[3] in the L1 cache, we conclude that the previous allocation decision was either an incorrect bypass decision or that the cache block was prematurely evicted due to a conflict and that the cache block should indeed be allocated in the L1 cache. This makes up for the problem identified for the AAA algorithm. However, there are two practical problems to be solved for such an algorithm: long timestamps are expensive to store as metadata and the threshold for a short enough reuse distance must be determined.

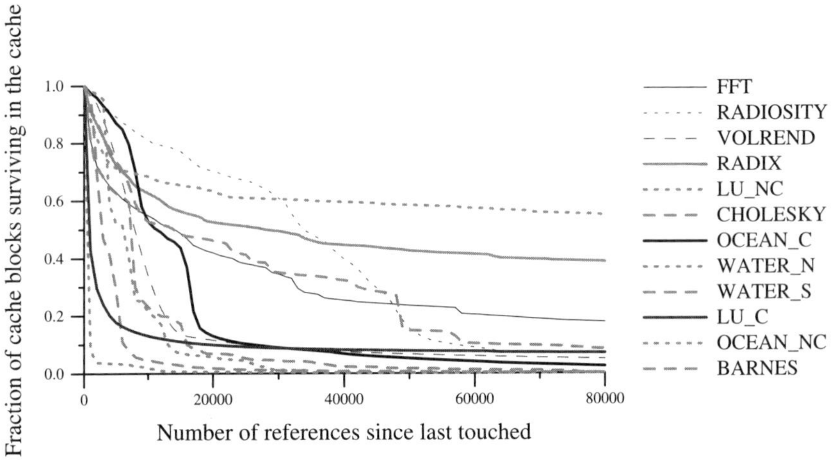

Fig. 4.4. Distribution of survival time in a cache for a conventional 32 kB 2-way cache with 64 byte cache blocks measured in number of references.

The problem is that the expected *survival time* in a cache varies for different applications, as can be seen in Figure 4.4. It shows the distribution of cache *survival time*, measured in number of memory references, for each replaced cache line in a conventional 2-way 32 kB cache. In other words, how

[2] The time of the last eviction from L0; see Figure 4.2

[3] Defined as the elapsed time between a cache block's last hit and its replacement.

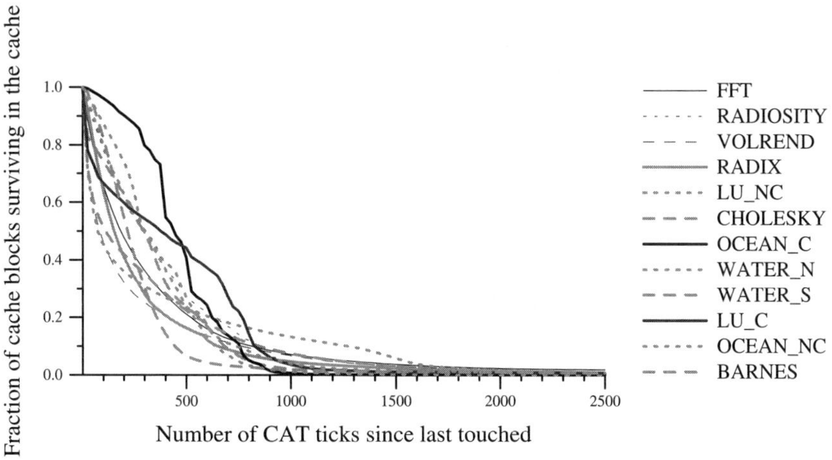

Fig. 4.5. Distribution of cache survival time for a conventional 32 kB 2-way cache with 64 byte cache blocks measured in cache allocation ticks (CAT).

long a time did each cache line survive untouched before replacement? As can be seen in Figure 4.4, there is not a generally applicable upper limit where the cache survival time converges across the applications and subsequently no universal *reuse distance* threshold to be used in our algorithm.

Using CAT Time

If we measure *reuse distance* in the time unit *cache allocation ticks* (CAT); (i.e., a time unit incremented each time a cache line is allocated in the cache), the applications share a similar behavior in terms of the upper bound for the survival time, as we can see in Figure 4.5. In the CAT time system, the *survival time* of a cache block is less than twice the number of blocks in the cache (i.e., 1024 in our example) for approximately 90% of the cache blocks over all the applications. We'll use this value as the *reuse threshold* in RASCAL. If a cache block has a *reuse distance* larger than the *reuse threshold*, we can conclude that it is unlikely that the cache block would have survived if allocated. We also decide not to allocate the cache block in L1 upon L0 eviction since we expect that the next *reuse distance* of the cache block will be similar to its previous reuse distance.

The intuitive explanation to why *survival time* measured in CAT time, instead of wall clock time, is more application-independent is helped by thinking about the average lifetime for a cache block in a cache. The lifetime[4] of a cache

[4] Lifetime is defined as the time from allocation to replacement.

block is on average B CAT, where B is the number of cache blocks that can reside in the cache.[5]. This holds since all the B objects in the cache age one CAT unit each time a cache object is replaced and since exactly one object is inserted and replaced in each time unit. In fact, the average lifetime is independent of the cache organization. Since the average lifetime B CAT extends to all cache organizations and since the average survival time by definition is always less than or equal to the average lifetime, the average survival time is always less than or equal to B.

The CAT time in RASCAL is implemented by a single counter in the L1 cache that is incremented for each L1 allocation. The value of the CAT time at L0 eviction is written into the cache block's metadata in L1 if allocated or in L2 if bypassed. The value does not change during the cache block's tenure in L1 and L2 and will remain the same until its next eviction from L0. At this point in time, its value will be compared to the current CAT time in order to make its next allocation decision.

Allocation History Counter

We have found that using a 3-bit *allocation history counter* provides more stable results than using a single *allocation history bit.* A cache block with a history counter set to zero is bypassed, while cache blocks with positive history counters are allocated. When a cache block is reused within the reuse threshold or hit during its L1 tenure, the allocation history counter is set to 7. If a cache block with a non-zero history counter is evicted without the hit-bit set, the history counter is decremented. A cache block generating an L2 miss is allocated in L1.

CAT Simulation Parameters

The CAT counter is implemented by a 5-bit CAT counter. We have found that using five bits generates a tolerable amount of false detections.[6] The RASCAL algorithm therefore requires a total of eight bits per cache block in L2. Note that the RASCAL CAT timestamp of the cache block is only accessed at the time of eviction from the L0 cache, which should be off the critical path. The reuse history bit is set on a cache hit, and the reuse history counter is set to 7 on a cache hit and decremented on L0 eviction. None of these operations should add to the critical path of an LRU cache. The MAT model will, however, need one associative lookup to find the counter and a counter increment for each cache hit. While it will be more costly to achieve

[5] This further assumes that the entire cache contains valid data and therefore does not hold for cold startup and multiprocessors

[6] The CAT is incremented every $\frac{reusethreshold}{2}$ replacement. Since we are using five timestamp bits, it will spin around every $\frac{reusethreshold}{2} \times 2^5$ replacement, which will lead to some false detections.

this without adding to the hit time of the cache, we still think it is doable and have not added any extra latency for the MAT hit time.

Figure 4.8 shows how the RASCAL allocation reduces the fraction of cache lines never touched before replacement from the L1 cache compared to a system that always allocates L0 victims in the L1 cache.

4.6 Experimental Results

Figures 4.6 and 4.7 show the miss rate reduction for the evaluated allocation schemes. The configuration used in the simulations presented in Figure 4.6 is the base configuration used in [JH99]. The MAT model was implemented with an infinite macro block table, instead of an MAT cache, an 8-bit access counter, and a 4-bit decrementing counter in the MAT decr_ctr model. The comparison is made between caches of the same size and organization and with identical L0 cache and bypass buffer. The RASCAL and AAA algorithms were evaluated with a 1 MB 4-way L2 cache. The RASCAL algorithm requires a total of 8 bits per cache block in the L2 cache, which corresponds to less than 2 percent SRAM overhead.[7]

As can be seen in Figure 4.6, the performance of the AAA algorithm is very good for some applications but extremely poor for other applications. The MAT model shows some improvement for the 16 kB direct-mapped cache, but for the 2-way associative 32 kB case the performance is worsened. As can be seen in Tables 4.2, 4.3, and 4.4, there exists a a general trend that the effectiveness of the MAT model decreases with higher associativity in the L1 cache. We believe that the reason for this is the effectiveness of the LRU replacement algorithm, which in itself makes sure that the least frequently used data are evicted first, thereby reducing the effect of less frequently used data evicting highly used data. The enhanced MAT model, MAT decr_ctr, show an improved performance compared to the original MAT model, but some applications still shows a miss ratio increase compared to a conventional cache. The RASCAL algorithm shows a strictly positive miss rate improvement over a conventional cache although for some applications the improvement is quite modest. In order to get an idea of how the overall performance is affected by the RASCAL algorithm, we have computed the memory system overhead in terms of a highly simplified CPI model, where the CPI memory overhead is defined as $ld\_fraction \times L1\_miss\_ratio \times (L2\_hit\_ratio \times L2\_hit\_penalty + L2\_miss\_ratio \times L2\_miss\_penalty)$ and measured how the memory system overhead is affected by the RASCAL algorithm. We have assumed an in-order superscalar CPU issuing on average two instructions per cycle, an L2 miss penalty of 150 cycles, and an L2 hit penalty of 15 cycles.

The memory overhead study also includes five SPEC CPU2000 benchmarks. As can be seen in Table 4.1, the memory overhead reduction for a

[7] Assuming a cache block size of 64 bytes.

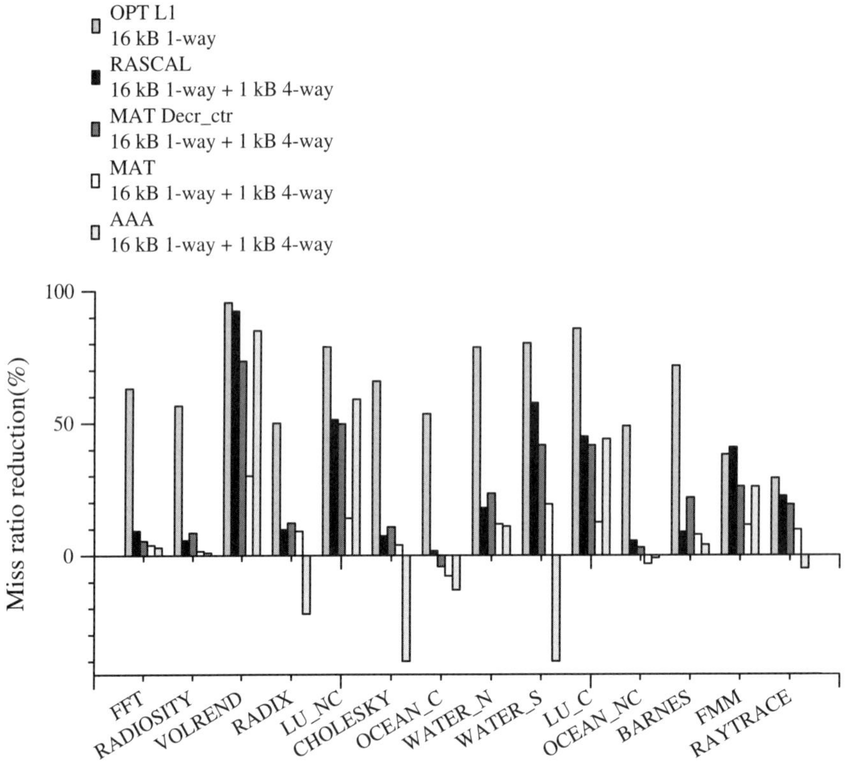

Fig. 4.6. Miss ratio reduction compared with a conventional cache (16 kB direct-mapped cache with a 32 byte block size) using 1 kB L0 cache and bypass buffer.

direct-mapped cache is substantial for a majority of the applications but decreases for more associative caches. The same observation can be made in Tables 4.2– 4.4, where the miss ratio reduction for the RASCAL algorithm and the MAT model is presented with varying cache block sizes and associativities for a 16 kB L1 cache. Also shown are the absolute miss rates for each applications. By comparing these results, we can observe that both RASCAL and MAT show a larger miss rate reduction when the cache block size is increased. This is due to the increase in capacity misses, which are targeted by the algorithms. The two SPEC benchmarks VPC_ROUTE_M and VPC_PLACE_M show the largest cut in memory overhead of all the applications.

4.7 Future Work

This chapter describes our initial work with the run-time adaptive selective cache allocation algorithm RASCAL. This field is largely unexplored to date. We believe that new algorithms can improve performance further with more aggressive bypassing schemes. We plan on continuing this work by studying

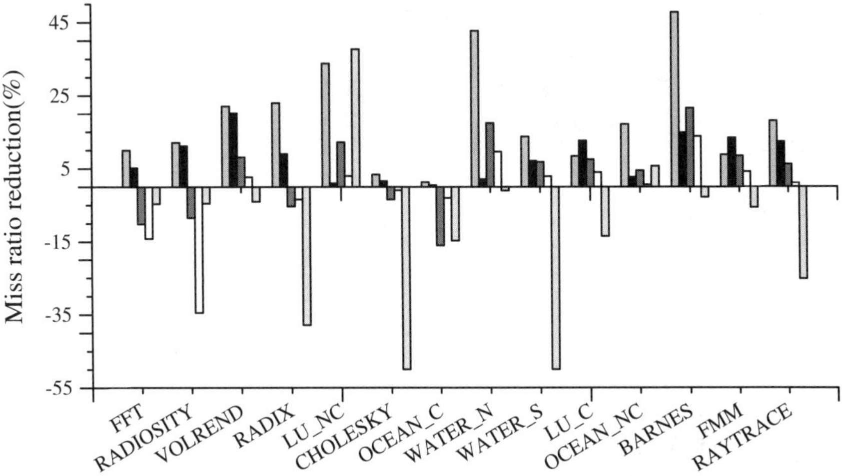

Fig. 4.7. Miss ratio reduction compared with a conventional cache (32 kB 2-way cache with a 64 byte block size).

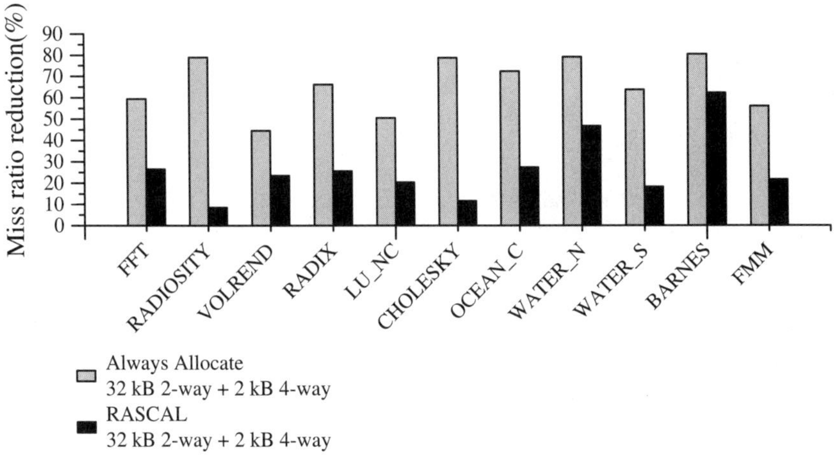

Fig. 4.8. Fraction of cache blocks never touched before replacement from the L1 cache. For all but one application more than half of the replaced objects are never touched in an L1 cache using an always-allocate scheme. RASCAL allocation reduces that number by about two-thirds.

dynamic threshold-adjustment algorithms. In our study, different applications benefited from different threshold settings. We would further like to combine this scheme, which is targeted at removing capacity misses, with schemes that are targeted at conflict misses, such as a victim cache. We also intend to extend our evaluation with more benchmarks with larger working sets, where there is potentially an even bigger need for selective allocation.

Table 4.1. Memory System overhead in terms of CPI.

128 byte linesize	**Conventional**	**RASCAL**		
	Memory	**Memory Overhead Reduction**		
Application	**Overhead [CPI]**	**1-w**	**2-w**	**4-w**
FFT	0.240	9%	2%	1%
RADIOSITY	1.662	4%	2%	2%
VOLREND	0.705	93%	14%	6%
RADIX	0.225	6%	3%	3%
LU_NC	1.149	59%	2%	0%
CHOLESKY	0.288	36%	6%	3%
OCEAN_C	0.863	3%	1%	1%
WATER_N	0.082	42%	3%	1%
WATER_S	0.059	66%	9%	1%
LU_C	0.095	55%	13%	0%
OCEAN_NC	0.223	14%	6%	1%
BARNES	0.175	14%	1%	1%
RAYTRACE	0.137	24%	8%	4%
EQUAKE_B	0.138	30%	4%	2%
VPR_PLACE_M	0.243	77%	67%	4 1%
VPR_ROUTE_M	0.435	28%	17%	1 1%
AMMP_B	3.231	0%	0%	0%
MCF_L	3.300	8%	1%	1%

4.8 Conclusion

We have demonstrated that a fourth cache property, *allocation policy*, is a potential cache enhancement scheme along with cache size, associativity and replacement strategy. Using an optimal allocation policy, a 2-way 32 kB cache was shown to outperform a cache with twice the associativity and perform comparably to 64 kB cache for many applications. We have also proposed a practical way to detect cache lines that would benefit from caching based on their past reuse history measured in the new time unit called *cache allocation ticks* (CAT). We have also proposed a practical low-cost implementation of the RASCAL algorithm, which has shown a stable performance improvement across all the studied benchmarks.

Acknowledgment

This work is funded by the PAMP research program, supported by the Swedish Foundation for Strategic Research.

	32 byte cache block								
	Miss ratio	Miss ratio reduction		Miss ratio	Miss ratio reduction		Miss ratio	Miss ratio reduction	
	1-w			2-w			4-w		
Application	CONV	RASCAL	MAT	CONV	RASCAL	MAT	CONV	RASCAL	MAT
FFT	0,0424	13%	11%	0,0341	6%	4%	0,0317	5%	0%
RADIOSITY	0,2462	11%	11%	0,2004	8%	3%	0,1779	5%	-3%
VOLREND	0,0849	93%	74%	0,0069	21%	16%	0,0054	8%	5%
RADIX	0,0383	16%	17%	0,0316	12%	7%	0,0284	9%	0%
LU_NC	0,2403	51%	50%	0,1181	1%	3%	0,1172	0%	1%
CHOLESKY	0,0856	9%	13%	0,0735	7%	11%	0,0670	4%	7%
OCEAN_C	0,1449	2%	-2%	0,1360	1%	-7%	0,1391	4%	-2%
WATER_N	0,0168	20%	28%	0,0157	1%	21%	0,0155	0%	12%
WATER_S	0,0086	61%	46%	0,0032	7%	8%	0,0031	2%	6%
LU_C	0,0310	63%	65%	0,0093	13%	14%	0,0076	1%	-1%
OCEAN_NC	0,0914	7%	4%	0,0853	5%	3%	0,0923	12%	11%
BARNES	0,0365	15%	23%	0,0340	14%	28%	0,0347	17%	36%
RAYTRACE	0,0288	28%	25%	0,0207	12%	14%	0,0184	8%	11%
EQUAKE_B	0,0177	31%	33%	0,0119	4%	8%	0,0115	3%	7%
VPR_PLACE_M	0,0624	89%	80%	0,0126	67%	47%	0,0058	37%	26%
VPR_ROUTE_M	0,0787	22%	19%	0,0622	9%	6%	0,0581	5%	2%
AMMP_B	0,5125	1%	2%	0,5074	0%	2%	0,5064	0%	2%
MCF_L	0,4004	5%	7%	0,3796	2%	2%	0,3763	1%	2%

Table 4.2. Absolute miss rates for a conventional cache and miss ratio reduction for RASCAL and MAT varied over different associativities using a 32 byte cache block size and 2 kB L0 cache and bypass buffer.

	64 byte cache block								
	Miss ratio	Miss ratio reduction		Miss ratio	Miss ratio reduction		Miss ratio	Miss ratio reduction	
	1-w			2-w			4-w		
Application	CONV	RASCAL	MAT	CONV	RASCAL	MAT	CONV	RASCAL	MAT
FFT	0,0292	19%	14%	0,0223	8%	4%	0,0208	7%	1%
RADIOSITY	0,1981	13%	11%	0,1591	12%	2%	0,1424	14%	2%
VOLREND	0,0955	94%	81%	0,0069	25%	21%	0,0053	11%	11%
RADIX	0,0410	13%	18%	0,0348	9%	10%	0,0322	9%	7%
LU_NC	0,2108	63%	60%	0,0785	2%	4%	0,0773	0%	3%
CHOLESKY	0,0573	26%	26%	0,0401	8%	9%	0,0364	5%	4%
OCEAN_C	0,0773	4%	-6%	0,0710	2%	-13%	0,0725	4%	-9%
WATER_N	0,0149	31%	29%	0,0106	1%	6%	0,0104	1%	2%
WATER_S	0,0087	70%	54%	0,0025	11%	10%	0,0023	2%	5%
LU_C	0,0297	71%	73%	0,0059	22%	18%	0,0043	1%	-9%
OCEAN_NC	0,0730	12%	12%	0,0649	2%	5%	0,0648	2%	5%
BARNES	0,0345	12%	20%	0,0324	4%	20%	0,0336	4%	24%
RAYTRACE	0,0236	33%	26%	0,0161	15%	14%	0,0140	9%	11%
EQUAKE_B	0,0173	46%	42%	0,0095	6%	10%	0,0090	3%	9%
VPR_PLACE_M	0,0692	86%	79%	0,0183	75%	62%	0,0066	49%	35%
VPR_ROUTE_M	0,0833	28%	23%	0,0611	13%	9%	0,0542	7%	2%
AMMP_B	0,5184	2%	2%	0,5130	0%	1%	0,5108	0%	1%
MCF_L	0,3233	5%	7%	0,3050	2%	3%	0,3020	2%	2%

Table 4.3. Absolute miss rates for a conventional cache and miss ratio reduction for RASCAL and MAT varied over different associativities using a 64 byte cache block size and 2 kB L0 cache and bypass buffer.

	128 byte cache block								
	Miss ratio	Miss ratio reduction		Miss ratio	Miss ratio reduction		Miss ratio	Miss ratio reduction	
	1-w			2-w			4-w		
Application	CONV	RASCAL	MAT	CONV	RASCAL	MAT	CONV	RASCAL	MAT
FFT	0,0231	32%	28%	0,0153	9%	13%	0,0144	7%	12%
RADIOSITY	0,1495	14%	13%	0,1202	10%	9%	0,1154	10%	13%
VOLREND	0,1509	97%	94%	0,0061	29%	22%	0,0047	15%	13%
RADIX	0,0443	11%	19%	0,0386	5%	12%	0,0371	5%	10%
LU_NC	0,1962	71%	68%	0,0591	2%	4%	0,0578	0%	3%
CHOLESKY	0,0477	51%	44%	0,0228	11%	11%	0,0203	6%	7%
OCEAN_C	0,0437	11%	0%	0,0376	3%	-9%	0,0381	4%	-6%
WATER_N	0,0160	49%	42%	0,0080	3%	3%	0,0077	1%	1%
WATER_S	0,0111	80%	65%	0,0022	19%	14%	0,0018	3%	3%
LU_C	0,0312	71%	77%	0,0045	39%	33%	0,0025	2%	-1%
OCEAN_NC	0,0681	25%	22%	0,0577	13%	10%	0,0513	2%	0%
BARNES	0,0302	17%	18%	0,0254	2%	8%	0,0256	1%	7%
RAYTRACE	0,0222	41%	33%	0,0138	16%	16%	0,0119	10%	14%
EQUAKE_B	0,0160	60%	50%	0,0069	13%	13%	0,0063	7%	9%
VPR_PLACE_M	0,0753	82%	74%	0,0277	79%	72%	0,0096	62%	51%
VPR_ROUTE_M	0,0970	30%	25%	0,0695	19%	15%	0,0585	13%	7%
AMMP_B	0,5171	1%	2%	0,5130	0%	1%	0,5114	0%	0%
MCF_L	0,2739	5%	7%	0,2578	1%	3%	0,2566	2%	3%

Table 4.4. Absolute miss rates for a conventional cache and miss ratio reduction for RASCAL and MAT varied over different associativities using a 128 byte cache block size and 2 kB L0 cache and bypass buffer.

References

[AHKB00] V. Agarwal, M. S. Hrishikesh, S. W. Keckler, and D. Burger. Clock rate versus ipc: The end of the road for conventional microarchitectures. In *ISCA00*, 2000.

[Bel66] L. A. Belady. A study of replacement algorithms for a virtual storage computer. *IBM Systems Journal*, 5:78–101, 1966.

[GAV95] A. Gonzalez, C. Aliagas, and M. Valero. A data cache with multiple caching strategies tuned to different types of locality. In *Proceedings of International Conference on Supercomputing*, pages 338–347, 1995.

[Hil87] M. D. Hill. *Aspects of Cache Memory and Instruction Buffer Performance*. Ph.D. thesis, University of California, Berkeley, 1987.

[JH97] T. Johnson and W. W. Hwu. Run-time adaptive cache hierarchy management via reference analysis. In *ISCA97*, pages 315–326, 1997.

[JH99] T. Johnson and W. W. Hwu. Run-time cache bypassing. *IEEE Transactions on Computers*, 48(12):1338–1354, December 1999.

[Joh98] T. Johnson. *Run-Time Adaptive Cache Management*. Ph.D. thesis, University of Illinois at Urbana-Champaign, 1998.

[Jou90] N. P. Jouppi. Improving direct-mapped cache performance by the addition of a small fully-associative cache and prefetch buffers. In *ISCA90*, 1990.

[KCZ+94] G. Kurpanek, K. Chan, J. Zheng, E. DeLano, and W. Bryg. PA7200, A PA-RISC processor with integrated high performance MP bus interface. In *Proceedings of CompCon*, 1994.

[KFML00] A. KleinOsowski, J. Flynn, N. Meares, and D. J. Lilja. Adapting the SPEC2000 benchmark suite for simulation-based computer architecture research. Workshop on Workload Characterization, International Conference on Computer Design, Austin.

[McF92] S. McFarling. Cache replacement with dynamic exclusion. In *ISCA92*, pages 191–200, 1992.

[MDG+98] P. S. Magnusson, F. Dahlgren, H. Grahn, M. Karlsson, F. Larsson, F. Lundholm, A. Moestedt, J. Nilsson, P. Stenstrom, and B. Werner. SimICS/sun4m: a virtual workstation. In *Proceedings of the 1998 USENIX Annual Technical Conference*, 1998.

[MMT96] V. Milutinovic, B. Markovic, and M. Tremblay. The split temporal spatial cache: initial performance analysis. In *Proceedings of SCIzzL-5*, pages 63–69, 1996.

[MT97] W. A. Najjar M. Tomasko, and S. Hadjiyiannis. Evaluation of a split scalar/array cache architecture. Technical Report TR-97-104, Department of Computer Science, Colorado State University, 1997.

[RD96] J. A. Rivers and E. S. Davidson. Reducing conflicts in direct-mapped caches with a temporality-based design. In *Proceedings of the 1996 International Conference on Parallel Processing*, 1996.

[RTT+98] J. Rivers, E. Tam, G. Tyson, E. Davidson, and M. Farrens. Utilizing reuse information in data cache management. In *Proceedings of the 1998 International Conference on Supercomputing*, pages 449–456, 1998.

[SA93] R. A. Sugumar and S. G. Abraham. Efficient simulation of caches under optimal replacement with applications to miss characterization. In *Proceedings of the 1993 ACM SIGMETRICS Conference on Measurement and Modeling of Computer Systems*, pages 24–35, 1993.

[SG99] J. Sanchez and A. Gonzalez. A locality sensitive multi-module cache with explicit management. In *Proceedings of the 1999 International Conference on Supercomputing*, pages 51–59, 1999.

[SJLW01] S. T. Srinivasan, R. D. Ju, A. R. Lebeck, and C. Wilkerson. Locality vs. criticality. In *ISCA01*, 2001.

[TFMP95] G. Tyson, M. Farrens, J. Matthews, and A. R. Pleszkun. A modified approach to data cache management. In *Proceedings of MICRO-28*, pages 93–103, 1995.

[WBL89] W. H. Wang, J. L. Baer, and H. M. Levy. Organization and performance of a two-level virtual - real cache hierarchy. In *ISCA89*, pages 140–148, 1989.

[WOT+95] S. Woo, M. Ohara, E. Torrie, J. P. Singh, and A. Gupta. The SPLASH-2 programs: characterization and methodological considerations. In *ISCA95*, 1995.

Part II

Power-Aware, Reliable, and Reconfigurable Memory

5

Power-Efficient Cache Coherence

Craig Saldanha and Mikko H. Lipasti

Department of Electrical and Computer Engineering
University of Wisconsin-Madison, Madison, WI, USA
saldanha@ece.wisc.edu, mikko@ece.wisc.edu

Abstract. Snoopy coherence implementations employ various forms of speculation to reduce cache miss latency and improve performance. We study the effects of reduced speculation on both performance and power consumption in a scalable snooping design. We find that significant potential exists for reducing energy consumption by using serial snooping for load misses. We report only a minor 6.25% increase for average cache miss latency for a set of commercial workloads, while finding substantial reductions in snoop-related activity. We also compare this implementation against a conventional directory protocol implementation and find that while a directory protocol effectively reduces power consumption due to message traffic, its overall energy consumption is unlikely to be lower than the serial snooping protocol due to lower performance (longer average load latency) and increased memory and directory references.

5.1 Introduction

In the recent past, researchers in both academia and industry have paid a great deal of attention to power consumption in computing systems [8]. Much of this attention has focused on architectural and circuit techniques for reducing on-chip processor power and energy consumption via techniques such as clock-gating [1], memory subsystem storage structure optimizations, system bus optimizations, and main memory access [5]. Recently, a study by Moshovos et al. examined the potential for filtering remote snoop requests by checking them against a small *Jetty* table to avoid tag lookups and reduce on-chip power consumption induced by remote cache misses [7]. We believe that approaches such as these, as well as many others not mentioned here, will help alleviate power consumption problems in future processor chips.

At the same time, market pressure for improved performance is driving designers to build shared memory systems with a large number of processors in them. The complexity and frequency of the processor interconnect that provides cache coherence to the software running on these systems are increasing rapidly, as is the power consumed by the interconnect. Interchip busses account for as much as 15–20% of total chip power [2]. There are several techniques that target coding and information compression as a means to reduce switching activity and thereby reduce power.

However, given that the energy to send a packet over a processor-to-processor interconnect is a function of the interconnect length, capacitance, and bus frequency, it is constant for a given system and circuit technology. Therefore the issue of power [1] consumption in the interconnect of a multiprocessor system must be dealt with at the architectural level by eliminating the transmission of unnecessary packets. This is the primary focus of our proposed serial snooping technique.

Various forms of speculation are routinely employed to reduce the latency of cache misses and overlap data fetch and transmission latency with checking for cache coherence. This chapter presents a case study of a hypothetical shared-memory system that is similar to two recent high-end server systems: the IBM S80 [3] and the SunFire 6800 [10]. We find that opportunities exist for reducing speculation in the cache coherence implementation of such a system while sacrificing very little performance (as measured by effective cache miss latency). The mechanisms we propose reduce the number of address transactions (or snoop commands), data fetches, and data transmissions that occur in the system.

5.2 Snoopy Coherence Protocols

In this section, we explain the principles of snoopy coherence protocols and the architectural trade-offs involved in the transmission of snoop packets and the subsequent tag array accesses and data fetch and transmission. In a snoopy coherence protocol where the nodes are connected by a shared bus (a single set of wires connecting a number of devices or a network that is logically equivalent), every node can observe all transactions on the bus. Coherence is then maintained by having all the cache controllers *snoop* on the bus and monitor the transactions.

The three distinct stages that occur to satisfy a cache miss are *snooping*, *data fetch* (from remote node or memory), and *data transmit* (also from remote node or memory). There is an opportunity for speculation at each of the three stages, and the degree of speculation at each stage enables an architectural trade-off between performance and power consumption. *Snooping:* Snooping protocols broadcast snoop packets to allow all nodes to see the snoop packet at the same time. This helps performance since remote tag lookups occur in parallel. This also means that the requesting node will see only a single tag array access latency while determining which nodes have a copy of the

[1] Throughout this chapter, we use the terms power and energy interchangeably since we do not vary the time base (i.e. bus frequency) needed to convert from one to the other.

requested data. Our simulations for a 4-way SMP with 4-way set-associative 8 MB L2 caches indicate that 32% of all load-miss-generated snoops, miss in all remote caches, an average 57% hit in a single remote cache and only about 3.5% find data in all the other caches. These results differ from those reported by Moshovos et al. [7] due to larger caches and different workloads studied but nevertheless indicate an opportunity for substantial power savings. Every time a snoop is sent to a node that does not contain the requested data, energy is wasted, both for the tag array access and to transmit the snoop packet across the bus. Thus, from a power-saving perspective, a useful alternative would be to serialize the transmission of snoops. That is, begin with the node closest to the requestor, and then propagate the snoop to the next successive node in the path only if previous nodes in the path have failed to satisfy the request. Depending on which node (or memory if all nodes miss) satisfies the request, there is the possibility for performance degradation since the requesting node now sees additional latency for each access that occurs serially. The total latency to satisfy the data request is no longer independent of which node will supply the data but is instead a function of how far the supplier of the data is from the requestor. The details of power savings and performance degradation associated with serial snooping are discussed in detail in Section 5.3.4.

Data Fetch: DRAM access latency constitutes the significant portion of total latency to satisfy a load miss from memory. By allowing the memory controller to start its DRAM access before the snoop responses from the remote nodes arrive, some of this latency can be overlapped with the remote node tag array accesses. Though this is advantageous from the point of view of maximizing performance, it contributes significantly to power consumption since the power associated with DRAM access can be on the order of 300 mW [5]. This power is wasted every time a load miss is satisfied from one of the remote caches. Hence, accessing DRAM non-speculatively after all the snoop responses have been combined saves the most power.

The speculative fetching of data can also be applied to caches at the remote nodes. There is an opportunity to improve performance by allowing the data array lookup to occur in parallel with the tag array look-up. This allows the data fetch latency to be overlapped with the tag array access latency, allowing the data to be supplied more quickly if there is a hit. Speculative fetching of the data prior to determining a tag array hit or miss can also consume excess energy when a miss occurs. This is nevertheless a viable trade-off when performance is at a premium, as is evident from the fact that speculative data-fetching techniques are employed in the IBM S80 [2][3] and Sun SunFire6800 [10] servers.

Data Transmit: Even with a speculative data fetch in parallel with the tag array lookup, the requesting node must still tolerate the latency of the combining logic that combines the snoop responses to determine which node will supply the data as well as the latency of the actual transmission of the data from the source node to the requesting node. To hide this latency, it is possible to speculatively transmit the data before the snoop response combining has taken place. We are unaware of a snoopy coherence protocol that speculatively transmits fetched data, but the SGI Origin2000, which implements a directory protocol speculatively, transmits data to the requestor if it finds that the directory state of the requested line is exclusive. Therefore, when minimizing the latency to satisfy a load miss is of primary importance, speculative transmission of data can be effective. The cost of doing so is the increased bus power and bandwidth consumption caused by the unnecessary transmission of data packets. For the purpose of our initial evaluation of performance and power, we will assume a sufficiently large bus bandwidth so that contention between nodes to transmit data can be ignored.

5.3 Methodology

In this section, we will describe the interconnect architecture that will form the basis of the power and performance discussions for our various schemes.

5.3.1 Address and Data Interconnect

For simplicity of discussion and simulation, we have modeled a 4-way SMP with a single processor per node. The proposed schemes, however, are easily scalable and can be applied to architectures with multiple processors per node as well as additional nodes. The architecture we are modeling has separate data and address interconnects. We assume that each processor is mounted on a separate board (in practical systems there would be more than one processor per board). These boards are then attached via the address and data interconnects through the backplane.

The address interconnect is based on the SunFire 6800 [10]. The interconnect forms a tree of point-to-point connections and is logically equivalent to a broadcast bus. In order to broadcast a snoop, the snoop packet must travel to the root node before it is reflected down to all of the leaf nodes. Each bus transaction needs to pass through two levels of switches to get from the source node to the destination node. Our system models the memory controller at the root node, which is similar to the IBM S80 design [3], rather than connected to the leaf nodes as in the SunFire 6800 [10]. Each link represents the delay to go from one block (either a node or a switch) to another. We assume a link delay equal to a single bus cycle of 7 ns. We also assume a single bus cycle to transmit a packet across a switch chip. These assumptions mirror the design assumptions of the SunFire 6800 [10].

The data interconnect also forms a tree of point-to-point links. Each board has a board-level switch that links each processor on board to the backplane switch. The backplane switch connects the individual boards. In our model each board has only a single processor and so a board-level switch may seem unnecessary. However, in an attempt to model a large-scale system, we include a board-level switch in our latency and power calculations since in larger commercial systems there will be more than a single processor per board. Each link or switch adds one 7 ns cycle of latency.

5.3.2 Types of Speculation

Our discussion on the architectural trade-offs involved in snoopy coherence protocols implies three degrees of freedom in their design: snooping, data fetch and data transmission. Snooping can be done either serially or in parallel. Parallel snooping is straightforward and simply implies that the snoop packets are broadcast, thereby arriving at every node in the system at the same time. In serial snooping, the snoop packet is sent to a single node at a time serially, starting with the node nearest to the requestor and proceeding until the request is satisfied or until all the nodes have been snooped. This is advantageous because the node closest to the requestor supplies the data when available, but more importantly, power is never wasted from either speculative tag and data array lookups or to transmit unnecessary snoop response packets and data. Non-speculative data fetch is done by a node only after the supplier of the data is determined by combining the snoop responses, while speculative data fetch involves performing the data array lookup in parallel with the tag array lookup. Lastly, speculative transmission of data allows the transmission of data to the requestor even before the results of the snoop responses have been determined by the combining network, while serial data transmission disallows this. Note that we consider serial snooping only for read operations. Serial snooping of write-related commands has consistency model implications that are beyond the scope of this chapter. Serial snooping of reads does not violate the PowerPC consistency model [6].

5.3.3 Parallel Snoop Protocols

We will now present a detailed analysis of several interesting cases; more detailed derivation of our results can be found in a technical report [9].

Parallel Snoop, Speculative Data Fetch, Speculative Data Transmit (PSS-FST). This is the most aggressive implementation of the snoopy coherence protocol. Snoop packets are broadcast to all nodes so that the tag array lookups for every node occur in parallel. Nodes access their tag and data arrays simultaneously so that in the event of a hit the data are ready for transmission to the requestor. The latencies involved to satisfy a data request that misses in the local cache can be explained with the help of Figure 5.1. The diagram uses a timeline to indicate the latencies involved in completing various operations and also shows the operations that occur serially and in parallel.

To explain the parallel snoop, speculative data fetch, and speculative transmit configuration, consider a read by P1 that missed in its local cache and is found in the M state in P3. We assume the start of the snoop transaction as time 0 since we are interested in knowing the latency between the time

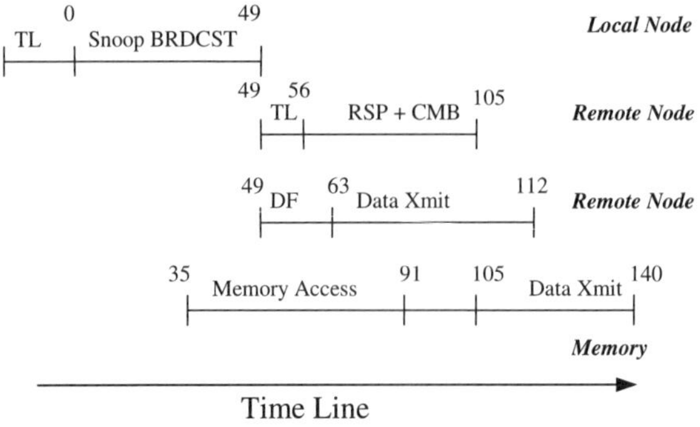

0: Data request misses in the local cache and a snoop is initiated.
35: Snoop packet reaches memory controller.
49: Snoop packet arrives simultaneously at all remote nodes.
Each node begins tag array lookup and data access in parallel.
56: Tag check completed. Snoop response available at remote node.
63: Data fetch complete. Data available in case of a hit.
91: Results of combining snoop responses available to memory controller.
105: Results of combining snoop responses available to remote nodes. Memory access also completes.
112: Data from remote nodes available to requestor.
140: Data from memory available to requestor.

Fig. 5.1. PSSFST coherence protocol

the snoop is sent out by the requestor and the time when it is satisfied either by a remote node or memory. At time 0, P1 sends its snoop packet out on the address interconnect. Since the interconnect is logically equivalent to a broadcast bus, the snoop request must travel to the root node before being reflected down to all of the branches. The packet passes through 2 switches and 3 links to get to the memory controller, while it must pass through 3 switches and 4 links to get to each remote node. Since each link as well as each switch has a single bus cycle latency, the snoop request is available at the memory controller at 35 ns (5 cycles) and at the remote node after 49 ns (7 cycles).

As soon as the snoop request is available, the memory controller begins the DRAM access, which has a 70 ns latency (we assume a slightly more conservative access latency than [5]). Similarly when the snoop reaches the remote nodes, the tag array lookup and the data-array access are started simultaneously. We assume a single bus cycle for a tag lookup and a 2-cycle latency for a data fetch operation to complete. At 56 ns the snoop responses are available at each remote node and must be sent to the combining logic. The combining of the snoop responses is done at the root node, and the process of combining incurs 1 bus cycle. The combining logic decides which node will supply the requested data or whether it will come from the memory. Since it takes 3 bus cycles to send responses from the remote nodes to the root node and a cycle to perform the combining, the result of the snoops is available at 84 ns. They take an additional cycle to be transmitted back to the memory controller and 3 additional cycles to be sent back to the remote nodes. Therefore, after 105 ns the results of the snoops are available at all the nodes. This is similar to the snoop response latency of 100 ns reported for the SunFire 6800 [10], which is consistent with the fact that the address interconnect structures in both systems are very similar.

Reviewing our data interconnect, the data need to traverse 4 links and 3 switches to travel from the source to the requestor. The data transmit is also done speculatively. Hence, 7 cycles later, at 112 ns, data from the remote nodes reaches P1. Note that if multiple nodes attempt to transmit data in parallel there will be contention on the bus. For the purpose of this study, we are assuming a sufficiently large bus bandwidth so that contention issues can be ignored. Also note that when cache line sizes are larger than the width of the data bus interconnects, then multiple data packets must be sent in response to a single snoop request. To simplify our analysis, all our discussions on latency and power account only for the critical packet from a remote node or memory to be transferred to the requestor in order to satisfy the load miss. The remaining data packets will be transferred non-speculatively and though they will contribute to the overall power consumption, their contribution will be the same for all of the schemes. Since we are performing a comparative study between different versions of the snoopy protocol rather than trying to estimate absolute values of power, these non-critical words can be excluded without affecting our relative comparisons.

Since the results of the snoop reach P1 at 105 ns, it knows in advance that it will accept data from P3 and discard data from other nodes. Figure 5.1 shows that if the requested data are present in any of the remote nodes, then the snoop request can be satisfied in 112 ns. If no remote node has a copy of the data then it takes an additional 28 ns to satisfy the request from memory. It is important to note that memory speculatively fetches its data but is never required to speculatively transmit its data. This is because the results of the snoop are available to the memory controller at 91 ns, before the DRAM access completes at 105 ns. This scheme offers the best performance but also consumes the most power because of the high degree of speculation involved.

To look at the overall power consumption of this configuration, we examine scenarios that will yield the worst case power consumption. The power consumptions of the various operations that are performed during a snoop transaction are represented by the following symbols:

- P_{link}: Power consumed to send a packet across a link in the address or data interconnect;
- P_{sw}: Power consumed to route packets across a switch;
- P_{tag}: Power consumed to do a tag array lookup;
- P_{cache}: Power consumed to fetch a block from the cache;
- P_{mem}: Power consumed to access DRAM.

The power consumption of this configuration is as follows.

If a remote processor node supplies the data:

P_{total}: $32P_{link} + 21P_{sw} + 3P_{tag} + 3P_{cache} + P_{mem}$

If memory supplies the data:

P_{total}: $23P_{link} + 14P_{sw} + 3P_{tag} + 3P_{cache} + P_{mem}$

Parallel Snoop, Speculative Data Fetch, Non-Speculative Data Transmit (PSSFNT). This configuration differs from the first (PSSFST) in that remote nodes speculatively fetch data in parallel with the tag lookup but they do not transmit data until the snoop responses have been combined and it is known which node will supply the data. By transmitting data non-speculatively, the latency to satisfy a request from a remote node is increased by 42 ns, but if the request is satisfied from memory there is no performance loss. This is intuitive since the memory controller receives the results of the snoop combining before it completes its DRAM access and therefore it does not have to speculatively transmit data even in the most aggressive configuration (PSSFST). Further details of this configuration can be found in [9].

The power consumption when a remote processor node supplies the data is:

P_{total}: $24P_{link} + 15P_{sw} + 3P_{tag} + 3P_{cache} + P_{mem}$

If memory supplies the data:

P_{total}: $23P_{link} + 14P_{sw} + 3P_{tag} + 3P_{cache} + P_{mem}$

Parallel Snoop, Non-Speculative Data Fetch, Non-Speculative Data Transmit (PSNFNT). This scheme is less aggressive than the previous two schemes since it disables speculative access from the memory and data cache. Data fetch occurs only after snoop responses have been combined and the node that will satisfy the request has been identified. The result of the reduced parallelism is an increased latency for both requests satisfied by remote node cache-cache transfers (168 ns) as well as those satisfied from memory (196 ns). The reduced speculation leads to significant power savings. This is because there is no power wasted by nodes that will not supply data to perform data cache accesses. Further details of this configuration can be found in [9].

The power consumption when a remote processor node supplies the data is:

P_{total}: $24P_{link} + 15P_{sw} + 3P_{tag} + P_{cache}$

If memory supplies the data:

P_{total}: $23P_{link} + 14P_{sw} + 3P_{tag} + P_{mem}$

5.3.4 Serial Snoop Protocols

In all the configurations we have presented so far we have assumed that snoops are broadcast on the address interconnect. With this broadcast technique, snoop packets are transmitted on every link since all nodes must see the snoop packet simultaneously. A more *power-aware* methodology for snoopy protocols is serial snooping. The basic idea is to prevent wasting power by transmitting snoop packets to nodes that either do not have a copy of the data or nodes that have a copy but are not responsible for sourcing the data as the result of a snoop.

Serial snooping works by transmitting a snoop packet only to the nearest node. If the nearest node has a valid copy, it sources the data to the requestor and snoop transaction ends without either the memory or any of the other remote nodes seeing the transaction. On the other hand, if the *nearest neighbor* is unable to satisfy the request, it forwards the request to the next level in the tree hierarchy.

This snooping methodology makes the assumption that the switches in the data interconnect are slightly more intelligent and are able to forward snoops to the appropriate nodes. Note again that we consider serial snooping only for read operations, which does not violate the rules of the PowerPC consistency model.

There are three serial snooping configurations that are more conservative in terms of speculation but offer significant opportunities for power saving. The configurations are serial snoop/speculative data fetch/speculative transmit (SSSFST), speculative fetch/nonspeculative transmit (SSSFNT), and nonspeculative fetch and transmit (SSNFNT). The following sections discuss the latency and power issues for a snoop initiated by a local miss in P1 and satisfied by P2, P3, P4, and Memory.

Requested Data are Sourced by P2. The snoop initiated by P1 takes 3 cycles to traverse 2 links and a switch to get to P2. The tag access completes and the results are available in the same cycle so that the data access can begin. Hence, in spite of the fact that the tag check and data access occur serially, they appear to be taking place in parallel. The results of the snoop reach P1 in 49 ns and the data that are non-speculatively fetched and transmitted reach P1 in 56 ns. The snoop never reaches the root node and therefore memory is never accessed. Thus, if a snoop request is satisfied within the same subtree by the nearest neighbor, there is a performance gain as well as power savings.

The power consumption for this configuration is:

P_{total}: $6P_{link} + 3P_{sw} + P_{tag} + P_{cache}$

Requested Data are Sourced by P3. This example describes the scenario of what happens when P2 is unable to satisfy the request from P1. P2 forwards the request to switch 1, which routes it to the root node and from there to memory and back down the tree to P3. P3 receives the snoop 8 bus cycles after it reached P2, which is the latency for P2 to do a lookup and retransmit the snoop. P3 determines that it has a copy of the requested data and transmits the snoop response and the data back to P1 at 140 ns. The snoop reaches the memory controller 2 cycles after it reaches the root node (63 ns after the transaction began). In this example, we have assumed that the memory does a speculative access to avoid the significant latency penalty if the data are not found in any of the caches.

This case obviously expends more power than when P2 sources the data because the snoop request travels to more nodes, but it is still significantly more power-efficient than the parallel snoop configurations. The power consumption of this configuration is as follows.

If memory does not speculatively fetch the data:

P_{total}: $16P_{link} + 10P_{sw} + 2P_{tag} + P_{cache}$

If memory fetches data speculatively:

P_{total}: $16P_{link} + 10P_{sw} + 2P_{tag} + P_{cache} + P_{mem}$

Requested Data are Sourced by P4. In this case, the load miss by P1 is satisfied by P4 or memory. Only after P2 and P3 have determined that they do not have a copy of the requested data does the snoop request reach P4. Therefore, 15 cycles (105 ns) after the snoop request originated from P1, P4 performs a tag lookup to determine if it has a copy of the requested data. P4 then transmits the data to P1. Data from P4 arrive at the requestor 168 ns after the transaction started. This is the maximum latency to satisfy a load miss from a remote cache. If the snoop request misses in all of the remote nodes then it must be satisfied from memory.

Requested Data are Sourced from Memory. The latency to satisfy a load miss from memory depends on the degree of speculation used by the memory controller. If the memory controller fetches data speculatively, it begins its DRAM access at 63 ns even before P3 has determined whether it experienced a hit or a miss. If the memory controller also transmits its data speculatively, then the latency to satisfy the load miss is 168 ns, which is the same as the latency for data obtained from P4.

The drawback of this scheme is that the power to perform the DRAM access as well as to transmit the data packet on the bus is wasted if either P3 or P4 experiences a hit. If the memory controller only performs a speculative data fetch but does not transmit the data speculatively, no power or bus bandwidth is wasted to transmit unnecessary packets but the load miss is satisfied in 182 ns. If the focus of the design were on conserving power, then the memory controller would not perform its DRAM access until it has determined that the snoop missed in all 4 remote nodes. Here, the load miss latency is 250 ns.

The power consumption for these cases is as follows:

If memory does not speculatively fetch the data:

P_{total}: $18P_{link} + 11P_{sw} + 3P_{tag} + P_{cache}$

If memory fetches data speculatively:

P_{total}: $18P_{link} + 11P_{sw} + 3P_{tag} + P_{cache} + P_{mem}$

If memory fetches and transmits data speculatively:

P_{total}: $21P_{link} + 12P_{sw} + 3P_{tag} + P_{cache} + P_{mem}$

If the snoop misses in all remote nodes and memory supplies the data:

P_{total}: $17P_{link} + 9P_{sw} + 3P_{tag} + P_{mem}$

5.4 Directory Protocols

It is straightforward to see the potential for power saving with the serial snooping protocol as compared to a more speculative parallel snooping protocol. However, serial snooping can provide a power-efficient alternative even to vastly different protocols such as a directory protocol. In this section, we will present an analysis of a directory protocol, while a comparative study of all three protocols (i.e., parallel snooping, serial snooping, and directory protocols) follows in Section 5.5.

Our analysis of directory protocols is based on the SGI Origin 2000 with some additional assumptions to facilitate a comparison with the serial and parallel snooping schemes. We model an interconnect structure identical to the snooping cases. The directory and all of the system memory are located at the root node. This differs from the approach of the SGI Origin 2000, which assumes system memory, and the directory is divided among the processor nodes. However, in order to maintain consistency across all the schemes discussed in this chapter and thereby facilitate comparison amoung the various protocols, we model the directory and memory at the root node. Comparison to systems with distributed memory and alternative interconnects is left to future work. As with the other protocols, we only consider read misses; issues and opportunities for handling stores are left to future work.

We will now provide a detailed analysis of the various conditions involved in satisfying a read request with the directory protocol outlined above. Our previous assumptions of a 7 ns bus cycle, a 1 bus cycle link traversal and tag lookup latency, a 2 cycle data cache access, and 10 cycle memory access latency remain unchanged. Our discussion on performance and power of the directory schemes will follow the same example of a data cache miss by node P1 being satisfied by P2, P3, P4, and memory.

Request Satisfied by Memory (Shared/Unowned State). As with other schemes, we measure latency from the time P1 misses in its local cache and initiates a network transaction to satisfy its request for data. In this case, we will assume that the requested data are found in the Unowned or Shared state. In either case, the request will be satisfied by memory at the root node with the same latency. It takes 35 ns (5 cycles) for P1's request to reach the root node as it traverses 3 links and 2 switches. At the root node, a directory lookup and a memory access are initiated simultaneously. Each of these completes in 10 cycles and therefore the state of the line and the data from memory are available at 105 ns. Additional power savings would be possible by serializing the directory lookup and memory fetch and avoiding the latter when it is not necessary. However, this would cause a dramatic increase in average load latency and hence we do not consider it further.

Since the line is in the Shared or Unknown state, the home node knows that it has the most recent copy of the data and is therefore responsible for sourcing these data to the requestor. It takes a further 5 cycles for these data to be transmitted back to the requestor. Hence, the data request from P1 is satisfied in 140 ns when the line is in the Shared or Unknown state.

The power consumed by this case is:

P_{total}: $6P_{link} + 4P_{sw} +$ PDir+ P_{mem}

Request Satisfied by P2 (Exclusive State). Now, we assume that the data that missed in P1's local cache reside in the local cache of P2. P1 initiates a network transaction to the home node. The request arrives at the home node after a 35 ns (5 cycle) latency. The home node initiates a directory lookup to determine the state of the line and its owner and also speculatively accesses memory. Both of these events complete after 10 cycles at 105 ns. The home node determines that the requested line is in the Exclusive state and resides at node P2. At this time it is unknown whether P2 has the line in the Clean or Dirty Exclusive state, so the home node speculatively transmits the data to the requestor. It also forwards the request to node P2. The data reach P1 at the same time that the request reaches P2 after traversing 3 links and 2 switches in 35 ns. P2 completes its ag lookup after 1 cycle or at time 147 ns after the transaction began at P1. If the line is Clean Exclusive, then P1 has the most recent copy of the data from memory and P2 need not wait for the data cache fetch to complete. It transmits a response to P1, which reaches P1 after 21 ns traversing 2 links and a switch. If the line is Dirty Exclusive then P2 has the most recent copy of the data. It must wait until the data fetch completes at 154 ns and then forward these data to P1 and to Memory. In this case, P1's miss is satisfied a cycle later at 175 ns.

The power consumed by this configuration is as follows:

If the requested data are Clean Exclusive:

P_{total}: $11P_{link} + 7P_{sw} + PDir + P_{mem} + P_{tag} + P_{cache}$

If the requested data are Dirty Exclusive:

P_{total}: $13P_{link} + 8P_{sw} + PDir + P_{mem} + P_{tag} + P_{cache}$

Request Satisfied by P3. In this analysis, we assume that P1's miss can be satisfied by P3 (or P4 since the cases are equivalent), which has the line in Clean or Dirty Exclusive state. As before, P1's request for data reaches the home node at 35 ns. The home node completes its directory lookup and speculatively transmits data back to P1 at 140 ns. It also forwards the request to the current owner, which we assume is P3 in this analysis. P3 does a local tag array lookup and a speculative data fetch.

The tag lookup completes at 147 ns and if the requested line is found in Clean Exclusive state then P3 may transmit these data immediately to P1 without waiting for the data fetch operation to complete. Data from P3 must traverse 4 links and 3 switches en route to P1 and hence arrive at the requestor after a 7 cycle (49 ns) delay. If the requested line is found in the Dirty Exclusive state, then P3 must wait until 154 ns for the data fetch to complete and then forward this data to P1 and memory. In this case P1's request is finally satisfied 203 ns after it missed locally.

The power consumed by this configuration is as follows:

If the requested data are Clean Exclusive:

P_{total}: $13P_{link} + 9P_{sw} + PDir + P_{mem} + P_{tag} + P_{cache}$

If the requested data are Dirty Exclusive:

P_{total}: $14P_{link} + 9P_{sw} + PDir + P_{mem} + P_{tag} + P_{cache}$

5.5 Simulation Results

We use an augmented version of the SimOS-PPC [4] full system simulator to collect statistics on load misses. We studied the behavior of load misses in four benchmarks: raytrace from the Splash-2 Benchmark suite, SPECweb99, SPECjbb2000, and TPC-W on a 4-way SMP with a 4-way set-associative 8 MB L2 cache with 128 byte lines.

Figure 5.2 shows a plot of average latencies to satisfy a load miss for the 7 configurations described in this chapter, starting with the most aggressive parallel snooping technique (PSSFST) and progressing through to the most conservative serial snooping technique (SSNFNT) along with the directory protocol for comparison. Figure 5.2 shows that the directory protocol performs poorly compared to the snooping techniques for read misses because of the directory lookup latency. Within the serial snooping techniques, the most aggressive configuration (SSSFST) has the lowest latency to satisfy a load miss, but the most conservative configuration (SSNFNT) does not have the worst performance. This is because the effectiveness of the serial snoop depends upon how many times a load miss can be satisfied by its nearest neighbor. When this is the case the latency to satisfy the load miss is 56 ns as compared to 112 ns in the most aggressive case (PSSFST) and 168 ns in the most conservative case with parallel snoop (PSNFNT). Even when the snoop request is satisfied by the next best node using the serial snooping technique, the latency to satisfy a node miss is 140 ns which is still less than the latencies for both parallel snoop cases with less than maximum speculation (i.e. PSSFNT and PSNFNT).

The latencies of serial snoop configurations depend on the location where the load miss is satisfied. Figure 5.2 shows that on average 31% of load misses are satisfied by the node nearest the requestor, 21% are satisfied by the next nearest node, 20% are satisfied by the farthest node, and 26% of all load misses are satisfied by memory. Figure 5.2 gives a clear indication that serial snoop performs worse than only the most speculative configuration, and the latency penalty is on average 6.25%, with the best case being only a 2.6% latency increase in raytrace. The performance penalty for the most conservative configuration (SSNFNT), which would yield maximum power savings, is on average 23% and in the best case 8.7% (also in raytrace). This indicates that serial snooping configurations provide opportunities for power savings and still perform better than some parallel snoop configurations.

It is intuitive that the power savings will increase as the degree of speculation is reduced. We quantify the power savings in terms of the reduction in activity; activity is represented by symbolic terms that correspond to the different types of activities that are included in the equations presented in Section 5.3. The power consumed for each of the seven configurations is based on statistics from our execution-driven simulation and is shown as a weighted sum of each of the different types of activities. The weights are determined according to the load miss distributions presented in Figure 5.2. To quantify

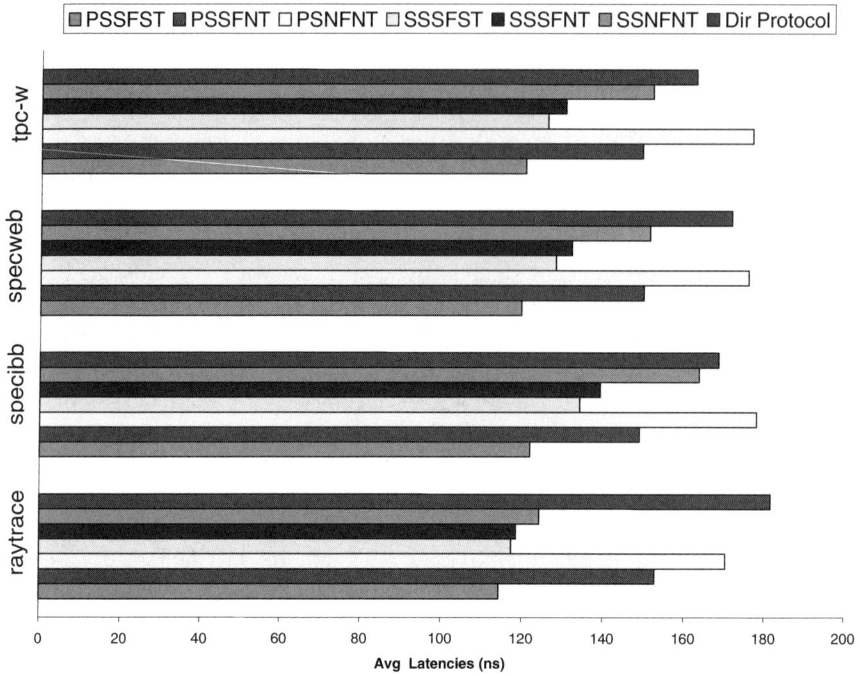

Fig. 5.2. Average load miss latency

power savings we compare each of the proposed configurations with the most speculative configuration, which consumes the most power. Table 5.1 summarizes the total power for each of the six cases as well as the savings relative to the baseline case (PSSFST).

Table 5.1. Weighted average power consumption $P_{total}(P_{save})$.

Configuration	P_{link}	P_{sw}	P_{tag}	P_{cache}	P_{mem}
PSSFST	46.8	19.2	3	3	1
PSSFNT	23.75 (23.05)	14.75 (4.5)	3	3	1
PSNFNT	23.75 (23.05)	14.75 (4.5)	3	0.736 (2.24)	0.264 (0.736)
SSSFST	14.2 (32.6)	7.9 (11.3)	2.16 (0.84)	0.74 (2.26)	0.69 (0.31)
SSSFNT	13.43 (33.37)	7.76 (11.44)	2.16 (0.83)	0.74 (2.26)	0.69 (0.31)
SSNFNT	13.43 (33.37)	7.76 (11.44)	2.16 (0.83)	0.74 (2.26)	0.26 (0.74)
Directory	10.47 (36.33)	6.73 (12.47)	1 (2)	1 (2)	$1 + 1P_{dir}$ $(-1P_{dir})$

The relative power consumption due to P_{link}, P_{sw}, P_{tag}, and P_{cache} decrease significantly as the degree of speculation decreases from parallel snooping configurations to serial snooping configurations. Table 5.1 shows low

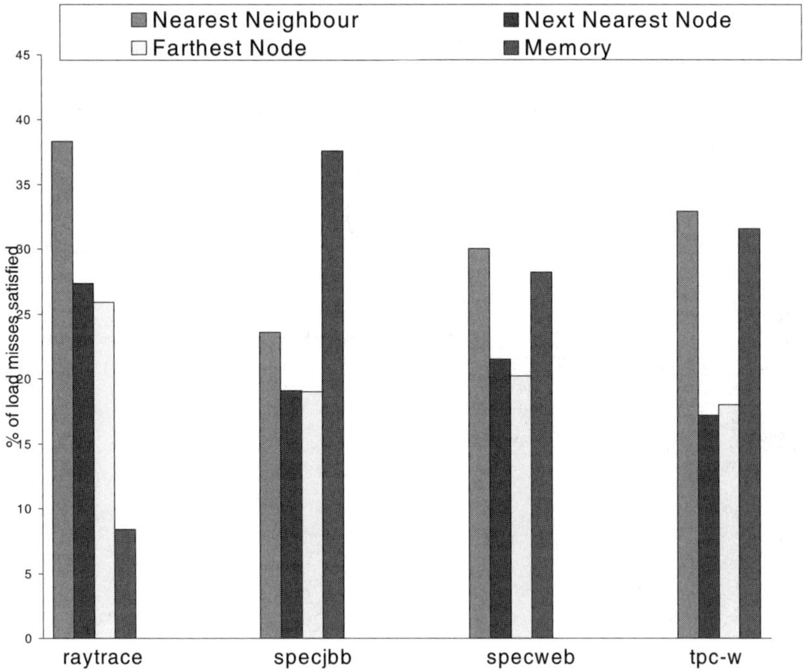

Fig. 5.3. Average load miss distribution

weights on P_{link}, P_{sw}, P_{tag}, and P_{cache} activities in the directory protocol. These weights are even less than our most efficient serial snooping technique. However, in the directory protocol, these low activities are negated by the constant power consumption associated with the directory and memory lookups, which have a higher power cost and thereby outweigh the potential savings. In the serial snooping technique, it is worthwhile to note the opportunity for power savings achieved by checking the nearest neighbor before forwarding a request to memory, as is evident by the drop in P_{mem}. It is clear that maximum power savings are achieved with no speculation in snooping, data fetch, and data transmit. However, it is more interesting to note that these savings are only slightly more than the savings obtained by using serial snooping with full speculation for memory. This technique is a clear winner with substantial power savings and minimal performance degradation.

5.6 Conclusion

The use of speculation to reduce latency is an important architectural consideration while designing coherency protocols for modern SMP systems. We have conducted a preliminary performance and power analysis for varying degrees of speculation in a scalable snooping protocol modeled after the IBM S80 and SunFire 6800 systems. We conclude that there is significant potential for power savings without severe performance degradation by reducing the degree of speculation in certain operations. Specifically, we find that employing serial snooping for read commands with speculative data fetch and transmit from memory provides substantial reduction in power consumption without significant performance overhead (only 6.25% latency increase) over both speculative snooping and directory protocol implementations.

We wish to thank IBM and Intel for their generous equipment and financial donations that have enabled much of this work. Finally, this work was supported in part by funding from the National Science Foundation under grants CCR-0073440, CCR-0083126, CCR-0133437, and EIA-0103670.

References

1. D. Albonesi. Dynamic IPC/clock rate optimization. In *Proceedings of ISCA-25*, pages 282–292, June 1998.
2. Jeff Brown. Personal communication, March 2001.
3. The RS/6000 enterprise server model S80 technology and architecture. technical white paper. 1999.
4. Tom Keller, Ann Marie Maynard, Rick Simpson, and Pat Bohrer. Simos-ppc full system simulator. http://www.research.ibm.com/arl/projects/simosPPC.html.
5. A. Lebeck, X. Fan, H. Jeng, and C. Ellis. Power aware page allocation. In *Proceedings of the Ninth International Conference on Architecture Support for Programming Languages and Operating Systems*, November 2000.
6. C. May, E. Silha, R. Simpson, and H. Warren. *The PowerPC Architecture: A Specification for a New Family of RISC Processors. Second Edition.* San Francisco: Morgan Kaufmann Publishers, Inc., 1994.
7. A. Moshovos, B. Falsafi, and A. Choudhary. JETTY: Filtering snoops for reduced energy consumption in smp servers. In *Proceedings of the 7th International Symposium on High- Performance Computer Architecture*, January 2001.
8. T. Mudge. Power: A first class design constraint for future architectures. *Computer*, 34(4):52–57, April 2001.
9. Craig Saldanha and Mikko H. Lipasti. Power efficient cache coherence. Technical report, Department of Electrical and Computer Engineering, University of Wisconsin-Madison, December 2002.
10. Sunfire 3800 - 6800 servers – computing the net effect. Technical White Paper. Available from www.sun.com/servers/white-papers, 2001.

6

Improving Power Efficiency with an Asymmetric Set-Associative Cache

Zhigang Hu[1], Stefanos Kaxiras[2], and Margaret Martonosi[3]

[1] T.J. Watson Research Center, IBM Corporation, Armonk, NY, USA
zhigangh@us.ibm.com
[2] Communication System and Software, Agere Systems, Allentown, PA, USA
kaxiras@agere.com
[3] Department of Electrical Engineering, Princeton University, Princeton, NJ, USA
mrm@ee.princeton.edu

Abstract. Data caches are widely used in general-purpose processors as a means to hide long memory latencies. Set-associativity in these caches helps programs avoid performance problems due to cache-mapping conflicts. Current set-associative caches are symmetric in the sense that each way has the same number of cache lines. Moreover, each way is searched in parallel so energy is consumed by all ways even though at most one way will hit. With this in mind, this chapter proposes an asymmetric cache structure in which the size of each way can be different. The ways of the cache are different powers of two and allow for a "tree-structured" cache in which extra associativity can be shared. We accomplish this by having two cache blocks from the larger ways align with individual cache blocks in the smaller ways. This structure achieves performance comparable to a conventional cache of similar size and equal associativity. Most notably, the asymmetric cache has the nice property that accesses hit in the smaller ways can immediately terminate accesses to larger ways so that power can be saved. For the SPEC2000 benchmarks, we found cache energy per access was reduced by as much as 23% on average. The characteristics of the asymmetric set-associative design (lowpower, uncompromised performance, compact layout) make them particularly attractive for low-power processors.

6.1 Introduction

To bridge the widening speed gap between the processor and the main memory, caches are widely employed in current general purpose microprocessors. For example, the Alpha 21264 processor [8] has a 64 kB, 2-way set-associative L1 data cache and an L1 instruction cache of the same size. Cache designers must consider many factors, including hit latency, miss rate, chip area, and power consumption. Balancing all these factors results in complex cache designs with multiple cache levels.

A key design choice for caches is the associativity. The associativity of a cache is the number of places in the cache where a block may reside. In the sim-

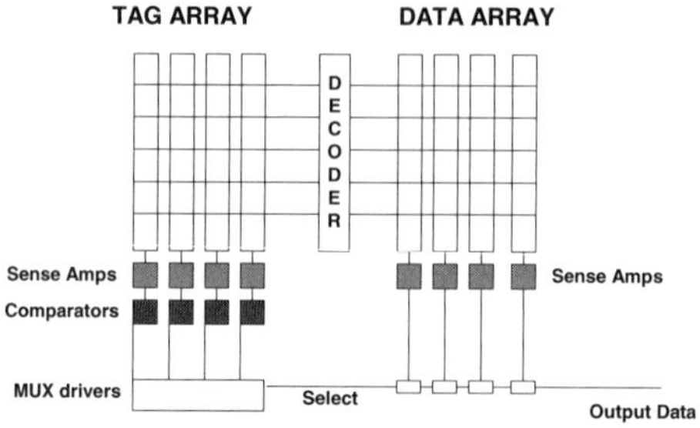

Fig. 6.1. The conventional cache organization.

plest form, a direct-mapped cache, there is only one place for each data block so the associativity is 1. More generally, in an n-way set-associative cache, a data block can appear in n different places, so to find a match all these n locations must be checked. Figure 6.1 shows a typical cache organization with associativity of 4. Increasing the associativity can improve the cache hit rate by reducing the mapping conflict between cache lines that interfer with each other. Hill and Smith [9] report that using a 2-way set-associative cache reduces the number of cache misses by about 30% compared to a direct-mapped cache. However, with conventional set-associative cache design, increasing associativity comes with a high cost of extended hit latency and extra power consumption.

Hit Latency: The latency of a set-associative cache is larger than that of a direct-mapped cache due to the delay associated with the multiplexing logic that selects the correct way. Based on the CACTI 3.0 [23] tool, Figure 6.2 gives the access latencies of three 16 kB caches with different associativities. When going from a direct-mapped cache to a 2-way set-associative cache, the cache latency is increased by about 25%. For many processors, cache latency is on the critical path, so increasing associativity could severely impact the cycle time. Furthermore, since memory reference instructions comprise about 1/3 of the total executed instructions, increasing cache latencies could result in a longer execution time, which will have a global impact on the performance and the power consumption of the whole microprocessor.

Power Consumption: In a conventional set-associative cache, all ways are searched in parallel. Since at most one way will hit, power is consumed by other ways without providing any useful data. Figure 6.2 shows that the average energy consumed per cache access to a 2-way 16 kB cache is about 51% higher than that of a direct-mapped cache. Increasing the associativity to 4 causes the access energy to increase by another 64%.

A major reason for the problems above is the symmetric organization and operation of conventional set-associative caches. In this organization, each way is physically designed to have the same number of cache lines. Furthermore, each way is activated simultaneously, their results come out at the same time, and selection hardware must be employed to decide which result to use. In

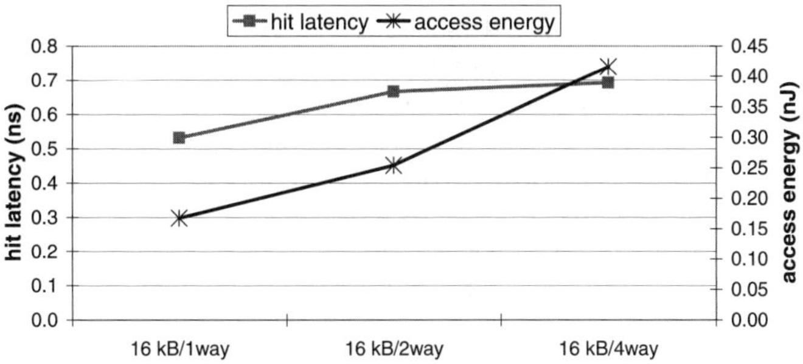

Fig. 6.2. The hit latency and energy per access for 16 kB caches with different associativities. From left to right: direct-mapped, 2-way set-associative, and 4-way set-associative.

this chapter, we propose a new cache architecture, called an *asymmetric cache*, that allows non-uniform sizes for each cache way.

An asymmetric cache uses larger sizes for some ways and smaller sizes for other ways. For instance, a 15 kB 4-way set-associative cache can have 4 ways, with sizes of 8 kB, 4 kB, 2 kB and 1 kB respectively. We describe how an access to this cache occurs and how LRU replacement can be implemented in such a cache. We show that asymmetric caches have similar performance compared to conventional caches of similar sizes and associativities. Furthermore, since in asymmetric caches smaller ways are faster, we show how a hit in smaller ways can immediately signal other larger ways to stop the lookup. This effect, similar to *short circuit evaluation* of boolean expressions, can reduce the average power consumed by the slower and larger ways. With this technique, the asymmetric cache described above achieves up to 23% energy savings compared to a 4-way conventional cache of similar size.

The structure of the chapter is as follows. In Section 6.2, we discuss related work and in Section 6.3 we explain the simulation environment and machine model used to evaluate our proposed structure. Next, in Section 6.4, we introduce in detail The structure of an asymmetric set-associative cache and discuss some advantages of this structure. In Section 6.5, we demonstrate our simulation results. Section 6.6 compares asymmetric caches with other design options and discusses our plans for future work. Finally, Section 6.7 summarizes this chapter.

6.2 Related Work

Caches have been the subject of much research. In general there are two main research categories. One category of research focuses on the internal structure and address-mapping design within a single cache. Group-associative caches [18] and DASC (Direct-mapped Access Set-associative Check) caches [22] are examples in this category. Both try to achieve the miss rate of a set-associative cache with the hit latency of a direct-mapped cache by combining an associative tag array with a direct-mapped data array. In a group-associative cache, a direct-mapped cache is dynamically partitioned into groups of cache lines. Each group functions as a set as in a conventional set-associative cache. Each memory block can map to any position within a group instead of a single position in a conventional direct-mapped cache. The exact position of this block is recorded in a directory that is accessed in parallel with a data/tag array. In DASC caches [22], the tag array is n-way set-associative but the data array is direct-mapped. For each memory request, data in the privileged location are optimistically used. If the tag check indicates a miss on the privileged location, all activities using the speculative data must be canceled. Since the tag array is set-associative, a hit on alternative locations can also be determined during the tag check. On a miss to all the alternative locations, the referenced data must be served from the next level of the memory hierarchy. Other work in this category includes the column-associative cache [1], skewed associativity cache [2], and the difference-bit cache [13].

Another category of cache research tries to split the data cache into typically two subcaches to capture different memory access patterns. Examples in this category include—among others—split temporal spatial data caches (STS) [17], split spatial/non-spatial caches [19], victim buffers [12] and filter caches [11]. A survey of this category of research can be found in [20].

Our work is similar to the skewed associativity work [2] in that each way is indexed differently. However, in asymmetric caches, the difference in indexing stems from the different size of each cache way but not by the deliberate use of different decoders for each way. Within each way, we retain the conventional index function to avoid adding new decoders. Since our work is focused on power consumption instead of miss rate, these two mechanisms are actually orthogonal to each other. It is possible to combine the two to achieve different trade-offs between power and performance.

Beyond research focusing on miss rate there is also research focusing on latency and power consumption. In an n-way set-associative cache, each cache line has n possible locations to be placed so the possibility that a useful cache line is driven out due to mapping conflict is reduced. However, compared to direct-mapped caches, conventional set-associative caches incur longer delay and higher power consumption for each cache access. These two problems have been the focus of much research [4, 5, 15, 27]. The general solution is to assign priorities either dynamically or statically to the possible locations. For each cache access, the location with the highest priority is first checked for a hit. If it is a hit, then the access is completed immediately without looking at other locations. If it is a miss, however, the remaining candidate locations are checked subsequently. This technique has been employed in some commercial processors [24, 26]. In the rest of this section, we describe two previous proposals to improve the energy inefficiency of set-associative caches.

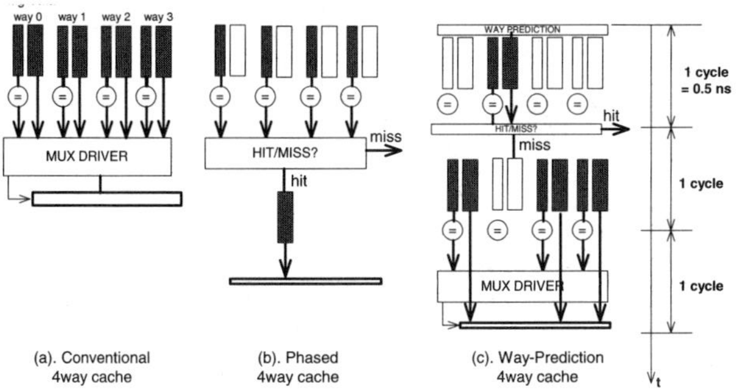

Fig. 6.3. Access procedure for different cache structures.

6.2.1 Phased Cache

In a phased cache, accesses to tags and data are serialized, as shown in Figure 6.3(b). During the first stage, all the tags in the selected set are examined in parallel. The data array is not touched in this step. If the tag comparison indicates that there is a hit, then the data array in the hit way is accessed during the second stage. Otherwise, the second stage is skipped and the next-level cache is accessed.

Phased caches can greatly reduce the energy consumed by each access since the tag array consumes much less energy than the data array. Also, only at most one way in the data array is activated for each cache access. However, in the common situation where there is a hit, the cache access latency is increased, which may delay the whole processor and lead to more energy consumed in other parts of the processor. Therefore, an evaluation of the phased cache must take the complete processor into account.

6.2.2 Way Prediction Cache

In a way prediction cache, as shown in Figure 6.3(c), one cache way is speculatively chosen by a predictor to be accessed before the other ways. If a hit is detected in the predicted way, the access latency and the power consumption are similar to that of a direct-mapped cache. On the other hand, if a miss is detected in the predicted way, the remaining ways are accessed in parallel as in conventional caches. A simple MRU (Most Recently Used) [4, 5, 10, 15] prediction policy is typically employed to exploit cache access locality. The effectiveness of a way prediction cache largely depends on the accuracy of the way prediction. Our simulations show that a simple MRU algorithm has a prediction rate of about 84%, which agrees with results in [10]. The way prediction hardware itself may, however, incur some extra latency and energy consumption.

Both phased caches and way prediction caches maintain the symmetric structure of conventional caches, but they modify the access procedure to

Table 6.1. Configuration of Simulated Processor.

General	
Clock Frequency Feature Size	2GHz (0.5ns cycle time) 0.1um
Processor Core	
Instruction Window Issue Width Functional Units	64-RUU, 32-LSQ 4 instructions per cycle 4 IntALU,1 IntMult, 4 FPALU,1 FPMult, 2 MemPorts
Memory Hierarchy	
L1 Dcache Size L1 Icache Size L2 Memory TLB Size	16KB, 4-way, 32 B blocks, 2-cycle 8KB, 1-way, 32 B blocks, 1-cycle 512KB, 8-way LRU, 64B blocks, 8-cycle latency 100 cycles 128-entry, 30-cycle miss penalty

trade extra latency for reduced power consumption. In this chapter, we propose a structurally asymmetric cache design that achieves a different trade-off between latency, power consumption, and design complexity. Before discussing this structure in detail, we first introduce the simulator and the benchmarks we used to evaluate our design.

6.3 Methodology and Modeling

Our performance results shown in this chapter are based on simulations using the SimpleScalar [3] tool set. The cache energy and timing results are obtained with CACTI 3.0 [23], which is an updated version of CACTI [25]. We augmented the cache model in SimpleScalar to simulate asymmetric caches, phased caches, and way-prediction caches. Our simulated processor is a 2 GHz 4-issue out-of-order processor based on 0.1 μ technology. The main parameters of this processor are shown in Table 6.1.

We evaluate our results using benchmarks from the SPEC CPU2000 benchmark suite [6]. The benchmarks are compiled and statically linked for the Alpha instruction set using the Compaq Alpha compiler with SPEC *peak* settings. For each program, we skip the first 1 billion instructions to avoid the initial startup behavior of the benchmarks. We then simulate the program until 2 billion instructions are committed. Our simulation is conducted with SimpleScalar's EIO traces using the reference input set to ensure reproducible results for each benchmark across multiple simulations.

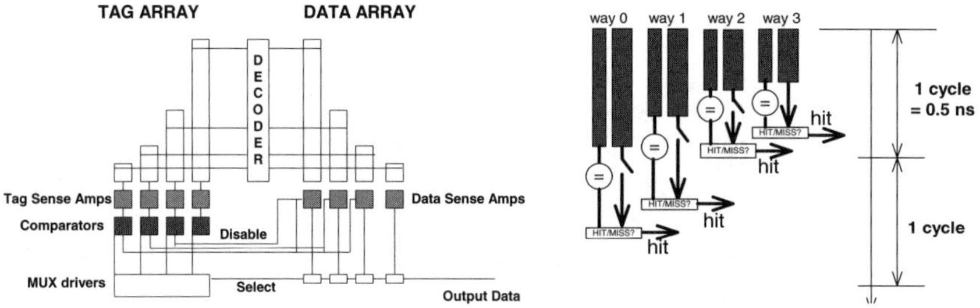

Fig. 6.4. Structure (left) and access procedure (right) of an asymmetric cache.

6.4 Asymmetric Set-Associative Cache

In this section, we will describe the basic structure, access policy, and replacement policy of asymmetric caches and analyze the latency and the power consumption associated with this design.

6.4.1 Structure

As the name implies, in an asymmetric set-associative cache, cache ways are of different sizes. Figure 6.4 shows the diagram of the asymmetric 4-way set-associative cache that is modeled in our simulation. In a 15 kB asymmetric cache with 32 byte cache lines, each of the four ways has 256, 128, 64, and 32 cache lines, respectively. Since the size of each way is different, decoder design becomes an issue for asymmetric caches. In conventional cache design, caches are broken into several smaller banks/blocks to balance the wire length of each direction [23, 25]. With this design, the large decoder shown in Figure 6.1 is actually made up of simpler subdecoders. By choosing sizes of each way to be powers of two, we can share these subdecoders among all ways. Thus, no extra decoders are required in asymmetric caches.

Due to the size difference of each way, asymmetric caches have the following characteristics.

1. Because of their smaller size, smaller ways are faster.
2. Tag comparisons in different ways happen at different speeds: hits are detected faster in smaller ways.
3. Smaller ways consume less power.

In the following subsections, we describe how an asymmetric cache is accessed and how replacement occurs. We also demonstrate how to take advantage of the asymmetry to achieve a new trade-off between performance and power consumption.

6.4.2 Access Policy

Figure 6.4 also depicts the access procedure of the asymmetric 4-way set-associative cache. Similarly to conventional set-associative caches, each way

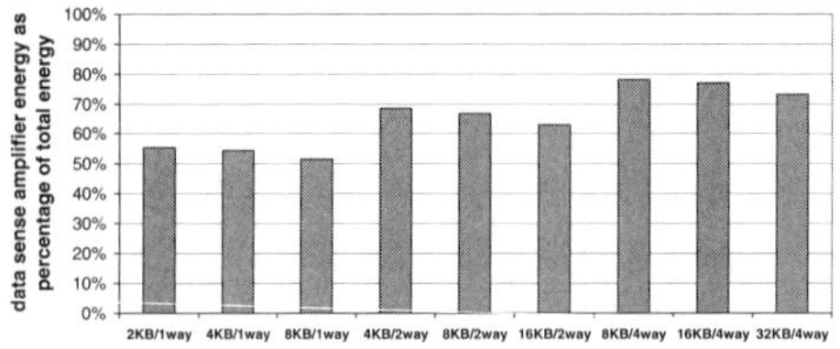

Fig. 6.5. The energy of data sense amplifiers as a percentage of total energy per cache access for various cache configurations.

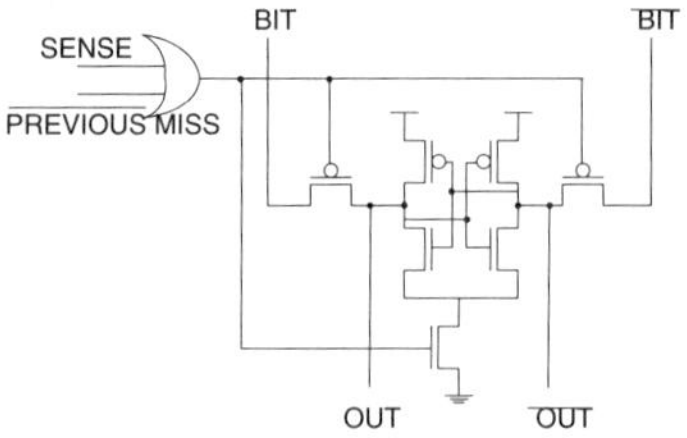

Fig. 6.6. Conventional sense amplifier augmented with a gated sense signal.

in asymmetric caches starts searching in parallel to look for a hit. Unlike conventional caches, however, asymmetric caches have different hit latencies for each way due to their size differences. In the situation when an access hits a smaller (thus faster) way, it is desirable to signal other slower ways to terminate their lookup. We refer to this mechanism as "shorting the lookups". This can reduce cache hit latency and power consumption.

Terminating a lookup can be conducted at various stages in a cache access. We can add termination control logic to the wordline, the bitline, the sense amplifier and the output drivers. The choice of the control point depends on the latency overhead and the power savings achieved. Figure 6.5 shows the percentage of cache energy per access attributed to data sense amplifiers for various caches with 32 byte cache line size in 0.1 μ technology. Across the different cache configurations, we observed that more than half of the energy per access is consumed on the data sense amplifiers. This suggests that to save power we should gate the data sense amplifiers and only activate them when needed.

In [23], control logic is proposed to gate the foot transistors of the sense amplifiers. In this section, we introduce an alternative way to gate the sense amplifiers. As shown in Figure 6.6, typical sense amplifier designs incorporate a *sense* signal that is pulled down (simultaneously with the wordline) to engage the sense amplifier [16]. Our approach is to gate the sense signal of the larger ways using the result (miss) from the smaller ways. Only in case of a miss in the smaller ways are the sense amplifiers enabled in the larger ways. We can cascade this gating signal from smaller to larger ways but we may delay a hit on the largest way. Alternatively, any hit in a smaller way disables sensing in all larger ways. We simulate the latter in our evaluations.

Gating the sense signal for a small period does not affect the correctness of the circuits as long as we are dealing with static RAM cells [7]. In this case, the static memory cell only enlarges the differential voltage in the bit and bit-bar lines, making it easier for the sense amplifier to amplify this to full swing down the road. The same is not true for dynamic RAM cells, however. There the sense signal has to be asserted simultaneously with the wordline signal since with the passage of time it becomes harder for the sense amps to detect the differential between the bit and bit-bar. Under such conditions, transient noise can easily introduce errors. Gating the data sense amplifiers will affect the hit latency and the power consumption of a cache access. We discuss this issue in detail below.

Hit Latency: Since the larger ways only activate their sense amplifiers after the tag comparison completes in all smaller ways, access latencies in these ways may increase. For the 15 kB asymmetric 4-way cache we simulated, our evaluation based on CACTI 3 shows that while the access to the two smaller ways (way 2 and way 3 in Figure 6.4) can be finished in a single clock cycle, the access to the two larger ways (way 0 and way 1 in Figure 6.4) needs two cycles to complete. Compared to a conventional 4-way cache, the hit latency to the smaller ways has a one-cycle advantage.

Power Consumption: The potential hit latency benefits can lead to improvements in a program's overall energy consumption and energy-delay product since they may reduce the program execution time. Moreover, our scheme for shorting cache lookups can be effective in reducing cache energy per hit, when hits occur in the smaller cache ways. As was explained above, if an access hits on a smaller way, the larger ways can be prevented from continuing their lookups. Thus, the energy consumed by the data sense amplifiers can be saved. In other words, early hits on faster ways are much more power-efficient than other hits. As shown in Section 6.5, this significantly reduces the total power consumption of asymmetric caches.

6.4.3 Replacement Policy

Because of the asymmetry among cache ways, conventional replacement algorithms are not directly applicable to an asymmetric cache. Replacement strategies in an asymmetric cache can affect where heavily accessed data are stored in the cache, thus impacting both performance and power consumption.

Since hits in a smaller way have smaller latency and lower power consumption, one might want to devise schemes in which the most heavily accessed data are dynamically pushed to the smallest ways. However, data movement within the cache would significantly increase the power consumption. In this chapter we examine asymmetric caches using simple LRU replacement policies without data movement.

An LRU replacement strategy helps to maintain low miss rates in set-associative caches, especially when power is a major concern and we want to

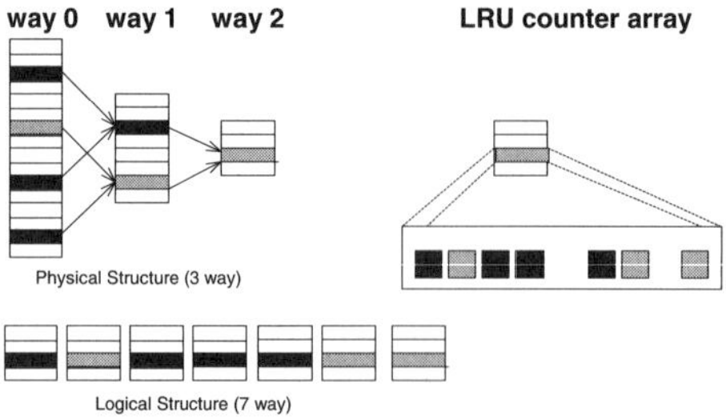

Fig. 6.7. An LRU counter-based replacement policy for an asymmetric cache.

minimize accesses to the outlying levels of the memory hierarchy. In asymmetric caches, LRU replacement is slightly more complex than in conventional caches. We illustrate this assuming an LRU implementation using N *modulo-N* counters per set, where N is the associativity. The counters are updated to preserve a total order within the set, the largest value indicating the LRU line in the set. Figure 6.7 shows the LRU scheme of a 3-way asymmetric cache. In the asymmetric cache, for the purpose of LRU replacement, we consider the number of sets to be equal to the number of lines in the smallest way. This is illustrated by the "logical structure" of the asymmetric cache shown in Figure 6.7. Each set, however, consists of more lines than the cache associativity. Specifically, each set contains all the alternative lines that map to the same line in the smallest way. Thus, the LRU array has only as many entries as the size of the smallest way but each entry contains more counters for the larger ways. Assume the asymmetric cache in the figure has 256, 128, and 64 cache lines for each way, respectively. Then there are just 64 LRU counter entries corresponding to the 64 lines of the smallest way. Each LRU counter entry, as shown on the right side of the figure, contains 4 LRU counters for the largest way (256 lines), 2 counters for the second largest (128 lines), and 1 counter for the smallest way (64 lines). When new data items are brought into the cache, a set of lines is selected according to the address of the new data. This address maps onto a single line in each of the 3 ways specifying a unique path in the mapping tree. Only the LRU counters that correspond to the specific mapping path are considered for the replacement decision. The evicted line is the one with the largest value among the counters selected. However, the LRU entry is updated with any access that corresponds to the mapping tree and therefore behaves as if it were not 3-way but 7-way set-associative. Overall, the LRU counters in a 3-way asymmetric cache are maintained like a 7-way conventional set-associative cache, but the victim selection is done similarly to a 3-way conventional cache.

While the paragraph above shows that the counter-based LRU replacement algorithm can be revised to work with asymmetric caches, it complicates the update and lookup operations of the LRU counters. Here we introduce an alternative way to implement a decay-based replacement algorithm that emulates a true LRU algorithm. Cache decay [14] uses 2-bit counters to gauge

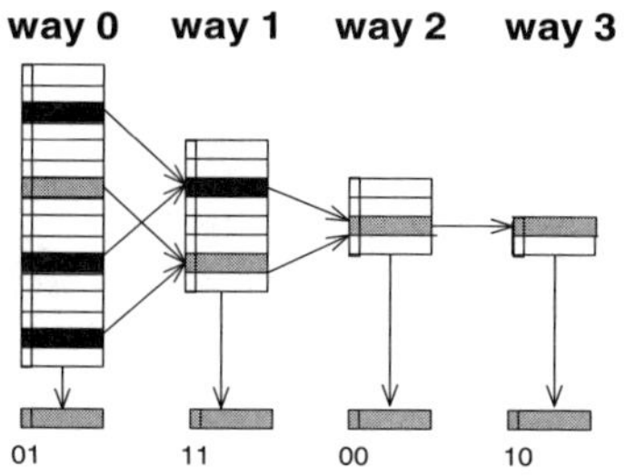

Fig. 6.8. A decay counter-based replacement policy for an asymmetric cache. The cache line with the longest idle time (i.e. largest decay counter value) is replaced.

the idle time of cache lines and proposes to shut off cache lines with long idle times to save cache leakage energy. These decay counters contain information similar to LRU counters. Specifically, within a cache set, the cache line with the largest idle time is the LRU block and, conversely, the one with the shortest idle time is the MRU block. This observation suggests that we can use the decay counters to approximate LRU counters. For each cache replacement, we evict the cache block with the largest decay counter value within the set (see Figure 6.8. Compared to the LRU implementation described in the previous paragraph, the update and lookup operations for the decay counters are much simpler. As in cache decay, we reset the decay counter with every cache line access and increase the counter with every global clock tick. During an eviction, all decay counters within a cache set are read out and the cache line with the largest counter value is chosen for replacement. In our simulation, we use a 2 bit local counter for each cache line and use a global cycle counter that ticks every 256 cycles. With these coarse-grained counters, an interesting situation could occur when more than one decay counter holds the same largest value within a cache set. In this situation, we consider all those cache lines with the largest counter value as candidates for replacement. Among these candidates, there is no further information to decide their exact LRU order, so we can assign priority based on their way sizes. Since accesses to smaller ways are faster and more energy-efficient, we prefer to place active cache lines in smaller ways. This leads to our first policy, where we always choose the smaller way to replace in case of equal counters. We call this policy *favor smaller ways*. Conversely, the *favor larger ways* policy tries to replace the larger way if the counters are the same. In comparison, we also considered an ideal implementation where the counter is very fine grained so that the situation where two decay counters are equal never occurs. We call this policy *ideal LRU*. Notice that the counter-based LRU algorithm shown in Figure 6.7 can be used to implement ideal LRU. In the next section, we will evaluate the performance and power consumption of these three policies.

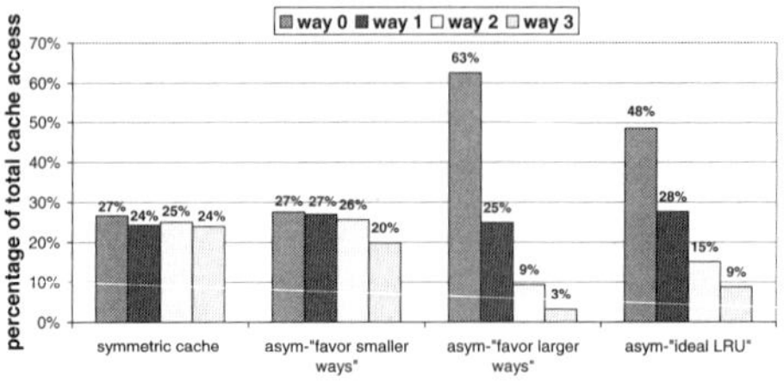

Fig. 6.9. Access to each way with a conventional symmetric cache and three asymmetric caches with different LRU implementations.

6.5 Results

In this section, we will examine simulation results for asymmetric caches compared to conventional symmetric caches. The conventional 4-way set-associative cache has a size of 16 kB and block size of 32 bytes, with each way having 128 cache lines. The 15 kB asymmetric caches have 256, 128, 64, and 32 cache lines for its 4 ways, respectively. For the conventional cache, we employ a true LRU algorithm. The asymmetric caches are evaluated with the three LRU algorithms we described in the previous section, including *favor smaller ways*, *favor larger ways* and *ideal LRU*.

6.5.1 Access Frequency to Each Way

Different flavors of LRU implementation lead to different distributions of cache accesses in each way. This effect is illustrated in Figure 6.9. As expected, in a conventional symmetric cache, the 4 ways are roughly equally exercised so each way has about 25% probability of being accessed. In asymmetric caches, with the "ideal LRU" algorithm, the access distribution to each way matches their relative sizes. In our simulated asymmetric caches, the distribution follows the "8:4:2:1" size ratio. More interesting distributions can be observed with the decay counter-based LRU implementations. When the algorithm favors smaller ways, these ways receive many more accesses than their sizes would suggest. Particularly in the sample configuration shown in this experiment, with a 256-cycle global counter and 2 bit local counters, the *favor smaller ways* LRU implementation achieved roughly equal distributions of accesses to each way, even though the size of the smallest way is only 1/8 of the largest way. Conversely, when the LRU algorithm favors larger ways, smaller ways are very infrequently accessed and the bulk of the accesses are directed to larger ways.

In the next two subsections, we will explore the effect of access policy and replacement policy on the performance and power consumption of asymmetric caches.

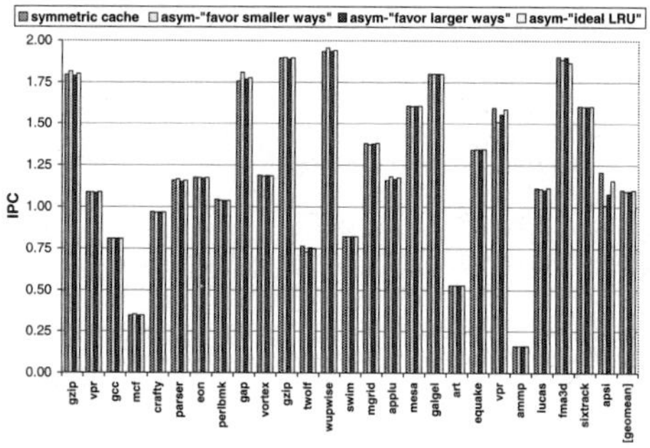

Fig. 6.10. IPC of asymmetric vs. conventional 4-way caches for SPEC2000.

6.5.2 Performance

Figure 6.10 depicts the IPC for SPEC2000 benchmarks with conventional vs. asymmetric 4-way 16 kB caches. In asymmetric caches, hits on smaller ways have lower latencies than on larger ways. However, the impact of this effect on performance is not significant for two reasons: the aggressive out-of-order execution and the fully pipelined data cache access. In [8], it has been estimated that increasing cache latency by 1 cycle degrades overall performance by about 4% for the Alpha 21264 microprocessor. We expect this effect to be even smaller for asymmetric caches since accesses hit smaller ways only part of the time. As shown in the figure, the average IPC difference is less than 1% comparing a 16 kB conventional symmetric cache and a 15 kB asymmetric cache with various LRU implementations. In benchmarks such as vpr and apsi, the cache size difference (15 kB vs. 16 kB) causes some recognizable IPC degradation, while in most other benchmarks, this effect is not significant. In many benchmarks, such as gzip, gap, wupwise, and applu, the IPC of "favor smaller way" outperforms other policies because more accesses hit on the smaller, faster ways. Overall, the performance is roughly stable among all the configurations because all the caches considered have similar size and all use an LRU replacement policy.

6.5.3 Power Consumption

This section compares the power consumption of our asymmetric caches with the similar-sized conventional 4-way cache. Since both caches are 4-way set-associative, we assume the energy consumed by the mux drivers and the output drivers is similar and small. Figure 6.1 and Figure 6.4 show that these drivers account for 1–2% energy in a 4-way cache. Thus, we exclude them from our comparison. Considering the *lookup-shorting* effect, hitting in the four ways (from the smallest to the largest way) in our sample asymmetric cache consumes about 50%, 66%, 83%, and 100% of the access energy of a conventional cache.

Table 6.2. Access frequency and per-access energy for asymmetric caches.

	Way 0 256 lines	Way 1 128 lines	Way 2 64 lines	Way 3 32 lines	Overall
(Favor smaller ways)					
Access frequency(%)	0.27	0.27	0.26	0.20	
Access energy	0.27	0.22	0.17	0.10	0.77
(Favor larger ways)					
Access frequency(%)	0.63	0.25	0.09	0.03	
Access energy	0.63	0.21	0.06	0.02	0.91
(Ideal LRU)					
Access frequency(%)	0.48	0.28	0.15	0.09	
Access energy	0.48	0.23	0.10	0.04	0.86

We estimate the energy per access of a conventional 4-way cache (excluding the mux drivers and output drives) as the sum of the access energies to each way. For the asymmetric cache, by applying lookup shorting, we avoid the data sense amplifier, energy in the larger cache ways if we determine in time that we have a hit in one of the smaller ways. Considering this effect, the energy saving of each way is roughly $prob(access\_in\_this\_way) * energy\_for\_hit\_on\_this\_way$. Based on this estimation, Table 6.2 shows average cache access energy considering the access frequency to each cache way. Compared to the conventional cache, an asymmetric cache achieves about 23%, 9% and 14% energy savings with *favor smaller ways*, *favor larger ways*, and *ideal LRU* replacement policies, respectively.

6.6 Discussion and Future Work

In this section we compare asymmetric caches to phased caches and way prediction caches and discuss some design issues associated with asymmetric caches. We also outline some directions for future work.

6.6.1 Comparing Asymmetric Caches to Previous Proposals

Asymmetric caches, like phased caches and way prediction caches, aim to achieve a new trade-off between latency, power consumption, and design complexity. Table 6.3 presents a detailed comparison of latency and power consumption for these cache schemes. For way prediction caches, there are two situations for a cache hit: hit on the predicted way or hit on other ways. For 4-way set-associative asymmetric caches, there are four situations for a cache hit: hit on each of the four ways, respectively. These situations incur different latency/power consumption values, as shown in the table.

Phased Caches: In phased caches, the lookups of the tag array and data array are serialized: the data array is accessed only when the tag comparison

Table 6.3. Comparison of power consumption and latency for asymmetric caches vs. conventional caches, phased caches, and way prediction caches. Note: Power is normalized to conventional caches.

	Caches	Conven.	Phased	WP	Asym
hit	Latency(cycles)	2	3	1/3	1/1/2/2
	Power	1	0.37	0.25/1	0.5/0.66/0.83/1
miss	Latency(cycles)	2	2	3	2
	Power	1	0.14	1	1

indicates a hit. As indicated by Table 6.3, the phased cache utilized less cache access power for both hits and misses. However, in the common case when there is a cache hit, the latency is one cycle longer than a conventional cache. This extra cycle latency is tolerable in L2 caches but is a rather big overhead for L1 caches, which are typically performance-constrained.

Way Prediction Caches: In way prediction caches, the lookup of one special way (typically the MRU way) is given priority over other ways. If it turns out that this way gets hit, then both the latency and the power consumption are improved. As in other predictive mechanisms, the effectiveness of way prediction caches is highly dependent on the accuracy of way prediction and the associated access pattern. If for some reason the access pattern is changed (for example, under a SMT environment), then the accuracy of way prediction might deteriorate and the extended latency associated with wrong way prediction could harm the overall performance.

Both phased caches and way prediction caches try to explicitly serialize the cache access process. On the contrary, asymmetric caches achieve implicit serialization through the size/speed differences among ways. It is tempting but difficult to reach a simple conclusion about which scheme is the best because each scheme targets a different balance and trade-off among many design factors such as latency, power consumption, and complexity. Together these schemes form a rich set of design choices for cache designers. In the next subsection, we discuss some design issues related to the evaluation of asymmetric caches vs. other cache structures.

6.6.2 Design Issues and Future Work

Instruction Scheduling: Load/store instructions bring challenges to the instruction scheduler because their latencies are variable and unknown at the time of scheduling. Since cache hits are typically more common than cache misses, current processors often optimistically issue a load-dependent instruction assuming the load will hit in the cache [21]. If it turns out that the load misses in the cache, the speculatively issued instructions are squashed and reissued after the load is completed. With way prediction and asymmetric caches, this strategy is further complicated because the hit latency depends on where the hit occurs. In this chapter, we assume a somewhat ideal scheduler that knows the exact cache access latency at the time of scheduling. Interesting future work would be to model a more realistic scheduler and evaluate its impact on the cache structures we discussed in this chapter, including phased caches, way prediction caches, and asymmetric caches.

Cycle Time Considerations: In the race to better performance and higher clock frequency, it can be very difficult to design a reasonably sized cache for a given cycle time. Instead, current L1 data caches are typically pipelined into two or more cycles. By allowing different latencies for each way, the asymmetric cache structure provides more flexibility for fitting the cache access time into a desired latency.

Area Savings: The idea of assigning different sizes to each way can be explored beyond achieving power savings. In this section, we briefly discuss the possibility of achieving area savings using this idea. Because of the rule of locality, the most recently used way (MRU way) is more likely to be re-accessed than the least recently used way (LRU way). This phenomenon has been explored by way prediction [10]. With an asymmetric cache structure, we can explore this phenomenon by moving data around so that the MRU line in a set is always placed in the largest way. Similarly, we can place the LRU line always in the smallest way. Thus, at the cost of extra data migrations among ways, an asymmetric cache could possibly achieve the miss rate of a much larger conventional cache. This scheme is especially suitable for L2 caches since the area savings there are more significant while extra data movements could be better tolerated. In this chapter, we did not explore this mechanism but it could be a promising direction for future work.

6.7 Conclusions

Current set-associative caches are physically symmetric. That is, all ways have the same number of cache lines. Moreover, current set-associative caches are operated symmetrically, which means all the ways are looked up in parallel. This results in both extended hit latency and increased power consumption compared to a direct-mapped cache. In this chapter we take a different approach: we propose set-associative caches in which different ways have different sizes. In these asymmetric caches, sizes of different ways are different powers of 2 and allow for a "tree-structured" cache. Extra associativity is shared by having two cache blocks from the larger ways align with individual cache blocks in the smaller ways. An LRU replacement policy can be implemented by treating all the items in a "mapping tree" as a single set with higher associativity. Replacement decisions take into account only the items that correspond to a single path within the mapping tree. An alternative LRU replacement is to use decay counters instead of LRU counters. The advantage of this implementation is that decay counters are easier to maintain for asymmetric caches.

Because of their different sizes, cache ways in asymmetric caches have different access times and power characteristics. In particular, smaller ways can be accessed faster and at the same time expend less energy. We can further exploit a hit on a fast cache way by "shorting" the lookups in the slower cache ways. Thus, asymmetric caches have the benefit of lower power consumption in the smaller ways while maintaining the performance of conventional caches. By immediately terminating lookups in larger ways when detecting a hit on smaller ways, the average cache access energy is reduced by as much as 23% for SPEC2000.

Asymmetric cache architectures do not require elaborate new hardware but rather are simple variations in the geometry of conventional set-associative caches. This approach results in power savings and with further optimizations could also provide higher performance at the same time.

References

1. Agarwal A and Pudar S (1992) Column-associative caches: A technique for reducing the miss rate of direct-mapped caches. In: Proceedings of the 20th Annual International Symposium on Computer Architecture.
2. Bodin F and Seznec A (1995) Skewed associativity enhances performance predictability. In: Proceedings of the 22nd Annual International Symposium on Computer Architecture.
3. Burger D, Austin T, and Bennett S (1996) Evaluating future microprocessors: The SimpleScalar tool set. Technical Report TR-1308, University of Wisconsin-Madison Computer Sciences Department.
4. Calder B, Grunwald D, and Emer J (1996) Predictive sequential associative cache. In: Proceedings of the 2nd Annual International Symposium on High Performance Computer Architecture.
5. Chang J H, Chao J, and So K (1987) Cache design of a sub-micron CMOS system370. In: Proceedings of the 14th Annual International Symposium on Computer Architecture.
6. SPEC Corporation (2000) WWW site http://www.spec.org.
7. Diodato P (2001) PersOnal communication.
8. Gwennap, L (1996) Digital 21264 sets new standard. Microprocessor Report, October 1996, pp. 11–16.
9. Hill M and Smith A (1989) Evaluating associativity in CPU caches. IEEE Transactions on Computers (38)12:1612–1630.
10. Inoue K, Ishihara T, and Murakami K (1999) Way-predicting set-associative cache for high performance and low energy consumption. In: Proceedings of the 1999 International Symposium on Low Power Electronics and Design.
11. Johnson M and Mangione-Smith W. (1997) The filter cache: An energy efficient memory structure. In: Proceedings of the 30th Annual International Symposium on Microarchitecture.
12. Jouppi N (1990) Improving direct-mapped cache performance by the addition of a small fully-associative cache and prefetch buffers. In: Proceedings of the 17th Annual International Symposium on Computer Architecture.

13. Juan T, Lang T, and Navarro J (1996) The difference-bit cache. In: Proceedings of the 23rd Annual International Symposium on Computer Architecture.
14. Kaxiras S, Hu Z, and Martonosi M (2001) Cache decay: exploiting generational behavior to reduce cache leakage power. In: Proceedings of the 28th Annual International Symposium on Computer Architecture.
15. Kessler R, Jooss R, Lebeck A, and Hill M (1989) Inexpensive implementation of set-associativity. In: Proceedings of the 16th Annual International Symposium on Computer Architecture, pp. 131-139.
16. Villa L, Zhang M, and Asanovic K (2000) Dynamic zero compression for cache energy reduction. In: Proceedings of the 33rd Annual IEEE/ACM International Symposium on Microarchitecture.
17. Milutinovic V, Markovic B and Tremblay M (1996) The split temporal/spacial cache: initial performance analysis. In: Proceedings of the SCIzzL-5.
18. Peir J, Lee Y, and Hsu W (1998) Capturing dynamic memory reference behavior with adaptive cache topology. In: Proceedings of the Eighth International Conference on Architectural Support for Programming Languages and Operating Systems.
19. Prvulovic M, Marinov D, Dimitrijevic Z and Milutinovic C (1999) The split spatial/non-spacial cache: a performance and complexity analysis. In: IEEE TCCA Newsletter.
20. Sahuquillo J and Pont A (2000) Splitting the data cache: a survey. IEEE Concurrency 8(3):30–35.
21. Seznec A (1993) A case for two-way skewed-associative caches. In: Proceedings of the 20th Annual International Symposium on Computer Architecture, pp. 169–178.
22. Seznec A (1995) DASC cache. In: Proceedings of the 1st Annual International Symposium on High Performance Computer Architecture.
23. Shivakumar P, and Jouppi N (2001) Cacti 3.0: An integrated cache timing, power, and area model. Technical Report 2001/2, Compaq Western Research Lab.
24. Tremblay M and O'Connor J (1996) UltraSparcI: A four-issue processor supporting multimedia. IEEE Micro (16)2:42–50.
25. Wilton S and Jouppi N (1994) An enhanced access and cycle time model for on-chip caches TR 1993/5, Compaq Western Research Lab.
26. Yeager K. (1996) The MIPS R10000 superscalar microprocessor. IEEE Micro (16)2:28–40.
27. Zhang C, Zhang X, Yan Y (1997) Two fast and high-associativity cache schemes. IEEE Micro (17)5:40–49.

7

Memory Issues in Hardware-Supported Software Safety

Diana Keen[2], Frederic T. Chong[1], Premkumar Devanbu[1], Matthew Farrens[1], Jeremy Brown[1], Jennifer Hollfelder[1], and Xiu Ting Zhuang[1]

[1] University of California at Davis, Davis, CA, USA
chong@cs.ucdavis.edu,devanbu@cs.ucdavis.edu,farrens@cs.ucdavis.edu, hollfeld@cs.ucdavis.edu, jbbrown@ucdavis.edu,xzhuang@ucdavis.edu
[2] California Polytechnic State University, San Luis Obispo, CA, USA
dkeen@csc.calpoly.edu

Abstract. Rising chip densities have led to dramatic improvements in the cost-performance ratio of processors. At the same time, software costs are burgeoning. Large software systems are expensive to develop and are riddled with errors. Certain types of defects (e.g., those related to memory access, concurrency, and security) are particularly difficult to locate and can have devastating consequences. We believe it is time to explore using some of the increasing silicon real estate to provide extra functionality to support software development. We propose dedicating a portion of these new transistors to provide hardware structures to enhance software development, make debugging more efficient, increase reliability, and provide run-time security.

Unfortunately, software safety tasks, such as checking pointer references, involve extensive bookkeeping, which results in unacceptably high overhead. We describe work in progress that attacks this overhead. In particular, we introduce a *hardware access table* (HAT) which accelerates table lookups critical to software monitoring tasks.

7.1 Introduction

For several decades now, advances in chip manufacturing technology have provided designers with an ever-increasing pool of available transistors. Designers have tended to use these transistors primarily to provide performance gains, yielding such innovations as out-of-order execution, multiple-issue pipelines, on-chip multi-threading, larger caches, branch prediction logic, etc.

At the same time, software development costs have skyrocketed. Large, complex software systems such as operating systems, databases, switching systems and desktop productivity applications are expensive, often behind schedule, and plagued with defects. In fact, maintenance and defect-removal costs are the major factor in the cost of developing large software systems.

When these contrasting trends in hardware and software are juxtaposed, the question naturally arises: Can some of the increasing bounty of real estate available on current and future chips be harvested to provide support for software development activities? This is the central focus of our work.

The specific software defects we will try to detect are dynamic memory access defects. These arise when a piece of data intended to be of one particular type is used as a different, incompatible type. This type of error has been called "unsafe" by Cardelli [1], and the effect is not always immediate and noticeable. The resulting failure may not occur until after quite a bit of additional computing has occurred, and the symptoms may have become much more diffuse. As a result, these defects are particularly pernicious and difficult to track down.

In type-unsafe languages such as C and C++, these errors are caused by the incorrect use of pointers. Strongly typed languages such as Java can prevent these errors by means of static type-checking combined with limited dynamic type checks. Unfortunately, because of legacy assets, efficiency, and available talent, it is likely that systems written in type-unsafe languages such as C or C++ will remain under active development or maintenance for the foreseeable future. In C and C++, the only way to detect memory access errors immediately is through dynamic checking, which has a very significant performance impact. Our central goal in this chapter is to reduce the performance impact of dynamic checking in C and C++ code by providing architectural support.

We present architectural support for dynamic checking that maximizes performance benefits while minimizing changes to commodity architectures. A critical issue is reducing the overhead of bookkeeping operations. During dynamic checking, each pointer reference in our target program could generate dozens of memory references and comparisons. These memory-related operations create a new kind of "memory wall" for software safety. The challenge is to provide dynamic checking without running 10 times slower or using 10 times more hardware. Towards this end, we introduce a *hardware access table* (HAT), which efficiently implements an associative memory by leveraging the existing level 2 cache. We demonstrate that this simple mechanism substantially reduces the overhead of our dynamic checking tasks, and we expect other applications to benefit in the future.

We begin in Section 7.2 with a summary of the historical context of this work. Section 7.3 presents some applications, followed by an overview of the architecture of our approach in Section 7.4. We look at the performance data in Section 7.5. We conclude and look at future directions in Section 7.6.

7.2 Historical Context

There has been a great deal of work done on the broad topic of software safety. Software safety, from our perspective, is concerned with executing untrusted (defective or malicious) code in a manner that quickly detects and rejects actions that compromise protected resources. The precise context can vary widely: the type of protected resource that might be of concern (kernel memory, other tasks' memory, file system, etc.), the trust model (mobile code, shrink-wrapped code, freeware, etc.), the available information (safety proofs, source code, signatures, trust policies), and the required performance, are all important dimensions of the design space. A wide range of solutions have been developed; they can be broadly classified into hardware- and software-based solutions.

Software-Based Safety. Strong typing, as used in languages such as Pascal, Haskell, or ML, ensures that an object identified as a certain type is always of that type during execution. Static type-checking, augmented with dynamic checks (e.g., for array accesses), ensures this property. This approach works when the source is available; this is the only way to be sure that a binary was correctly compiled from a source. Claims made about a binary that arrives *sans* source cannot be verified. Proof-carrying code [2], perhaps derived by a compiler, can provide binaries that have *statically verifiable* properties. Unfortunately, such information-enriched binaries may risk revealing important intellectual property contained in the data-structure definitions and invariants[3]. More recently, Xu et al. [5] proposed a static analysis approach to checking, type safety of binaries; the scaleability of this approach is not yet clear.

Dynamic methods use run-time checks to detect errors such as array bounds overflow or security policy violations. Approaches include source or binary instrumention [6], or run-time environments such as the Java Virtual Machine. Generally, run-time monitoring entails substantial performance penalties, often up to 5x slowdown. Our work is focused precisely on *specialized architectural mechanisms for accelerating current software-based dynamic-checking methods.*

Hardware-Based Safety. Hardware-based approaches use hardware resources to accelerate run-time checking. The LISP-specific Symbolics [7] provided hardware support for four types (list, atom, integer, and NIL) via two extra tag bits. This mechanism was also used implicitly for bounds checking. Hardware tagging a language with an unbounded number of types is resource-intensive in terms of extra memory that is used and intimately affects the entire design of the processor. Changing a commodity processor such as the Intel Pentium to include tagging would be prohibitively expensive. Sun's Pico-Java for Java provides hardware support for an efficient stack but no acceleration for run-time checking. The ambitious Intel iAPX432 project processor aimed to provide a rich set of run-time checks to support the ADA language. However, the sophisticated run-time checking resulted in memory accesses that were quite slow.

[3] The structure of data is the key to understanding programs. See Brooks [3] or Raymond [4].

While inspired by previous efforts, our designs are based on certain technical and business observations about current processor architectures:

1. Current processor designs are complex and finely tuned; adapting one of these designs to add run-time checks will require extensive design and verification time.
2. While providing tagged data types is the most direct means of accelerating run-time checking, our goal is to provide a solution that can be integrated with modern microprocessors at minimal cost. It is impractical to discard the substantial investment in these processors.
3. Much of the software written today is in C or C++ largely because of their efficiency, which is lost with inserted run-time checks.

Our goal was to provide hardware that is non-intrusive to the processor core (to reduce design time) and can dramatically improve the performance of C or C++ with run-time checks.

Now, we describe the applications that we examined in detail along with relevant work that forms the baseline for our approach.

7.3 Motivating Applications

7.3.1 Pointer Safety

Normally, a pointer is associated with a memory location of a particular type. If a pointer should (through accident or malice) point to a location of a different type, it may be said to be *unsafe*. Unsafe pointers are a common source of mysterious software failures. Memory corruption due to an unsafe pointer is notoriously difficult to trace because the effects may not become apparent for quite a while after the first pointer wrote in the wrong location. In addition, programmers often fail to check user input before use. Particularly with arrays, this can leave programs vulnerable to attacks resulting from buffer overflows. Both of these types of mistakes are easily missed in testing.

There are different approaches to mitigating or eliminating the risk of unsafe pointers. We review these approaches and place our work in context.

Software-Based Safety

Strongly typed languages with static checking provide pointer safety, often with only a limited need for dynamic checking. Strongly typed languages, including functional languages such as Haskell and ML (for reasons beyond the scope of this chapter) have yet to gain the momentum that Java has. Finally, as mentioned earlier, the massive momentum behind C and C++ is unlikely to abate for quite a while.

Static Analysis. Wagner [8] and others describe algorithms to analyze the source code of a program to find potential errors with buffer overflows. The software is analyzed using a method based on linear programming to locate potential problems. His method makes worst-case assumptions about inputs, resulting in many false positives. In sendmail, their tool reported 44 *probable* bugs. Four were bugs, whereas forty were false positives. Though this may help a programmer perform a more methodical search of the source code to determine that the code is secure, it still requires the programmer to invest a great deal of time to find bugs. As experience with checking tools such as Lint indicates, busy programmers are unlikely to embrace checking tools that produce a large number of wild geese.

Sandboxing with Segments. The memory management system of the processor could be harnessed to provide pointer safety. One could allocate segments in segmented memory to confine pointers within the proper segment; the memory management hardware would then cause an interrupt when the pointer crosses a segment boundary. This would prevent some errors since buffers would only be allowed to write into other buffers and could not corrupt the stack through normal string operations. It does not, however, stop them from overwriting each other; if different types of data are in the same segment, an unsafe pointer would not be prevented from corrupting data within its own segment. It also may not always be practical to allocate a separate segment for each type of data used in the program. In addition, not all hardware provides such a mechanism.

Augmented Pointer Representation. Several approaches have placed information with pointers to aid in bounds checking. Safe Pointers [9], bcc [10], and rtcc [11] all use this approach. While this is a fairly low-overhead approach that can be employed on current C programs, it is not compatible with legacy codes that cannot be recompiled or that have programmer make assumptions about the representation of pointers.

Another approach associates the pointer with the object at the time it is used, increasing compatibility. Cbounds [12] allows good compatibility with legacy code – if the pointer has been changed by unchecked code, then the object will not be in the memory table, and it can choose not to flag that object. When a pointer is used, an object lookup is performed to make sure it is within a valid object. When a pointer is altered through pointer arithmetic, the original and new values are checked to make sure they are both part of the same object. However, there are problems with efficiency since the object must be found each time a pointer is checked.

A separate process can also be used to make sure that accesses do not go out of the bounds of the arrays. In one proposal [13], a *shadow process* is created. If there are free processors, it runs on a separate processor. This reduced program contains only instructions relevant to these pointer addresses and obtains run-time information from the main program.

Our approach is most similar in spirit to augmenting pointers. However, we use some lightweight hardware mechanisms to accelerate the purely software approaches described above.

Safe Pointers Implementation

For our study, we use the augmented pointer representation as proposed in [9]. Each pointer has associated information about the object to which it points. This "safe pointer" structure contains the current value of the pointer, base (starting address) of the object, the size of the object, and a unique identifier (ID) of the object.

Each time a pointer is used, two checks must occur. A spatial validity check is performed to make sure the value of the pointer is within the bounds of the object. A temporal validity check is also performed to make sure the referred object is still live; i.e., it has not been freed and perhaps reallocated for a new instance of a different (or even the same) type. The information required for the spatial check is contained within the augmented pointer data structure. However, this information is insufficient to determine temporal validity; what if the memory has been reallocated to a different object? So, for temporal validity, we must maintain a separate temporal hash table that indicates whether an object with a specific ID is still allocated and has not yet been freed. To correctly perform the checks each time a pointer is used, these data structures must be kept up to date. Whenever a pointer is assigned to another pointer, the safe pointer structure is copied automatically. When a pointer is assigned to the address of an object, the information about the object must be placed in the safe pointer structure.

The unique IDs are generated by a global counter, which is incremented upon every object allocation. The counter is also incremented when a new stack frame is created in response to a procedure call. Local, stack-allocated objects are given the ID of the current active stack frame. Stack object sizes are calculated at compile time unless the allocation routine is called, in which case the routine is instrumented. Heap allocations are determined at run time. The ID and base of both are obtained at run time. For global objects, all the information is known at compile time. As long as an object is active, its ID is entered in the temporal hash table; once the object is freed (upon explicit deallocation for heap objects and a stack pop for stack objects), the ID is expunged from the hash table.

The code must be instrumented both to maintain these data structures and to check pointer validity. Static analysis is performed on the source code to identify (conservatively) the relevant locations, and we then insert instrumentation as follows.

- Inserted code updates the hash table every time a heap pointer is freed or allocated. Likewise, when a subroutine is entered or exited, we update the hash table.
- Every time a pointer is assigned, we update the associated safe pointer data structure.
- We insert code to perform the requisite checks each time a pointer is used.

- If setjmp is called, the current stack is recorded with a tag. When the corresponding longjmp is called, all of the stack IDs between the longjmp stack and the tagged stack are removed from the ID table.

This purely software-based mechanism is accelerated by specialized hardware components that we introduce in Section 7.4.

In the next section, we present the evaluation suite of programs used in our experiments.

7.3.2 Test Programs

We chose a variety of applications to determine the performance of our safety mechanisms. Our performance evaluations were obtained using cycle-by-cycle simulation. We used SMTsim [14], a simulator for a simultaneous multithreaded processor.

To evaluate our monitoring mechanisms, we used several applications that require dynamic run-time checks to guarantee security. Library calls such as `gets`, `strcpy`, `strcmp`, etc., were instrumented, as well as the individual applications. A summary of the static characteristics of the test programs is given in Table 7.1, and the applications are discussed below.

Table 7.1. Static characteristics of test programs.

Application	Src Lines	Accesses	Assigns	Allocs
Quicksort	45	10	4	4
MinSpan	215	50	49	7
Fingerd	58	13	10	4
MatMult	11	3	0	3
Bridge	2000	224	51	28

1. Quicksort
   The general quicksort algorithm takes a pointer to an array, lower and upper bounds, and a comparison function. Any function may be passed in as the comparison function. Ten thousand random numbers were sorted.
2. Fingerd
   The finger daemon, `Fingerd`, responds to remote `finger` command requests. Version 5.3 was simulated, which contains the vulnerability used by a worm in November 1988 to cripple computers around the world. The worm used a classic buffer overflow attack. Buffer overflows are common errors, so we use `Fingerd` to represent a class of applications that have had similar bugs. The bug in `Fingerd` is caused by the `stdio.h` routine `gets` rather than the program itself. Performance was measured by running the loop 100 times with different value inputs. (It should be noted

that when we run `Fingerd` with an input that causes a buffer overflow, our hardware-enhanced monitor promptly flags it!)

3. Bridge
   Bridge is a classical min-max branch-and-bound game search that plays bridge with full knowledge of each player's cards. A branch-and-bound min-max search dynamically constructs a search tree. The full algorithm is not relevant; suffice to say that the program is deeply recursive, with frequent pointer and array accesses to varied indices. This program was written for a contest in an undergraduate Artificial Intelligence course in 1996. When we ran the safe pointer monitor on the bridge code, it found an array access with an index of -1. Prior testing had not exposed this defect but dynamic pointer checking did.
4. MinSpan
   MinSpan is a minimum spanning tree generator using Prim's algorithm. To create the input graph, we began with 500 nodes and, given a desired connectivity, used a random number generator to determine whether there was an edge between each pair of nodes. If an edge was present, we used a random weight. A binary heap was used to store the nodes that had not yet been connected.
5. MatMult
   MatMult is a classic matrix multiply algorithm. Two 40 by 40 double-precision floating point matrices of randomly generated numbers are multiplied. This was selected because it has a very tight loop.

7.4 Architectural Mechanisms

Previous work in software-based solutions for safety has entailed substantial overhead. Our goal is to exploit current trends in microprocessor design to substantially reduce this overhead. We discovered that a substantial portion of the time due to checking was spent in hash table lookups. We propose a hardware accelerated table (HAT) to accelerate these hash table accesses. Our goal is to provide hardware support that can be integrated into commodity microprocessors at low cost.

7.4.1 Hardware Accelerated Table

To determine whether an object is still alive, the monitor process looks up the ID in a hash table. If it is present, then the object is still alive. Program measurements indicated that these table lookups comprise a substantial fraction of the monitor process execution time. In order to reduce the impact of these lookups, we investigated using a hardware structure called a Hardware Accelerated Table (HAT). The HAT is designed to improve performance in two ways. First, by implementing the hash table lookup in hardware, we can perform in a single cycle what would take several instructions in software.

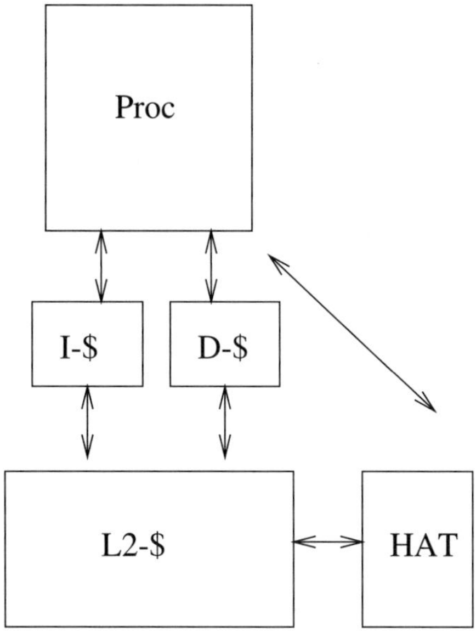

Fig. 7.1. The HAT and its relationship to chip components.

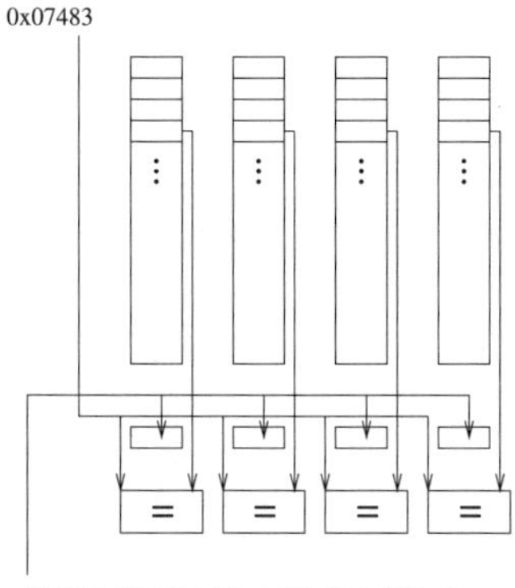

Fig. 7.2. The HAT architecture.

Second, we reduce the memory pressure between the core and L1 cache by providing a cache and by interfacing with the L2 cache, essentially providing a (very small) extra L1 cache. Figure 7.1 shows the HAT and its relationship to the chip components.

The hash table is mapped onto hardware in the following fashion: The hash function is a mask of bits 2 through x, where x is determined by the number of sets in the cache. We ignore the lowest two bits because if the keys are memory addresses, the lower bits are 0's. We do not want to lose all of the lower bits since the keys may be integers. This hash function determines which set in the HAT to search. The search proceeds as a normal cache access does — parallel hardware is employed depending on the degree of associativity in the cache. Our simulations showed that there was very little increase in hit rate when moving from four to eight-way associativity, so we chose four-way associativity. The entries in the HAT are treated as a cache — they are the most recently used items for that entry.

A difficulty arises when the entry is not found in the HAT. Where can the extra entries be stored? With a normal cache, the search is continued at the lower level with the address. In our case, we have a key that has no relation to a memory address. The HAT must allocate its own memory to store the extra entries. Each set has a pointer associated with it that gives the memory address of the next set of data associated with the current set. Because the HAT is far away from the core, we interface with the L2 cache. This can introduce consistency issues if two things occur: the L1 cache is not write-through *and* the user code itself is altering the HAT internal overflow area. We make sure that when memory is allocated to the HAT, it is removed from the L1 cache. Then, because the HAT allocates its own memory and this memory is not part of a data structure to which the user program has access, the only way the user program can touch internal HAT data is through program error. If we were running this safe pointers application, we would discover and flag this erroneous access before it occurred.

Once the HAT has allocated and filled this overflow area, we need to search it to find the relevant entry. If the item is not in the HAT's cache, we read in the overflow line from the L2 cache. We continue to use our 4-way associative comparison for overflow entries. Figure 7.2 shows the temporary holding places in which data from the L2 cache are held. When an L2 cache line is read in, four tags are compared during each cycle. The last entry in the cache line is a pointer that points to the location of the next set of overflow entries. If the L2 cache line size is small compared to the size of a HAT entry, we can make an optimization that several cache lines are allocated together, necessitating one pointer at the end of all of the cache lines rather than one pointer per cache line. This was the case in our simulation environment since the Alpha microprocessor uses 64-bit addresses. It takes a single cycle to perform the actual cache access (in the event of a cache hit), another cycle to transfer the data from the L2 cache to the HAT, and one additional cycle for every four entries in the cache line. In our case, the cache line size is 64 bytes, and each address is 8 bytes. This means each entry is 16 bytes. Only four entries fit on each line. This makes every cache line take a minimum of three cycles to consume. In the last cache line of each allocated block, the last entry is a pointer. We allocated in four-line blocks, giving us fifteen entries that we can search with four cache accesses (twelve cycles). The search ends when the key matches or we reach the end of a linked list.

The HAT has two jobs: One is to determine from what location in memory to read the next four entries, and the other is to search the current entries to find a match. The HAT will provide lookups, insertions, and deletions through a special instruction using a register-based interface:

```
HAT_lookup <key_register> <dest_register>
HAT_insert <key_register> <data_register>
HAT_remove <key_register> <dest_register>
```

When designing the HAT, we had to deal withthe following issues.

- The size of the HAT is static.
- The access time of the HAT is proportional to its size.
- Placing an extra component in the core of the processor will most likely increase wire delays, slowing down the processor clock and substantially increasing processor complexity and design time.
- Placing an extra component away from the core of the processor will increase the delay for accessing that particular component.
- The HAT must support speculative accesses.

In order to minimize the effect on the processor design, we placed the HAT next to the L2 cache. This makes the delay to and from the processor large but minimizes the delay for fetches into the cache. We set the HAT size to 4 kB because we found that with 64 buckets, 90% of the queries lie within the first four entries.

HAT operations are assumed to take six cycles in our results, distributed in the following manner because we place the logic next to the level 2 cache rather than in the processor core, we charge one cycle in wire delay to send the request to the HAT. In cycle 2, the HAT is searched. If the element is not currently in the HAT, and there is overflow allocated, the search continues from the L2 cache. It takes three cycles to access the L2 cache, transfer the line, and search the line. This is because of the close proximity to the L2 cache. If the entry is found in the first overflow line from the L2 cache, the result is returned in cycle 6. In reality, the average access time was between three and four cycles, but we used the larger six cycle latency estimate to account for our small application sizes.

In order to support speculation, we used the same approach as memory accesses. An insert is analogous to a store, and a find is analogous to a load. If an insert precedes a find, then the find needs to return the value used in the insert. The rules are identical to those of loads and stores except that the address is the key read in from the register rather than a calculated value. With this in mind, we share the load/store resources with the HAT resources. The load/store unit is used to obtain the address (key). Zero is always the offset since we want the key in the register, not a calculated value based on the register. We also share the load/store reorder/speculative buffer. We must add one bit to distinguish between HAT operations and memory instructions. When performing a find, we first look in the outstanding previous operations to see if there is an insert with the same key. If not, then the find is sent to the HAT component. Since a find does not change the state of the HAT, except for what values are being cached, this is safe. An insert, however, may not be sent to the HAT until commit time. Since we are reducing overall memory traffic, we expect performance to increase even while sharing ld/st resources. Each HAT command would have produced at least one (and often many) memory requests. Future work will investigate the impact of this sharing in greater detail.

The HAT is similar in spirit to victim caches [15] and has a goal similar to pointer-based prefetching [16]. However, the HAT takes an additional step in supporting comparison operations that provide the user an efficient implementation of an associative memory. With such a low cost and efficient mechanism, it is our hope that users will be free to choose the more natural model of keys and data over hashing and addresses.

7.5 Results

In this section, we provide cycle-accurate simulation results of our mechanisms incorporated into a next-generation microprocessor. Specifically, we examine a system based upon the Alpha 21464 [17], Compaq's next-generation high-performance microprocessor.

Table 7.2. Simulation parameters.

Parameter	Value
CPU Clock	1 GHz
CPU Configuration	8 wide
Line Size	64 bytes
L1 Access Time	1 cycle
L1 I-Cache	32 kB
L1 D-Cache	32 kB
L2 Access Time	6 cycles
L2 Cache	1 MB
L3 Access Time	12 cycles
L3 Cache	4 MB
L3 Miss Penalty	62 cycles
HAT Access Time	3 cycles
HAT Cache	8 kB
HAT Miss Penalty	3 cycles/line
HAT Avg. Latency	6 cycles

Our simulation infrastructure is based upon SMTsim [14], a cycle-by-cycle simulator implementing a next-generation Alpha microprocessor. The system parameters are as shown in Table 7.2.

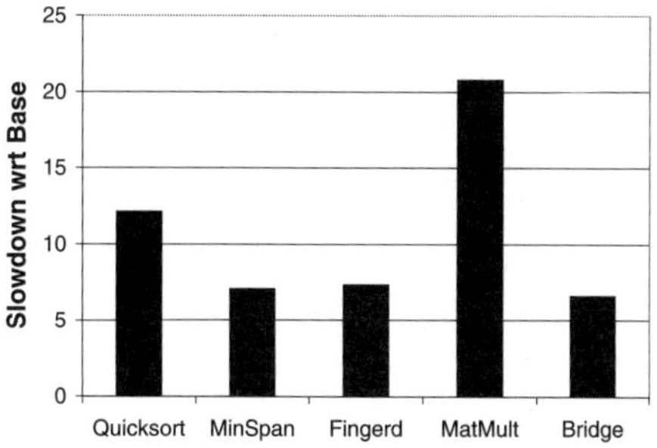

Fig. 7.3. Baseline performance of instrumented code.

In Figure 7.3, we begin with measurements of software implementations of our safety checks on the baseline Alpha microprocessor system *without* hardware modifications. We observe that performance can be substantially degraded by software monitoring. We also note that our implementation of a minimum spanning tree, while not the original code, exhibits results comparable to Austin et al. [9]. Quicksort and MatMult perform poorly because the inserted code is too high of a percentage of the overall execution.

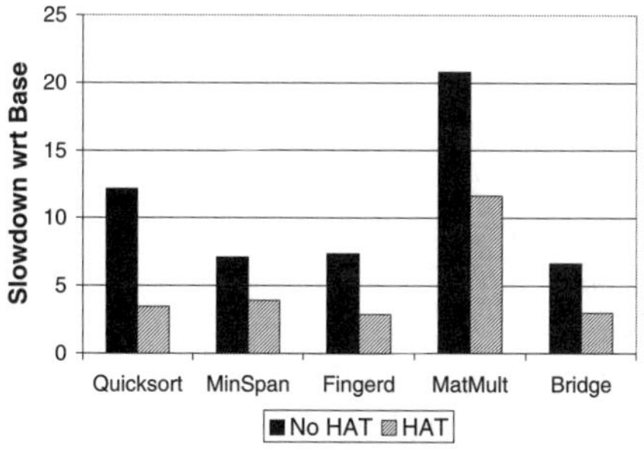

Fig. 7.4. Performance of inserted code with HAT.

A major factor in software monitor overhead for safe pointers is a lookup of the unique ID in a hash table to check whether the object is still alive. In Figure 7.4, we show the results of attacking this overhead using the hardware HAT mechanism. Performance improvements are evident: We note approximately a factor of 2 improvement in all cases, due to a substantial reduction in lookup overhead.

7.5.1 Implications

It is clear that our mechanism provides a doubling of the performance on pointer safety monitoring, and that will immediately benefit programmers.

Several artificially seeded defects in different programs, corresponding to various types of unsafe pointer usage, were all detected as expected. In addition, our system identified a previously unknown defect in the bridge program, and it properly detected a violation and exited when we attacked the simulated `Fingerd` with a buffer overflow attack.

Although we obtain a $2x$ improvement with the HAT compared to instrumented code without the HAT, we are still in slowdown ranges just acceptable for debugging purposes and completely unacceptable for production codes. Except for the highly array-intensive matrix multiply, we have come from a $5x$–$12x$ slowdown to a $2x$-$4x$ one. With improved static analysis, we anticipate performance closer to the uninstrumented program, and static analysis should improve matrix multiply enormously with its predictable access pattern. We believe that this makes it feasible to use pointer safety monitoring consistently throughout development, thus enhancing the ability of programmers to debug code.

But what would be the cost of adding this feature to current chips? It should be quite modest for two reasons. First, because we have placed the HAT quite far away from the processor core, we have not thrown off the delicate timing in the core. We have not forced components in the core to change position. To add HAT instructions to the load/store functional unit and reorder buffer, there would be some design involved, but the changes are fairly straightforward since the HAT instructions behave in the same manner in the core. The HAT itself is very small and simple; we estimate that it would take up only about 2-5% of the area of current chips and an even smaller amount of the next generation of chips. There is a modest impact due to adding the control and data paths for the three extra instructions.

So overall, the additional cost impact on the final CPU would be quite small—so much so that the monitoring function could simply be added to commodity processors with a negligible impact on the cost of the final workstation. On the other hand, as noted in the beginning of the chapter, the cost savings resulting from reduced debugging time could be far more significant. When we consider that the overall cost of a computer system includes the cost of the software, we believe that this approach has the potential to significantly *reduce* the overall cost of the system based on savings in software development costs alone.

All in all, we believe that our results indicate hardware support for safety monitoring such as the one we have discussed above is an attractive design option for future microprocessors.

7.6 Conclusions

As hardware speeds increase and costs decrease, software development is consuming an increasing proportion of overall system costs. Certain types of defects are very difficult to debug — for example, defects related to unsafe pointers in popular languages such as C or C++. Dynamic pointer safety monitoring can effectively and quickly trap such errors but entails a high performance penalty. In this chapter, we presented a hardware technique that can be used to improve memory performance and lower performance penalties. The use of a simple hardware accelerated hash table can speed up pointer checking by about a factor of 2. With the addition of sophisticated static analysis, the speed can increase even further. Our work continues with investigations of other hardware techniques and other monitoring applications, such as security policy enforcement over untrusted binaries [18].

Acknowledgments

We would like to thank Shubu Mukherjee and Compaq for the Alpha computers used for this research. This work is supported by an NSF CAREER award to Fred Chong, by NSF grant CCR-9812415, by an NPSC fellowship to Diana Keen, and by grants from the UC Davis Academic Senate.

References

1. L. Cardelli, "Type systems," in *The Computer Science and Engineering Handbook* (A. B. Tucker, ed.), pp. 2208–2236, Boca Raton: CRC Press, 1997.
2. G. Necula, "Proof-carrying code," in *Proceedings of POPL 97*, ACM SIGPLAN, 97.
3. F. Brooks, *The Mythical Man-Month: Essays on Software Engineering.* Reading, MA: Addison-Wesley, 2000.
4. E. Raymond and B. Young, *The Cathedral and the Bazaar: Musings on Linux and Open Source by an Accidental Revolutionary.* Sebastopol, CA: O'Reilly & Associates, 2000.
5. Z. Xu, T. Reps, and B. Miller, "Typestate checking of machine code," in *Proceedings of ESOP 2001: European Symposium on Programming*, 2001.
6. R. Wahbe, S. Lucco, T. Anderson, and S. Graham, "Efficient software-based fault isolation," in *Proceedings of the Symposium on Operating Systems Principles*, 1993.
7. Symbolics Technical Summary. http://kogs-www.informatik.uni-hamburg.de/ moeller/symbolics-info/symbolics-tech-summary.html.
8. D. Wagner et al., "A first step towards automated detection of buffer overrun vulnerabilities," in *Network and Distributed System Security Symposium*, 2000.
9. T. M. Austin, S. E. Breach, and G. S. Sohi, "Efficient detection of all pointers and array access errors," in *Proceedings of the Conference on Programming Language Design and Implementation*, 1994.
10. S. Kendall, "Bcc: run-time checking for c programs," in *USENIX Toronto 1989 Summer Conference Proceedings*, 1983.
11. J. L. Steffen, "Adding run-time checking to the portable c compiler," in *Software — Practice and Experience*, 1992.

12. R. W. M. Jones and P. H. J. Kelly, "Backwards-compatible bounds checking for arrays and pointers in c programs," in *Third International Workshop on Automated Debugging*, 1997.
13. H. Patil and C. Fischer, "Low-cost, concurrent checking of pointer and array accesses in c programs," in *Software - Practice and Experience*, 1997.
14. S. J. Eggers, J. S. Emer, H. M. Levy, J. L. Lo, R. L. Stamm, and D. M. Tullsen, "Simultaneous multithreading: A platform for next-generation processors," *IEEE Micro*, 17(5):12–26, September-October 1997.
15. N. Jouppi, "Improving direct-mapped cache performance by addition of a small fully associative cache and prefetch buffers," in *Proceedings of the 17th International Symposium on Computer Architecture* (Seattle, WA), 1990.
16. L. Zhang et al., "Pointer-based prefetching within the Impulse adaptable memory controller: Initial results," in *Proceedings of the ISCA-2000 Workshop on Solving the Memory Wall Problem*, June 2000.
17. R. Merritt, "Microprocessor forum: Designers cut fresh paths to parallelism," *EE Times*, October 1999.
18. D. S. Wallach, A. W. Appel, and E. W. Felten, "Safkasi: A security mechanism for language-based systems," in *ACM Transactions on Software Engineering and Methodology*, 9(4):341–378, 2000.

8

Reconfigurable Memory Module in the RAMP System for Stream Processing

Vason P. Srinii[1,2], John Thendean[2], Jan M. Rabaey[2]

[1] Data Flux Systems, Berkeley, CA, USA
[2] EECS Department, University of California, Berkeley, CA, USA
srini@eecs.berkeley.edu, jmt@eecs.berkeley.edu, jan@eecs.berkeley.edu

Abstract. A memory module with logic to support random access (RAM), FIFO access (FIFO), delay line implementation (DELAY), and lookup table implementation (LUT) is described in this chapter. The memory module can be reconfigured statically to be in one of the four modes (RAM, FIFO, DELAY, LUT) and is part of a system containing reconfigurable clusters of memory and processors, called RAMP. Each cluster in RAMP has a memory module, four computation processors, and an I/O processor that communicate using a handshake protocol. The memory module uses a self-timed memory array with separate data lines for read and write. The memory array consists of rows of memory cells and a dummy row circuit that mimics the worst case delay in accessing the memory. This dummy circuit generates a done signal when read/write has been completed.

Asynchronous communication between a processor and the memory module can be achieved using the done signal also. This allows the memory module to be used in other systems as a form of asynchronous FIFO. The size of the memory array is $256x16$. To obtain a larger memory size, the memory module is designed such that it can be cascaded. A read cycle time of 5 ns is estimated using a 0.25 micron CMOS technology. The memory module can be used for doing a convolution function in image processing, implementing a sample data buffer, digital filtering, and color conversion in a digital camera or video camera. It is also useful in storing lookup tables needed in DCT, FFT/IFFT (twiddle factor), and video compression algorithms.

8.1 Introduction

The need for high-performance and low-power microprocessors for many of the media applications involving images, sound, and video has been recognized by many computer companies and research organizations. Processors such as Philips' TriMedia, Texas Instrument's TMS320C6000, Analog Device's Sharc, and Hewlett Packard/ST's Lx have been introduced to meet the performance requirements. The datapaths in these processors are optimized to provide extremely high performance on certain kinds of arithmetic-intensive algorithms.

However, a powerful datapath is only a part of the solution for high performance. To keep the datapath fed with data and to store the results of datapath operations, the processors require the ability to move large amounts of data to and from memory quickly. Thus, the organization of memory, latency, and its interconnection with the processor's datapath are critical factors in determining processor performance. It is known that any off-chip communication is expensive in terms of power, delay, and area. To drive a signal off-chip, a large amount of current is required to drive the capacitor on the I/O pads and any external capacitors. Therefore, having to move data to and from chip to off-chip memory will not be an efficient implementation. Many high performance DSP and media processors have on-chip memory. Commercial general purpose digital signal processors such as Motorola's DSP56000 family and TI's TMS320C6000 family have separate on-chip memory for program and data. With on-chip memory, the memory bandwidth can be increased and off-chip traffic can be reduced.

Finite Impulse Response (FIR) filter implementation is the simplest example to clearly illustrate the memory requirement of DSP processors. A single FIR tap computation requires four accesses to memory — instruction fetch, read data from the delay line, read the appropriate filter coefficient, and write data to the next location in the delay line to shift data through the delay line. A similar pattern of memory accesses occurs in 2-D convolution and filter computations in image processing. The memory accesses involved are random access, table lookup, and delay line. In this chapter we discuss the architecture and design of a memory module that is part of a reconfigurable cluster of memory and processor (RAMP) system capable of delivering tens of giga operations per second and uses low-power techniques. The RAMP system combines on a single chip many stream data processors, memory modules with builtin logic and controllers, I/O processors, and a conventional superscalar processor. The parallel stream data processors compute on the multiple data streams using an MIMD model of computation, and the superscalar processor performs the coordination of parallel tasks, sequential computations, and communication with the memory system. The execution time for any instruction is one cycle. An overview of the RAMP system is given in Section 8.2 . Section 8.3 contains an overview of the cluster architecture in the RAMP. The architecture of the memory module is described in Section 8.4. The blocks of the datapath are described in Section 8.5. The storage array of the memory module is also described in this section. The hardware support for data communication between the memory module and other processors and buffering are also described in Section 8.5. The FSM controllers used in the control part of the memory module are described in Section 8.6. A brief description of the blocks used for communicating data and control tokens is included in Section 8.7. The programming of the memory module as well as other processors is done using a scan chain register in each cluster, and reconfiguration is achieved using the scan chain register after bringing the processors in a cluster to a freeze state. The 55 bits forming the scan chain register of a memory module are explained in Section 8.8. The bits of the scan chain register are used by the blocks described in Sections 8.5 to 8.8. Forward references to Section 8.8 appear throughout the chapter. The detailed timing diagram resulting from functional and timing simulations is described in Section 8.9.

8.2 RAMP Architecture

Real-time audio/video communication and image processing using wired and wireless networks involve handling data coming in streams at a high rate from sensors, cameras, antennas, and networks. Physical (PHY) layer components in high-data-rate wireless networks using standards such as IEEE 802.11ag, Hiperlan2 (wireless LAN), and IEEE 802.16ab (wireless MAN) also require processing data coming in streams from one or more antennas. Temporary storage and fast access to data streams are important to keep the overall system performance at a high level. In the case of wireless LANs such as IEEE 802.11ag and wireless MANs such as IEEE 802.161b, other factors such as low power and low cost are also important. This means some of the PHY components might operate at different clock rates and some of the components might be turned off to save power. A block diagram of PHY components involved in a WLAN/WMAN system is shown in Figure 8.1. Each component in the diagram gets control tokens from the control processor. This is shown by thin lines with arrows on one end. The point-to-point interconnection is shown by thick lines between PHY components. Data width conversion, serial to parallel conversion, and buffering functions are shown using thin rectangles. Functions that do computation are shown by squares. The thick lines show data token communication between blocks.

Dealing with different clock domains in a single chip is a challenging activity. One way to handle the communication of data across different clock domains is to use asynchronous FIFOs at the interfaces. A memory module with built-in logic and a controller to support random access (RAM), FIFO access (FIFO), delay line implementation (DELAY), and lookup table implementation (LUT) is proposed to handle the data communication between processors in different clock domains and also the LUT and delay line requirements of DSP algorithms. The memory module can be reconfigured to be in one of the four (RAM, FIFO, DELAY, LUT) modes and is part of a system containing reconfigurable clusters of the memory and processors called RAMP. RAMP is proposed as a low-power and high-performance reconfigurable parallel processing system with the needed partitioning, placement, and routing (PPR) software so that the application above can be mapped to processors on one or more chips. A block diagram of RAMP is shown in Figure 8.2.

A RAMP system comprises a hierarchical interconnection of clusters of processors and memory modules. The block diagram shows 16 clusters interconnected by 16 data buses to form a crossbar-like network. The controller processor in Figure 8.2 is the unit responsible for dynamically reconfigur-

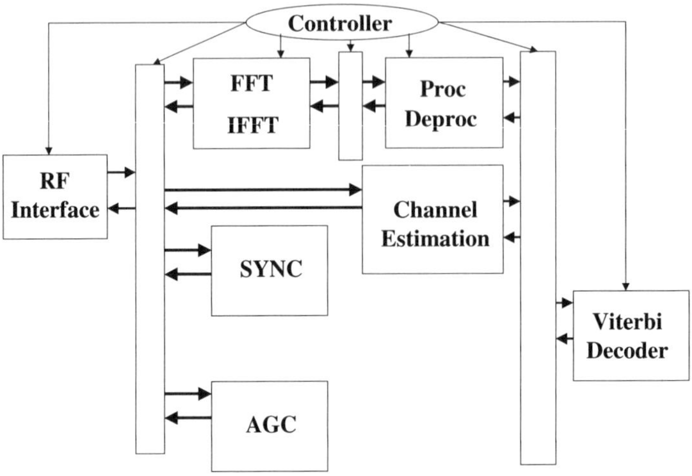

Fig. 8.1. Block diagram of a WLAN/WMAN.

ing the clusters by sending configuration tokens over 8-bit buses, supplying data streams from external memory or the network to the memory modules,

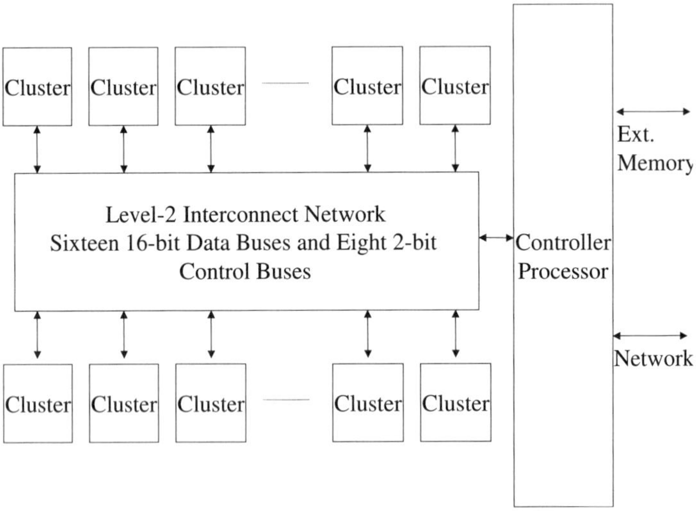

Fig. 8.2. RAMP VLSI building block with 16 clusters and external connections.

and storing results in external memory. The memory modules in the clusters can also receive data from cameras, and sensors and supply results to tape recorders or other recorders and display monitors using I/O modules. Each cluster is designed to be reconfigurable independent of other clusters. One of the key features of RAMP is the separation of information flow into three separate entities: data tokens, control tokens, and configuration tokens. The configuration tokens are used to set up the processors, memory modules, I/O modules, and interconnection networks at load time or reconfiguration time. The control tokens are generated by programs. Each cluster in RAMP has a memory module, four computation processors, and an I/O processor. The architecture and design of the reconfigurable memory module are the focus of this chapter. All the units within a cluster communicate data with a delay of one cycle using a simple send/receive handshake protocol. By limiting the number of clusters in a chip to 16, intercluster communication delay can also be kept at one cycle without slowing the processor. The implementation of the protocol using a single wire, buffers, and queue controllers in sending and receiving units is discussed. Since the memory module can be configured to be in one of the four modes, control logic is needed to switch between these modes and also to perform the operations in each of the modes. Four finite state machines (FSMs) have been designed to support the four operating modes of the memory modules. The details of the FSMs and other control parts of the memory module are described. The storage array for the memory module is based on a self-timed low-power SRAM design. The programming and reconfiguration of the memory module are supported using a scan chain register and control signals. The datapath, controllers, and storage array of the memory module have been integrated and simulated at the VHDL level and transistor level to verify functionality and timing. RAMP has its foundations in a PADDI-2 [1] chip containing 48 nanoprocessors. A nanoprocessor is used to interface the PADDI-2 chip and the external memory. The nanoprocessor handles the single-cycle interprocessor communication protocol. In the RAMP system, memory is on-chip and partitioned so that a part of it is available in each cluster to support locality of data in applications. Based on analyzing DSP algorithms [1, 2, 3], simulation studies, and experiments [4], it was determined that performance could be improved if memory could be organized to fit the four commonly used memory accesses in signal processing — RAM, lookup table, FIFO, and delay line. We decided to enhance the storage array in a memory block with logic and controllers to support the four commonly used accesses and the single-cycle interprocessor communication protocol.

8.3 Cluster Architecture

A cluster containing processors, memory, and an I/O interface is the building block of a RAMP system. A block diagram of a cluster in RAMP is shown in Figure 8.3.

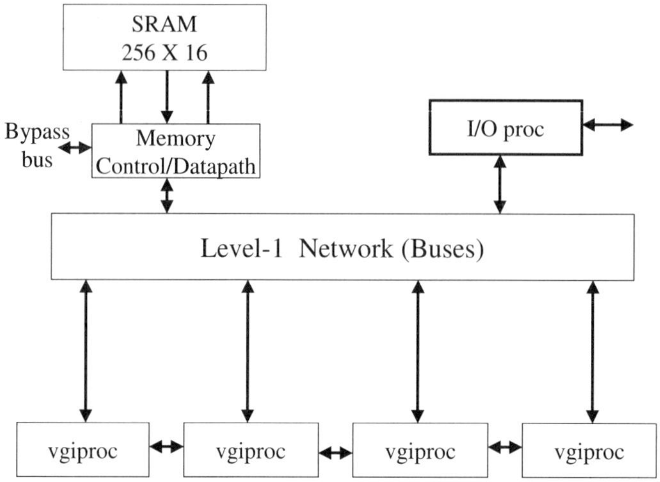

Fig. 8.3. Cluster architecture with a memory module, VGI processors and an I/O processor.

It contains four processors, called *VGI processors*, that can do video, graphics, image processing, and digital communication computations on streams of data [5, 6]. A memory module containing a storage array ($256x16$ words) and controllers for implementing the four commonly used memory accesses is the second major part of the cluster. The third part of the cluster is an I/O processor that sends and receives data from external devices using a two-cycle communication delay protocol. The I/O processor communicates with VGI processors and memory modules using a single-cycle communication delay protocol. All six processors in a cluster have a three-stage pipeline in their datapaths and there is a system clock. Although the prototype memory module has a $256x16$ SRAM, it is not a limitation. The storage array can be increased in size, and the controllers can be resynthesized by changing the parameters of delay lines, queue length, and counters. Communication between the processors in a cluster is done through six data token buses (16 bits) and four control token buses (2 bits) in the Level-1 communication network and the associated handshake lines. The single-cycle delay communication protocol for the memory module and I/O processor is the same as that of the VGI processor. From Figure 8.3, we can see that the memory module's control and datapath are the interface between other processors and the storage array. The memory module handles all the timing requirements to read and write into the storage array. It also handles data addressing in the FIFO and delay line modes. Using a Level-1 network, the processors in a cluster can communicate with other clusters on a RAMP chip using an intercluster network, called a Level-2 interconnection network, containing 16 data token buses and eight control token buses. This is done by setting the switches (50 switches in all) between the Level-2 network and Level-1 network. Adjacent processors in a cluster can communicate data using the bypass buses, thus leaving the resources in the Level-1 network for intercluster and nonadjacent processor communication. One of the novel features of the RAMP architecture is the single-cycle communication protocol between processors in a chip using a send/receive handshake protocol. This protocol is implemented using a bidirectional handshake line for each data token bus and control token bus and the two phases of the system clock. During the execution stage, a processor wanting to communicate data to another processor pulls the handshake line high when the clock is low. If the receiver is not ready it can pull down the handshake line when the clock goes high on the next cycle (communication stage). At the end of the clock high, the success of the transaction is evaluated. If the handshake line is high, then the transaction is successful. Otherwise it is unsuccessful. A sender can retry the transaction when the clock is low. The details of the protocol and its implementation are in Sections 8.5 and 8.6.

8.4 Memory Module Architecture

The memory module has a datapath and a control section. A block diagram of the memory module is shown in Figure 8.4. The datapath has a three-stage pipeline similar to that of the VGI processor and I/O processor comprising fetch, memory access, and communicate. The fetch and communicate stages are needed to synchronize the memory module with a VGI processor. This avoids the need for a special protocol when a VGI processor communicates with the memory. The additional two stages impose a two-clock latency when read is requested and a one-clock latency for the write process. Since requests are usually pipelined, the latency occurs only on the first request. In the following section the architecture of the memory module is explained. The datapath structure is described first and then the controller block.

8.5 Datapath Structure

The memory module's datapath consists of the following blocks: meml1insel, memlin, data queue, mempipelat, storage array, memlout, address pointer and counter as shown in Figure 8.4. We have retained some of the cryptic names for the blocks to maintain consistency with the names in design schematics and netlists. The following subsections describe in detail the functions of each block.

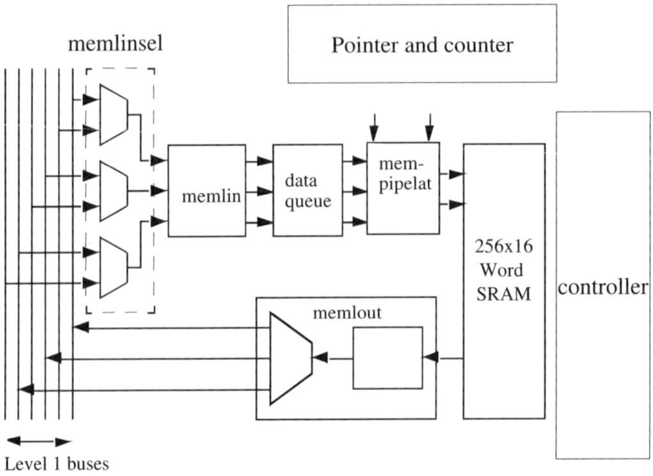

Fig. 8.4. Block diagram of a Memory Module.

8.5.1 Meml1insel Block

Meml1insel is the interface between buses in the Level-1 network and memory module. It consists of three multiplexers that select three out of six Level-1 buses. The three outputs of this block are read address, write address, and write data. The bus assignment is done by setting the associated Level-1 configuration switches in the scan chain register (bits $memscni < 5 : 0 >$ in the scan register of the memory module). The Memlin block consists of two 8-bit registers for the read and write addresses and one 16-bit register for write data. During the communicate cycle, the sender drives the output data on the Level-1 bus. On the same cycle, the receiver copies the data into the master of the memlin register. During the fetch cycle, the data in memlin will be transferred into registers in the data queue block. Memlin is the communication data buffer at the receiver. In the Memlin block, data and address sources can be selected from the bypass buses or the Level-1 buses. To select the address or data source from bypass buses, the associated memsbpi bits in the scan chain register ($memsbpi < 2 : 0 >$) should be asserted.

8.5.2 Data Queue

The data queue consists of three two-deep queues, one for read addresses, one for write addresses, and the other for written data. The queues are important because of the two cycle delay for a request to be processed. For example, when a read is requested, whether the read data can be sent out or not is not known until two cycles after the request is received. During those two cycles, additional requests are being accepted and processed. If the memory module fails to send the read data, the processor will stall; data queues are used to buffer the requests that have been received before the stall comes. A queue consists of two registers, ro and r1. When there is no pipeline stall, data will always be placed to the head of the queue, r1. The 2-to-1 mux between r0 and r1 is used to bypass r0, to allow data from memlin to appear directly to r1. The second 2-to-1 mux is used to allow data from memlin to go directly into the pipeline register (mempipelat). Therefore, when no stall pipe occurs, data from memlin can be fetched into r1 and the pipeline register at the same time.

8.5.3 Pipeline Register

The pipeline register (mempipelat) plays two major roles. During program execution, mempipelat is used to supply a stable address and data to the storage array block, as shown in Figure 8.4. Like the data queue, mempipelat consists of two 8-bit registers for the read and write addresses and one 16-bit register for write data. The read address register and write data register are also part of the scan chain register and are used to load data into the storage array during the scan-in process and to read out the memory content during the scan-out process. The data register is also used to initialize the read and write pointer for FIFO and delay line operation. The two major roles of the mempipelat block are explained in the next two subsections using the control signals of a cluster and two scan chain register bits.

Mempipelat as a Scan Chain Register

During the scan process, data can be loaded into the storage array (e.g. sine or cosine table) or read out, and the address pointers can be initialized. To store data in the storage array, the data and address are scanned into data and address registers. The read/write enable (rwen) bit and memory update (memupdate) bit of the scan chain register should be asserted as well. When the scan update (supdate) control signal comes, data in the scan register will be loaded into the location specified by the address register. To read out the content of a memory location, first the address has to be scanned in, and the read/write enable bit (rwen) and memory update (memupdate) bit should be disabled. When the supdate signal comes, data in the address location will be loaded into the data register and can be scanned out later. The data register is also used to initialize read and write pointers for FIFO and delay line operation. Read and write pointers are each 8 bits wide, while the data register is 16 bits wide. Cascading read and write pointers, we get data that is 16 bits wide. Therefore, by connecting the upper byte of the data register to the write pointer register and the lower byte to the read pointer register, we can initialize the pointer registers. The memory update (memupdate) bit of the scan chain is used to distinguish this operation from loading data into the storage array. When pointer initialization is intended, the memupdate bit is not asserted. The read/write enable (rwen) bit, however, has to be asserted.

Mempipelat as a Pipeline Register

As a pipeline register, mempipelat is used to supply a stable address and data to the storage array unit. Whether data in mempipelat can advance or not is controlled by the advance signal, which comes from the queue controller block. The advance signal is asserted when neither the stall pipe nor save signal is asserted. The save signal comes from the access controller and is asserted when the the access controller cannot serve a request. The section on access controller explains more about the function of this signal. The address output of mempipelat can come from two sources. In the RAM and LUT modes, this address comes from Level-1 buses. In FIFO and delay line modes, the address comes from the read or write pointer.

8.5.4 Storage Array Block

The $256x16$ word SRAM in Figure 8.4 is the storage array of a memory module. This storage array is based on the self-timed SRAM designed by Burstein [7]. It has separate buses for input data and output data and a single address bus. The storage consists of memory cells and a dummy circuit that mimics the worst case delay in the memory block. This dummy circuit generates a done signal that indicates that a read/write has been completed. This signal is intended for asynchronous design. In this design, only the memory cell array is used. The done signal is not used. Although the prototype has a $256x16$ SRAM, a generator is available [8] for extending the size of the storage array.

8.5.5 Memlout Block

Memlout consists of a data register to hold data read from the storage array and switches that connect to Level-1 buses. Data in the register can be driven to three of the six Level-1 buses so that they can be sent to other processors. Level-1 output switches are configured using scan chain register bits ($memscno < 2 : 0 >$). When a receiver is not ready to receive data in the memlout register, then memlout block will preserve its data to be resent during the next cycle. The output of memlout is also extended to bypass buses. Therefore, if the receiving processor is next to the memory module, the data transfer can be done through the bypass buses, which frees up the Level-1 buses for other processors.

8.5.6 Pointer and Counter

This block contains two up counters for the read pointer and write pointer, one up/down counter to count the number of data stored in the array, and a memflag unit, which outputs fullnn and emptynn signals when the memory is full or empty. The read pointer is incremented every time a read request is processed and no stall pipe is present. The same is true for the write pointer. It is incremented every time a write request is processed. The pointers are always pointing to the next read and write addresses to be read and written. The counter is incremented every time a write is executed and decremented when a read is executed. Memflag is used to indicate that FIFO or the delay line is full or empty. Full is asserted when the counter value is the same as the value of the delay set in the scan chain register. For FIFO, in order to use the whole memory as FIFO, one would have to specify the number of the delay as 256. Shorter FIFO can be specified by setting the value of delay in the scan chain to be less than 256. Empty is asserted when the counter value reaches one and the read request is being executed. The read and write pointer blocks can be initialized during the scan chain as described in the mempipelat discussion in Section 8.5.3.

8.6 Controller

The controller of a memory module (see Figure 8.4) can be divided into three major blocks: queue controller, memory access controller, and output controller. A block diagram of the controller is shown in Figure 8.5 with all the control signals and communication blocks. The control signals are used in the FSMs of the major blocks. The signals gstall and clk are global control signals. The function of each block is described in the following subsections.

8.6.1 Handshake Queue

Each bus carrying data tokens or control tokens has a handshake signal associated with it. The handshake signal also carries information about what operation is to be performed on the data — read or write. Since data in the datapath go through a queue, there needs to be the same queue for the handshake signal so that the data and their associated handshake signal can propagate in parallel in the memory module.

8.6.2 Queue Controller

The queue controller decides where the data in the memlin register will be stored in the data queue block. If there is no stall pipe, data will be placed at the head of the queue. There are three queue controllers: one for the read

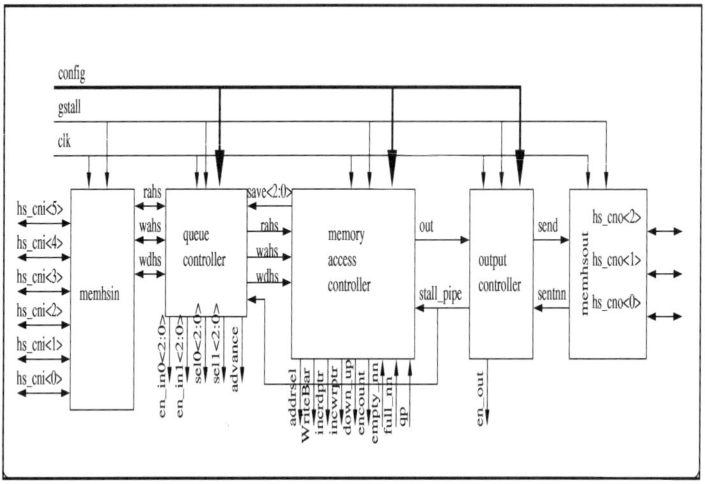

Fig. 8.5. Controller unit of a memory module.

address, one for the write address and the other for write data. Queue controllers also decide whether incoming data can be accepted. When a queue is full, the queue controller will pull down the handshake line to indicate to the sender that no data can be accepted. An advance signal is generated using the following logic:

$$advance = not(or(stallpipe, save)), \tag{8.1}$$

where save is a signal from the access controller that tells the queue controller that the data at the head of the queue have not been serviced because another process is being executed. As an example, consider a situation where read and write requests arrive simultaneously at the access controller. If the priority is given to write over read, then write will be performed and save will be generated for the read address queue controller.

8.6.3 Memory Access Controller

The memory access controller is the key block of the memory module. The four modes of the memory module are implemented in this block. The operation mode of the memory access controller is configured using configuration ($config < 1 : 0 >$) bits of the scan chain register. The memory access controller communicates with the queue controller using the save signal. Whenever a request (read/write) cannot be serviced by the memory access controller, it will assert the save signal. This will result in the advance signal being deasserted and the data in the data queue and pipeline register blocks will be preserved. For example, if the memory access controller simultaneously receives read and write requests, depending on the priority, either read or write will be selected and the other request has to wait. If write is performed, then the save signal for the read queue controller will be asserted and vice versa for read. The memory access controller communicates with the output controller through the the out signal. When a read is performed, out signal is asserted, signaling the output controller to prepare to send out the data read from the storage array. The four modes of the memory access controller are described using FSMs in the next four subsections. The control signals shown in Figure 8.5 are used in deriving inputs that cause state transitions.

RAM Mode

When configured in the RAM mode, the memory access controller treats the storage array as a random access memory. It can accept any read and write operation. Simultaneous read and write requests are resolved using the queue priority bit of the scan chain register. This means that the user determines the read or write priority. When the queue priority bit is asserted, priority is given to the read request and, when the bit is low, priority is given to the write request. For a write request to be executed, both write address and write data have to be available to the access controller.

Lookup Table Mode

The lookup table (LUT) mode is similar to the RAM mode except that write is not allowed during execution. In the LUT mode, the storage array is loaded with a table during the scan in process. The procedure for scanning is described in the mempipelat section (Section 8.5.3).

FIFO Mode

In FIFO mode, addresses for read and write come from read and write pointer blocks. Only the write data come from Level-1 buses. The read request is communicated using the read handshake line, and the write request is communicated using the write data handshake. Since the write address comes from the write pointer, it is assumed to be always ready. So, in FIFO mode, the write address handshake signal is ignored. Simultaneous read and write requests can occur in FIFO mode. This is resolved using the queue priority bit as in the RAM mode. Fullnn and emptynn signals from memflag block tell the access controller when the FIFO is full or empty. Full occurs when the counter value reaches the number of the delay in the scan chain register. Empty occurs when the counter value reaches one and the access controller is in read mode.

Delay Line Mode

Like the FIFO controller, the sources for the addresses of the delay line controller are read and write pointer blocks. What makes the delay line different from FIFO is that delay line controller does not accept a read request. Read will be executed automatically once the delay line is full. This is indicated by the fullnn signal from the memflag block. The write address is assumed to be ready every time write data is available. So, a write request is communicated using write data handshake signal only. Since simultaneous read and write is not possible when the controller is operating in delay line mode, the queue priority bit is simply ignored.

8.6.4 Output Controller

The output controller, shown in Figure 8.5, receives the out signal from the memory access controller every time the access controller is in the read state. When the request comes, the controller will assert the output handshake line to signal the receiver of outgoing data during clock low. When clock high comes, the output controller observes the handshake line to determine if the send is successful. If the handshake line is pulled down any time during clock high, the send is unsuccessful and the controller will try to resend the data during the next cycle. In this case, the stall_pipe signal is asserted for the memory module, which will stall other activities.

8.7 Handshake Blocks

These blocks implement the Level-1 network's handshake lines that interface with the memory module controller. At the input side we have the input handshake block (memhsin), and at the output side we have the output handshake block (memhsout), as shown in Figure 8.5.

8.7.1 Input Handshake Block

Like the meml1insel block in Figure 8.4, the input handshake block consists of Level-1 configuration switches that select three out of six handshake lines from Level-1 handshake lines. These switches are configured using the same scan chain bits used to configure Level-1 switches in meml1insel ($memscni < 5:0 >$). The three output handshake lines are read address handshake (rahs), write address handshake (wahs), and write data handshake (wdhs). The order of handshake assignments is the same as the address and data assignment in the meml1insel block. The input handshake block receives the full signal from the queue controller. When full is asserted, it will pull the associated handshake low during clock high.

8.7.2 Output Handshake Block

The output handshake block consists of Level-1 output configuration switches like those in the memlout block (see Figure 8.4). When there are data to be sent out, the output controller will assert a send signal (see Figure 8.5). The output handshake block will drive this signal across the communication network to other processors. The output handshake block can fan out this signal to at most three other processors.

8.8 Scan Chain Register

Programming of the memory module is done using the scan chain register. The memory module scan chain register is 55 bits long. It is divided into three blocks, memscni (26 bits), mempipelat (26 bits), and memscno (3 bits). The physical locations of the bits of the scan chain register are scattered among the blocks of the memory module. Memscni contains 6 bits for selecting a Level-1 network's six buses, 3 bits for activating bypass buses to supply data tokens, 1 bit for selecting read/write to counter, 3 bits for selecting read/write to queue register, 2 bits for selecting read and write address source, 2 bits for operation mode selection (00 = RAM, 01= LUT, 10 = FIFO, 11 = delay), 1 bit for queue priority assignment, and 8 bits for FIFO or delay line size. Scan register in mempipelat consists of an 8-bit address register, 16-bit data register, read/write enable (rwen) bit, and memupdate bit. Address and data registers are used to load the storage array with data or to read out content of memory. The second function of the data register is to initialize read and write pointer registers in the datapath's counter unit. The read/write (rwen) bit indicates that the data in the data register are to be loaded either into memory or the pointer register. Together with the read/write bit, memupdate indicates that the data in the data register is to be loaded into the storage array. The memscno block contains 3 bits to control Level-1 output select switches. The operation of the scan chain register is controlled by two cluster level control signals, sen and supdate, that are generated from primary input signals gstall, tms, reset, and clk.

8.9 Design Verification

All the blocks of the memory module have been designed and functionally simulated at the RTL level using a VHDL simulator. Many blocks in the control part of the memory module have been synthesized. The remaining blocks have been custom designed. The physical layout of the entire memory module has been completed using custom layout tools, and it is included in Figure 8.7. The storage array occupies the two quadrants on the right side of the layout. The datapath occupies the bottom left quadrant, and the control occupies the top left quadrant. The physical layout has been extracted, verified, and a transistor level netlist generated for use with Timemill simulations. The operation of the the memory module has been verified using Timemill simulations. The following example illustrates the data propagation in memory module. We assume the memory module is configured in RAM mode (memconfig = 00). There are three requests that arrive consecutively at the memory module. They are labeled 1, 2, and 3 in Figure 8.6. Request 1 is a read operation, request 2 is a write operation, and request 3 is a read operation. The three requests can come from a VGI processor, another memory module, or an I/O processor. On a read request, output data are sent out to another processor and the receiving processor is assumed ready to receive the data. Figure 8.6 shows the timing diagram of data through the memory module's datapath.

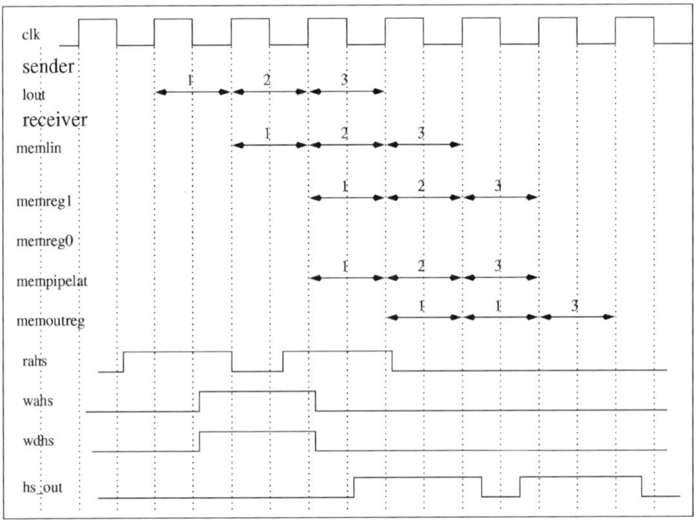

Fig. 8.6. RAM data propagation through the memory module datapath.

During the communication cycle, data 1 are driven onto Level-1 buses to the input of the memory module. These data are copied by memlin and driven to the data queue in the fetch cycle of the memory module. Data 1 is a read request as indicated by the rahs line. Since no data are yet stored in the queue, data 1 will advance to memreg1 and mempipelat. At the same time, memlin is accepting the next data, 2. Data 2 is a write request, as indicated by both the wahs and wdhs lines. For a write request, both wahs and wdhs have to be high to be processed. In the next cycle, mempipelat drives the data 1 request to the storage array and a memory read is executed. Data 2 are advanced to memreg1 and the third read request, data 3, is communicated. At the beginning of the next cycle, the data 1 result appears at the output register. These data are being driven on the Level-1 bus to a receiving processor. Notice that the output handshake line (hs_out) has been pulled high during the clock low in the previous cycle to tell the receiver processor of the arrival of the data 1 result. At the same time, the write request of data 2 is executed and data 2 operation is completed. Data 3 are transferred to memreg1 and mempipelat during this clock cycle. Since data 2 do not produce any output, hs_out is pulled low by the output controller at the next clock cycle to tell the receiver that no data are being communicated. On the same cycle data 3 is executed and the output is stored in the output register. The output handshake line again is asserted when the clock goes low to inform the receiver of the availability of data. During the next cycle, data 3 results are communicated to the receiver. In this example, we can clearly see the latency of read and write requests. A read request, indicated by data 1 in the example, incurs a two clock-cycle latency. When data 1 appear at the output of memlin during the first clock cycle, data 1 is transferred to mempipelat. At the second clock cycle, the memory read is performed. At the end of this clock cycle, the data 1 result is available at the output register, which will be sent to the receiver when the next clock cycle comes. A write request, indicated by data 2, only incurs one clock cycle latency. When data 2 is available at the output of memlin during the first cycle, data 2 is transferred into mempipelat. At the second clock cycle, the memory write is performed and the request is completed.

8.10 Conclusion

The design, simulation, and implementation of the memory module turned out to be almost twice as complex as the processor module in the RAMP architecture. The memory access controller, the queues used for buffering, the handshake protocol, and the two additional pipeline stages (fetch and communicate) contributed to the complexity. The design has been done so that when the size of the storage is changed to a multiple of 256 words, most of the parts of the memory module can be reused after changing the sizes of the read pointer, write pointer, and counter. The presence of integrated memory modules improved the performance of the RAMP system for FIR filters, convolution, and DCT. This leads us to conclude that memory modules with logic will form an integral part of future processor clusters in RAMP-like architectures.

Acknowledgments

The authors wish to thank Brian Richards, Matt Armstrong, and Roy Sutton for their comments and many ideas. The authors are grateful to Bob Brodersen for his support and encouragement at the Berkeley Wireless Research Center (BWRC). Additional thanks go to Gary Kelson and Kevin Zimmerman.

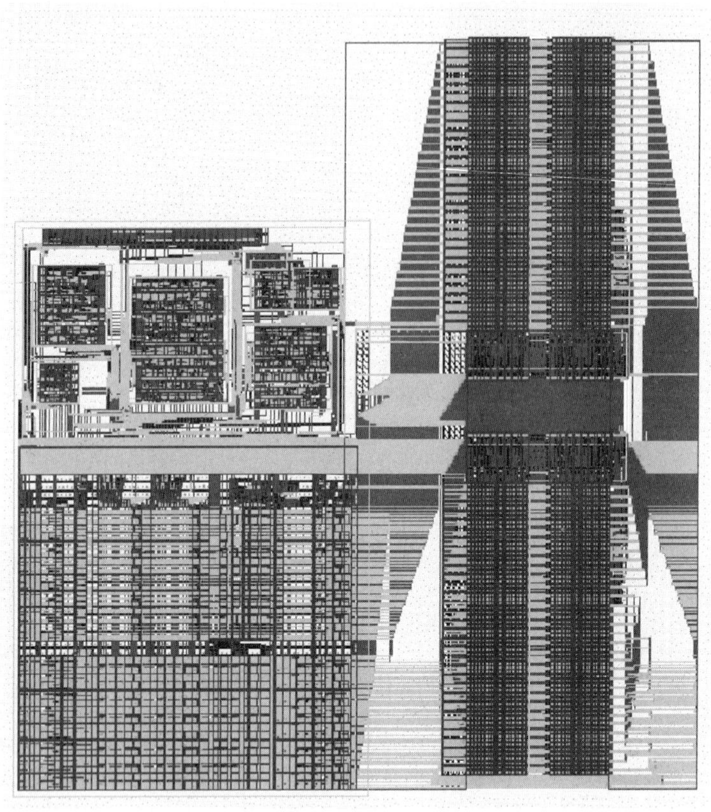

Fig. 8.7. Layout of a RAMP memory module.

References

1. Yeung A (1995) PADDI-2 Architecture and Implementation, Ph.D. Thesis, University of California, Berkeley, CA, June 1995.
2. Lapsley P, Bier J, Shoham A, Lee E A (1994) DSP Processor Fundamentals: Architectures and Features, Berkeley Design Technology, Inc., Berkeley, CA, Chapter 4.
3. Ifeachor E, Jervis B (1993) Digital Signal Processing: A Practical Approach, Addison-Wesley, Wokingham, England.
4. Srini V P, Sutton R A, Rabaey J M (1998) Multiple Processor DSP System Using PADDI-2, In: Proceedings of Design Automation conference, San Francisco, CA, June 1998.
5. Pini D M, (1997) A Parallel Processor for High Performance Digital Signal Processing Master's Thesis, University of California, Berkeley, CA, May 1997.

6. Srini V P, Thendean J, Ueng S, Rabaey J M (1998) A Parallel DSP with Memory and I/O Processors, In: Proceedings of the SPIE Conference, San Diego, CA, July 1998.
7. Burstein A J (1997) Speech Recognition for Portable Multimedia Terminals ERL Memorandum No. UCB/ERL M97/14, University of California, Berkeley, CA, Feb 1997.
8. Walker N (1999) Integrated Circuit Module Generator, Master's Thesis, University of California, Berkeley, CA, May 1999.

Part III

Software-Based Memory Tuning

9

Performance of Memory Expansion Technology (MXT)

Dan E. Poff, Mohammad Banikazemi, Robert Saccone, Hubertus Franke, Bulent Abali, and T. Basil Smith

IBM T.J.Watson Research Center
P.O. Box 218,
Yorktown Heights, NY, USA
{poff@us.ibm.com,mb@us.ibm.com,rsaccone@us.ibm.com,frankeh@us.ibm.com, abali@us.ibm.com,tbsmith@us.ibm.com}

Abstract. A novel memory subsystem called Memory Expansion Technology (MXT) has been built for fast hardware compression of main memory contents. This allows a system with memory expansion to present a *real* memory larger than the physically available memory. This chapter provides an overview of the memory compression architecture, the OS support, and an analysis of the performance impact of memory compression while running multiple benchmarks. Results show that the hardware compression of main memory has a negligible penalty compared to an uncompressed memory, and for memory starved applications it increases performance significantly. We also show that an applications' memory contents can be compressed usually by a factor of 2.

9.1 Introduction

Data compression techniques are extensively used in computer systems to save storage space or bandwidth. Both hardware- and software-based compression techniques are used for storing data on magnetic media or for transmission over network links. While compression techniques are prevalent in various forms, hardware compression of main memory contents has not been used to date due to its complexity. The primary motivation for using a compressed main memory system is savings in memory cost and space savings for tightly packed systems, such as for 1U (1.75") thin, rack-mounted systems. Compression increases the amount of memory, or in cost-sensitive applications it provides the expected amount of memory at a smaller cost. Recent advances in parallel compression-decompression algorithms coupled with improvements in the silicon density and speed make main memory compression practical [12, 8, 13, 1]. A high-end, Pentium-based server class system with hardware-compressed main memory support, called the Memory Expansion Technology (MXT), has been designed and built [13].

In this chapter, we present a brief overview of the hardware and software technologies required to enable the MXT technology and provide detailed performance results and main memory compressibility of several benchmarks. Results show that two-to-one compression (2:1) is practical for most applications and that the performance impact of compression is insignificant, and for memory starved applications main memory compression improves performance significantly. Two-to-one compression effectively doubles the amount of memory; or in cost-sensitive applications it provides the expected amount of memory for half the expected cost or even less. Larger memory configurations require more expensive, higher-density memory modules due to the four memory-slot limit of a typical system. Therefore, an additional cost benefit of MXT is being able to use less expensive, lower-density modules. Observations show that main memory contents of most systems, operating system and applications included, are compressible. Relatively few applications' data that are already compressed or encrypted cannot be further compressed.

In the MXT system, a compressed memory/L3 cache controller chip is central to the operation of the compressed main memory [13]. The MXT architecture adds a level to the conventional memory hierarchy. Real addresses are the conventional memory addresses seen on the processor external bus. Physical addresses are the addresses used behind the controller chip for addressing the compressed memory, also referred to as physical memory in this chapter. The controller performs the real-to-physical address translation and compression/decompression of L3 cache lines. The processors are off-the-shelf Intel processors. They run with no changes in the processor or bus architecture. Standard operating systems such as Windows NT, Windows 2000, and Linux run on the new architecture with no changes for the most part. However, a corner case exists in which physical memory may be exhausted due to incompressible data. Standard operating systems are unaware of this problem. Hence, software support is needed to prevent the physical memory exhaustion. The amount of physical memory required changes with the compressibility of the memory contents. For example, a program starting with zero-filled buffers will require more physical memory as the buffers are loaded from the disk. Hence, the physical memory requirements change as the program runs, requiring constant monitoring and tuning as well as a recovery process if memory usage approaches the limit of the physical size. This corner case and the compressed memory management are handled by small modifications in the Linux kernel and by a set of user-level services and a device driver in the Windows NT and Windows 2000 operating systems.

The main contributions of this chapter are as follows. We provide an overview of the memory compression hardware and software support. Combined software/hardware design allows applications to run and take advantage of compression transparently. Using benchmarks, we show the cost/performance benefits of doubling the memory size due to compression. We further show that a number of applications' main memory contents can be compressed effectively.

The rest of this chapter is organized as follows. In Section 9.2, an overview of the MXT hardware is presented. The memory management software support added to the Linux and the Windows operating systems is discussed in Section 9.3. In Section 9.4, we present the experimental results of various industry benchmarks on the MXT system and examine the compressibility of various applications' memory contents. Related work is discussed in Section 9.5 and conclusions are presented in Section 9.6.

9.2 Overview of MXT Hardware

In an MXT system, the physical memory (SDRAM) contains compressed data and can be up to 16 GB in size. A third level cache (L3) is introduced. The L3 cache is a shared, 32 MB, 4-way set-associative write-back cache with 1 kB line size and is made of double data rate (DDR) SDRAM. The L3 cache contains uncompressed cached lines and hides the latency of accessing the compressed memory. The L3 Cache/Compressed Memory Controller (Champion North Bridge CNB 3.0 HE component of the Pinnacle server chipset developed in cooperation with Serverworks) is central to the operation of the MXT system. The L3 cache appears as the main memory to the processors and I/O devices, and its operation is transparent to them. The controller compresses 1 kB cache lines before writing them into the physical memory.

The compression algorithm is a parallelized generalization [8] of the Lempel-Ziv algorithm known as LZ1. The compression scheme stores compressed cache lines to the physical memory in a variable length format. The unit of storage in physical memory is a 256 byte sector. Depending on its compressibility, a 1 kB cache line may occupy 0 to 4 sectors in the physical memory. Due to this variable length format, the controller must translate real addresses to physical addresses. A 1 kB cache line (real) address is mapped to 0 to 4 sector (physical) addresses in the physical memory. The real address is the conventional address seen on the processor chip's external bus. The physical address is used for addressing the sectors in the compressed physical memory. The memory controller performs real-to-physical address translation by a lookup in the Compression Translation Table (CTT), which is kept (uncompressed) at a reserved location in the physical memory. The CTT size is 1/64th of the real memory size.

Each 1 kB cache line address maps to one entry in the CTT, and each CTT entry is 16 bytes long (therefore, the 64 to 1 ratio between and the real memory size and the CTT size). A CTT entry contains control flags and four physical addresses, each pointing to a 256 byte sector in the physical memory. Different physical memory occupancies result from compressing 1 kB cache lines with different compression characteristics. For example, a 1 kB cache line that does not compress occupies 4 sectors, i.e. 1 kB of physical memory. A cache line that compresses by 2:1 will occupy only two sectors in the physical memory (512 bytes), and the CTT entry will contain two addresses pointing to those sectors.

The remaining two pointers will be null. For a cache line that compresses to less than 120 bits (for example a cache line full of zeros), a special CTT format called trivial line format exists. In this format, the compressed data are stored entirely in the CTT entry replacing the four address pointers. Therefore, a trivial line of 1 kB occupies only 16 bytes in the physical memory, resulting in a compression ratio of 64:1. Another memory-saving optimization implemented in the controller is sharing of sectors by cohort cache lines. If two 1 kB cache lines are in the same 4 kB page, they are called cohorts. Two cohorts may share a sector provided that space exists in the sector. The compression operations described so far are done entirely in hardware, with no software intervention.

In addition to the operation above, the compressed memory controller provides fast page operations, such as page moving and page zeroing, which perform significantly faster than if issued through regular memory operations. Fast page operations work on 4 kB pages, same as in the x86 architecture. The speed increase is achieved merely by updating pointers in the CTT entries, rather than moving bulk data with the processor.

The decompression latency is brought down significantly through the use of parallel compression techniques and the utilization of a deep memory hierarchy. Memory hierarchies employing multiple cache levels have been used for many years to reduce the effect of main memory access times, particularly as the disparity has grown in the past decade between processor bus speeds and memory bus speeds. In the MXT architecture, the additional L3 cache captures many accesses that would go to the main memory for miss retrieval. The sizes of L2 to L3 are 256 kB and 32 MB, respectively, leading to a low global miss rate. In addition, the L3 cache is shared, four-way set-associative, and write-back. The L3 cache size is limited by the L3 directory size that can be supported on the controller.

Another aspect of this architecture is the real-to-physical address translation performed by the MXT memory controller. The translation is performed transparently to the processors, I/O devices, and software. This has the advantage of being able to use stock CPUs and I/O peripherals and without any changes in the software (except for the memory management subsystem of the OS). The translation is performed only for L3 cache misses, which are in the low single digits due to the large L3 size. For current processor/memory organizations, combining real-to-physical address translation with virtual-to-real address translation appears neither useful nor practical unless processors and memory controllers become integrated on a single chip in the future.

The additional cost for the MXT memory controller is estimated at approximately $60-100 plus the cost for the L3 cache SDRAM. In return, for a 2 GB system supporting 4 GB of real memory, the system is approximately $2400 cheaper based on the memory prices effective at the time of writing this chapter. Readers are referred to [13, 7] for much more comprehensive discussions of various issues related to the MXT memory controller.

9.3 The MXT Memory Management Software

Compressed memory hardware allows an operating system to use a larger amount of real memory than physically exists. During the boot process, the hardware BIOS reports a larger memory size than the installed physical memory. For example, in an MXT system with 512 MB of installed SDRAM, the BIOS may report having 1 GB of memory to the operating system. The main problem in such a system occurs when applications fill the memory with incompressible data, although more memory than physically available has been committed. In these situations, the common OS is unaware that the physical memory may be running out. For example, a 1024 MB system may have only 600 MB allocated and therefore may appear to have 424 MB free memory. However, due to low compressibility of the allocated memory, the physical memory usage may be near the 512 MB physical memory limit. Therefore, if the free memory is allocated, or if compressibility of the already allocated 600 MB further decreases, then the system will run out of physical memory, even though it appears to the OS that there is 424 MB free memory. Common operating systems do not distinguish between real and compressed physical memory, nor do they deal with out-of-physical-memory conditions. The MXT memory management software addresses these problems. The general mechanisms underlying the MXT memory management software that prevent physical memory from running out can be described as follows:

- Detect physical memory utilization
  1. Either by polling or through interrupts, it detects physical memory utilization and exhaustion.
  2. Detect excessive I/O activity to adjust various thresholds to ensure forward progress [6].
- Reclaim real memory and zero out freed pages to reduce utilization
  1. Pageable pages
     a) Make VMM believe that it is running out of memory and cause shrinking of file caches, and cause the paging daemon to move dirty pages to the swap disk. Pages freed are cleared with zeros, therefore physical utilization decreases or
     b) Dispatch memory eater tasks/processes that allocate big chunks of memory, stealing them from other processes. Then, clear the pages while holding on to them as long as the physical utilization is high.
  2. Non-pageable pages (e.g. drivers and kernel extensions)
     a) Reserve an amount in physical memory equal to the non-pageable memory size.
     b) Force drivers to free memory (e.g. MXT aware drivers).
- Steal CPU cycles to prevent further increase in utilization either by
  1. Descheduling processes or
  2. Decreasing process priorities or

3. Activating a set of busy threads (one per CPU) to block processes from running.

In Linux, minor changes to the kernel were made in order to implement these mechanisms. For Windows NT and Windows 2000, since kernel source code is generally not available, a combination of a device driver and user-level services were implemented. The particular details of these implementations under Linux and Windows 2000 are described in [8].

9.4 Performance Evaluation

The MXT memory system uses a relatively long 1 kB compression block size to be able to compress efficiently since shorter blocks may not compress well. Due to the compression and decompression operations performed on these blocks in the memory controller, memory access times are longer than usual. The 32 MB L3 cache contains uncompressed (1 kB) lines to reduce the effective access times by locally serving most of the main memory requests. Since this type of memory organization is relatively new, we present in the following a detailed performance analysis using SPECint2000, the SPECweb99, and a DB2 database regression test. In these experiments, we use MXT systems with dual 733 MHz Pentium III processors and a single disk drive. Dependent on the benchmark, we run both Linux and Windows 2000 and different memory sizes ranging from 512 MB to 2 GB physical memory. The MXT hardware was an early prototype that had some of the performance-enhancing features disabled, such as bus defer response and processor IOQ depth limited to 1, due to hardware bugs. We compared the MXT hardware to a standard system with similar hardware characteristics except with no compression or L3 support.

9.4.1 SPECint2000 Results

The SPECint2000 benchmark suite was designed by the SPEC consortium to measure the performance of the CPU and the memory (http://www.spec.org/osg/cpu2000/) and requires approximately 256 MB of memory. There are 12 integer benchmarks in the suite. These are the *crafty* chess program, *twolf* place and route simulation, *eon* ray tracing, *vpr* circuit placement and routing, *parser* natural language processing, *gcc* compiler, *mcf* minimum cost network flow solver, *vortex* object-oriented database, *perlbmk* perl utility, *gap* computational group theory, *bzip2* data compression utility, and *gzip* data compression utility benchmarks.

We ran the benchmarks three times, once on the standard system and twice on the MXT system with the compression on and off. The difference between the standard and the MXT with compression-off results demonstrates the performance impact of the L3 cache. The difference between compression off and compression-on results gives the performance impact of the compression-decompression hardware. The MXT system has a boot option that permits compression to be turned off. In that case, the system operates as a standard with an L3 cache and with non-compressed memory. Since compression/decompression hardware is disabled, the memory access latency is expected to be different from that of the compression-on case. We also recorded the number of L3 requests and L3 misses using the performance counters built into the memory controller chip.

Main results of the SPECint2000 experiments are shown in Figure 9.1. Due to strict reporting requirements of the SPEC consortium, we cannot publish the actual execution times. Therefore, we normalized the compression-on and compression-off results relative to the standard system results. Results show that on the average, MXT with compression-on is 1.3% faster than a standard system. The individual benchmarks *twolf*, *vpr*, *parser*, *gcc*, and *bzip2* perform 4.0 to 8.3% faster on the MXT system, as shown in Figure 9.1. *Mcf* runs 1.1% faster on MXT. The L3 miss rates (Figure 9.2) and L3 request rates (Figure 9.3) for these six benchmarks reveal the reason: their miss rates are relatively small, but their L3 request rates are the highest among the twelve benchmarks. In other words, the working set of these six benchmarks fit in the 32 MB L3 cache, and since they make a large number of L3 requests, the L3 cache comprising double data rate (DDR) SDRAM gives a slight performance advantage over the standard system comprising regular SDRAM. On the contrary, the benchmarks *vortex*, *gzip*, and *gap*, respectively run 2.1%, 2.4%, and 10% slower on the MXT system than the standard system. Figure 9.2 shows that these three benchmarks have the highest miss rates among the twelve benchmarks. *Gap* has the worst performance and the highest miss rate. It also has the highest misses/second metric, which is 2.6 times greater than the next highest.

Another observation is the relatively small L3 request rates for *crafty* and *eon*, which indicate that their working sets entirely fit in the L1 and L2 caches. Therefore, the L3 cache does not impact the performance of *crafty* and *eon*, which reveals itself as a negligible difference in their SPEC rates in Figure 9.1. Comparisons between MXT with compression and without compression show that the compression-on case is 0.4% faster than the compression-off case on the average. Figure 9.1 shows that *vpr* and *twolf* have the greatest difference in favor of the compression-on case. One possible explanation is that cache misses of these two benchmarks may result in a large number of trivial line compressions and decompressions. As explained before, a trivial line is an L3 cache line that compresses to less than 120 bits and therefore is stored in a 16 byte CTT entry. Compression and decompression of trivial lines may have a smaller overhead than that of a line occupying a sector (256 bytes) or more in the physical memory. For example, cold cache misses at the beginning of execution will almost always result in trivial line compressions because the memory is filled with zeros initially. The compression-off case runs faster than the compression-on case for the *gap* and *vortex* benchmarks by 1.5% and 1.9%,

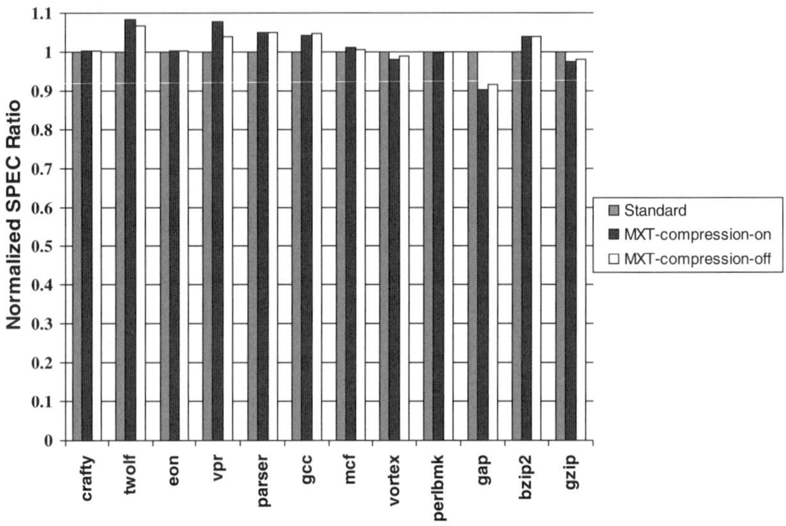

Fig. 9.1. SPECint2000 results for three system configurations.

respectively. These have the first and third highest miss rates and first and second highest misses per second.

In summary, the impact of the L3 cache and memory compression for the set of benchmarks is negligibly small considering that MXT doubles the amount of memory.

9.4.2 SPECweb99 Results

In this test, we measure the performance of Web serving using the SPECweb99 benchmark comparing an MXT system with a standard system. The operating system is Linux and the Web server is TUX 2.0. The fileset of SPECweb99 was generated with the test option of *wafgen.c* enabled to make the files compressible. The standard SPECweb99 benchmark uses random character strings as the file content, which is not realistic. Web content is generally compressible by a factor of 2, as shown later in Figure 9.9 and also in [3]. Web benchmarks, including SPECweb99, need to be changed to present a more realistic Web content. Two system configurations with varying memory sizes and a different number of gigabit ethernet adapters are analyzed. The left columns in Figure 9.4 show the achievable number of connections per second for the adapter (1EthGb) configurations. Since the SPEC consortium has strict rules for reporting results, we are not providing absolute numbers

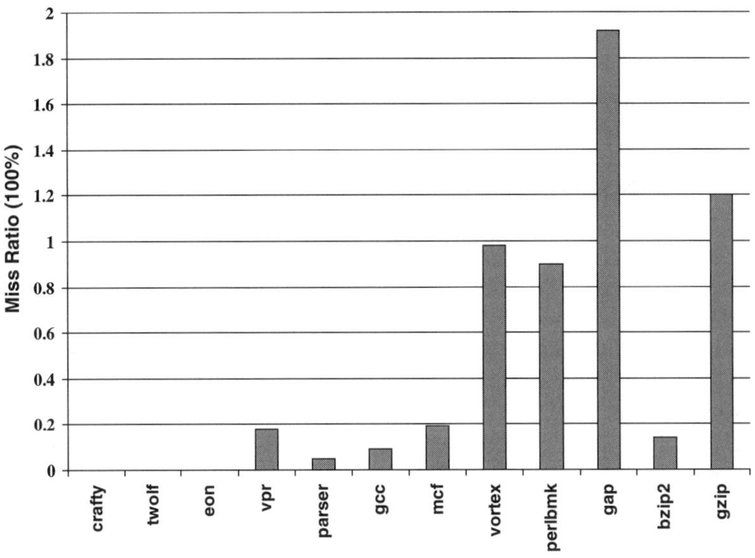

Fig. 9.2. L3 miss ratio for SPECint2000 under MXT.

of achievable connections but only relative numbers normalized with respect to the leftmost column (512 MB MXT+1EthGB). Adding further memory to the system does not substantially increase the performance, as the system is bandwidth-limited. However, we observe that MXT can provide roughly the same performance with half the physical memory configured in the standard box. Adding an additional adapter in the 2EthGB configuration moves the bandwidth limitation from the 1 GB memory size to the 2 GB memory size. Again we observe that the same performance can be achieved under MXT with half the memory size of the standard box. We further note that at the same physical memory size, the MXT systems delivers twice the performance. At this operating point, the I/O bandwidth is not the limiting factor. Instead, under MXT, the OS is capable of keeping a significantly higher number of Web pages in the file cache (due to the compression) and thus does not have to fetch them as frequently from the disk.

9.4.3 DB2 Database Benchmark Results

The MXT system has been measured running an insurance company database schema. This configuration is primarily used within IBM as a quick regression

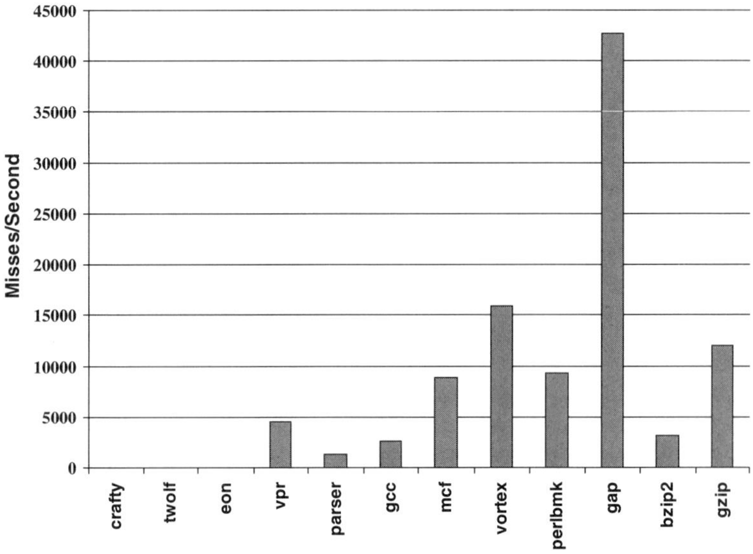

Fig. 9.3. L3 request rates for SPECint2000.

test for ascertaining the impact of DBMS design changes.[1] It is substantially less costly and quicker to run than complex benchmarks such as TPC-C but is coarsely representative of the performance characteristics that might be expected. Several configurations were run on the prototype hardware: 512 MB with MXT off, 512 MB (1 GB expanded) with MXT on, 1 GB with MXT off, 1 GB with MXT on (2 GB expanded), and 2 GB with MXT on (4 GB expanded). Benchmarks ran on the Windows 2000 operating system. Two runs were made for each configuration, a cold run where the file cache is initially empty, and immediately following that a second warm run, where the buffers have been warmed by the preceding cold run.

Figure 9.5 shows the performance benefits of MXT. For the 512 MB system when compression is on, it doubles the effective amount of memory and the benchmark runs 25% faster than in the compression-off case. For the 1 GB system when compression is on, it doubles the effective amount of memory to 2 GB and the benchmark runs 66% faster than in the compression-off case. It is interesting to note that the benefit of larger memory is more pronounced for this workload for larger memory sizes and is indicative of both the smaller 512 MB memory and 1 GB memory configurations being memory

[1] See http://www.ibm.com/software/data/db2/ for more information on configuring DB2

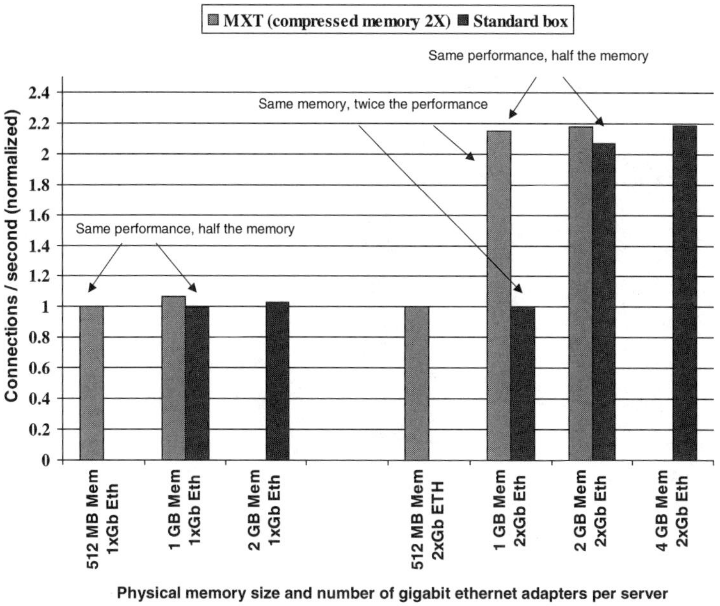

Fig. 9.4. SPECweb99 performance comparison.

starved. Finally, the 2 GB configuration (4 GB with compression-on) contains the entire database in memory. The performance improvement in this case is 300%. Figure 9.5 also shows *performance twins* and *cost twins* to emphasize the benefits of MXT. Performance twins perform nearly identically; however, the MXT-on twin costs less since its memory requirements are one-half that of the standard system. Cost twins have the same amount of physical memory; however, the MXT-on twin performs better due to the doubling of the memory.

Figure 9.6 shows runtimes of the individual DB2 queries in a 4 GB system after warmup. The database is in memory at this point, so most I/O is eliminated. Generally, queries run a bit faster with compression on. query 16 is an exception. This result is explained in Figures 9.7 and 9.8, which detail L3 cache accesses and misses for queries 7 and 16. Query 7 has much higher L3 access and miss rates, and the compression ratio for this database is 2.68:1, resulting in improved bandwidth between the L3 cache and main memory with compression on.

However, the standard system generally runs faster. The standard system used the same processors, twice the amount of SDRAM used in MXT, and a similar memory controller, except with no compression or L3 support. On this early MXT prototype, performance-enhancing features of the processor bus were disabled due to hardware bugs, such as bus defer response and IOQ

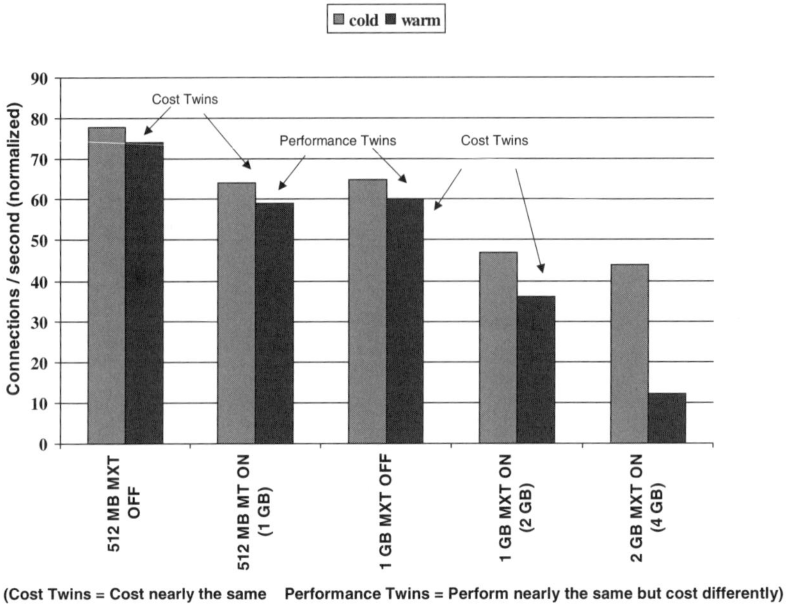

Fig. 9.5. Database benchmark results for five different configurations.

depth limited to 1, which is one possible explanation. Another possibility is higher L3 miss rates degrading overall performance compared to a standard system without an L3 cache.

9.4.4 Compressibility of Applications

Now that the performance of the MXT system is established, we turn our attention to the compressibility of the main memory contents of various applications. We measured the compression ratios on the actual MXT hardware whenever possible. We used an estimation tool when MXT hardware was not available. The estimation tool samples the live memory contents while the application is running on a standard computer and predicts the compression ratio.

On the MXT hardware, the real and physical memory utilizations were recorded using an instrumentation register of the memory controller. The Sectors Used Register (SUR) reports to the operating system the amount of physical memory in use. A sampler program every two seconds reads the SUR register and the real memory utilization as reported by the OS and saves them in a file to be processed later. The measured memory values are for the entire memory. Therefore, in addition to the benchmark application's memory utilization, the measurements include possibly large data structures

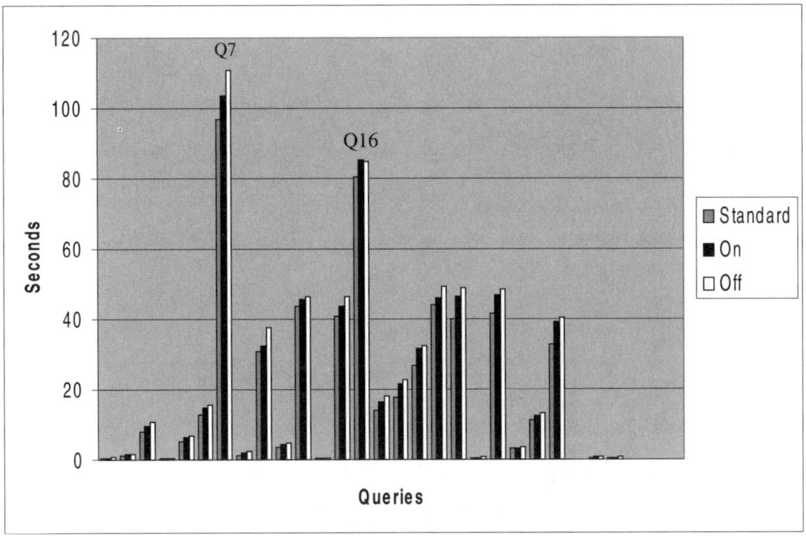

Fig. 9.6. DB2 query runtimes.

such as the file cache and buffer cache that the OS maintains for efficient use of the system. In a post-processing step, we took the average of the samples to produce the average compression ratio of a given benchmark.

Figure 9.9 shows the compression ratios for a few applications. Synopsis, Photoshop, MSDN Install, and DB2, compression ratios were measured on the MXT hardware with the Windows 2000 operating system. The Synopsis tool is used as a step in automating chip design. Photoshop compressibility varies significantly depending on the properties of the images being processed. Teiresias, from IBM Research, is an efficient algorithm for finding patterns in genetic structures. Teiresias ran on a stock PC, and the compressibility was measured by an estimation tool that sampled the memory contents. This compressibility measurement was taken while analyzing the *E coli* DNA. Microsoft Developer Network (MSDN) installations and most software installations compress poorly since the CD-ROM files are already compressed. The install program itself consumes only 4 MB. However, the associated file cache or NT standby pages fill the remainder of the memory. The DB2 result is for an insurance company database schema. SPEC CPU 2000 is the average of the 12 integer benchmarks in the SPEC suite. The live Web server used by IBM PC company customers is www.pc.ibm.com. This result was obtained on

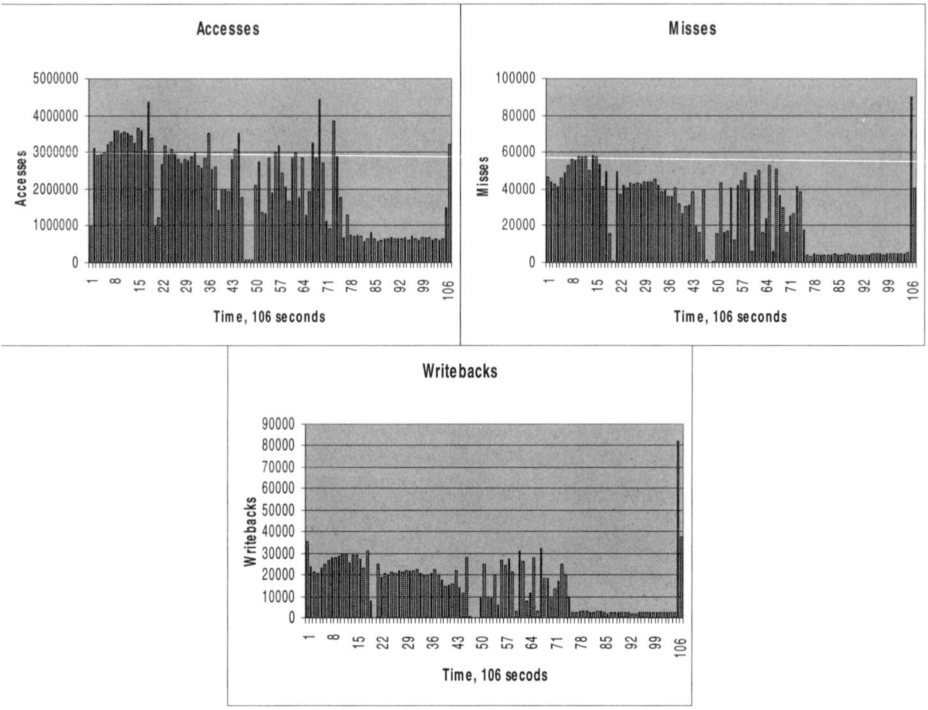

Fig. 9.7. Query 7 L3 accesses vs. misses.

a production Web server, and we used the estimation tool to sample memory contents.

Figure 9.10 shows the compressibility of the DB2 insurance database over time. The set of DB2 queries was run three times. The first run, a cold run, took 44 minutes, reading the database from disk. The second and third runs took 12 minutes each, following 20 minutes idle time. The average compressibility was 2.68:1. Overall, the compressibility of applications, particularly those that require large memories (Web serving, databases), is at least 2:1. This justifies running the MXT system at a 2:1 real-to-physical ratio, and one should not expect the physical exhaustion mechanism to kick in other than in emergency situations.

9.5 Related Work

A novel approach to compression that yields parallel speedup while maintaining the compression efficiency of sequential approaches is presented in [8]. The internal design of compressed random access memories is discussed in [7]. The

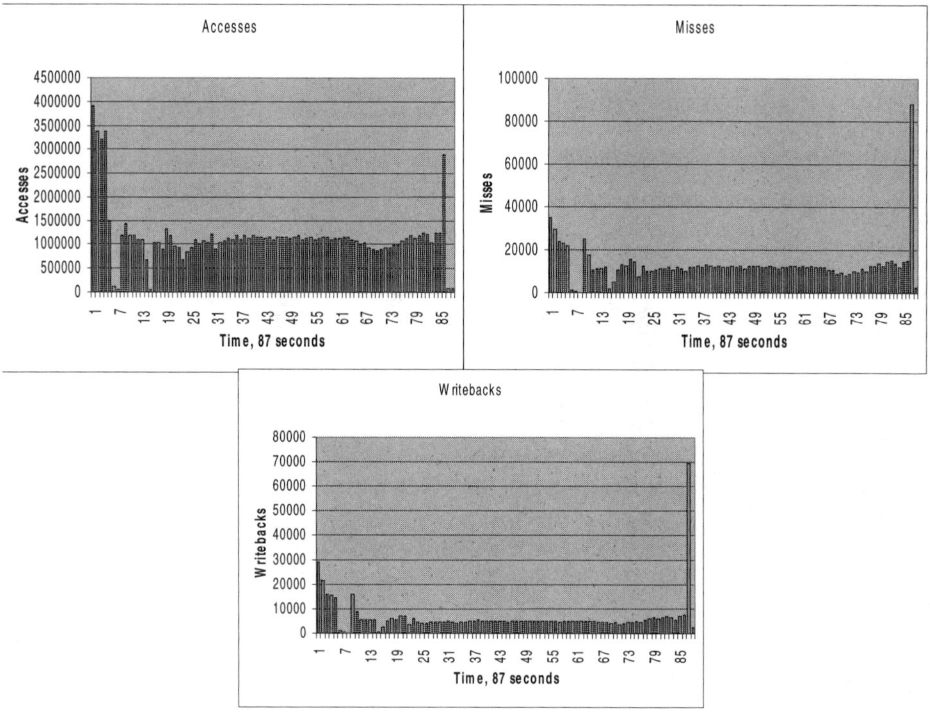

Fig. 9.8. Query 16 L3 accesses vs. misses.

issues of effective memory management in a compressed memory system are considered in [6]. In particular, a method for estimating the number of page frames as a function of physical memory utilization is described. Furthermore, the authors model the residency of outstanding I/O as they transfer data into the memory when streamed through a cache, thus potentially forcing cache writebacks that could increase the physical memory utilization. Using a time decay model, the system behavior is evaluated using simulation. A set of algorithms and data structures for compressed memory machines is presented in [5].

An approach to compression that removes the tight constraints of latency and bandwidth is discussed in [14]. This is accomplished by devising an architecture with two pseudo-levels — compressed and uncompressed memory — and the CPU operates only from the uncompressed region where the most frequently used pages are stored. The concept of the compression cache, an intermediate level in the memory hierarchy that serves as a paging store, is introduced in [10]. The authors introduce this concept to take advantage of the improving speed of processors versus disk and note that the grow-

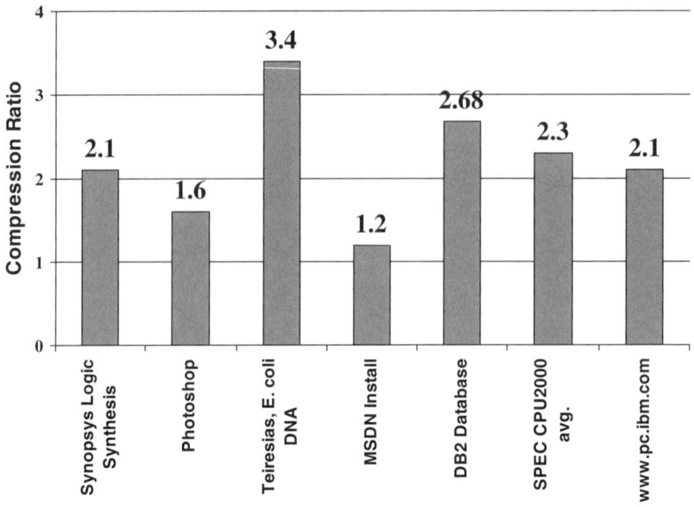

Fig. 9.9. Compressibility of various applications.

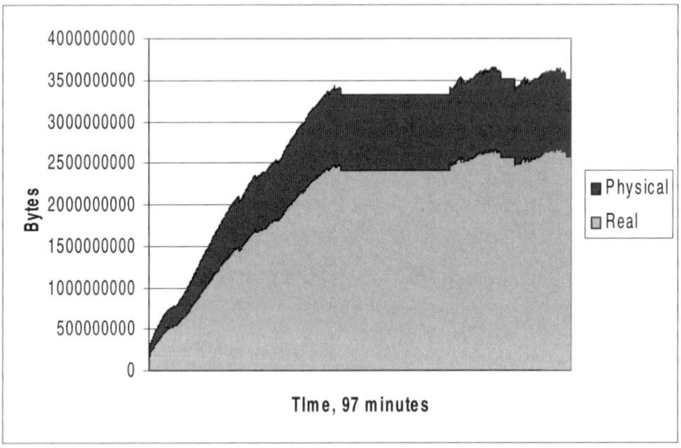

Fig. 9.10. DB2 compressibility: real vs. physical memory utilization.

ing disparity between these system elements makes compression close to the processor an appealing feature. In contrast, our approach allows the entire memory to be compressed, unlike in [10], and it does not partition the main memory as compressed and uncompressed as in [14]. The TinyRISC effort in which compression is used to reduce embedded system code size is discussed in [11]. Compression techniques for increasing branch prediction accuracy in microprocessors are discussed in [4] and [9].

9.6 Conclusions

In this chapter we described and evaluated a computer system with hardware main memory compression that effectively doubles the size of the main memory. We gave a brief overview of the MXT hardware and software technologies. We measured the impact of compression on the application performance and determined that the hardware compression has a negligible penalty over uncompressed hardware. We measured real and physical memory utilization of various applications and determined that main memory contents can be compressed usually by a factor of 2 or greater. Overall, MXT provides a compelling argument to either increase performance through increased real memory size at the same price as standard systems or to reduce the cost of the system while retaining the same performance characteristics of standard systems.

References

1. B. Abali and H. Franke. Operating System Support for Fast Hardware Compression of Main Memory. In *Memory Wall Workshop*, June 2000, also published as IBM Research Report No. RC21964, IBM, Yorktown Heights, NY.
2. B. Abali, H. Franke, D.E. Poff, R. Saccone, C. Schulz, L. Herger, and T.B. Smith. Memory Expansion Technology (MXT): Software Support and Performance. *IBM Journal of Research and Development*, 2:287–302, 2001.
3. B. Abali, H. Franke, D.E. Poff, X. Shen, and T.B. Smith. Performance of Hardware Compressed Main Memory. In *Proceedings of The Seventh International Symposium on High Performance Computer Architecture (HPCA-7)*, pages 73–81, January 2001.
4. I.-C.K. Chen, J.T. Coffey, and T.N. Mudge. Analysis of Branch Prediction via Data Compression. *Computer Architecture News*, 24:128–137, October 1996.
5. P. Franaszek, P. Heidelberger, D.E. Poff, and J. Robinson. Algorithms and Data Structures for Compressed Memory Machines. *IBM Journal of Research and Development*, 2:245–258, 2001.
6. P. Franaszek, P. Heidelberger, and M. Wazlowski. On Management of Free Space in Compressed Memory Systems. In *Proceedings of the ACM Sigmetrics Conference*, pages 113–121, June 1999.
7. P. Franaszek and J. Robinson. On Internal Organizations in Compressed Random Access Memories. *IBM Journal of Research and Development*, 2:259–270, 2001.

8. P. Franaszek, J. Robinson, and J. Thomas. Compression architecture for system memory application. In *Proceedings of the Data Compression Conference (DCC)*, pages 200–209, 1996.
9. J. Kalamatianos and D.R. Kaeli. Predicting Indirect Branches via Data Compression. In *Proceedings of the Annual International Symposium on Microarchitecture*, pages 272–281, 1998.
10. M. Kjelso, M. Gooch, and S. Jones. Empirical Study of Memory Data: Characteristics and Compressibility. *IEE Proceedings on Computers and Digital Techniques*, 45(1):63–67, 1998.
11. S.Y. Larin and T.M. Conte. Compiler-Driven Cached Code Compression Schemes for Embedded ILP Processors. In *Proceedings of the Annual International Symposium on Microarchitecture*, pages 82–92, 1999.
12. D. A. Luick, J.D. Brown, K.H. Haselhorst, S.W. Kerchberger, and W.P. Hovis. Compression Architecture for System Memory Application. US Patent 5,812,817, 1998.
13. R. Tremaine, P. Franaszek, J. Robinson, C. Schulz, T.B. Smith, M. Wazlowski, and M. Bland. IBM Memory eXpansion Technology (MXT). *IBM Journal of Research and Development*, 2:271–286, 2001.
14. P. Wilson, S. Kaplan, and Y. Smaragdakis. The Case for Compressed Caching in Virtual Memory Systems. In *Proceedings of the USENIX Annual Technical Conference*, 1999.

10

Profile-Tuned Heap Access

Efe Yardımcı[1] and David Kaeli[2]

[1] Department of Information and Computer Science, University of California, Irvine, CA, USA eyardimc@ics.uci.edu

[2] Department of Electrical and Computer Engineering, Northeastern University, Boston, MA, USA kaeli@ece.neu.edu

Abstract. As memory latencies continue to grow, effective use of cache memories is necessary. A disproportionate number of cache misses are caused by accesses to dynamically allocated memory, and a small number of heap objects account for a large percentage of heap misses.

In this chapter we describe two methods that attempt to increase cache utility using profile-guided allocation of heap objects. In our first approach, we have modified an existing malloc library to allocate heap objects with the aim of reducing first-level data cache conflicts. Our allocation routines utilize information about the target cache architecture. We use program behavior obtained from profiling to classify objects and allocate them to regions in the cache where they will potentially cause fewer cache conflicts. We perform our work on a Compaq Alpha 21264 processor as our target architecture.

In our second approach, we explicitly guide allocation of objects to increase spatial locality. We maintain *Temporal Relationship Graphs* (TRGs) for subsets of objects and allocate objects that are observed to have strong temporal interaction into localized regions in the heap to increase spatial locality. We introduce the concept of allocation *phases* to capture the allocation of objects and the temporal relationship displayed by accesses to those objects.

To motivate this work, we provide an evaluation of the differences between heap-based and nonheap-based accesses. We show that by using a procedure-stack-based predictor as the input to the allocator, we can achieve speedups of up to 5.5%.

10.1 Introduction

Memory latency has become increasingly important as the gap between processor speeds and memory speeds grows [12, 24]. Many methods have been proposed to overcome this disparity, such as the design of sophisticated cache memory hierarchies and cache prefetching algorithms. A memory hierarchy can hide much of the memory latency only if a large percentage of the memory accesses result in cache hits. As the gap between processor and memory speeds continues to grow, this percentage must also increase.

For the purposes of this chapter we divide memory into two categories:

1. heap
2. nonheap.

Heap objects are allocated dynamically. Accesses to the heap region differ in nature from statically allocated objects (e.g., arrays). References to heap objects access nonconsecutive elements at noncontiguous memory locations. Operations such as sorting and insertion/deletion can alter the overall structure of linked data structures at runtime. This inherent lack of spatial locality reduces the efficiency of conventional prefetching methods in pointer-intensive applications. Temporal locality may also be lacking [10], as a traversal through a linked data structure may involve visiting enough nodes to displace a node from the cache before it is revisited (i.e., exhausting the cache's capacity).

When we look at the characteristics of memory accesses to the heap region as compared to accesses to other regions (mainly to the data segment and the stack segment), several issues stand out. First, a disproportionate number of cache misses are caused by accesses to the heap region, as seen in Table 10.1. For example, in equake, a simulation of seismic wave propagation from the SPEC2000fp suite, almost 90% of all cache misses are caused by accesses to dynamically allocated memory. However, the number of accesses to the heap region only comprises 19% of all accesses.

Table 10.1. Number of heap accesses and heap misses as a percentage of the total number of memory accesses and cache misses, respectively. A 64 kB 2-way set-associative, level-1 data cache is modeled.

Program	twolf	equake	ammp	power	tsp	em3d
Percentage of heap accesses over all accesses	13.3	19.2	21.8	0.5	11.9	43.9
Percentage of heap cache misses over all misses	49.6	88.8	86.2	18.1	30.5	92.2

Another interesting characteristic of accesses to dynamically allocated memory is that increases in cache size do not significantly reduce collision and capacity misses for heap references — not nearly as well as they remedy misses for accesses to statically allocated structures. In experiments involving several benchmark suites, we found that accesses to linked data structures that miss in the cache actually make up an increasingly disproportionate number of the total misses with increasing cache size, as seen in Figure 10.1.

When we look at the source of the misses in the heap region (the blocks that are accessed when a cache miss occurs in the heap region), we notice that a small number of objects account for a large percentage of the misses [19]. This is significant in that it shows why assigning a random address to heap objects (which in practice approximates the case in most malloc implementations) might lead to problems in the memory hierarchy. When multiple objects with

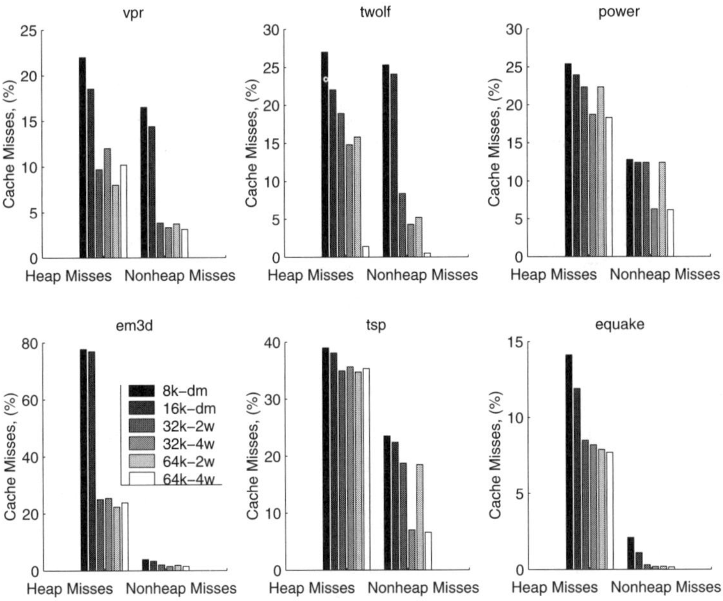

Fig. 10.1. Cache miss rates for nonheap segment and heap segment accesses with varying cache sizes and associativities.

high reference counts are mapped to addresses that conflict in the cache, a significant number of misses can occur.

Table 10.2. Utilization of heap memory during program execution. The Final footprint column refers to memory still residing in the heap at program termination.

Program	Total bytes allocated	Max footprint in bytes	Final footprint in bytes
em3d	1,289,800	1,289,800	244,880
power	468,944	468,944	468,944
tsp	1,836,592	1,836,592	1,835,752
twolf	10,245,722	2,470,941	1,092,089
ammp	30,626,152	26,400,656	23,479,132
equake	13,230,080	9,244,200	7,142,543

In general, existing allocation routines tend to balance allocation speed and memory usage. Preserving locality has not been a major concern [22]. Also, the footprint of dynamically allocated objects tends to be larger than the size of the data segment, even though the number of accesses to the heap region is generally smaller than the number of accesses to the data segment. As observed in the benchmarks listed in Table 10.2 (executed with midsized inputs), the heap footprint does not fit in a large (64 kB, two-way set-associative) L1 cache. A different memory allocation algorithm can greatly influence memory layout. There is a lot that can be done to improve the spatial and temporal localities of heap-based data structures. These observations are the premise of our work.

We have developed two different profile-guided approaches to allocating heap objects to improve heap behavior. As previously mentioned, mapping two blocks with high reference counts to the same cache line will cause a significant number of cache misses. The objective of the first method is to identify and reduce potential cache collisions. In the second method, we attempt to develop a novel way of classifying consecutive allocations (i.e., *phases*) and use this information to determine the state of the program at both profile and allocation times.

Both of our approaches use profile-guided optimization. Our profile guidance is based on characteristics obtained during a profile run. All of our analysis uses different training and testing inputs. To tie the profiled state to an actual program runtime state, we develop a *state predictor*. We utilize information about the program call stack and the allocated heap object size to uniquely identify program states associated with heap allocations.

This chapter is organized as follows. Section 10.2 briefly reviews related work. Section 10.3 explains our state predictor and discusses how we use it to guide our cache-conscious memory allocator. Section 10.4 presents runtime and simulation results. Section 10.5 summarizes the contributions of this work and suggests directions for future work.

10.2 Related Work

There have been a number of previous projects that have considered reordering code and data. Hashemi et al. [13] use a *Call Graph* (CG) to guide procedure placement. This algorithm has been used as the basis for reordering in a number of reordering algorithms [14, 18]. In [14, 15], two temporal-based procedure reordering algorithms are proposed. Both of these algorithms build a graph whose edge weights capture the temporal interaction between procedure pairs. The graph is called a *Temporal Relationship Graph* (TRG) in [14] and a *Conflict Miss Graph* (CMG) in [15]. Placement is done using *cache line coloring* based on either a locally optimal search [14] or greedy heuristics [15].

In [16], Kalamatianos et al. describe code reordering applied over a complete memory hierarchy. Besides trying to minimize conflicts in multiple caches, they also use heuristics in order to improve spatial locality at the page level. Simulation results clearly motivate the need for mapping procedures over the entire cache hierarchy of a system.

There has been a considerable amount of research on the effects of garbage collection on cache performance and locality [8, 9, 19, 23]. Chilimbi and

Larus [5] have studied reordering the objects in memory during a garbage collection cycle. More recently, Chilimbi [6] describes a methodology for changing the organization of pointer-based data structures to improve cache performance. The main focus of this work was to show the benefits of packing small structures into cache lines.

Kistler and Franz [17] describe a method of improving the memory-hierarchy performance at runtime by continuously adapting the internal storage layout of heap objects. The work perhaps closest to ours is that of Seidl and Zorn [20], in which they use profiling to classify objects into categories (highly referenced, not referenced) and attempt to reduce page faults by allocating objects in the same category into the same segment (thus improving reference locality).

10.3 Algorithms

For the first part of our experiments, we obtained and modified dlmalloc, a version of malloc/free/realloc written and released to the public domain by Doug Lea who was a primary author of libg++, the GNU C++ library. For the TRG-guided allocation part of our research, we have written our own malloc library — one that was more suited to the specific allocation strategy we wished to pursue.

We use a range of benchmarks taken from multiple suites. Table 10.3 lists the programs used in this work. We utilize the ATOM [21] instrumentation tool to instrument binaries for profile extraction. ATOM allows us to insert analysis code in these programs without significantly perturbing the integrity of the runtime dynamics. Results were obtained by running the executables with the modified allocation libraries on an Alpha 21264 (Miata) workstation. The 21264 provides a 64 kB 2-way set-associative L1 cache.

All benchmarks were compiled with the native Compaq *cc* compiler using the -O2 level of optimization. In this work, we evaluated improvements in data layout by changing the program inputs between profiling and performance runs. This helps to ensure that our algorithms are insensitive to changes in program input. For the SPEC benchmarks, we profiled using the smallest set of inputs provided and obtained our performance speedups using the medium-sized inputs provided. The inputs for the OLDEN benchmarks were scaled to provide a short profiling input, and the normal inputs were used during the performance runs.

10.3.1 State Predictor Implementation

State predictors form the interface between the profile data and the target program execution. The effectiveness of profile-guided reordering is based on the premise that the profile is representative of the target execution. To produce a profile, a program is run with a training input set to train predictors

Table 10.3. Benchmarks evaluated in this work.

Program	Benchmark Suite	Description
em3d	OLDEN	EM wave propagation in a 3D object
power	OLDEN	Power pricing optimizer
tsp	OLDEN	Traveling salesman problem
twolf	SPEC2000int	Place and route simulator
equake	SPEC2000fp	Simulation of seismic wave propagation
ammp	SPEC2000fp	Modeling large systems of molecules

used to identify similar program states in the target (same program, different input set) execution. We then detect performance problems (i.e., cache conflicts) that were encountered during the profile run and then anticipate (and potentially remedy) these problems when they are detected in the target execution. Detection is dependent on our ability to identify a similar program state.

We will make our decisions to perform reordering at heap allocation time. Among the possible sets of program information we could obtain at allocation time include the *stack pointer*, the *procedure call stack*, the *allocation size*, and the *allocation call site*. We have evaluated these possible predictors used singly as well as in combination.

The value of the stack pointer at allocation time is easy to implement as a predictor. The call stack is harder to implement but provides a great deal of information about the program state. The implementation of a low-overhead call stack-based predictor should actually be trivial; using lightweight binary instrumentation to implement such a mechanism could provide negligible overhead as the instrumentation granularity would be at the procedure level.

Tracking object allocation size is also easy to implement but used alone provides very little useful information. When used together with the call stack state, it can outperform most other state predictors. We have also experimented using the *malloc* call site address within a procedure as a very accurate predictor mechanism. This has proven to be costly to implement, and combined usage of the call stack and allocation size has given comparable results. In our experiments, we have obtained the best results with the call stack state predictor combined with the allocation size.

10.3.2 Phases of Allocation

In the TRG-guided allocation part of our work, one of our premises has been that the sequence of allocation events can be separated into distinct slices capturing unique patterns of accesses. It follows that when one object among a sequence of consecutively allocated objects is accessed, the other objects will be accessed as well (a form of *sequence locality*).

We decided to exploit this fact by identifying *phases* of allocation. We keep a FILO buffer of predictor states, and whenever a phase is entered into the buffer (a phase is entered at each allocation) that is not currently in the buffer, we identify this as the beginning of a new phase. All the allocations are entered as belonging to this phase. A phase can contain a large number of allocations, but can have at most $n - 1$ distinct state types, where n is the size of the state buffer. We use a buffer length of 10 for the results in this chapter (this value was determined through experimentation).

These phases are used extensively in the TRG-guided allocation part of our work, both in the profiling and execution stages. It is essential that we maintain a TRG among the states of each phase. We define the *signature* of a phase as the contents of the state buffer at the time the new phase is entered and use these signatures to identify multiple occurrences of a phase.

10.3.3 Profile Creation

We used the ATOM instrumentation tool to obtain our profiling results. We have also used ATOM to perform runtime call stack tracking for the target execution. During the target execution, we access a separately indexed *State Table* used to track and guide allocation states of the target execution.

Miss Profile Creation

A *miss profile* is created during the profiling step, which can be indexed by a State Table entry. The profile is essentially a conflict table, holding conflict information occurring between each predictor state for the cache under consideration. In all experiments our target architecture was the Alpha 21264, which has a 64 kB 2-way set-associative level-1 data cache.

During the creation of this graph, we also found it useful to keep a separate TRG graph that records temporal interaction between conflict table entries. The TRG is used to prune entries where low temporal interaction is observed. While we recognize that pruning may be susceptible to changes in program input, we have found this not to be the case in the programs studied.

TRG Profile Creation

We maintain a TRG graph for each phase of the profiling step. We had seen that multiple occurrences of the same phase exhibit very similar temporal access patterns. Therefore we update the weights of the TRG edges of a phase for all instances of the same observed phase; however, we only identify the temporal interaction between the states of a certain phase. So if states 2 and 3 of a phase exhibit high temporal interaction, we update the TRG graph. For another phase with the same signature (thus an instance of the same phase), we update the same temporal relationship graph. We ignore interaction between states of two separate instances of a phase since this interaction occurs very infrequently.

10.3.4 Implementation of Miss-Profile-Guided Allocation

As mentioned previously, we used the dlmalloc allocation library as a basis to implement our first strategy. This allocator holds several bins and tries to match allocation requests with each bin before trying to allocate in the wilderness block, (the highest address heap block, placed between the heap region and the unmapped region; this block is always free and is the only block whose size can grow freely). Whenever a call is made to malloc, our modified malloc waits until free space is found. Then the Conflict Table is checked with the predictor number obtained from the State Table.

The entry in the Conflict Table corresponding to the predictor state is checked if there is a potential collision with the free block. If a conflict is found in the Conflict Table, the block is released and the next available bin is checked until either:

- a conflict-free address is found, or
- the wilderness block is reached.

If we reach the wilderness block, and the address is also found in the Conflict Table (and thus, a collision could occur in the future), our allocation algorithm checks the next sequential cache line to see if it is free of conflict. This is repeated until a cache line is reached that is not among the addresses in the current state's Conflict Table entry. If during this step we find that the end of the wilderness block is reached, a call is made to sbrk() and the wilderness block is extended.

Once a suitable address is found, the region starting from the original address up to the nonconflicting address is allocated. The actual allocation is done at the address immediately following this region. The previously allocated buffer is then freed, causing minimal space wastage (though possibly some limited fragmentation).

10.3.5 Implementation of TRG-Profile-Guided Allocation

For the TRG-profile-guided allocation, we have written our own complete malloc library — one that was more suited to the explicit placement of selected objects. As in the miss-profile-guided results, we maintain a table of objects, but now we record the states within various phases that exhibited strong temporal interaction and should be allocated considering the placement of one another (i.e., close though not overlapping in the address space). We use a simplified version of the State Table used in the miss profiling step, this time holding only the allocation number of highly accessed states of selected phases.

Our allocator keeps separate bins for directed allocation. Into each bin, we allocate a storage arena where we allocate objects that we would like to be in close proximity to one another. From the profiling stage, we have produced a list of states that should be allocated close together. When we come across one of these states, we direct allocation to the associated bin. When a bin is full, we simply request more memory from the operating system for the bin. Since we know beforehand the required number of bins (based on the number of profiled states), the headers are allocated at compile time and we are assured of having as many bins as are needed.

10.4 Results

The results we obtained from using our allocation algorithms during runtime have given us a good indication of the potential value of our mechanisms. Despite the overhead introduced to the allocation mechanisms, in each case we were able to achieve actual speedup figures. The TRG profiling method is a novel method that exhibits a strong opportunity for improvement.

Table 10.4. Execution time speedups relative to the original execution. All runtimes were obtained on a Compaq Alpha 21264 workstation.

Program	twolf	equake	ammp	power	tsp	em3d
Speedup,miss profiling	3.1%	5.5%	2.8%	1.9%	1.0%	0.85%
Speedup,TRG profiling	1.0%	3.1%	2.5%	2.1%	1.3%	1.9 %

The results shown in Table 10.4 were obtained by running the original and optimized versions of the benchmarks 10 times discarding the longest and shortest recorded times, and averaging the remaining execution times.

Table 10.5. Miss rates for a 64 kB 2-way set-associative data cache. Results were obtained using ATOM.

Program	twolf	equake	ammp	power	tsp	em3d
Miss rate, original	14.6%	9.2%	18.0%	27.3%	12.6%	29.2%
Miss rate,TRG profiling	14.3%	7.1%	16.2%	16.2%	12.5%	27.3%

Table 10.5 shows cache miss rates for the original and TRG-optimized executions. The TRG-guided allocation provides a significant reduction in miss rates for a number of the programs.

10.5 Conclusion

In this chapter we have proposed and evaluated two techniques that attempt to increase cache performance through guided allocation of heap memory objects. To effectively use profile guidance during allocation, we must be able to accurately map the profiled state to the target execution state.

Our methodology identifies blocks or machine states (indicators to conflict-causing blocks) by using a profile and information about the target cache to direct the memory allocator. In our first method, we have modified an existing malloc routine to use a profile and attempt to allocate objects at addresses where they will incur fewer cache conflicts. In the second method, we restricted the reallocation address of an object based on a TRG graph, avoiding mapping temporally local heap objects to the same portion of the cache.

Our preliminary results show we can obtain good speedups using an efficient greedy algorithm to partition the conflict graph and perform cache-conscious memory allocation. Our results give us confidence in the validity of our TRG-guided policies and provide motivation to carry the work further.

We believe our TRG-profile-guided allocation strategy can be improved upon substantially by employing more aggressive graph partitioning algorithms. We plan to take into account the hot and cold regions within highly referenced states and allow for conflicting states' cold regions to overlap in the cache. We also plan to look at the sensitivity of our policies for different inputs.

Acknowledgments

This work has been supported by NSF grant CCR-9900615, by Compaq Computer, and by Mercury Computer Systems.

References

1. Ball T, Larus J (1996) Efficient path profiling. In: Proceedings of the 29th Annual International Symposium on Microarchitecture (MICRO-29), Paris, France, pp. 46–57.
2. Barrett D, Zorn B (1993) Using lifetime predictors to improve memory allocation performance. In: Proceedings of the SIGPLAN Conference on Programming Language Design and Implementation, pp. 187–196.
3. Calder B, Grunwald D, Zorn B (1994) Quantifying behavioral differences between C and C++ programs. Journal of Programming Languages 2(4):313–351.
4. Carlisle M (1996) Olden: parallelizing programs with dynamic data structures on distributed-memory machines. Ph.D. Thesis, Department of Computer Science, Princeton University, Princeton, NJ.
5. Chilimbi T, Larus J (1998) Using generational garbage collection to implement cache-conscious data placement. In: Proceedings of the ACM International Symposium on Memory Management, pp. 37–48.
6. Chilimbi T, Davidson B, Larus J (1999) Cache-conscious structure definition. In: Proceedings of the SIGPLAN Conference on Programming Language Design and Implementation, pp. 13–24.

7. Cohn D, Singh S (1996) Predicting lifetimes in dynamically allocated memory. Advances in Neural Information Processing Systems, 9(8):932–938.
8. Courts R (1988) Improving locality of reference in a garbage collecting memory management system. Communications of the ACM 31(9):1128–1138.
9. Diwan A, Tarditi D, Moss E (1994) Memory subsystem performance of programs using copying garbage collection. In: Proceedings of the 21st ACM SIGPLAN-SIGACT Symposium on Principles of Programming Languages, pp. 1–14.
10. Ghiya R (1998) Putting pointer analysis to work. Ph.D. Thesis, School of Computer Science, McGill University, Montreal, Canada.
11. Grove D, Dean J, Garret C, Chambers C (1995) Profile-guided receiver class prediction. In: Proceedings of the Conference on Object-Oriented Programming Systems, Languages, and Applications, pp. 108–123.
12. Hadimioglu H, Kaeli D, Lombardi F (2001) Introduction to the special issue on high performance memory systems. IEEE Transactions on Computers 50(11):1103–1104.
13. Hashemi A, Kaeli D, Calder B (1997) Efficient procedure mapping using cache line coloring. In: Proceedings of the SIGPLAN Conference on Programming Language, Design and Implementation, pp. 171–182.
14. Gloy N, Blackwell T, Smith M, Calder B (1999) Procedure placement using temporal-ordering information. ACM Transactions on Programming Languages 21(5):997–1027.
15. Kalamatianos J, Khalafi A, Kaeli D, Meleis W (1999) Analysis of temporal-based program behavior for improved cache performance. IEEE Transactions on Computers 48(2):168–175.
16. Kalamatianos J, Kaeli D (2000) Accurate simulation and evaluation of code reordering. In: Proceedings of IEEE ISPASS, pp. 45–54.
17. Kistler T, Franz M (1999) The case for dynamic optimization: Improving memory-hierarchy performance by continuously adapting the internal storage layout of heap objects at run-time. Technical Report No. 99–21, Department of Information and Computer Science, University of California, Irvine.
18. Ramirez A, Barroso L, Gharachorloo K, Cohn R, Larriba-Pey J, Lowney G, Valero M (2001) Code layout optimizations for transaction processing workloads. In: Proceedings of the 28th International Symposium on Computer Architecture, pp. 155–164.
19. Reinhold M (1997) Cache performance of garbage-collected programs. In: Proceedings of the SIGPLAN Conference on Programming Language Design and Implementation, pp. 206–217.
20. Seidl M, Zorn B (1997) Predicting references to dynamically allocated objects. Technical Report CU–CS–826–97, Department of Computer Science, University of Colorado, Boulder, CO.
21. Sristava A, Eustace A (1994) ATOM: A system for building customized program analysis tools. In: Proceedings of the SIGPLAN Conference on Programming Language Design and Implementation, pp. 196–205.
22. Wilson P, Johnstone M, Neely M, Boles D (1995) Dynamic storage allocation: A survey and critical review. Lecture Notes in Computer Science 986:1–115, Springer-Verlag, Berlin Heidelberg New York.
23. Wilson P, Lam M, Moher T (1991) Effective "static-graph" reorganization to improve locality in garbage-collected systems. In: Proceedings of the SIGPLAN

Conference on Programming Language Design and Implementation, pp. 177–191.
24. Wulf W, McKee S (1995) Hitting the memory wall: Implications of the obvious. Computer Architecture News 23(1):20–24/

11

Array Merging: A Technique for Improving Cache and TLB Behavior

Daniela Genius[1], Siddhartha Chatterjee[2], and Alvin R. Lebeck[3]

[1] INRIA, Rocquencourt, France
[2] IBM T.J. Watson Research Laboratory, Yorktown Heights, NY, USA
[3] Duke University, Durham, NC, USA*

Abstract. Many data layout techniques for cache optimization reduce data cache miss rates significantly while only marginally improving run time. This chapter suggests a systematic approach to array merging, a simple but highly effective optimization with a beneficial effect on the memory hierarchy. The run time trade-off can be kept small while improving on cache and particularly on misses in the translation look-aside buffer (TLB). One of the SPEC95 benchmarks is analyzed in detail, with encouraging experimental results.

11.1 Introduction

It is common knowledge that the memory bottleneck has become increasingly acute in recent years. For decades now, *memory hierarchies* have been inserted between the processor and main memory. Scientific computing applications access large portions of memory in regular patterns and are particularly sensitive to memory hierarchy misses. A standard technique to overcome such misses is to change the loop structure. In addition, the data layout can be changed. In order to avoid large page tables, virtual memory often uses translation look-aside buffers (TLBs), special caches keeping the address translations ready. These, too, can become an important source of performance degradation.

This chapter suggests a simple *array merging* scheme to achieve better page utilization in the fully associative TLB while also preventing cross interference in the cache hierarchy levels. The focus is on scientific FORTRAN codes without pointers or procedure calls. The remainder of this chapter is organized as follows. Section 11.2 contains related work. Section 11.3 introduces basic terminology. Section 11.4 presents the method, while Section 11.5 provides a case study. Section 11.6 gives detailed experimental results for this

* This work was performed when the first author was a postdoctoral researcher, the second author was a professor at University of North Carolina at Chapel Hill, and all three authors were with the TUNE project sponsored by DARPA.

example on four different memory hierarchies. The chapter concludes by outlining future work. A longer version of the work presented here can be found in a technical report of UNC [9].

11.2 Related Work

The well-established compiler approach to improving memory hierarchy behavior is to apply loop transformations, usually focusing on improvement for the first-level data cache [14]. As shown in [8], some techniques such as *iteration space tiling*, while largely improving on capacity misses, can lead to an increase in cache conflicts for certain tile sizes. A loop transformation affects all arrays in the loop, sometimes destroying good locality for one array while enhancing it for the other. Furthermore, conflicts are difficult to control at the loop transformation level. Most *data layout* approaches such as matrix transposition and stride reordering [7] use techniques that try to reorder data according to the access structure for better spatial reuse. However, these techniques neglect cache conflicts, and some might even increase them. [4] In the mid-1990s, several researchers established *padding* [4, 15, 17] as a data layout technique for avoiding cache conflicts. Originating from memory bank conflict avoidance in the highly interleaved memory systems on vector computers without a cache [5], this technique advocates the insertion of gaps filled with unused data (the *pad*) into data structures in order to prevent interferences.

Ghosh et al. used cache miss equations [11] to select both padding and tile size. Characteristic of padding is the possible inflation of data structures: pad sizes that are optimal with respect to cache conflicts can become quite large so that there is an imminent danger of exceeding the capacity of higher memory hierarchy levels, leading to TLB misses. An alternative approach to prevent arrays from interfering with each other is to *merge* them by alternately taking elements of each one; obviously this eliminates any chance of them interfering, but it glues them together permanently. Although the technique is acknowledged as a standard technique for hand optimization in the computer architecture literature [12], it has not yet found its way into compilers. By profiling, Lebeck and Wood reveal the opportunities for merging on a significant fraction of the SPEC92 floating point benchmarks in [13]. The authors combine an ad hoc merging with other optimizations for half of the benchmarks with good run time improvements. There have also been suggestions for merging into cache blocks. An approach based on a data flow analysis appears in the master's thesis of Rawat [16] but handles direct-mapped caches only and treats arrays as a whole. Thus, cache miss rates are significantly overestimated. Calder et al. [6] use a variant of merging for heap allocation.

[4] As an example, take the matrix multiplication code $C_{i,j} = C_{i,j} + A_{i,k} * B_{k,j}$. Transposing A for column-wise access forces accesses to A and B into cadence, which for certain array sizes causes a conflict in every iteration.

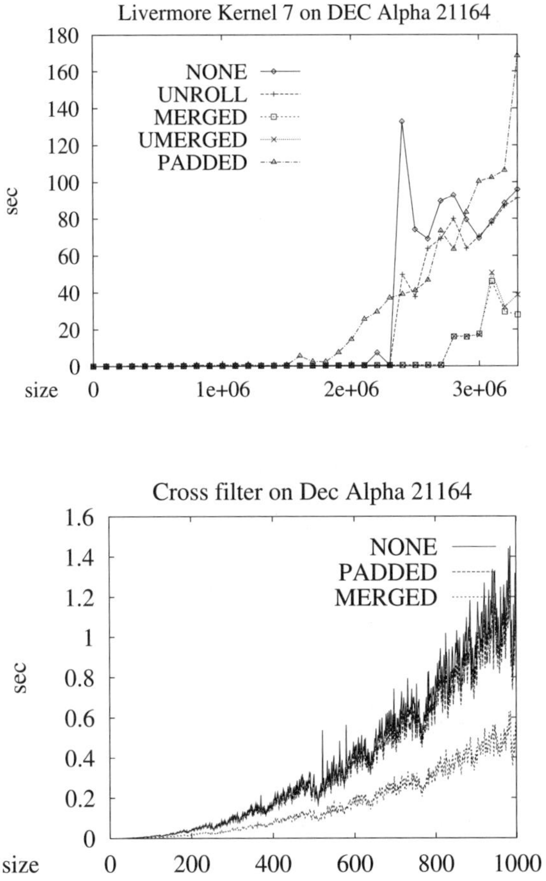

Fig. 11.1. Run times for Livermore kernel 7 and the cross filter on Alpha 21164.

In [10] merging is applied to simple pointered data structures such as linked lists and hash tables, with a beneficial effect on data cache behavior.

During previous experimentation, we experienced extremely encouraging results for merging with some smaller codes. Livermore kernel 7 (Figure 11.1 top) is a fragment of a hydrology kernel consisting of a single loop sequentially accessing four arrays; also, unrolled variants (UNROLL, UMERGE) are shown. If only inter-array padding can be applied, small to medium array sizes merging and padding yield approximately the same run times. Yet, an interesting effect can be observed for large arrays: as the TLB is fully associative and the accesses traverse the array sequentially, every new page has already been evicted; we call this TLB *thrashing*. The sharp increase in run time usually attributed to TLB thrashing is postponed for merged code, while for the padded code, the overall size of the portion of memory required is inflated, causing worse page utilization and an earlier onset of thrashing. For the cross filter, padding makes no difference compared to the unoptimized layout — the two curves are approximately the same and can hardly be discerned in the graph. On the other hand, merging improves run time by up to a factor of 2 (Figure 11.1 bottom). The remainder of the chapter will show that while it does not inflate the array size, merging is cheap at compile time and suitable for inter-loop optimization.

11.3 Basic Notions

Data cache hierarchies in Harvard architectures have separate first level data and instruction caches. In an n-level memory hierarchy [12], we have the parameters A, B, C of **A**ssociativity, **B**lock size, and **C**apacity on each level. The first level data cache is denoted as the L1 cache with parameters A_1, B_1, C_1, and so forth.

In scientific codes, common data types on 32 bit architectures are of size 4 bytes and size 8 bytes, determining B_0. Block sizes B in the cache vary between 16 and 128 bytes.

Associativity A gives the number of choices given when a block is mapped to a level of the memory hierarchy. For *direct mappings* ($A = 1$), the address m completely determines the cache location $m \bmod \frac{C}{B}$. *Full associativity* ($A = \frac{C}{B}$), on the other hand, is expensive to implement, and associativities $A > 8$ generally only marginally improve performance [12]. The set is selected by $m \bmod \frac{C}{B*A}$. Within a set, replacement algorithms such as LRU and FIFO apply.

Let us assume the *inclusion property* holds, i.e. a block present in levels i is also present in level 1 to $i-1$. Whenever a block requested by the program is not present in level i, a *cache miss* occurs. In this case, the block containing the requested location is loaded from level $i+1$. For higher levels, the time required to retrieve the block, the *memory latency*, grows by orders of magnitude.

Virtual addresses are translated to physical addresses with the help of the TLB, which works like a small cache with very large block size. B_{TLB} is the size of a portion of memory that is addressed through one TLB entry (here 8 or 16 kB). All accesses go to the TLB. As a consequence, while there are fewer misses on higher cache levels due to hits in the lower levels, this does not extend to the TLB. TLB misses are known to occur rarely (at a percentage lower than 1%) on typical programs as can be found in the Hennessy/Patterson test suite. However, if they occur, they cause a high penalty of at least 20 cycles [12].

A *data access* is a dynamic instance of a reference. A single reference can either read from or write to memory. A FORTRAN assignment can cause several references (e.g. `A(i) = B(i+1)` causes two references: a load to the address of array variable `B(i+1)` and a store to `A(i)`). The classical model [21] considers loop nests where *access vectors* are affine mappings of the loop index vector $\mathbf{i} = (i_1, \ldots, i_s)^T$. Let $\mathbf{d}$ be a vector of constants, and let n be the array dimensionality. The access matrix J relates n array dimensions and s loop indexes:

$$\begin{bmatrix} j_{1,1} & \cdots & j_{1,s} \\ \vdots & & \vdots \\ j_{n,1} & \cdots & j_{n,s} \end{bmatrix} \begin{bmatrix} i_1 \\ \vdots \\ i_s \end{bmatrix} + \begin{bmatrix} d_1 \\ \vdots \\ d_n \end{bmatrix} .$$

References are called *uniformly generated* if their accesses differ only in $\mathbf{d}$. Arrays containing only such references are *uniformly referenced.*

One distinguishes between *temporal reuse* and *spatial reuse.* Temporal reuse refers to the same data item, while spatial reuse refers to any item in the same cache line. If there are r references in a program, temporal reuse can ideally improve by a factor of r for the same element. Spatial reuse can only improve up to $\lfloor \frac{B}{B_0} \rfloor$, when all elements of the line are reused. Let us define the *reuse distance* as the number of loop iterations between two temporal reuses. Even with locality, in caches where $A < \frac{C}{B}$, *conflicts* can occur. They often destroy reuse by evicting a cache block that is still used. *Self-interference* denotes conflicts between blocks that stem from the same array, and *cross interference* denotes conflicts between cache blocks from different arrays. *Thrashing* denotes the situation in which a block is evicted on every iteration; this can occur with cross interference in uniformly referenced arrays.

11.3.1 Stencil Codes

Stencil codes exhibit uniformly generated references, opening opportunities for reuse.

Typical examples are filter algorithms, most Livermore kernels, and a large part of every collection of SPEC floating point benchmarks. In Figure 11.2, consider loops of nesting depth two. Each dimension represents one loop index, each line a stride of size one. Stencil (a) occurs e.g. in multigrid algorithms, (b) occurs e.g. in successive overrelaxation, and (c) and (d) are typical templates in various image filters and many of the Livermore kernels. In [18] it is shown that impressive results can be obtained with an additional merging for multigrid algorithms. In Figure 11.2, the reuse distance is N for (a)+(b), N resp. $2N$ for (c) and (d).

11.3.2 Data Layout

The *data layout* for an n-dimensional array a can follow any (injective) function $L : \mathbb{N}^n \rightarrow \mathbb{N}$. Compilers usually allocate contiguous memory space from

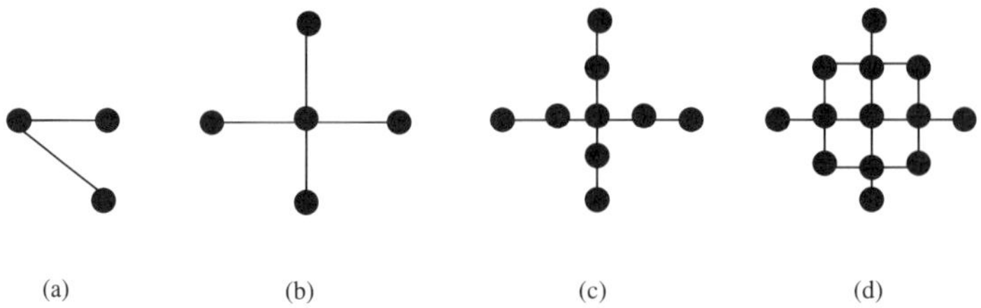

Fig. 11.2. Stencils: (a) 3-point, (b) 5-point, (c) 9-point, and (d) 13-point.

an arbitrary starting address, with some alignment on a cache line or virtual memory page boundary. FORTRAN compilers use column major layout; i.e. for two-dimensional arrays array element $A_{k,l}$ is mapped to virtual memory address $o+k+N*l$, where N is the length of the column and o is the starting address offset. The basic idea of a compiler-directed data placement is to place data at suitable memory locations at compile time such that at run time they are loaded into the desired cache blocks.

11.4 Cache-conscious Merging

Using classical compiler techniques, we analyze for *uniformly* generated references. In contrast to the classical notion, we also consider references to *different* array to be uniform if they satisfy the condition from section 11.3. Moreover, two array accesses are considered. Let us assume that simple data layout transformations have already taken place.

Definition 1 (uniformity). *Let $i_1, \ldots, i_n$ be the loop index vector, $k =$ the dimensions of an array. Accesses are* uniform in dimension k, *denoted by $u_{k,m}$ for some i_m with $m \leq n$, if dimension k is accessed only by references uniformly generated from one loop index i_m. They are in particular* innermost uniform, *denoted by $u_{k,n}$, if dimension k is accessed only by references uniformly generated from loop index i_n. Arrays $A_1, \ldots, A_l$ that satisfy condition u are in relation $u(A_1, \ldots, A_l)$.*

As a simple example, an array access `A[i,j+1]` in a loop nest with index vector (i, j) is uniform in both dimensions but not innermost uniform.

Definition 2 (togetherness). *Arrays A_1, A_2 are accessed* together *if they are in the same loop nest and satisfy the uniformity condition, $A_1, A_2 \in u(A_1, \ldots, A_l)$ for example. We denote this by $t_u(A_1, A_2)$.*

While togetherness with respect to the innermost dimension is obviously profitable if the traversal of the innermost loop coincides with the array layout in memory and stride $\leq B$, the use of the other kinds of uniformity is not so obvious. To transform these into k, n-uniformity, classical techniques such as *loop fusion* are applied [3]. However, innermost uniformity can lead to cache thrashing because accesses traverse the array in cadence.

11.4.1 A Conservative Heuristic

A general problem with data reordering is that it is also a *global* transformation: what is profitable for one loop nest might be damaging cache behavior for subsequent loop nests. If only one array of a merge set is accessed in another loop nest, spatial locality is violated. There is no such thing as a low-cost operation for copying data into a different layout pattern between loop nests, although some of this effort could be hidden behind high-latency floating point operations. Replication, too, is out of the question for large datasets. Thus, this chapter chooses a conservative heuristic as a first approximation. The number of merged arrays l for an l-way merging should always be a power of 2 or a multiple thereof to avoid unused space in a cache block. Most of the caches in our study are either direct-mapped or 2-way associative. Thus, we restrict to *2-way merging*, hoping to make up for the benefits of 2-way associativity in a direct-mapped cache. We maintain a list of loop nest levels and arrays that are accessed therein. The heuristic merges the arrays if they are used uniformly in all of the loops. In order to identify individual loops, we label them by tuples $id = i_{1,1}, \ldots, i_{s,p}$, respectively, i referring to the loop index, s referring to the nest level, p to the pth instance of a loop over index i. By this, we capture the individual loop nests.

Heuristic: If two arrays A, A' are accessed uniformly wrt. dimension n in all individual loop nests described by tuple id (i.e. $A, A' \in u_{k,n}(A_1, \ldots, A_l)$ holds for at least one k, n), then $t(A, \ldots, A') \leftrightarrow u_{k,m}(A, \ldots, A') \in \bigcap u_{k,n}$.

While the above works well with the codes we have examined so far, a less conservative heuristic might want to allow for a less strict criterion than the set intersection. This necessitates a cost measure to assess the trade-off between miss reduction and the possible loss of spatial locality. The cautious choice of 2-way merging will reduce the risk of violating spatial locality in that case: at most, $\frac{B}{2}$ elements are wasted.

11.4.2 Modifications to Code and Data

The code is currently modified by a simple preprocessing, compile time transformation as planned. Like the analysis, this procedure is rather straightforward. First, the compound array is given a new name, which is replaced throughout the program. Then, memory for a merge set is allocated together by simply changing the size N to *2*N* for the dimension concerned. Finally, index calculations are replaced. Care must be taken not to incur too much additional cost — the FORTRAN compiler is very sensitive to index operations because it can highly optimize the usual expressions. Experience shows that doubling the stride and boundary of a loop is the cheapest way. Figure 11.3 shows the pseudo-code of the overall algorithm for analysis and source code transformation.

In: *maxid* number of loop nests
  $Vars$ list of variables in loop nest k
Out: 2-way merge sets

For k= 1 to *maxid*
  For-all $Vars$
  analyze uniformity with standard algorithms
  distinguish $u_{k,m}$ for array dimensions $k = 1$ to n
  End for-all
End for
For k= 1 to *maxid*
  If $A, A' \in u_{k,m}(k)$ for any k
  Then $t(A, A')$
End for
/*build tentative togetherness relations*/
For all pairs A, A'
  For k= 1 **to** *maxid*
    If $A, A' \in Vars \wedge A, A' \notin t'$
    Then delete $t(A, A')$
    Endif
  /*delete unless together in every loop nest*/
    If $t(A, A'), t(A, A'')$ for $A \neq A' \neq A''$
  /*if two combinations of same array survive*/
  /*keep the more frequently used pair*/
      Then If $|t(A, A')| \leq |t(A, A'')|$
      Then delete A, A' **Endif**
  End for
End for-all
For-all $t(A, A')$
  /*apply transformations to FORTRAN code*/
  $A, A' \rightarrow$ `M`$\circ A \circ A'$
  /*rename compound array prefixed by `M` (merge)*/
  `[`N_1`]...[`N_n`]`$\rightarrow$ `[2*`N_1`]...[`N_n`]`
  /*double innermost dimension size*/
  `DO 10 I = 1,N`$\rightarrow$`DO 10 I = 1,2*N,2`
  /*modify loop bounds and stride*/
  $A(f(I_s), \ldots, f(I_1)) \rightarrow A^*(f(I_s - 1), \ldots, f(I_1))$
  /*modify indexes within compound array A^* */
End for-all

Fig. 11.3. Conservative 2-way merging algorithm

Note that while possibly endangering spatial locality if used too aggressively, merging can actually enhance spatial locality in cases where innermost $(k, n\text{-})$ uniformity cannot be achieved otherwise. By merging l accesses that are k, m-uniform for $m < n$, (i.e., they are accessed in the same loop iteration), spatial reuse can be improved by a factor of $\lfloor \frac{B}{l} \rfloor$.

11.5 Case study

Mesh generation with Thompson solver, better known as `tomcatv` within the SPEC92 and SPEC95 floating point benchmarks, is infamous for its bad cache behavior and thus has become a favorite target for cache optimization. Though smallest in code size of the entire benchmark suite, it behaves extremely badly in the cache, both of which make it suitable for presentation here. `Tomcatv` is a typical *stencil code* (see Section 11.2): It has loop nest depth two (not counting the outermost iteration loop) and exhibits four-point stencil patterns and a simple two-point stencil. The code is made up of seven individual loop

1:	$J_{1,1}$	$I_{2,1}$: X,Y,RX,RY,AA,DD	1:	$J_{1,1}$	$I_{2,1}$:	X,Y,RX,RY	
2:	$J_{1,2}$	$I_{2,2}$: RX,RY	2:	$J_{1,1}$	$I_{2,2}$:	X,Y,RX,RY,AA,DD	
3:		$I_{1,1}$: D	3:	$J_{1,1}$	$I_{2,3}$:	RX,RY	
4:	$J_{1,3}$	$I_{2,3}$: AA,DD,RX,RY,D	4:		$I_{1,1}$:	D	
5:	$J_{1,4}$	$I_{2,4}$: RX,RY,D	5:	$J_{1,1}$	$I_{2,4}$:	AA,DD,RX,RY,D	$N \rightarrow 1$
6:	$J_{1,5}$	$I_{2,5}$: RX,RY,AA,D	6:	$J_{1,1}$:		RX,RY,D	
7:	$J_{1,6}$	$I_{2,6}$: X,Y,RX,RY	7:	$J_{1,2}$	$I_{2,5}$:	RX,RY,AA,D	$N \rightarrow 1$

Fig. 11.4. (Left) original loops; (right) after loop fusion, reuse distance improvement .

nests ($id = 1, \ldots, 7$), six of which iterate over both index variables I and J. The first step is to apply loop fusion in order to nest a sequence of I-loops within a J-loop, so that several traversals of one array column are completed before the next is accessed. This changes uniformity from type J to type I and improves temporal locality. However, the danger of cache thrashing has increased: what before was only erratic now becomes imminent because accesses run in cadence.

Figure 11.4 shows an abstraction of the code. On the left, loops are shown before loop fusion and on the right after loop fusion. In both cases there are seven distinct loop nests (denoted by lines 1: to 7: in the first column). We abstract from the actual loop structure by denoting the loop indices I and J in the second and third columns. The first subscript shows the depth (usually 1 for J, 2 for I). The second subscripts are only used to distinguish between the independent instances of I and J. $I_{2,5}$ for example means the fifth instance of the loop index I at depth 2. Loop 3 (loop 4 after fusion) goes

Original loops	Fused loops
1: $J_{1,1}$ $I_{2,1}$: $u_J(X,Y), u_I(X,Y), u_J(RX,RY,AA,DD), u_I(RX,RY,AA,DD)$	1: $J_{1,1}$ $I_{2,1}$: $u_J(X,Y), u_I(X,Y), u_J(RX,RY), u_I(RX,RY)$
2: $J_{1,2}$ $I_{2,2}$: $u_J(RX,RY), u_I(RX,RY)$	2: $J_{1,1}$ $I_{2,2}$: $u_J(X,Y), u_I(X,Y), u_J(RX,RY,AA,DD), u_I(RX,RY,AA,DD)$
3: $I_{1,1}$: D	3: $J_{1,1}$ $I_{2,3}$: $u_J(RX,RY), u_I(RX,RY)$
4: $J_{1,3}$ $I_{2,3}$: $u_J(AA,DD,RX,RY,D)$	4: $I_{1,1}$: D
5: $J_{1,4}$ $I_{2,4}$: $u_J(RX,RY,D), u_I(RX,RY,D)$	5: $J_{1,1}$ $I_{2,4}$: $u_I(AA,DD,RX,RY,D)$
6: $J_{1,5}$ $I_{2,5}$: $u_J(RX,RY,AA,D), u_I(AA,D)$	6: $J_{1,1}$: $u_J(RX,RY,D), u_I(RX,RY,D)$
7: $J_{1,6}$ $I_{2,6}$: $u_J(X,Y,RX,RY), u_I(X,Y,RX,RY)$	7: $J_{1,2}$ $I_{2,5}$: $u_I(RX,RY,AA,D), u_J(AA,D)$

Fig. 11.5. Uniformity and togetherness: (left) original and (right) fused loops.

over I only, so here I has depth 1. All arrays that occur in a loop nest are shown in the fourth column. The biggest change occurs in loops 5 and 7, where uniformity of all references with respect to the inner loop is achieved. $N \rightarrow 1$ stands for the improvement of reuse distances through loop fusion: instead of in two iterations of the outer loop that are N iterations of the inner loop apart, accesses happen in the same iteration. Figure 11.5 shows the analysis result for the accesses before and after loop fusion. All arrays that are uniform with respect to I and J are placed together in a set u_I or u_J, respectively. Arrays that share a set u_I are innermost uniform. As a result of applying the algorithm in Figure 11.3, only $t(X,Y)$ and $t(RX,RY)$ remain as merge sets, because they are always used together.

```
REAL*8  MXY(2*NMAX,NMAX)
...
DO    10   J = 1,N
  DO    10    I = 1,2*N,2
    READ(...) MXY(I-1,J),MXY(I,J)
...
DO    50   I = 2,2*N-3,+2
           XX = MXY(I+2,J)-MXY(I-2,J)
           YX = MXY(I+3,J)-MXY(I-1,J)
...
```

name	modifications
none	original program
merge2	merge RX,RY
merge2+2	merge RX,RY and X,Y
pad	inter- and intra-padding
fusion	loop fusion
fusion2	loop fusion + merge2
fusion2+2	loop fusion + merge2+2
fpad	loop fusion + inter-padding

Fig. 11.6. (Left) code for array merging; (right) code variants.

Other candidates such as $t(AA,D)$ are evicted because D is also used alone in loop nest 4. In [13] only X and Y are merged, whereas RX and RY are accessed much more frequently. On the left of the table, the loop identifiers are shown, on the right the access structure for the arrays. AA and D are not merged in this conservative heuristic because it would incur a penalty in loops where only D and not AA is accessed (as is the case for loop 4). In the case of `tomcatv`, indexing is most efficiently hidden within the loop index. Figure 11.6 shows on its left the modified code fragments for declaring, reading in, and accessing the new merged array MXY. On the right, the techniques have been applied; *none* denotes the original code taken as is from SPEC. In addition we examine merging X and Y without loop fusion (*merge2*) and *merge2+2*, where additionally RX and RY are merged, as would be the result of our algorithm. The abbreviation *fusion2* corresponds to the technique applied in [13], where only X and Y are merged in addition to loop fusion. For merging X, Y and RX, RY in addition to fusion, *fusion2+2*, the best results for the direct-mapped cache and TLB are expected. As shown in [17], only inter-array padding is applicable to the fused loops (*fpad*), while the original loop structure is viable for both inter- and intra-array padding (*pad*).

11.6 Experimental Results

With the goal of obtaining insight into the response of different architectures to merging, we present a comparison for one benchmark, `tomcatv` from Section 11.5, in full detail. Table 11.1 summarizes the characteristics of the architectures used in this study. The memory hierarchy level capacity C_i is always a power of 2; the number of arrays in loop nests of the codes we surveyed is usually large, indicating the imminent threat of cross interference and even more potential for merging. For a realistic assessment of the benefits, it is necessary to select a high-level compiler optimization. Compiler optimization may well interact badly with the program and data layout transformations employed. Optimization level is -fast for Alpha 21164 and SPARC, -O4 for

Table 11.1. Machine configurations: *single-processor mode, **virtual memory page size. Cache sizes refer to the data cache hierarchy only.

Machine	Alpha 500au	Alpha DS10	Ultra-10	SGI Origin*
CPU	Alpha 21164	Alpha 21264	UltraSparc-II	MIPS R12000
Clock rate	500 MHz	466MHz	300MHz	300MHz
L1 (A/B/C)	1/32 B/8 kB	2/64 B/64 kB	1/32 B/16 KB	2/32 B/32 kB
L2 (A/B/C)	3/64 B/96 kB	1/64 B/2 MB	1/64 B/512 KB	1/6 4B/8MB
L3 (A/B/C)	1/64 B/4 MB	-/-/-	-/-/-	-/-/-
TLB (A)	64	128	64	64
MM (B**/C)	*8 K/256 MB	8 K/512 MB	8 K/320 MB	16 K/16 GB
Compiler (option)	f77 (-fast)	f77 (-O4)	f77 (-fast)	f77 (-O3)
Operating System	Digital Unix 4.0D	FreeBSD4.0	SunOS5.7	Irix 6.5.3

Alpha 21264 (highest available under freeBSD) and -O3 for the SGI (as recommended for most reliable use of the tool set). The benchmark uses 513*513 arrays of `REAL` type 8 byte elements, and the maximal number of iterations is set to 750 (both the original SPEC95 settings). We examine eight variants of `tomcatv`.

For measuring the cache miss rates on the Alphas, we used a simulation based on ATOM [20], a tool that instruments binaries. The TLB is evaluated directly via the hardware counters with the help of Digital's *dcpi* [2]. Fastcache on SPARC also uses a binary-driven simulation that was developed within the Wisconsin tool set together with the tools used in [13] for profiling. The Mips R12000 features a variety of tools [19] that allow a convenient inspection of the hardware counters.

11.6.1 Run Times

For reasons of trade-off as discussed in the previous section, it is crucial to also give run times; a correlation should be observable. Table 11.2 shows measured run times for the entire program (750 iterations as in the SPEC95 suite, array size 513*513). It can be observed that merging has more potential when combined with loop fusion because it avoids thrashing. The results are good with respect to the Alphas' memory hierarchies (up to 28% improvement on the 21164, 36% on the 21264). Intra-array padding (as part of *pad*) incurs high run time penalties on all architectures, as FORTRAN cannot optimize the additional index operations appropriately. With loop fusion, *fpad* can only use inter-array padding, which has practically no additional run-time cost (a dummy array is introduced during declaration[17]) but also no benefit except in the rare cases where several arrays would have mapped to a starting address that maps to the same cache line.

Table 11.2. Run times (sec) for `tomcatv` 513*513.

Architecture	21164	21264	UltraSparc	R12000
none	180	127	237	135
merge2	168	119	227	136
merge2+2	162	111	248	128
pad	180	108	245	133
fusion	144	104	173	95
fusion2	137	91	217	95
fusion2+2	129	81	198	110
fpad	131	94	198	94

The UltraSparc run time degrades with merging, unexpectedly for a purely direct-mapped architecture with comparatively small caches. Also, this is out of proportion to the observed miss rates. With this architecture, our results

Table 11.3. Miss rates for `tomcatv` on the four target architectures. Dn means data cache level n, and all numbers are percentages.

Alpha21164					UltraSparc-10			
MH level	D1	D2	D3	TLB	MH level	D1	D2	TLB
none	62.1	13.0	3.83	0.052	none	14.6	3.62	0.029
merge2	53.0	11.3	4.10	0.046	merge2	11.6	3.65	0.028
merge2+2	45.4	5.27	3.71	0.041	merge2+2	19.9	3.86	0.030
pad	48.8	5.81	3.85	0.052	pad	14.7	3.84	0.039
fusion	62.9	5.05	2.64	0.057	fusion	14.5	3.17	0.020
fusion2	28.8	7.36	2.99	0.048	fusion2	15.6	2.43	0.017
fusion2+2	41.3	3.56	3.75	0.042	fusion2+2	16.7	2.56	0.018
fpad	47.6	5.17	2.85	0.056	fpad	14.3	2.16	0.019
Alpha21264					R12000			
MH level	D1	D2		TLB	MH level	D1	D2	TLB
none	22.6	11.3		0.049	none	15.8	1.09	0.027
merge2	20.9	11.3		0.038	merge2	15.9	1.59	0.026
merge2+2	14.7	11.1		0.021	merge2+2	15.0	1.60	0.026
pad	14.1	4.58		0.058	pad	10.9	1.22	0.031
fusion	26.1	5.3		0.055	fusion	17.8	1.26	0.009
fusion2	18.6	3.03		0.044	fusion2	18.2	1.25	0.008
fusion2+2	17.4	4.15		0.036	fusion2+2	16.3	1.70	0.009
fpad	13.4	4.50		0.049	fpad	15.4	1.31	0.009

indicate that pure loop fusion performs best, but more research is required to dig out the reasons. On the powerful SGI Origin memory hierarchy for high-performance graphics demands, *fusion2+2* improves run time only by 18.5%, while *fusion2* improves it by over 29%.

11.6.2 Miss Rates

For validation, we also show the miss rates. Table 11.3 shows detailed miss rate results for all code variants and architectures. The Alpha 21164 has a very small, direct-mapped L1 data cache, which badly interacts with the total of eight relatively small arrays. Here, Lebeck and Wood's *fusion2* beats all other methods, except that merging both X, Y and RX, RY exhibit significantly fewer TLB misses. The Alpha 21264 shows the most significant benefits from merging, particularly for *merge2+2* and *fusion2+2*, by our heuristic. This is surprising because it features a 2-way associative L1 data cache and a very large L2 cache (see Table 11.1). Actually, SPEC chose an array size of 513, accounting for a loop index range of 512. A power of 2, this interacts pathologically with the power of 2 cache size. Intra-array padding is specialized in avoiding this case, which is reflected by the good results.

The SPARC performs poorly with both padding and merging, which is equally surprising for a memory hierarchy with comparatively limited facilities compared to the large profits obtained for the Alpha 21264. For the SGI, D1 miss rates increase for all optimized variants. Loop fusion without merging and *fusion2* yield the best results, in spite of suffering from worse L1 cache behavior. For nearly all merged variants, however, TLB misses are reduced.

In summary, the run-time improvements do not always show a perfect correlation to the changes in miss rates. Where they improve significantly however, this coincides with the TLB miss reduction. Note that this chapter represents preliminary work and is limited to one case study. Other results with array merging, obtained by a different approach based on analysis of data structures, can be found in [10].

11.7 Conclusions

This chapter presents a systematic compiler approach to array merging in nested loops. We have shown that for a large class of scientific codes characterized by stencil accesses, merging can be profitably combined with standard techniques, meanwhile avoiding some of the dangers of other data layout approaches. While it is known that padding interacts well with tiling [15], merging can exploit the benefits of loop fusion to a larger extent. As shown in the case study, systematic merging can significantly reduce misses on all levels of the memory hierarchy, including the TLB. Although much more work is required to gain full insight into the interaction with current high-performance memory hierarchies, compilers, and operating systems, the overall experimental results so far are extremely encouraging.

Although compile time is not an issue in this chapter, merging is often much cheaper than padding: at most the same analysis power is required, and merging does not require a compile-time search for pad size. Merging can be easily handled with today's compiler techniques. Encouraged by the experimental results, we are currently integrating the analysis and heuristic into a large, widely used research compiler framework. TLB misses due to scattering of data over pages are a major problem also in non-scientific code, where first approaches exist for merging of simple data structures [10]. Inter-loop analysis techniques, such as the matrix-based work of Ahmed et al. [1] can likely be used to extend inter-loop-nest analysis beyond the current heuristic.

References

1. Ahmed N, Mateev N, Pingali K (2000) Synthesizing Transformations for Locality Enhancement of Imperfectly-Nested Loop Nests. In: Proceedings of the International Conference on Supercomputing.
2. Anderson J, Berc L, Dean J, Ghemawat S, Henzinger M, Leung S-T, Sites RL, Vandevoorde M, Waldspurger C, Weihl W (1997) Continuous Profiling: Where Have All the Cycles Gone? ACM Transactions on Computer Systems 15(4):357–390.

3. Bacon D, Graham S, Sharp O (1994) Compiler Transformations for High-Performance Computing. ACM Computing Surveys 26(4):345–420.
4. Bacon D, Chow J-H, Dz-ching R, Muthukumar K, Sarkar V (1994) A Compiler Framework for Restructuring Data Declarations to Enhance Cache and TLB Effectiveness. In: Proceedings of CASCON, pp. 270–282.
5. Burnett G, Coffman E (1970) A Study of Interleaved Memory Systems. In: Proceedings of AFIPS 1970 Spring Joint Computer Conference, pp. 467–474.
6. Calder B, Krintz C, John S, Austin T (1998) Cache-Conscious Data Placement. ACM SIGPLAN Notices 33(11):139–149.
7. Cierniak M, Li W (1997) Interprocedural Array Remapping. In: Proceedings of PACT, pp. 146–155.
8. Coleman S, McKinley K (1995) Tile Size Selection Using Cache Organization and Data Layout ACM SIGPLAN Conference on Programming Language Design and Implementation. ACM SIGPLAN Notices 30(6):279–290.
9. Genius D (2000) A Case for Array Merging in Memory Hierarchies, Technical Report, University of North Carolina at Chapel Hill.
10. Genius D, Trapp M, Zimmermann W (1998) An Approach to Improve Locality Using Sandwich Types In: Proceedings Types in Compilation Workshop. Springer, Berlin Heidelberg New York, pp. 194–215.
11. Ghosh S, Martonosi M, Malik S (1997) Cache Miss Equations: An Analytical Representation of Cache Misses. In: Proceedings of the 11th International Conference on Supercomputing. ACM Press, New York, pp. 317–324.
12. Hennessy JL, Patterson DA (1996) Computer Architecture — A Quantitative Approach (2nd edition), Morgan Kaufmann, San Francisco.
13. Lebeck A, Wood D (1994) Cache Profiling and the SPEC Benchmarks: A Case Study. IEEE Computer 27(10):15–26.
14. McKinley K, Carr S, Tseng C-W (1996) Improving Data Locality with Loop Transformations ACM TOPLAS 18(4):424–453.
15. Panda P, Nakamura H, Dutt N, Nicolau A (1997) Improving Cache Performance Through Tiling and Data Alignment. In: Proceedings of IRREGULAR 1997. Springer, Berlin Heidelberg New York, pp. 167–185.
16. Rawat J (1993) Static Analysis of Cache Performance for Real-Time Programming Thesis, Iowa State University, Iowa City, IA.
17. Rivera G, Tseng C-W (1998) Data Transformations for Eliminating Conflict Misses. In: Proceedings of ACM SIGPLAN Conference on Programming Language Design and Implementation.
18. Sellappa S, Chatterjee S (2001) Cache-Efficient Multigrid Algorithms. In: Proceedings of the 2001 International Conference on Computational Science.
19. Silicon Graphics Inc. (1996) Performance Analysis using the MIPS R10000 Performance Counters.
20. Srivastava A, Eustace A (1994) ATOM: A system for building customized program analysis tools. In: Proceedings of ACM SIGPLAN Conference on Programming Language Design and Implementation, pp. 196–205.
21. Wolfe M J (1996) High Performance Compilers for Parallel Computing. Addison-Wesley, Reading, MA.

Software Logging under Speculative Parallelization

María Jesús Garzarán[1], Milos Prvulovic[2], José María Llabería[3], Víctor Viñals[1], Lawrence Rauchwerger[4], and Josep Torrellas[2]

[1] Universidad de Zaragoza, Spain
garzaran@posta.unizar.es,victor@posta.unizar.es
[2] University of Illinois, Urbana-Champaign, Urbana, IL, USA
prvulovi@cs.uiuc.edu, torrellas@cs.uiuc.edu
[3] Universitat Politècnica de Catalunya, Barcelona, Spain llaberia@ac.upc.es
[4] Texas A&M University, College Station, TX, USA rwerger@cs.tamu.edu

Abstract. Speculative parallelization aggressively runs hard-to-analyze codes in parallel. Speculative tasks generate an unsafe state, which is typically buffered in caches. Often, a cache may have to buffer the state of several tasks and, as a result, it may have to hold multiple versions of the same variable. Modifying the cache to hold such multiple versions adds complexity and may increase the hit time. It is better to use logging, where the cache only stores the last versions of variables while the log keeps the older ones. Logging also helps to reduce the size of the speculative state to be retained in caches.

This chapter explores efficient software-only logging for speculative parallelization. We show that such an approach is very attractive for programs with tasks that create multiple versions of the same variable. Using simulations of a 16-processor CC-NUMA, we show that the execution time of such programs on a system with software logging is on average 36% shorter than on a system where caches can only hold a single version of any given variable. Furthermore, execution takes only 10% longer than in a system with hardware support for logging.

12.1 Introduction

Speculative thread-level parallelization attempts to extract parallelism from hard-to-analyze codes such as those with pointers, indirectly indexed structures, interprocedural dependences, or input-dependent patterns. The idea is to break the code into tasks and speculatively run some of them in parallel. A combination of software and hardware support tracks memory accesses at run time and, if a dependence violation occurs, the state is repaired and parallel execution resumes. Many different schemes have been proposed, ranging from software-only [9, 16, 17] to hardware-based [4, 7, 8, 10, 12, 13, 14, 15, 18, 20,

21, 23, 25], and targeting small systems [7, 8, 10, 13, 14, 18, 21] or scalable ones [4, 9, 15, 16, 17, 20, 23, 25].

As a speculative task runs, it generates a state that cannot be merged with the the main memory because it is unsafe. Different schemes handle the buffering of the speculative state differently. In some schemes, each task uses its own private range of storage addresses [9, 16, 17, 24]. In most schemes, however, tasks buffer the speculative state dynamically in caches [4, 8, 13, 20], write buffers [10, 21], or special buffers [7, 15]. If the cache or buffer overflows due to conflicts or insufficient capacity, the processor has to stall or squash the task.

The size of the speculative state to be buffered by a processor depends on the working set size of individual tasks and on the load imbalance between tasks. Indeed, task load imbalance may force a processor to buffer the state of several speculative tasks at a time, which increases the overall speculative state size. Many of these tasks may be finished but are still speculative because a predecessor task is still running.

Buffering the speculative state of several tasks at a time may be challenging. Specifically, such a state may contain individual variables that have been written by several tasks. Such variables are common in applications that have quasi-privatization access patterns. In this case, the buffer must be organized to hold several speculative versions of the same variable. Furthermore, for these variables, it is preferable to keep the last version more handy since it is more likely to be needed next.

Past work on speculative parallelization takes different approaches to handling this multi-version problem. Many schemes do not address this issue. Thus, it must be assumed that the processor stalls or squashes the task before creating a second local version of a speculative variable. Other schemes propose redesigning the cache to hold multiple speculative versions of the variable; e.g. in different ways of a set-associative cache [4, 19]. This approach complicates cache operation and may increase cache hit time. Finally, other schemes propose to store only the last versions in the cache and automatically displace older speculative versions to a hardware-managed undo log [23, 25]. With logging, before a task overwrites a speculative version generated by a previous task, the hardware saves the version in the log. Logging is attractive because it reduces the size of the speculative state to be retained in caches and keeps the last versions more handy. However, this solution requires non-trivial hardware support.

Since logging has advantages but also has a noticeable hardware cost, this chapter explores buffering multiple versions through efficient software-only logging. Logs are declared as plain user data structures and are managed in software. We present one efficient implementation. Simulations of a 16-processor CC-NUMA show that software logging is very attractive for programs with tasks that create multiple versions of the same variable. The execution time of such programs on a system with software logging is on average 36% shorter than on a system where caches can only hold a single version of any given variable. Furthermore, execution takes only 10% longer than in a system with hardware support for logging.

This chapter is organized as follows: Section 12.2 introduces speculative parallelization and versioning; Section 12.3 introduces the speculation protocol used; Section 12.4 presents efficient software logging; Section 12.5 discusses our evaluation environment; and Section 12.6 presents the evaluation.

12.2 Speculative Parallelization and Versioning

12.2.1 Basics of Speculative Parallelization

When several tasks run under speculative parallelization, they have a relative order imposed by the sequential code they come from. Consequently, we use the terms predecessor and successor tasks. If we give increasing IDs to successor tasks, the lowest-ID task still running is called non-speculative, while its successors are called speculative.

The set of variables that a speculative task writes is typically kept buffered away in the cache [4, 8, 13, 20], write buffer [10, 21], or special buffers [7, 15]. These variables cannot be merged with main memory because they are unsafe. They are called speculative state variables. Only when the task becomes non-speculative can its speculative state be merged with the main memory.

When the non-speculative task finishes, it commits. Any state that it kept buffered can be merged with memory and the non-speculative status is passed to a successor task. When a speculative task finishes, it cannot commit. The processor on which it ran can start to execute another speculative task, but the cache has to be able to hold the speculative state from the two (or more) uncommitted tasks. Thus, in order to distinguish which of these tasks produced a particular cached variable, we associate a task-ID field with each variable (or line) in the cache.

12.2.2 Multiple Local Speculative Versions

In some cases, the speculative tasks that share a given cache as a reservoir for their speculative state may try to generate multiple versions of the same variable. This occurs, for example, in codes with quasi-privatization access patterns. In this case, if we have a simple cache, we may decide to support only a single version of each variable and, when a second local version is about to be created, stall the processor or squash the task.

One alternative approach that has been proposed is to redesign the cache to hold multiple versions of the same variable at a time [4, 19]. The cache must be able to buffer several lines with the same address tag but different task-IDs. For example, Figure 12.1 (a) shows a cache with three versions of line 0x400 generated by task-IDs i, j, and k. These lines can go into different ways of the same set in a set-associative cache [4, 19].

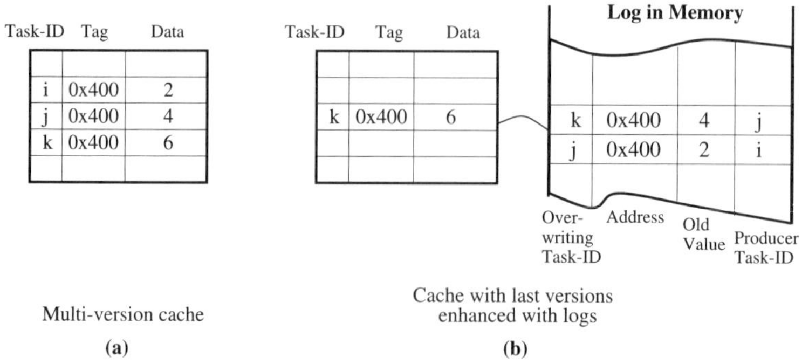

Fig. 12.1. Two ways of keeping multiple local speculative versions.

Unfortunately, this approach adds complexity to the cache. In addition, the extra comparisons needed affect a sensitive timing path and may increase the cache hit latency. Moreover, since all the versions share the cache, the chance of line displacements due to capacity or conflict increases. The result may be lower performance since existing schemes typically prevent the displacement of speculative versions to memory by either squashing the task or stalling the processor.

A final shortcoming of this approach is that it makes it equally hard to access any of the versions of a given variable. Instead, we would like to be able to access the *last* version of the variable faster. Such a version is the one generated by the youngest task that ran on the processor and wrote the variable. It is the version that will be needed to satisfy any subsequent load by this task or younger ones.

The older versions are much less likely to be accessed. For example, they may be accessed by a read request from an old task running on a second processor. Since we expect these events to be relatively infrequent, we could afford to make accesses to non-last versions a bit slower.

Our proposed approach is to keep *last* versions in the cache and copy *non-last* versions to a software *log structure* mapped to the virtual space of the application. A natural implementation of the log is a list of records that are placed in memory contiguously in real time. In general, a log record includes the previous version of the variable (before it is overwritten), its address, the producer task-ID, and the overwriting task-ID. Log records can be displaced from the cache and possibly even bypass it to minimize space contention with last versions. Figure 12.1 (b) shows a cache with its associated log organization in memory. Version k is the last one.

12.2.3 Application Behavior

There are many applications that require individual processors to buffer multiple speculative versions of the same variable. These applications tend to

```
specul_par_do i
  do j = 1, i-1
    xdt(j) = ...
  enddo
  Compute L
  do j = 1, L
    ... = xdt(ind(j))
  enddo
enddo
```

(a) Bdna

```
specul_par_do i
  do j
    do k
      work(k) = work (f(i,j,k))
    enddo
    call foo(work(j))
  enddo
enddo
```

(b) Apsi

```
specul_par_do i
  while (sptr > 0) do
    ... = stack(sptr)
    do j
      if (cond)
        stack(sptr) = ...
        Compute sptr
    enddo
  enddo
enddo
```

(c) Tree

Fig. 12.2. Examples of non-analyzable loops that exhibit quasi-privatization access patterns. The outermost loop is speculatively run in parallel.

exhibit quasi-privatization access patterns. Under this pattern, tasks create new versions of a given variable without reading older versions. Of course, the pattern should not be fully analyzable since otherwise the compiler would have privatized the variable and the tasks could execute in parallel without speculation.

Figure 12.2 shows simplified loops taken from the applications used later in this chapter that exhibit quasi-privatization access patterns. The arrays accessed with quasi-privatization patterns are *xdt()*, *work()*, and *stack()*. These loops are speculatively parallelized because the compiler cannot prove that iterations are independent.

Applications with these patterns have a higher tendency to require the buffering of multiple versions per processor if the tasks exhibit load imbalance. In this case, processors that execute short tasks accumulate many speculative versions. Note that the imbalance may be intrinsic to the application or can come from external causes that selectively delay the execution of some tasks. Such causes can be operating system interrupts or tasks from a different application grabbing a processor.

Table 12.1 estimates the weight of quasi-privatizable data and the load imbalance in our applications (discussed in Section 12.5.2) running on our simulated 16-processor architecture of Section 12.5.1. Column *Priv* shows how much data generated by task $i-1$ were speculatively written by task i without reading it first. This quantity estimates the amount of quasi-privatizable data in task i. The table also shows the rest of the data speculatively written by task i (*Other*) and the sum of the two items (*Total*). From the table, we see that tasks in *P3m*, *Tree*, *Apsi*, and *Bdna* write a lot of quasi-privatizable data, both in absolute and relative terms. In *Dsmc3d* and *Track*, they do not.

Table 12.1. Application characteristics that affect the need for individual processors to buffer multiple versions of the same variable. The data corresponds to 16-processor runs.

Appl	Spec Written Footprint per Task (kB)			# Uncommitted Tasks per Proc		Need Multiple-Version Buffer?
	Priv	Other	Total	Maximum	Average	
P3m	1.5	0.2	1.7	100	50.0	Yes
Tree	0.9	0.0	0.9	8	1.5	Yes
Apsi	12.0	8.0	20.0	4	1.8	Yes
Bdna	23.5	0.2	23.7	4	1.6	Yes
Dsmcd3d	0.0	0.8	0.8	3	1.1	No
Track	0.0	2.3	2.3	4	1.3	No
Average	6.3	1.9	8.2	20.5	9.5	–

Columns 5–6 show the number of uncommitted tasks that keep their speculative state buffered per individual processor at a time. The table shows the maximum and average values for the execution of the applications. Large values in these two columns suggest load imbalance. These columns show that each processor may need to buffer the state of more than one speculative task at a time. Even if we redesigned a set-associative cache to keep each version of a given variable in a different bank, the cache would require too high an associativity in *P3m* and *Tree*. *Apsi* and *Bdna* are less imbalanced, although they can still require up to four versions of the same variable to be buffered per processor. Thus, we expect that *P3m*, *Tree*, *Apsi*, and *Bdna* will benefit from multiple-version buffering supports.

12.3 Speculation Protocol Used

In [23], speculative accesses are marked with special load and store instructions that trigger the protocol. In each node, the first speculative access to a shared data page prompts the OS to allocate a page of *local time stamps* in the local memory of the node. These time stamps will record, for each word, the ID of the youngest local task that writes the word (*PMaxW*) and the ID of the youngest local task that reads it without writing it first (*PMaxR1st*). The latter operation is also called *exposed load*. These local time stamps are needed by the protocol and are automatically updated by dependence-detecting hardware with small overhead [23].

12.4 Efficient Software Logging

12.4.1 Log Operations

A logging system must support four operations, namely saving a new record in the log (*Insertion*), finding a record in the log (*Retrieval*), unwinding the log to undo tasks (*Recovery*), and freeing up log records after their information is useless for retrieval or recovery (*Recycle*).

Figure 12.3 shows simple per-processor software structures that we use for logging. The log buffer is broken down into fixed-sized sectors that will be used to log individual tasks. The compiler estimates the size of the sectors and log buffer based on the number of writes in a task and the number of tasks per processor that are likely to be uncommitted at a time, respectively.

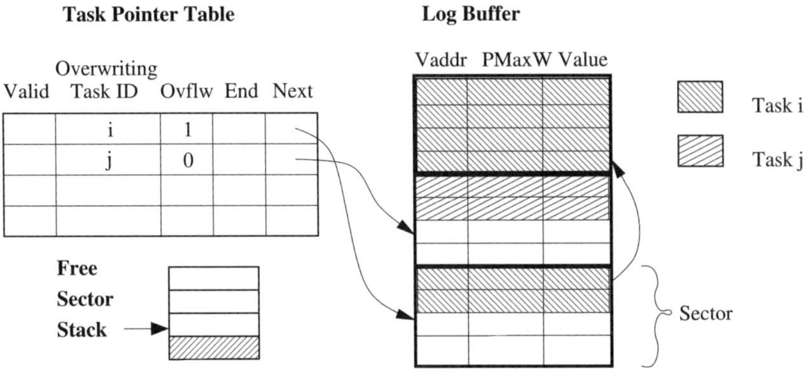

Fig. 12.3. Simple per-processor software structures that we use for logging.

When a task starts running, it is dynamically assigned an entry in the Task Pointer Table and one sector in the Log Buffer. Free sectors are obtained from the Free Sector Stack. Each entry in the Task Pointer Table has two pointer fields: Next, which points to the next entry to fill, and End which points to the end entry to check for overflow. If the task needs more entries than a sector, we dynamically assign another sector and link it to the previous one while we set the Overflow bit and update the End pointer. If the Free Sector Stack runs out of entries, we resize the Log Buffer and Stack accordingly.

Insertion. Insertion is the most overhead-sensitive operation since it occurs frequently. At compile time, the compiler instruments stores in the code with instructions to save a log record. As shown in Figure 12.3, a record includes the following information about the variable that is about to be updated: its virtual address (the only one the software knows), its value before the update, and its producer Task-ID (*PMaxW*). *PMaxW* is obtained from the local time stamp page (Section 12.3). After the record is inserted at run time, the Next pointer is incremented. At the end of a task, all the records that it generated are in contiguous locations in one or more sectors, easily retrievable through the Task Pointer Table with the task ID.

Recycle. When a processor finishes a task, it tries to commit it [23]. Based on the resulting value of the commit point, it can identify which of the entries in its Task Pointer Table correspond to committed tasks. The data in those tasks' sectors will not be needed in the future and, therefore, the sectors can be recycled. Consequently, we invalidate the corresponding Task Pointer Table entries and return the sectors to the Free Sector Stack.

Recovery and **Retrieval.** Recovery occurs when we need to undo tasks after the detection of an out-of-order RAW dependence. Retrieval occurs when an in-order RAW dependence cannot simply be satisfied by the underlying coherence protocol because the requested version is not in a cache: another task running on the producer processor has overwritten the variable pushing the desired version into the log. Since these two cases happen infrequently, we solve them with software exception handlers that access the logs.

12.4.2 Insertion Overhead

Inserting a record in the log of Figure 12.3 involves collecting the items to save, saving them in sequence using the *Next* pointer, and advancing the pointer. Figure 12.4 shows the MIPS assembly instructions added before every speculative store that we log. All memory accesses in the figure are non-speculative. Overall, we need 9 instructions: 1 to check for sector overflow, 6 to collect and insert the information, 1 to increment the pointer, and 1 to update the cached time stamp.

Figure 12.4 shows two special instructions, namely *load half-word time stamp (lh_ts)* and *store half-word time stamp (sh_ts)*. These are special instructions that load the 16-bit *PMaxW* local time stamp of the variable, and update it (the cached copy only), respectively. *lh_ts* loads the time stamp so that it can be saved in the log. *sh_ts* updates the cached copy with the ID of the executing task. This is done to prevent the cached copy from becoming stale. The reason is that the time stamp pages in memory are read and updated in hardware by the speculation protocol as it tries to detect dependence violations (Section 12.3). They cannot be updated in software.

We can reduce the overhead of the instrumentation by noting that the log only needs to save the value overwritten by the *first store* to the variable in the task. Consequently, for variables accessed with speculative accesses, we can modify the instrumentation in Figure 12.4 to dynamically test whether or not a store is a first store in the task and log it only if it is. Such testing can be done by comparing the *PMaxW* of the variable with the ID of the executing task. If they are the same, the store is not a first store. A detailed discussion of this topic is beyond the scope of this chapter.

```
            ; r1 = upper limit of the sector. r5 = ID of the executing task
            ; r2 = address in memory to insert the log record.
            ; offset(r3) = address of the variable to update.
            bgt   r1, r2, insertion          ; check for sector overflow
            ... allocate another sector
insertion:
            addu  r4, r3, offset             ; compute address of variable
            sw    r4, 0(r2)                  ; store in log
            lh_ts r4, offset(r3)             ; load the 16-bit PMaxW time stamp
            sw    r4, 4(r2)                  ; store as a full word in log
            lw    r4, offset(r3)             ; load value of variable
            sw    r4, 8(r2)                  ; store in log
            addu  r2, r2, log_record_size    ; increment pointer
            sh_ts r5, offset(r3)             ; update cached PMaxW
```

Fig. 12.4. Instructions added before an instrumented speculative store.

12.4.3 Alternative: Hardware-Only Logging

In the evaluation section, we will compare our software logging system to a hardware-only implementation of logging described in [25]. The latter uses a logging module embedded in the directory controller of each node. Log record insertion is done in the background with no overhead visible to the program. Similarly, recycling has practically no overhead. The log is kept in memory, thereby avoiding cache pollution.

12.5 Evaluation Methodology

12.5.1 Simulation Environment

We use an execution-driven simulation system based on MINT [22] to model in detail a CC-NUMA with 16 nodes. Each node contains a fraction of the shared memory and directory as well as a 4-issue dynamic superscalar. The processor has a 32-entry instruction window and 4 Int, 2 FP, and 2 Ld/St units. It supports 8 pending loads and 16 stores. It also has a 2 k-entry BTB with 2-bit saturating counters. Each node has a 2-way 32 kB L1 D-cache and a 4-way 2Mb L2 cache, both with 64 byte lines and a write-back policy. Contention is accurately modeled. The average no-contention round-trip latencies from the processor to the on-chip L1 cache, L2 cache, memory in the local node, and memory in a remote node that is 2 and 3 protocol hops away are 1, 12, 60, 208, and 291 cycles, respectively.

We use release consistency and a cache coherence protocol like that of DASH. Pages of shared data are allocated round-robin across the nodes. We choose this allocation because our applications have irregular access patterns and the tasks are dynamically scheduled; it is virtually impossible to optimize shared data allocation at compile time. Private data are allocated locally.

For speculation, we use the protocol of Section 12.3. In the evaluation, we simulate all software overhead, including allocation and recycling of log sectors, and the dynamic scheduling and committing of tasks. We wrote software handlers for parallel recovery after a dependence violation and to retrieve data from logs. In addition, a processor that allocates a page of time stamps is penalized with 4,000 cycles.

12.5.2 Workload

We use a set of scientific applications where a large fraction of the code is not analyzable by a parallelizing compiler. These applications are: *Apsi* from SPECfp2000 [11], *Track* and *Bdna* from Perfect [2], *Dsmc3d* from HPF-2 [5], *P3m* from NCSA, and *Tree* from the University of Hawaii [1]. We use the Polaris parallelizing compiler [3] to identify the non-analyzable sections and prepare them for speculative parallelization. The source of non-analyzability is that the dependence structure is either too complicated or unknown because it depends on input data. For example, the code often has doubly subscripted accesses to arrays. The code also has sections that have complex control flow, with conditionals that depend on array values and jump to code sections that modify the same or other arrays. In these sections, Polaris marks the speculative references, which will trigger speculation protocol actions. Polaris also identifies store instructions that may need to be logged, and we instrument them according to Section 12.4.

Table 12.2. Application characteristics. In *Apsi*, we use an input grid of $512x1x64$. In *P3m*, while the loop has 97,336 iterations, we only use the first 9,000 iterations in the evaluation. Finally, in *Dsmc3d*, the data correspond to unrolling the loop 15 times.

Appl	Non-Analyzable Sections (Loops)	% of Tseq	# of Invoc	Iters per Invoc	Instruc per Iter
P3m	*pp_do100*	56.5	1	97336	69165
Tree	*accel_do10*	79.1	41	1024	28746
Apsi	*run_do[20,30,40,50,60,100]*	29.3	900	63	102639
Bdna	*actfor_do240*	44.2	1	1499	103339
Dsmc3d	*move3_goto100*	41.2	80	46777	5442
Track	*nlfilt_do300*	58.1	56	502	5577
Average		51.4	180	24533	52484

Table 12.2 shows the non-analyzable sections in each application. These sections are loops. The table lists the weight of these loops relative to the total

sequential execution time of the application (%Tseq), with the I/O excluded. This value, which is obtained on a single-processor Sun Ultra 5 workstation, is on average 51.4%. The table also shows the number of invocations of these loops during program execution, the average number of iterations per invocation, and the average number of instructions per iteration. Note that all the data presented in the evaluation, including speedups, refer only to the code sections in the table.

12.6 Evaluation

We compare multi-processors that support no logging, software logging, or hardware logging. Under no logging, a node can only hold in its cache hierarchy a single version for each variable; if the processor is about to overwrite a local version produced by an uncommitted task, the processor stalls. For software logging, we use our scheme of Sections 12.4.1 and 12.4.2. Finally, for hardware logging, we use the support of Section 12.4.3.

Figure 12.5 compares the execution time of these three systems, called *NoLog*, *Sw*, and *Hw*, respectively. They run on 16 processors. For each application, the bars are normalized to *NoLog* and broken down into execution of instructions (*Useful*), waiting on data, control, and structural pipeline hazards (*Hazard*), synchronization (*Sync*), waiting on data from the memory system (*Memory*), and stall when attempting to overwrite an uncommitted version in *NoLog* (*Stall*). A sixth category, measuring the execution of software handlers for data recovery and retrieval, is too small to be seen. Finally, the numbers on top of each bar show the speedup relative to the sequential execution of the code, with all the application data placed on the local memory of the single active processor.

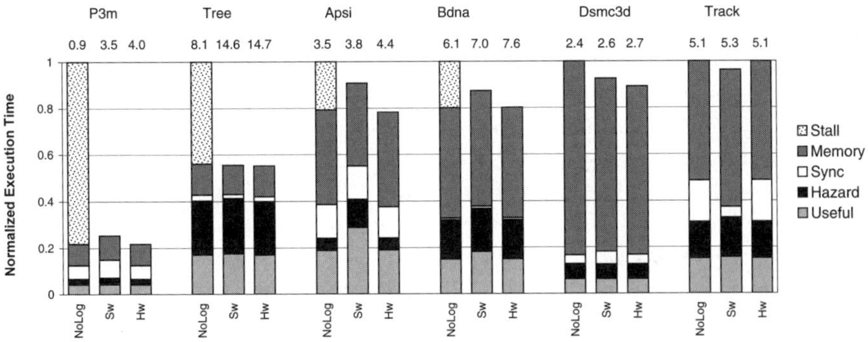

Fig. 12.5. Execution time on a 16-node multiprocessor with different logging supports.

A comparison between *NoLog* and *Sw* reveals the benefits of software logging. With software logging, processors do not stall when they overwrite local uncommitted versions. Thus, *Stall* disappears. However, software logging introduces extra instructions and memory system accesses to generate and maintain the log. As a result, it tends to have higher *Useful* and *Memory* times. Indirectly, the other times (*Hazard* and *Sync*) may also increase.

To understand these results, note that logging is most beneficial in applications that have both quasi-privatization access patterns and load imbalance. *P3m*, *Tree*, *Apsi*, and *Bdna* have quasi-privatization patterns and, of these, *P3m* and *Tree* have the largest imbalances. These observations are consistent with Figure 12.5. The figure shows that *P3m*, *Tree*, and, to a lesser extent, *Apsi* and *Bdna* have *Stall* under *NoLog*. *Sw* removes all *Stall* and speeds up these applications, especially *P3m* and *Tree*. For *Dsmc3d* and *Track*, the difference between *NoLog* and *Sw* is an indirect effect of the different data layouts, which cause different cache conflicts, and the different execution timings, which result in different dependence violations being found at run time. Overall, software logging is effective: *Sw* is on average 36% faster than *NoLog* for the four applications with quasi-privatization patterns. If we take the average of all the applications, the speedup of the 16-processor execution increases from 4.3 under *NoLog* to 6.1 under *Sw*.

The *Hw* system also eliminates the *Stall* time like the *Sw* system. Furthermore, it induces negligible overhead. The cost, of course, is special hardware support. Comparing *Sw* to *Hw*, we see the overhead of software logging. From Figure 12.5, we see that this overhead is very modest. Indeed, for the four applications with quasi-privatization patterns, the average overhead is only 9% of the *Sw* execution time. Therefore, we conclude that software logging is efficient as well as effective.

12.7 Related Work

Different schemes handle speculative state buffering differently. For instance, some schemes do not buffer the speculative state because they do not allow on-the-fly repair on a violation [9, 16, 24]. If a violation occurs, the state rolls back to the beginning of the speculative section. The schemes that support on-the-fly repair typically buffer the state in caches [4, 8, 13, 20], write buffers [10, 21], or special buffers [7, 15]. In some schemes, a new task cannot start on a processor until the task that previously ran there commits [7, 8, 13, 14, 21]. In this case, there is no need to support the speculative state from multiple tasks in the buffer.

Several schemes support several uncommitted tasks on a processor, including Run-Time Speculation (RTS) [25], Hydra [10], Stampede [20], and MDT [4]. In RTS, they handle multiple versions with hardware logs. In Hydra, a new buffer is allocated when a new task starts to execute. The applications that they use only need up to 2 kB of buffering storage. In Stampede, they suggest either to exploit cache associativity to hold multiple versions or to stall or squash the task [19]. However, since their applications do not need support for multiple writers [20], they do not evaluate this issue. In MDT, they also exploit cache associativity, aided by a victim cache, to keep multiple versions [4].

Finally, logging is also used in the schemes presented in SUDS [6] and RTS [25]. RTS uses hardware logs as described in Section 12.4.3. The SUDS system, proposed for RAW, uses software logs that only keep a single version per variable [6].

12.8 Conclusion

A good solution to buffer a speculative state with multi-version variables is to enhance a cache hierarchy with logs. In this chapter we showed that software logging is inexpensive and delivers high performance for applications with quasi-privatization patterns and load imbalance. Using simulations of a 16-processor CC-NUMA, we show that the execution time of such applications on a system with software logging is on average 36% shorter than on a system where caches can only hold a single version of any given variable. Furthermore, execution takes only 10% longer than in a system with hardware support for logging.

Acknowledgments

This work was supported in part by the National Science Foundation under grants CCR-9970488, EIA-9975018, EIA-0081307, and EIA-0072102; by the CICYT of Spain under grant TIC 2001-0995-C02-02; and by gifts from IBM and Intel.

References

1. J. E. Barnes. ftp://hubble.ifa.hawaii.edu/pub/barnes/treecode/. University of Hawaii, 1994.
2. M. Berry et al. The Perfect Club Benchmarks: Effective Performance Evaluation of Supercomputers. *International Journal of Supercomputer Applications*, 3(3):5–40, Fall 1989.
3. W. Blume, R. Doallo, R. Eigenmann, J. Grout, J. Hoeflinger, T. Lawrence, J. Lee, D. Padua, Y. Paek, B. Pottenger, L. Rauchwerger, and P. Tu. Advanced Program Restructuring for High-Performance Computers with Polaris. *IEEE Computer*, 29(12):78–82, December 1996.
4. M. Cintra, J. F. Martinez, and J. Torrellas. Architectural Support for Scalable Speculative Parallelization in Shared-Memory Multiprocessors. In *Proceedings of the 27th Annual International Symposium on Computer Architecture*, pages 13–24, June 2000.

5. I. Duff, R. Schreiber, and P. Havlak. HPF-2 Scope of Activities and Motivating Applications. Technical Report CRPC-TR94492, Rice University, November 1994.
6. M. Frank, W. Lee, and S. Amarasinghe. A Software Framework for Supporting General Purpose Applications on Raw Computation Fabrics. Technical Report MIT/LCS Technical Memo 619, July 2001.
7. M. Franklin and G. S. Sohi. ARB: A Hardware Mechanism for Dynamic Reordering of Memory References. *IEEE Transactions on Computers*, 45(5):552–571, May 1996.
8. S. Gopal, T. N. Vijaykumar, J. E. Smith, and G. S. Sohi. Speculative Versioning Cache. In *Proceedings of the 4th International Symposium on High-Performance Computer Architecture*, pages 195–205, February 1998.
9. M. Gupta and R. Nim. Techniques for Speculative Run-Time Parallelization of Loops. In *Proceedings of Supercomputing 1998*, pages 1–12, November 1998.
10. L. Hammond, M. Willey, and K. Olukotun. Data Speculation Support for a Chip Multiprocessor. In *8th International Conference on Architectural Support for Programming Languages and Operating Systems*, pages 58–69, October 1998.
11. J. L. Henning. SPEC CPU2000: Measuring Performance in the New Millennium. *IEEE Computer*, 33(7):28–35, July 2000.
12. T. Knight. An Architecture for Mostly Functional Languages. In *ACM Lisp and Functional Programming Conference*, pages 500–519, August 1986.
13. V. Krishnan and J. Torrellas. A Chip-Multiprocessor Architecture with Speculative Multithreading. *IEEE Transactions on Computers, Special Issue on Multithreaded Architectures*, 48(9)866–880, September 1999.
14. P. Marcuello and A. González. Clustered Speculative Multithreaded Processors. In *Proceedings of the 1999 International Conference on Supercomputing (ICS'99)*, pages 365–372, June 1999.
15. M. Prvulovic, M. J. Garzarán, L. Rauchwerger, and J. Torrellas. Removing Architectural Bottlenecks to the Scalability of Speculative Parallelization. In *Proceedings of the 28th Annual International Symposium on Computer Architecture*, pages 204–215, July 2001.
16. L. Rauchwerger and D. Padua. The LRPD Test: Speculative Run-Time Parallelization of Loops with Privatization and Reduction Parallelization. In *Proceedings of the SIGPLAN 1995 Conference on Programming Language Design and Implementation*, pages 218–232, June 1995.
17. P. Rundberg and P. Stenström. Low-Cost Thread-Level Data Dependence Speculation on Multiprocessors. In *Fourth Workshop on Multithreaded Execution, Architecture and Compilation*, December 2000.
18. G. S. Sohi, S. Breach, and S. Vajapeyam. Multiscalar Processors. In *Proceedings of the 22nd Annual International Symposium on Computer Architecture*, pages 414–425, June 1995.
19. J. G. Steffan, C. B. Colohan, and T. C. Mowry. Architectural Support for Thread-Level Data Speculation. Technical report, CMU-CS-97-188, School of Computer Science, Carnegie Mellon University, November 1997.
20. J. G. Steffan, C. B. Colohan, A. Zhai, and T. C. Mowry. A Scalable Approach to Thread-Level Speculation. In *Proceedings of the 27th Annual International Symposium on Computer Architecture*, pages 1–12, June 2000.
21. J. Y. Tsai, J. Huang, C. Amlo, D. Lilja, and P. C.Yew. The Superthreaded Processor Architecture. *IEEE Transactions on Computers, Special Issue on Multithreaded Architectures*, 48(9):881–902, September 1999.
22. J. Veenstra and R. Fowler. MINT: A Front End for Efficient Simulation of Shared-Memory Multiprocessors. In *Proceedings of the Second International*

Workshop on Modeling, Analysis, and Simulation of Computer and Telecommunication Systems (MASCOTS'94), pages 201–207, January 1994.

23. Y. Zhang. Hardware for Speculative Run-Time Parallelization in DSM Multiprocessors. Ph.D. Thesis, University of Illinois at Urbana-Champaign, Department of Electrical and Computer Engineering, May 1999.
24. Y. Zhang, L. Rauchwerger, and J. Torrellas. Hardware for Speculative Run-Time Parallelization in Distributed Shared-Memory Multiprocessors. In *Proceedings of the 4th International Symposium on High-Performance Computer Architecture (HPCA)*, pages 162–174, February 1998.
25. Y. Zhang, L. Rauchwerger, and J. Torrellas. Hardware for Speculative Parallelization of Partially-Parallel Loops in DSM Multiprocessors. In *Proceedings of the 5th International Symposium on High-Performance Computer Architecture (HPCA)*, pages 135–139, January 1999.

Part IV

Architecture-Based Memory Tuning

13

An Analysis of Scalar Memory Accesses in Embedded and Multimedia Systems*

Osman S. Unsal[1], Zhenlin Wang[2], Israel Koren[1], C. Mani Krishna[1], and Csaba Andras Moritz[1]

[1] Department of Electrical and Computer Engineering, University of Massachusetts, Amherst, MA, USA
[2] Department of Computer Science, University of Massachusetts, Amherst, MA, USA

Abstract. In an earlier chapter about the FlexCache project [24], we described our vision of a multipartitioned cache where memory accesses are separated based on their static predictability and memory footprint, and managed with various compiler-controlled techniques supported by instruction set architecture extensions or with traditional hardware control.

In line with that vision, this paper describes our work in progress related to the memory performance and memory management of scalars. Our focus in this paper is embedded and multimedia architectures, but the methodology described can be applied to other classes of applications.

In particular, we establish the minimum size of a memory partition that would allow us to map and manage all scalar accesses in a program statically and describe compiler techniques to automate the extraction of this information. We evaluate the impact of register file size on the volume of scalar-related memory accesses and its impact on the applications' overall cache performance. We study the cache behavior of scalar accesses for embedded architectures, including reduction in cache misses due to separation of scalars from other types of memory accesses. Additionally, we develop an energy-efficient data caching strategy for multimedia processors, based on our scalar partitioning approach.

13.1 Introduction and Motivation

The recent proliferation of palmtops, MP3 players, and Internet-enabled wireless phones has ignited interest in embedded and multimedia systems. These systems have to be fast and energy-efficient. As such, they have tight memory/processing requirements. Therefore, understanding their memory/caching behavior is of paramount importance.

In an earlier paper about the FlexCache project [24], we described our vision of a multipartitioned cache where memory accesses are separated based on their static

* Supported in part by NSF grant EIA-0102696.

predictability and memory footprint and managed with various compiler-controlled techniques. This chapter addresses the cache behavior of scalar accesses and its memory footprint in order to enable a fully static memory management in a logical memory partition.

Although prior studies into memory behavior of arrays for embedded and multimedia systems have been conducted, the study of the memory footprint of scalars has lagged behind. Here we report our ongoing work in closing this gap. This chapter presents techniques and results for scalar memory accesses in embedded and multimedia systems. Our preliminary results show promise, and we hope that this work will heighten interest in this area.

This research spans compiler and architectural domains. Our particular contributions in this chapter are threefold:

- First, we experimentally establish the memory size requirements of scalars for embedded and multimedia systems. We present a new compiler algorithm to automatically extract this information, as would be required in a multipartitioned cache.
- Second, by separating scalar accesses from array accesses, we expect decreased cache interference and improved static predictability. This aspect is especially important for hard deadline embedded systems.
- Third, we study the energy implications of partitioning the scalars from nonscalars in media processors. In particular, we compare the energy consumption of a regular data cache with a multipartioned one in which scalars are exclusively assigned to *scratchpad* memory.

The rest of this chapter is organized as follows. In Section 13.2, we provide a brief literature survey and reiterate our motivation. Section 13.3 describes the experimental setup, and we include baseline cases for both embedded and media processors. Section 13.4 provides the results, and we consider separate case studies for embedded (Section 13.4.4) and media (Section 13.4.5) processors. In Section 13.5 we conclude with a brief summary and a synopsis of future work.

13.2 Previous Work

This work builds upon the framework in [23, 24]. Previous memory behavior research efforts primarily targeted array structures [17, 26]. Delazuz et al. [12] discuss energy-directed compiler optimizations for array data structures on partitioned memory architectures; they use the SUIF compiler framework for their analysis. On the other hand, architectural support to improve memory behavior includes split caches, which were discussed in [22]. Albonesi [2] proposed selective cache ways, a vertical cache-partitioning scheme. Benini et al. [4] discuss an optimal SRAM partitioning scheme for an embedded system-on-a-chip. Kin et al. [16] study a small L0 cache that saves energy while reducing performance by 21%. Lee and Tyson [19] use the Mediabench benchmarks and have a coarse-granularity partitioning scheme: they opt for dividing the cache along OS regions for energy reduction. Chiou et al. [10] employ a software-controlled cache and use a partitioning scheme based on cache ways. A recent paper by Huang et al. [15] also uses a way-prediction scheme; their cache partitioning includes a specialized stack cache, and compiler implementation concerns are addressed. Mueller [25] sketched some broad ideas on compiler support for cache partitioning. Combined compiler/architectural efforts toward increasing cache locality [21] have also exclusively focused on arrays. For multimedia systems, one previous work has considered reconfigurable caches [27] using the recently introduced Mediabench benchmark in the performance analysis, with comments on compiler-controlled memory. Burlin [9] concentrates on optimizing stack frame layout in embedded systems. Cooper and Harvey [11] look at compiler-controlled memory. Their analysis includes spill memory requirements for some SPEC'89 and SPEC'95 applications. Engblom [13] and Lee et al. [18] discuss why SPEC is not a suitable benchmark for embedded systems.

The research above, although preoccupied primarily with memory behavior of arrays, provided valuable pointers for our work. In this chapter, we consider scalar memory accesses, not only array or spill memory accesses, and we target embedded systems running a suite of media applications. We develop a compiler heuristic to calculate the memory requirements of scalars and discuss the impact of architectural design choices for embedded and multimedia systems on scalars.

13.3 Experimental Setup

We use the recently developed Mediabench benchmarks [18] in our experiments. Mediabench is a collection of popular embedded applications for communications and multimedia. We chose Mediabench since other benchmarks such as SPECint, DSPstone, or Dhrystone are not suitable for embedded or multimedia systems [6, 13].

We needed a detailed compiler framework that would give us sufficient feedback, be easy to understand, and allow us to change the source code for our modifications. With this in mind, we chose the SUIF/Machsuif suite as our compiler framework. SUIF [28] does high-level passes, while Machsuif [20] makes machine-specific optimizations. Our main focus is Machsuif's register allocator pass, Raga. Raga makes the transition from virtual registers into real registers and performs register allocation. The allocation uses a graph coloring heuristic to assign registers to temporaries. We have made modifications to Raga to annotate scalar memory accesses. The resulting annotated assembler code targets the Alpha processor. We have amended the assembler code by inserting NOP instructions around the scalar memory operations, thus *marking* them. The scalar memory accesses consist of spills and register promotion related memory accesses.

We used the Simplescalar tool suite [7] to run the Alpha binaries and collect the results. We have modified Simplescalar to recognize the scalar memory operations in the *marked* code. Simplescalar was modified to squash the marker instructions on fetch, therefore the marker instructions do not impact the results in any way. Our baseline machine model is a single-issue in-order processor. Lee et. al. [19] use an identical Simplescalar configuration in their power dissipation analysis of region-based caches for embedded processors. Most embedded processors employ an in-order microarchitecture. Using an out-of-order, non-blocking load type of microarchitecture would, to some degree, decrease the performance penalty of scalar/non-scalar conflict cache misses. We use the Wattch [8] tool suite to run the binaries and collect the energy results. Wattch is built on top of the Simplescalar framework. We use the activity sensitive conditional clocking power model in Wattch, i.e., the cache consumes power when it is accessed.

For embedded processors, we did a survey of cache sizes to determine the baseline. As Table 13.1 indicates, embedded processor data cache sizes are usually small. Therefore, we have selected a data cache size of 2 kB for our experiments with embedded systems.

Table 13.1. Data cache sizes for typical embedded CPUs. SRAM scratchpad areas are available in the Samsung ARM7, Hitachi SH-II and Fujitsu SparcLite.

Processor	Cache Size	Processor	Cache Size
Samsung ARM7	2 kB	SparcLite	2 kB
PA-RISC HP	1 kB to 2 kB	Power PC 403GA	1 kB
Hitachi SH-II	4 kB unified	Coldfire 5102	1 kB
Embedded Pentium	8 kB	MIPS Jade	1 to 8 kB
Sandcraft SR-1-GX	8 kB		

On the other hand, as Table 13.2 indicates, the trend is towards larger caches for media processors. Therefore, for media processors, we have selected a 64 kB 2-way cache as our baseline. The table also indicates that media processors do not typically have L2 data caches. Therefore, we only have L1 caches in our baseline architecture. However, our framework is applicable to media processors with L2 caches as well. In this case, one issue that must be addressed is the consistency between the L2 cache and the L1 data + scratchpad. Namely, the block fetched from L2 into the L1 caches could contain a mix of scalar and non-scalar data. We avoid this problem by keeping the block sizes the same across the caches. If the block sizes were different, then the issue could be addressed by clustering the scalar data to the beginning of the address space and padding them appropriately to the size of the L2 cache block size and boundary.

Table 13.2. Cache configurations for typical media processors.

Processor	L1 Cache	L2 Cache
ARM ARM10	32 kB	None
Transmeta Crusoe TM3200	32 kB	None
Transmeta Crusoe TM5400	64 kB	256 kB
Intel StrongARM SA-110	16 kB	None
Equator Map-CA	32 kB	None
Intel StrongArm 110	16 kB	None
Intel StrongARM 1100	8 kB	None

13.4 Results

13.4.1 Motivational Example

We start with a motivational example. Consider the sample program in Figure 13.1. The program consists of x scalar variables being written in a chain-dependent fashion, after which a single array element is written per loop iteration. We define the scalar miss ratio to be the ratio of scalar misses to total misses. Consider the scalar miss ratio for 32 scalars, which is 34%. When we increase the number of scalars to 64, the ratio increases to 46%, although the memory footprint of 32 additional scalars is small. This points to the fact that interference between the scalar and array accesses are chiefly responsible for the increase in the scalar miss ratio. Therefore, if we can separate the array accesses from the scalar accesses, this ratio and the overall miss rate will decrease. Next, we present our results based on Mediabench applications for embedded systems.

```
main( ) {
  loop {
    scalar_accesses;
    array_access[ ];
    }
  }
```

	Number of scalar temporaries		
	32	64	96
Scalar Miss Ratio	0.34	0.46	0.47

	Number of scalar temporaries		
	32	64	96
Scalar Footprint%	1.55	3.10	4.65

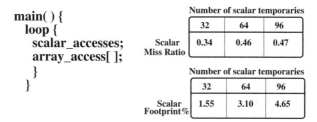

Fig. 13.1. Scalar misses for the synthetic example. Here the integer array is of size 2048, and the columns denote the number of scalar variables in the example. Scalar operations are of the form $Variable_{n+1} = Variable_n \mp constant$. There is a single array access per loop iteration. The loop is iterated 100,000 times. The cache is 2 kB direct-mapped.

13.4.2 Memory Size

We use two yardsticks for experimental evaluation of the scalar memory size requirements of media applications. The first of these is the static memory evaluation. It is static in the sense that the results were extracted by a compile-time analysis of assembler code. We isolated the scalar memory operations in every routine. We then determined the granularity of data by instruction analysis; i.e., the granularity is 8 if the move is a quadword instruction, 2 if it is a word instruction, and so on. We then identified the unique scalar accesses by counting multiple accesses into the same memory location only once and by taking the maximum of the pertaining granularities. The results given in the first column of Table 13.3 indicate that memory size requirements are modest.

Table 13.3. The memory size requirements.

(In Bytes)	Static	Dynamic	(In Bytes)	Static	Dynamic
ADPCM	0	0	EPIC	321	203
G721 Encode	48	32	GSM	202	146
JPEG Encode	502	83	MPEG Encode	2125	604
PEGWIT	98	16	RASTA	618	152
PGP	394	358	MESA	2191	770

However, the static estimate is pessimistic since not all of the data space is traversed during execution. We therefore developed a second yardstick, a dynamic memory evaluation that provides a tighter, more robust bound. We recompiled the

Mediabench benchmarks to record runtime routine use information. We executed each benchmark with its default input set and extracted the *dynamic* call-tree information by using the *gprof* profiling utility. Then, for every routine, we noted the scalar memory requirements as in the static technique. Traversing the tree from the root to each leaf, adding up the unique scalar accesses from each routine, and finding the critical path, (i.e., the path with the maximum size requirement) yields the result. We supply the *dynamic* call-tree for the EPIC application in Figure 13.2 as an example of this process. The memory requirements thus obtained are shown in the second column of Table 13.3. The results suggest that the memory footprint of scalars in media applications for embedded systems is quite small. These results will guide the choice of our architectural optimization schemes. We next present our compiler technique to automate the scalar memory size estimation.

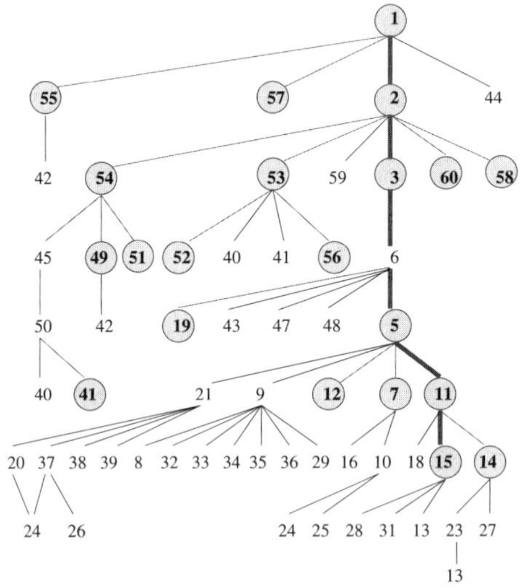

Fig. 13.2. Call-tree and the critical path for the EPIC benchmark. Here the routines are numbered from 1 (the function *main*) to 60. The routines with scalar memory accesses are circled and the path with bold lines is the critical path.

Intuitively, the upper bound of the size of the scalar buffer is the maximum of the distinct scalars along all program execution paths. An algorithm that accurately calculates this bound needs inter-procedural analysis and a complex data-flow analysis. Here we present a good approximation. Our algorithm conservatively assumes that the scalars along all paths are distinct. It simply adds the number of bytes needed for each scalar. Of concern here are loops in the control flow graph and recursive calls in the call graph. We can reuse the scalar space for loops and need only count it once. To accomplish this, the algorithm first marks back edges in the control flow graph that are not going to be traversed. For recursive calls, when there is no register promotion on stack accesses, such as parameters and local variables, the compiler can still ignore the recursion because the scalar buffer can be reused. Otherwise, it will be impossible to compute the upper bound because the depth of recursion is usually unknown at compile time. However, stack accesses for recursive calls usually have no reuse. We can assume that the buffer replacement policy can take care of those scalars. Therefore, in our algorithm, we also count the space for recursive calls only once by ignoring back edges in the call graph.

Our algorithm is divided into two phases. The first phase calculates the bound for each routine, ignoring all routine calls. The second phase traverses the call graph to compute an upper bound for the whole program. In this algorithm, we assume there are three attributes for each basic block and call node, *resolved*, *scalarBound*, and *localScalarSize*. The *localScalarSize* of a basic block is the total number of bytes for all scalars in the basic block. The *localScalarSize* of a routine is its scalar buffer upper bound without taking routine calls into account. The *scalarBound* of a basic block is the scalar bound along all simple paths from the entry block to the current block in the control flow graph. The *scalarBound* of a routine is the scalar bound along all simple paths from the *main* routine to the current routine in the call graph. We say that a basic block or a routine is *resolved* when its *scalarBound* is known. Assuming there are N routines in a program and the maximal number of basic blocks of a routine is M, then the complexity of the algorithms is $O(NM^2 + N^2)$.

13.4.3 Register File Size

For memory analysis of arrays, optimizing the cache is more important than the register file architecture since array accesses seldom use registers. However, for scalars the situation is different. The register file size can have a direct impact on spills and thus impact performance. We therefore analyze the impact of register file sizes on scalars. We take a two-step approach: first, we do a survey of the register file sizes for *current* embedded CPUs and use these results to drive our experiment. Second, we gauge the impact of expanded register file sizes in *future* embedded processors.

Table 13.4 shows the register file sizes on some typical embedded CPUs: the size ranges between 16 and 32 except for the embedded Pentium which has 8 general-purpose registers. We therefore varied the register file size from 16 to 32 in our experiments. We modified Machsuif passes and architectural definitions to output binaries for different register file sizes. Then, we noted the static number of scalars inserted into the instruction stream. The results in Figure 13.3 show that there are a considerable number of scalar memory accesses for 16 registers. Another point is that for some particular benchmarks (e.g., JPEG Encode), the number of scalar memory accesses is more dramatically decreased than others as more registers become available. This is because the register pressure is more unevenly distributed in those benchmarks, i.e., only a few routines exhibit intense register pressure. Once those are relieved through additional registers, the decrease in scalar register spills is more steep.

Usually, the current methods and techniques used in general microprocessors migrate to embedded systems with a couple of years time lag. We believe that the integer register file sizes will follow the same trend. Therefore, we project the embedded CPU integer register file size to grow to 64, 128, and maybe 256. We extended our analysis by modifying Machsuif to output code for larger register file sizes. The results are shown in Figure 13.4. Note that for large register file sizes all the register spills are eliminated, the only remaining scalar memory operations are related to register promotion. This is the reason for the flattening out of the scalar memory

Algorithm 1 Find Routine Scalar Memory Requirement from CFG

```
Require: localScalarSize of block
  /* Phase 1 */
  /* For each routine, traverse its control flow graph */
  for each routine do
    calculate scalar bound for each basic block;
    mark back edges in CFG;
    /* Add the entry back block to workList */
    E = entry basic block;
    E.scalarBound = E.localScalarSize;
    E.resolved = true;
    workList = successors of E;
    while !empty(workList) do
      B = next element in workList;
      allResolved = true;
      maxBound = 0;
      /* check if all B's predecessors are resolved */
      for each predecessor P of B do
        if the edge (P,B) is not marked and P is not resolved then
          allResolved = false;
          break;
        else
          maxBound = max(maxBound, P.scalarBound);
        end if
      end for
      if allResolved then
        remove B from workList;
        B.resolved = true;
        B.scalarBound = maxBound + B.localScalarSize;
        add all unresolved successors of B to workList;
      end if
    end while
    set localScalarSize of the current routine as scalarBound of its exit block
  end for
```

Table 13.4. Integer register file sizes in current embedded CPUs.

Processor	Register File Size	Processor	Register File Size
Samsung ARM7	15	SparcLite	32
PA-RISC HP	16+16	Power PC 403GA	32
Hitachi SH-II	16	Coldfire 5102	16
Embedded Pentium	8	MIPS Jade	32
Sandcraft SR-1-GX	32		

accesses. The implication is that, as far as scalars in media applications are concerned, increasing the register file size will not bring any additional benefits. This is especially true for register file sizes larger than 64. Thus, we experimentally establish what has been an industry insight with general-purpose CPUs [5]. This provides guidance to the designers of future embedded/multimedia CPUs. The number of in-

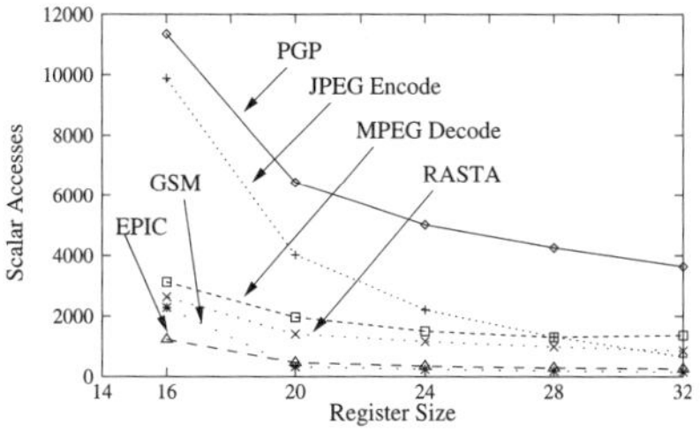

Fig. 13.3. Number of scalar memory accesses With register file size.

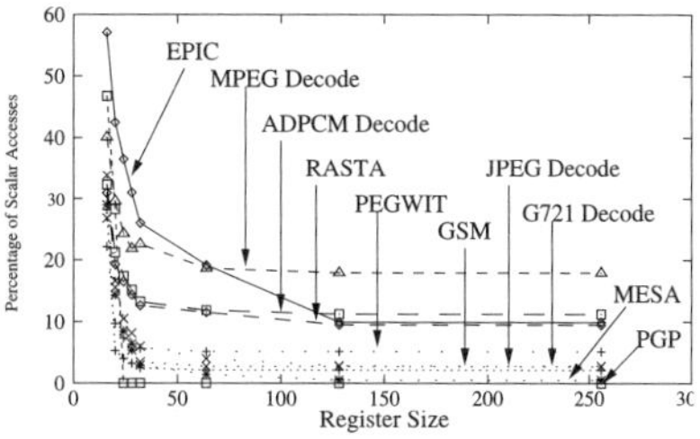

Fig. 13.4. Percentage of scalar memory accesses for extended register file size.

teger general-purpose registers should be at most 64; the additional chip real estate could be devoted to other functional units (e.g., caches) that offer better incremental performance.

Our analysis also includes a cross-architectural comparison, as seen in Figure 13.5. We used an Intel X86-family targeted version of Simplescalar for this analysis. The 8-register X86 has significantly more scalar memory accesses than the 32-register Alpha. This is due to Machsuif's register allocator, Raga. Raga is based on a graph coloring heuristic and, as argued in [1], register allocation based on graph-coloring is sensitive to the number of registers, in particular when the number of available registers is low. Here, we experimentally verify this argument. *Therefore, compiler designers for embedded CPUs, which typically have fewer registers, should develop new register allocation heuristics.* Work in this direction has already started [1]. We also comment on an important property leading to a dual conclusion. Sometimes, increasing the register file size can increase scalar memory accesses. This may seem counterintuitive at first. However, consider Figure 13.6 for the MPEG benchmark. As the register size is increased from 28 to 32, the number of scalar memory accesses actually increases. This is due to the graph-coloring heuristic used in Raga to assign registers. The use of this heuristic creates a phenomenon similar to the Belady anomaly in paging [3]. The conclusion that can be drawn is that *embedded CPU designers should be aware of the characteristics of their target compiler in choosing their design point.* In summary, the experiments above show that the compiler/architecture coupling in embedded systems is stronger than previously assumed and should be considered at the design phase.

13.4.4 Case Study: Scalar Data Remapping for Embedded Processors

We assume that the reorganization and separation of scalar and array accesses are compiler level tasks. As mentioned in Section 13.2, there are several cache reorganization options for scalars. Vertical or horizontal partitioning [2], which partition the cache along cache ways and lines, respectively, can be used. Another option is to use a scratchpad SRAM area and direct the scalar memory accesses to this partition. Here, an appropriate partitioning option must be selected. Vertical partitioning schemes are wasteful: the existing cache has to be divided into a power of 2, and our results indicate that the memory footprint of the scalars in embedded media applications is small. Instead, we advocate the use of a scratchpad SRAM area. Separate SRAMs are widely used in DSPs: they are typically used to hold

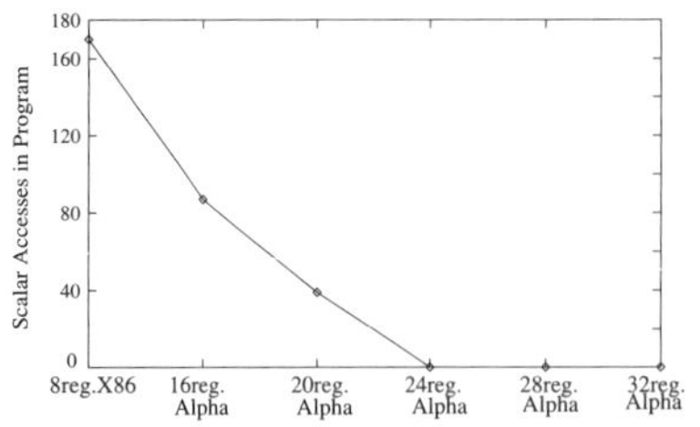

Fig. 13.5. Scalar accesses for IntelX86 and Alpha.

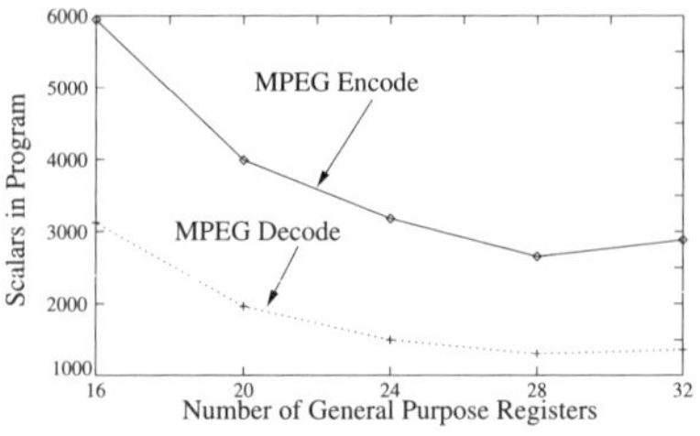

Fig. 13.6. Effect of register coloring heuristic.

frequently used data such as floating-point constants. A scratchpad SRAM guarantees single-cycle access time to scalars since there are no cache misses. Moreover, the on-chip scratchpad SRAMs have small sizes, making this scheme ideal for data with a small memory footprint such as the scalars in embedded media applications. This is also beneficial for a software-directed approach since as shown in [24], every hardware partition can be logically partitioned and the scalar buffer area can be implemented as a logical partition. We assume the SRAM area to be sufficient to hold all the scalar data. No architectural modifications are necessary since many embedded processors have a scratchpad buffer area, see Table 13.1.

Therefore, if the embedded processor is equipped with a scratchpad SRAM area, the scalar memory accesses can be annotated by the compiler and remapped to the scratchpad. If not, then the Instruction Set Architecture (ISA) can be augmented by special load-store instructions that would channel the scalar data to a separate cache area. The modifications to the compiler are minimal and consist of statically determining the application memory size and mapping the scalar accesses to the special load-store instructions.

We ran the Mediabench benchmarks with the baseline cache settings; we compared this with the same cache settings but with the scalar accesses being redirected to the SRAM buffer area by the compiler. We stress that capacity misses are not an issue here: Fritts et al. [14] have shown that data working set sizes of the considered benchmarks are very small. The results for selected benchmarks are presented in Table 13.5. The improvement depends on the particular benchmark and ranges between 0.6 and 9.5%. This improvement is more pronounced for the benchmarks that have a significant percentage of scalars in their memory accesses. Our results also affirm that scratchpad warmup costs are extremely small compared to the number of cache misses.

We also replicated our experiments for a 2 kB 2-way cache organization. Table 13.6 shows the results. Note that the percentage improvements due to remapping of scalars to the scratchpad are similar to the direct-mapped cache results.

13.4.5 Case Study: Scratchpad Energy Savings for Media Processors

Unless otherwise stated, all the results in this section are with a scratchpad of size 1024 bytes, and the baseline cache is 64 kB 2-way associative. We ran the benchmarks

Table 13.5. The number of misses for the baseline and for a design with a scalar SRAM buffer are shown in the first and third columns, respectively. The second column shows the baseline miss rate. The percentage drop in miss rate for remapping scalars to the scratchpad is given in the fourth column. The fifth column is the percentage of scalar accesses to total memory accesses. The last column shows the scratchpad buffer warmup costs, i.e., the cost associated with promoting scalars from the main memory to the scratchpad SRAM.

	Baseline	Miss (%)	Partitioned	Improvement(%)	Scalars(%)	Warmup
EPIC	1753939	13.6	1589065	9.5	32.0	15598
G721	1377675	2.0	1369395	0.6	4.5	9
GSM	239914	0.5	230549	3.9	2.3	19
JPEG	228644	9.3	224185	1.9	1.1	21
RASTA	216173	6.9	203373	5.9	16.0	59

Table 13.6. The results for the 2-way associative cache. The first column shows the baseline miss rate. The percentage reduction in miss rate due to remapping is shown in the second column.

	Miss Rate(%)	Improvement(%)
EPIC	12.7	6.0
G721	1.2	0.1
GSM	0.5	5.5
JPEG	5.9	1.6
RASTA	5.3	9.2

using the modified Wattch/Simplescalar and collected the data cache energy results. Figure 13.7 shows the percentage energy savings for our 32 general-purpose register media processor model. We save 10.7% energy on average by using our scheme.

Many media processors, such as the ARM, have a smaller number of registers, usually 16. Therefore, we have repeated our energy analysis for a 16-register version of our media processor. For 16 registers we have significantly more scalar memory accesses due to register pressure. The results are also shown in Figure 13.7. Our technique in this case saves an average of 38.2% in energy.

In fact, we show that we can be just as energy-efficient with a 16-register media processor with a scratchpad SRAM as with a 32-register processor with no scratchpad, see Figure 13.8. Actually, the overall energy savings are even greater since we just concentrate on the data cache energy consumption: a 16-register file consumes substantially less power than a 32-register file.

13.5 Conclusion and Future Work

We have performed an analysis of scalars in embedded systems. We established the memory requirements of scalars in embedded applications and presented a compiler algorithm to extract this information. We then discussed several architectural issues pertaining to scalars in embedded systems.

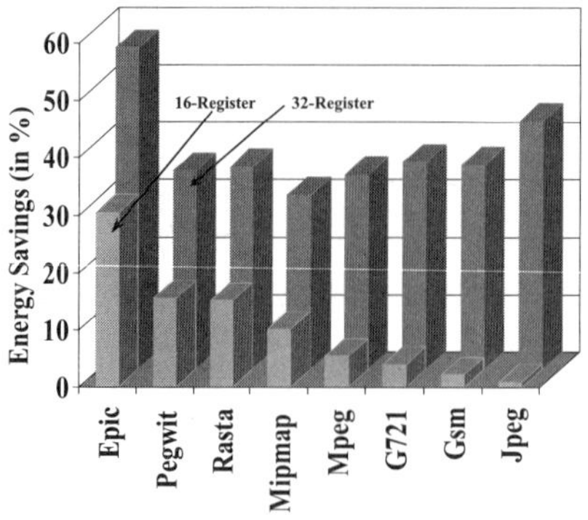

Fig. 13.7. Scratchpad Energy Savings.

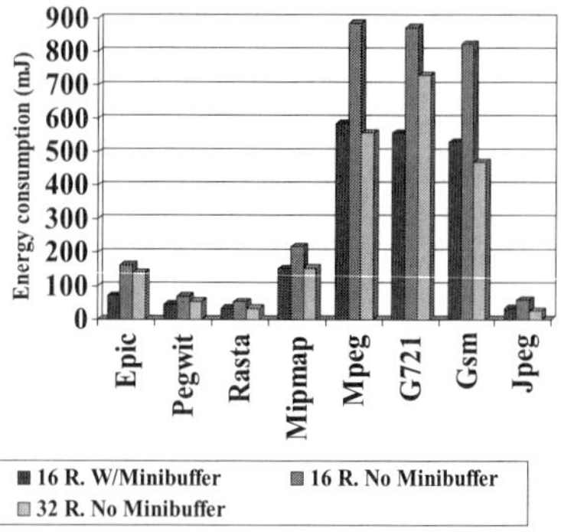

Fig. 13.8. A 16-register architecture with a scratchpad can be more energy-efficient than a 32-register architecture without a scratchpad.

This is ongoing work in line with our vision of creating memory systems with logical partitions where accesses are being mapped based on their static properties [24]. In particular, we are integrating our technique with other compiler/architectural techniques that handle diverse types of memory accesses.

References

1. Appel AW, George L (2001) Optimal Spilling for CISC Machines with Few Registers, In: Proceedings of the ACM SIGPLAN Conference on Programming Language Design and Implementation, pp. 243–253.
2. Albonesi DH (1999) Selective Cache Ways: On-Demand Cache Resource Allocation, In: Proceedings of the 32nd International Symposium on Microarchitecture, MICRO32, pp. 248–258.
3. Belady LA (1966) A Study of Replacement Algorithms for a Virtual-Storage Computer, IBM Systems Journal, 5(2):78–101.
4. Benini L, Macii A, Poncino M (2000) A Recursive Algorithm for Low-Power Memory Partitioning, In: Proceedings of the International Symposium on Low Power Electronics and Design, ISLPED'00, Rapallo, Italy, pp. 78–83.
5. Bhandarkar DP (1996) Alpha Implementations and Architecture, Complete Reference Guide, Digital Press, Newton, MA, pp. 42–43.
6. Bishop B, Kelliher T, Irwin N (1999) A Detailed Analysis of MediaBench, In: Proceedings of the IEEE Workshop on Signal Processing Systems, Taipei, Taiwan, IEEE, New York.
7. Burger D, Austin TD (1997) The Simplescalar Tool Set, Version 2.0, University of Wisconsin-Madison Computer Sciences Department Technical Report #1342.
8. Brooks D, Tiwari V, Martonosi M (2000) Wattch: A Framework for Architectural-Level Power Analysis and Optimizations, In: Proceedings of the 27th International Symposium on Computer Architecture, ISCA'00, Vancouver, Canada, pp. 83–94.
9. Burlin J (2000) Optimizing Stack Frame Layout for Embedded Systems, Masters Thesis, Computing Science Department, Uppsala University, Uppsala, Sweden.

10. Chiou D, Jain P, Rudolph L, Devadas S (2000) Application-Specific Memory Management for Embedded Systems Using Software-Controlled Caches, In: Proceedings of the 37th Design Automation Conference, DAC'00, Los Angeles, CA, pp. 416–419.
11. Cooper KD, Harvey TJ (1998) Compiler-Controlled Memory, In: Proceedings of the Eighth International Conference on Architectural Support for Programming Languages and Systems (ASPLOS-VIII), pp. 2–11.
12. Delaluz V, Kandemir M, Vijaykrishnan N, Irwin MJ (2000) Energy-Oriented Compiler Optimizations for Partitioned Memory Architectures, In: Proceedings of the International Conference on Compilers, Architectures, and Synthesis for Embedded Systems CASES'00, San Jose, CA, pp. 138–147.
13. Engblom J (1999) Why SpecInt95 Should Not Be Used to Benchmark Embedded Systems Tools, In: Proceedings of the ACM SIGPLAN Workshop on Languages, Compilers and Tools for Embedded Systems (LCTES'99), pp. 96–103.
14. Fritts J, Wolf W, Liu B (1999) Understanding Multimedia Application Characteristics for Designing Programmable Media Processors, In: Proceedings of SPIE, Multimedia Hardware Architectures, San Jose, CA, pp. 2–13.
15. Huang M, Renau J, Torrellas J (2001) L1 Cache Decomposition for Energy Efficient Processors, In: Proceedings of the International Symposium on Low-Power Electronics and Design, ISLPED'01, Huntington Beach, CA, pp. 10–15.
16. Kin J, Gupta M, Mangione-Smith WH (1997) The Filter Cache: An Energy Efficient Memory Structure, In: Proceeedings of the 30th Annual Symposium on Microarchitecture, MICRO30, pp. 184–193.
17. Kulkarni C, Catthoor F, De Man H (2000) Advanced Data Layout Organization for Multi-Media Applications, In: Workshop on Parallel and Distributed Computing in Image Processing, Video Processing, and Multimedia (PDIVM 2000), Cancun, Mexico.
18. Lee C, Potkonjak M, Mangione-Smith WH (1997) Mediabench: A Tool for Evaluating and Synthesizing Multimedia and Communications Systems, In: Proceedings of the 30th Annual International Symposium on Microarchitecture, MICRO30, pp. 330–335.
19. Lee HS, Tyson GS (2000) Region-Based Caching: An Energy Delay Efficient Memory Architecture for Embedded Processors, In: Proceedings of PACM (CASES'00), San Jose, CA, pp. 120–127.
20. http://www.eecs.harvard.edu/hube/software/software.html.
21. Memik G, Kandemir M, Haldar M, Choudhary A (1999) A Selective Hardware/Compiler Approach for Improving Cache Locality, Northwestern University Technical Report CPDC-TR-9909-016.
22. Milutinovich V, Tomasevic M, Markovic B, Tremblay M (1996) The Split Temporal / Spatial Cache: Initial Performance Analysis, In: Proceedings of SCIzzL-5, Santa Clara, CA, pp. 63–69.
23. Moritz CA, Frank M, Amarasinghe S (2000) FlexCache: A Framework for Compiler Generated Data Caching, In: Proceedings of the Second Workshop on Intelligent Memory Systems, IRAM'00, Held in Conjunction with ASPLOS-IX, Cambridge, MA.
24. Moritz CA, Frank M, Amarasinghe S (2001) FlexCache: A Framework for Compiler Generated Data Caching, Lecture Notes in Computer Science, Springer-Verlag, Berlin.
25. Mueller F (1995) Compiler Support for Software-Based Cache Partitioning, In: Proceedings of the ACM SIGPLAN Workshop on Languages, Compilers and Tools for Real-Time Systems, La Jolla, CA, pp. 125–133.

26. O'Boyle M, Knijnenburg P (1996) Non-Singular Data Transformations: Definition, Validity, Applications, In: Proceedings of the 6th Workshop on Compilers for Parallel Computers (CPC'96), Aachen, Germany, pp. 287–297.
27. Ranganathan P, Adve S, Jouppi NP (2000) Reconfigurable Caches and Their Application to Media Processing, In: Proceedings of the 27th International Symposium on Computer Architecture (ISCA-27), pp. 214–224.
28. http://suif.stanford.edu/.

14

Bandwidth-Based Prefetching for Constant-Stride Arrays *

Steven O. Hobbs, John S. Pieper, and Stephen C. Root

Intel Corporation, Shrewsbury, MA, USA
steven.hobbs@intel.com, john.pieper@intel.com, steve.root@intel.com

Abstract. We describe a new algorithm for prefetching arrays that are accessed with a compile-time known constant stride. We demonstrate a hardware limitation that has not previously been dealt with (limited off-chip bandwidth) and show its effect on prefetching. Our new algorithm is designed to cope with this hardware limitation. The new algorithm generates prefetches that are more efficient than the standard algorithm because it avoids cache conflicts and issues prefetches based on the machine's ability to process memory transactions in parallel. As a bonus, the new algorithm is independent of the time to execute an iteration. This allows the compiler to perform prefetch analysis early, before good estimates of execution time are available. The result is that we prefetch as far ahead as is profitable given machine resources, but no farther. We show the performance gained by prefetching for our algorithm and for the traditional algorithm on the SPEC CPU2000 floating-point benchmarks. The new algorithm is demonstrably faster for this set of programs.

14.1 Introduction

Modern microprocessors are limited in two important ways that should affect prefetching: the number of simultaneously in-flight memory references is small, and the associativity of their caches is also small.

We will first show evidence of this first machine limitation, which has not been well-understood by the compiler community. We will then explain its impact on prefetch strategy and describe a new technique for dealing with this limitation.

The second limitation (cache associativity) is obvious, but techniques for dealing with it have not yet been developed. We offer an algorithm for finding some cache conflicts at compile time, allowing the compiler to avoid introducing conflicts.

The prefetching we describe in this chapter is the standard prefetching typically applied to arrays that are accessed in inner loops. The compiler can easily predict which data elements will be accessed some number of iterations in the future. Standard strength-reduction techniques applied to array address arithmetic are all that

* This work was done at Compaq Computer Corporation.

is required. The compiler can prefetch such an access by inserting a prefetch instruction into the loop that targets an address equal to that of the original access plus a constant offset. This offset is called the prefetch distance.

The techniques described here have the further restriction that array subscripts have a known constant stride in the innermost loop. Array references not meeting this criterion are not considered for prefetching by our technique. Arrays are only rarely accessed with non-constant strides, so we were willing to trade off the prefetching of variable-stride accesses to get better analysis of the common case. Array references with non-constant strides can be considered in the same framework, but cache conflict analysis is not possible, and reuse analysis is significantly changed from the simple algorithms presented here.

14.2 Previous Work

Our work builds upon previous work in the area of constant-stride array prefetching. Porterfield [2, 9] first described software prefetching and how it allows the memory system to operate in parallel with the processor. He issued prefetches for every array reference with an inductive subscript, one loop iteration ahead. Selvidge [11] described how the compiler could heuristically detect classes of memory references that tend to cause cache misses. Selvidge used pattern recognition on the data-flow graph to detect opportunities to prefetch constant-stride array accesses, indirection arrays, and linked-list structures. He offered the traditional distance computation, in which prefetching distance is computed in terms of the number of loop iterations required to hide memory latency. Our work focuses on deeper analysis of constant-stride array accesses, and we consider how the hardware performs memory references rather than the execution time of the loop.

Mowry [7, 8] first discussed the idea of computing leading and trailing references to avoid the overhead of prefetching references that will likely be cache hits. These works also discuss the relationship of prefetching with loop blocking and software pipelining.

Santhanam [3, 10] described generating prefetches on a low-level intermediate representation that gives them a more accurate computation of the time taken by a loop iteration. Santhanam described the problems large-stride accesses cause and handled them separately from small-stride accesses. This work also handles cache alignment issues. In our work, prefetching is performed after strength reduction, on a higher-level, machine-independent intermediate language. We do not need to compute iteration times, so our techniques can successfully be used on high-level intermediate representations. We show how to use unified algorithms for handling prefetch analysis regardless of the length of the stride. We follow Santhanam's example in allowing the unroller to eliminate redundant prefetch operations. Our software pipeliner does not insert prefetch instructions if they have already been inserted but is free to schedule them. Santhanam described the problems associated with cache conflicts (and memory bank conflicts) but did not offer a solution.

Others have studied prefetching for linked lists and other non-linear access patterns [4, 5, 6]. These papers do not address the hardware limitations addressed in this chapter, instead focusing on the harder problems of deciding when and how to prefetch such irregular access patterns.

14.3 Off-Chip Bandwidth

Modern microprocessors have the first few levels of the memory hierarchy on-chip (registers and caches). The main memory of general-purpose computer systems is still too large to fit on the same chip as the CPU, however, so memory references that miss the cache must go off-chip. Early microprocessors allowed only one reference to be off-chip at a time. More recent processors have improved on this. In the Alpha family, for instance, the 21064 allowed two off-chip references, but the processor stalled when the second reference left the chip. The 21164 allowed two simultaneous off-chip references with no stalls. The 21264 allows up to eight simultaneous off-chip references.

The number of outstanding references is limited by the hardware because the hardware has to keep track of each reference and match the data as they return to the instruction that requested them. The number of references is kept small in part because of the size of the hardware resources used for tracking but to a larger extent because of the practical limits of parallelism in a typical memory system. The impact of this limitation is that it is not profitable for the compiler to insert prefetches very far ahead. If the prefetches are very far ahead, the hardware simply stalls most of the prefetches (or it may drop them). In essence, the common view that prefetches are used to reduce memory latency is misleading because the hardware limits how far ahead a prefetch can be effectively issued.

Figure 14.1 shows the average time (in processor clocks) for an Alpha 21264 processor to execute a single iteration of a pointer-chasing loop. An array of pointers is initialized so that each element points one cache line further down the array. Making the chain circular at a given distance varies the length of the pointer chain (i.e., the dataset size). We use pointer chains rather than a simple array access so that the loads are dependent and must be issued in order. One iteration consists of a load through the pointer, a prefetch at a given offset from the pointer, a counter decrement, and a branch back to the top of the loop.

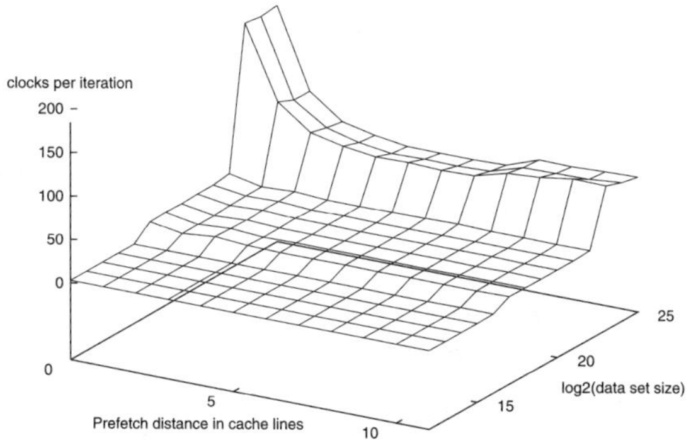

Fig. 14.1. Prefetching on the Alpha 21264.

For small pointer chains, the whole chain stays in the first-level cache and prefetching doesn't help. For longer pointer chains, prefetching does improve the time per iteration. Prefetching one line ahead helps a lot, while the improvement from four lines ahead to five lines ahead is small. A slight stall can be noticed when the processor has to keep eight or more references in flight simultaneously. This is an effect of the interleaved memory system in the 525 MHz GS140 on which this test was run; other Alpha systems do not show this effect.

Figure 14.2 shows the same experiment on a Pentium III processor, which allows four references to be in flight simultaneously. The results are similar. Prefetching one cache line ahead helps a lot. The second and third help a little, but the benefit from increasing the prefetch distance from three lines ahead to four is small.

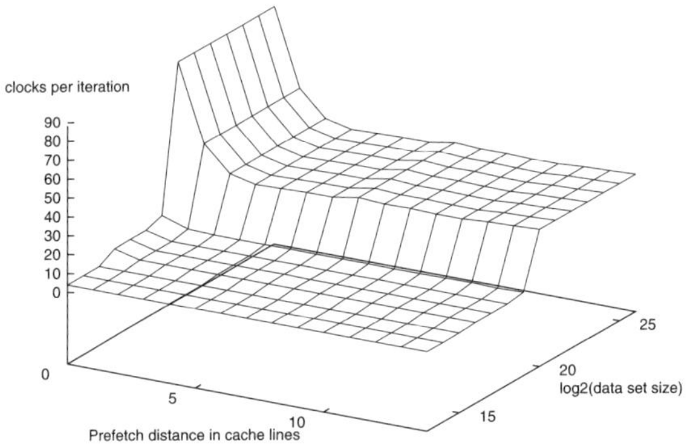

Fig. 14.2. Prefetching on the Pentium III.

Notice also that once the pointer chains are larger than the first-level cache, no amount of prefetching can hide the full latency of the memory system. The performance of this kernel is limited by memory bandwidth. It is not possible to hide the full memory latency, because the processor can issue memory requests faster than the memory system can respond. This suggests that calculating prefetch distances to hide the full memory latency is illusory and doesn't match the reality of what the machine actually does.

Our distance algorithm is based on this observation. Prefetching cannot be used to lower memory latency in all cases. Instead, prefetches are a flexible method of smoothing the demand for memory bandwidth. Prefetch instructions do not return data to the programmer-visible machine state, so they do not have dependencies. This means that both the compiler and the hardware can move prefetches across other instructions freely. This allows the prefetches to be issued when the memory system would otherwise be idle. This reduces the burstiness of memory requests and increases the overall utilization of the memory system, leading to higher net bandwidth. In this model, prefetch distances do not need to hide the full memory latency. Instead, prefetch distances are calculated to be the largest distance that does not over saturate the memory system. We refer to this as bandwidth-based prefetching as opposed to the traditional model of latency-based prefetching.

14.4 Cache Conflicts

A cache conflict occurs in a k-way set-associative cache when the same cache element needs to hold more than k data items. Cache conflicts can occur between data items in active use. Conflicts can also occur between active data and data that are either being prefetched or have been prefetched but are not yet in use. Conflicts are even possible between multiple prefetched data items.

The result of a conflict is that some data that should be kept in the cache is not kept. This means either that prefetch data are flushed, so that the prefetch was wasted, or real data were flushed, so that the prefetch caused an extra cache miss. To reduce cache conflicts, the compiler can take two steps: it can analyze the access patterns and try to avoid some conflicts, and it can reduce the prefetch distances to reduce their cache footprint and lower the probability of conflict.

14.4.1 Statically Detectable Conflicts

Memory references to the same data structure or to different structures with known constant offsets give us the opportunity to detect cache conflicts at compile time. Simple examples are common blocks in Fortran or file-scope data defined in the same file in C (the C language does not require contiguous data layout, but if the data are placed by the compiler, the compiler may well know the offset from one variable to the next). Using this information together with a model of the cache and a known stride, the compiler can detect many possible conflicts at compile time. It can then avoid issuing a prefetch that would result in a conflict.

14.4.2 Dynamically Detectable Conflicts

When there are accesses to data that do not share a common base address, the starting offsets are not known. The compiler cannot determine whether conflicts occur statically. The compiler can still minimize the probability of a run-time cache conflict in two ways:

- It can keep prefetch distances as small as possible, while retaining their effectiveness.
- It can notice when the probability of a cache conflict gets high and give up prefetching in those loops.

As we will see later, our prefetch distance calculation algorithm keeps the prefetch distances no larger than what the hardware can profitably issue. This reduces the cache footprint of the prefetched data, thus reducing the probability of a cache conflict.

We also count the number of distinct memory reference streams in a loop and suppress prefetching when the probability of a cache conflict is high.

14.5 Algorithm Details

The four main phases of our algorithm are (1) prefetch candidate identification, (2) reuse analysis to determine leading and trailing references, (3) distance calculation, and finally (4) prefetch insertion. Each of these phases is described below.

14.5.1 Prefetch Candidate Identification

In the GEM compiler [1], prefetching is driven off of the strength-reduction phase. Strength reduction identifies groups of references with a common base address (either references to the same array or to different arrays with a known relative offset) and a common stride. This is helpful because the Alpha architecture allows register-plus-offset addressing, and a single register can be used to generate addresses for several references sharing both a base address and stride by giving each reference a different offset. Our technique requires the further restriction that the stride be a compile-time constant. A set of references sharing a base address and a common stride are called a reference group.

14.5.2 Reuse Analysis

An important part of prefetch analysis is finding the set of references that do not need to be prefetched. Many references can be shown to touch the same data as other nearby references. These references are called trailing references. Trailing references do not cause cache misses and so need not be prefetched.

Reuse analysis identifies temporal and spatial locality. Locality is particularly important when it occurs among the members of a reference group, because then it will occur on every iteration of the loop. Mowry [7, 8] describes reuse analysis in terms of localized iteration spaces by computing a particular solution to the difference between two array index equations. Our algorithm uses the relative-offset information already produced by the strength-reduction phase.

Reuse analysis is performed separately for each reference group. The analysis is a two-step process. In the initialization step, the references within a group are sorted by their relative offsets. The largest offset seen is remembered since it provides a useful bound for the second step.

The second step is to determine which references trail other references. The references are walked in order from smallest to largest. For each reference, the set of offsets that the reference will access over time is computed by adding successive multiples of the stride (this is why we require a compile-time constant stride). The offsets thus computed are called induced offsets. For each induced offset, a window just less than one cache line wide is checked. If a reference is found in that window, then the original reference trails the reference in the window. Induced offsets are computed out as far as the maximum useful prefetch distance for the machine; that is, the length of a cache line times the maximum number of simultaneous off-chip references.

Note that for strides smaller than a cache line, sorting the references and using a linear scan works fine. However, for large strides, a linear scan causes the algorithm to become $O(n^2)$. This is because from a given reference, we add a multiple of the stride (which may be quite large) and then compute the result modulo the cache size. In general, this takes us to a random spot in the cache, and we have to search linearly to find that spot.

In our technique, inserting the references into a B-tree indexed by relative offset performs the sorting step. We can then look up any cache address in time proportional to $log(n)$, where n is the number of references in a group. The normal B-tree structure is augmented by a pointer chain that allows the references to also be walked in linear order to make checking the window fast.

Note that when the stride is smaller than a cache line, there is significant overlap in the windows from one stride step to the next. A simple way to remove redundant checks is to keep a lower bound and an upper bound on the range of offsets to be checked. The lower bound never needs to be smaller than the biggest offset we have already checked, nor smaller than the induced offset minus the length of one cache line. Similarly, the upper bound need not be larger than the minimum of the largest offset, or one cache line beyond the induced offset. The pseudo-code of Figure 14.3 gives details.

```
for each reference in sorted order
  begin
  nextAddress = reference->offset;
  checkedAddress = nextAddress;
  maxPrefetch = max(cacheLineLength,stride)*prefetchMaxLines;
  stopAddress= min(largestOffsetSeen,reference->offset+maxPrefetch);
  lowerBound = max(checkedAddress+1,nextAddress-cacheLineLength+1);
  upperBound = min(stopAddress, nextAddress+cacheLineLength-1);
  while(lowerBound <= stopAddress)
    begin
    lookup = LookupOffsetLessThanOrEqualTo(lowerBound);
    while (lookup != null)
      begin
      if lookup->offset > upperBound then
        exit while;
      else if lookup->offset >= lowerBound then
        // "reference" trails "lookup"
        reference->leadingReference = false;
        skip to the next reference;
      else
        lookup = lookup->next;                // follow linear order
      end;
    checkedAddress = upperBound;
    nextAddress = nextAddress + stride;
    lowerBound= max(checkedAddress+1,nextAddress-cacheLineLength+1);
    upperBound = min(stopAddress, nextAddress+cacheLineLength-1);
    end;
  end;
```

Fig. 14.3. Pseudo-code for reuse analysis.

When the second walk has been completed, any references that have not been marked as trailing references are leading references. We keep the list of trailing references for each leading reference for use during prefetch insertion.

14.5.3 Cache Conflict Detection

Given a reference group with a known constant stride and a model of the cache, it is straightforward to detect if there are any cache conflicts among members of the same reference group. From the relative offsets, we compute a new set of offsets called cache offsets, which are just the relative offsets modulo the cache set size. Cache conflicts can be modeled by inserting all of the references into a model of the cache and checking how many references fall into the same cache line but have different relative offsets and thus would require being put into a different set. If the number of sets required exceeds the available associativity, a conflict will occur.

This is extended to prefetch data by considering where prefetch data will fall into the cache model over several iterations (up to the maximum profitable prefetch distance, just as for reuse analysis). First, all of the original references are placed into the cache model. We then consider prefetches one line ahead, two lines ahead, and so forth, until either a conflict is detected or the maximum prefetch distance is reached. For each reference group, we note the maximum prefetch distance (in cache lines) for which no conflicts occur.

The preferred implementation once again relies on B-trees since we once again add multiples of the stride to each reference and look up where they go in the cache. This allows us to handle strides larger than a cache line with a single unified algorithm.

14.5.4 Prefetch Distance Calculation

The traditional technique for calculating prefetch distances is to compute the number of iterations ahead that the prefetch must be issued and then to multiply that by the stride of the reference. The number of iterations is computed by estimating the time it takes to execute one iteration of the loop: the number of iterations is equal to the time a memory reference takes divided by the time to execute one iteration. Unfortunately, this means prefetches must be inserted fairly late, when good estimates of execution time are available. Further, this approach ignores the limits of the hardware. For stride-one accesses, the distance computed is often small enough that the hardware limit is met. For instance, on an Alpha 21264, the cache line size is 64 bytes. For stride-one double-precision data, there are eight data items per cache line. The chip supports eight outstanding references, so the maximum effective prefetch distance is 64 iterations ahead. On a system where memory is 128 clocks away, the traditional method over prefetches only if an iteration takes less than two clocks (this assumes there is only one reference being prefetched; for two references, the loop would have to execute in less than four clocks on average). For large-stride accesses, every iteration touches a new line, so every iteration potentially causes an off-chip reference. The traditional method over prefetches whenever the average loop iteration time (ignoring memory) is less than the average memory access time.

Our algorithm computes distances in a way that attempts to keep the total number of prefetches in flight about equal to the number supported by the hardware. First, each leading reference is given a minimum number of off-chip references (currently, we use two per leading reference for the 21264 and one per leading reference for the 21164). Then, if the total number of simultaneous off-chip references is less than the hardware allows, each leading reference is given an additional off-chip reference if it can take it without causing a known cache conflict. The prefetch distance is then the number of off-chip references assigned to a leading reference multiplied by the cache line size or the stride (whichever is larger).

This has the effect of dividing the available off-chip bandwidth evenly among the leading references in a loop. The processor resources are not oversubscribed unless the minimum distance times the number of leading references exceeds the number of profitable off-chip references.

There is one additional mechanism we apply to the distance calculation. If the number of reference groups exceeds a threshold based on the cache size, we abort prefetching altogether. The reason for this is that when the number of reference groups gets high, the probability that some pair of groups has a conflict increases. Prefetching only worsens the effects of cache conflicts. This prefetch throttling is applied in our compiler based on the number of reference groups and is independent of the prefetch distance calculation that would otherwise be used.

14.5.5 Prefetch Insertion

Prefetch analysis is performed just prior to loop unrolling. We insert an intermediate language representation of prefetches during the loop-unrolling phase. This allows the unroller to remove redundant prefetches and to consider the intended prefetches when determining how much to unroll. As the unroller copies the loop body, it inserts a prefetch operation for a leading reference when it is encountered. Some of the prefetches may be redundant and can be eliminated following Santhanam's method [3, 10].

Prefetching just the leading reference may not be enough to ensure that all references are prefetched when the stride is larger than a cache line, due to cache alignment issues. As an example, imagine two references just less than one cache line apart. With a stride of two cache lines, the probability of the data lining up in the cache so that both references are in the same line is fairly small. In order to be sure the second reference is prefetched, both references must be prefetched.

Using the list of trailing references produced by reuse analysis, we can decide which references to prefetch. The leading reference is always prefetched. The list of trailing references is then examined, and the most trailing reference that is not more than a full cache line behind the leading reference is also prefetched. This new reference establishes a new baseline, and the next reference not more than a full cache line back is prefetched, and so forth, until the list of trailers is exhausted. This guarantees that every cache line that might be accessed in one iteration is prefetched, regardless of the alignment of the data in the cache.

Leading references are annotated by reuse analysis prior to loop unrolling. However, the loop unroller does not blindly insert a prefetch into every unrolled copy of the loop body. Instead, it performs a simple version of reuse analysis to eliminate redundant prefetches. It inserts a prefetch into the last iteration of the unrolled loop and into the next preceding iteration that is at least a cache line away. Thus, the compiler inserts one prefetch per cache line in the unrolled loop body.

If no unrolling is done, there will be one prefetch in each iteration for every leading reference. Unrolling the loop allows prefetches within a cache line of each other to be removed. The unroller considers this removal of redundant prefetch instructions in its heuristics for choosing the unroll amount. The ideal unrolling amount for prefetching gives exactly one prefetch per cache line. The unroller computes how many prefetches can be saved for a given unroll amount and factors that into choosing the best unroll amount for the loop.

14.6 Evaluation

The algorithm presented here has been implemented in the GEM backend [1], which is the optimizer and code generator for all of Compaq Computer Corporation's compiler products. We also implemented traditional, time-based prefetch distance calculation. We compare the performance of the generated code for SPEC CPU2000 floating-point benchmarks using a set of switches typical for a SPEC submission from Compaq. The reference data set was used. The programs were compiled three different ways: with the new prefetch algorithm, with the traditional time-based algorithm, and with prefetching suppressed. Figure 14.4 shows the relative improvement gained by traditional latency-based distance calculation versus the relative improvement gained by our new algorithm based on off-chip bandwidth for both base and peak runs. These runs were done on a 667 MHz 21264-based Compaq XP1000 workstation. For the four benchmarks on the left, prefetching is a significant win, improving run times by up to 40%. For the others, prefetching is a minor gain, or occasionally a minor loss.

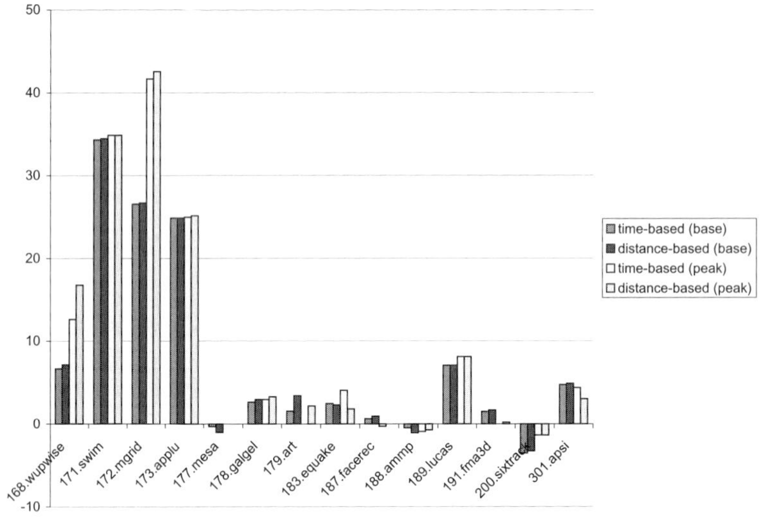

Fig. 14.4. Percentage improvement in execution time with different prefetch distance calculations.

Distance-based prefetching is just as effective as time-based prefetching. In fact, distance-based prefetching often wins slightly over time-based prefetching, most notably in 168.wupwise peak (4%) and 179.art (about 2% for both base and peak). In 168.wupwise, more than half the execution time is spent in the routine zgemm.

This routine performs matrix-matrix multiplication on complex data. In one loop that stores zeroes into a 2-D complex array, the execution time of an iteration is just the time to do two 8-byte stores, and so the prefetch distance chosen is 5552 bytes ahead with time-based prefetching. The 21264 target processor supports eight off-chip references to 64-byte cache lines, so the distance-based prefetch choices are a more reasonable distance of 512 bytes ahead.

The one consistent loss is in 183.equake. Equake is a C program that heap-allocates the important multidimensional arrays. The stride of the data arrays is not a compile-time known constant, so compiler-inserted prefetching is ineffective and the program is memory-bandwidth bound. The compiler is able to insert prefetches for an outer array of pointers, but prefetching these pointers only interferes with the unprefetched data stream. In this case, time-based prefetching chooses a smaller distance, because our implementation of distance-based prefetching does not model all the non-prefetchable references. If we modeled the effect of all the unprefetchable references in the hot loops, we could choose a more appropriate prefetch distance. (As a side note, hardware is easily able to detect the access pattern at run time and prefetch effectively, as shown by recent Pentium IV and Power3 SPEC CPU2000 results.)

Figure 14.5 shows the effect of removing pieces of our prefetch algorithm on the shorter-running SPEC CPU95 floating-point benchmarks. These results are base runs, done without the KAP preprocessor and with the only optimization switch being "-arch ev6" to identify which version of the Alpha architecture is being targeted. Again, the reference data set was used. KAP was not used for this experiment because it pads arrays so that our cache analyzer does not find any conflicts. Since these benchmarks tend to fit in the second-level cache, prefetching is less important overall than it is in CPU2000. Five runs were done: a baseline run, and four runs each removing an optimization. The results of those four are plotted, scaled relative to the base run with full optimization.

The worst slowdown occurs when redundant prefetch removal in the unroller is disabled ("noredundant"). This means that obviously redundant prefetches (usually to consecutive memory locations) are not eliminated. Disabling the redundant prefetch elimination has two effects: the execution time cost of the redundant prefetches that must be executed and the loss of unrolling since the prefetches no longer encourage the unroller to choose larger unroll amounts. The loss of unrolling also reduces instruction-level parallelism and can affect other optimizations. To eliminate this effect, we can force the unroller to choose unroll amounts based on eliminating redundant prefetch instructions even though the prefetch instructions are not eliminated ("noredundant+unroll"). The loop unroller heuristics were tuned with redundant prefetch elimination on. For most programs, the unroll amount chosen when redundant prefetches are eliminated normally is better than what the unroller would choose while ignoring the possible prefetch savings. The exception is 146.wave5: here the unrolling is useful principally for redundant prefetch elimination and isn't profitable on its own (that is, the compiler can choose a better unroll amount while ignoring the prefetches that can be eliminated).

Cache conflict detection makes a significant (4%) win in 103.su2cor but otherwise has little effect. Su2cor declares many arrays with dimensions that are powers of 2 or nearly powers of 2. The compiler is able to detect this and avoid inserting a prefetch that would cause cache conflicts.

Reuse analysis (eliminating redundant prefetches by identifying trailing references) doesn't have a large effect in our compiler because source programs don't tend to contain many separate references to the same cache line. Loop unrolling,

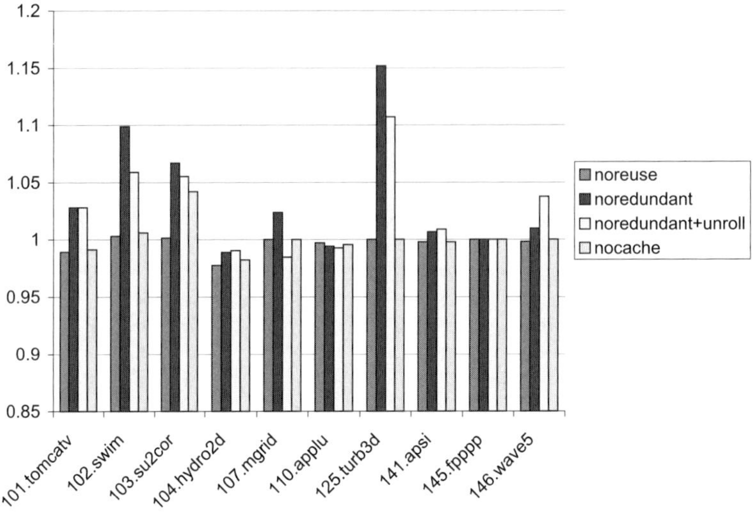

Fig. 14.5. Effects of different analyses on SPEC CPU95 floating-point benchmarks.

however, introduces many such references, so the redundant prefetch elimination it performs is very important. This optimization would be part of reuse analysis if that analysis were performed after loop unrolling.

14.7 Conclusion

We have demonstrated an important limitation of current microprocessors: the number of simultaneous off-chip memory references is limited to a small fixed number. We have shown that this leads to over prefetching using the traditional prefetch algorithm. We have outlined a new bandwidth-aware algorithm that handles both small-stride accesses and large-stride accesses without oversubscribing machine resources. The new algorithm does not need accurate estimates of loop execution time. Instead, it models how many references will be off-chip during execution of the loop. We also describe an algorithm that detects some cache conflicts at compile time and avoids issuing a prefetch that would cause a cache conflict. When cache conflicts are present, avoiding additional conflict can save up to 4% of overall execution time. The distance-based prefetching algorithm also avoids cache conflicts at run time by limiting prefetch distances to match the ability of the hardware to sustain off-chip references.

The single most important prefetch optimization is the use of loop unrolling to eliminate multiple prefetches to the same cache line. The strides of the prefetches in the loop are an important indicator of a good unroll amount. Redundant prefetches can slow execution time by up to 15%.

Acknowledgments

Special thanks to Jeannie Lieb, who ran the CPU2000 benchmarks for us. This work would not have been possible without Jeannie and the rest of the GEM compiler team.

References

1. Blickstein, D., et al. The GEM Optimizing Compiler System. Digital Technical Journal, 4(4):121–136, 1992.
2. Callahan, D., Kennedy, K., and Porterfield, A. Software Prefetching. In Proceedings of the Fourth International Conference on Architectural Support for Programming Languages and Operating Systems, pages 40–52. Association for Computing Machinery, New York, April 1991.
3. Gornish, E., and Hsu, W.-C., and Santhanam, V. Data Prefetching on the HP PA-8000. In: Proceedings of the 24th International Symposium on Computer Architecture, pages 264–273. Association for Computing Machinery, New York, 1997.
4. Luk, C-K., and Mowry, T. Automatic Compiler-Inserted Prefetching for Pointer-Based Applications. IEEE Transactions on Computers, 48(2):134–141, February 1999.
5. Luk, C-K., and Mowry, T. Compiler-Based Prefetching for Recursive Data Structures. In Proceedings of the Seventh International Conference on Architectural Support for Programming Languages and Operating Systems, pages 226–233, October 1996.
6. Moshovos, A., Roth, A., and Sohi, G. Dependence Based Prefetching for Linked Data Structures. In Proceedings of the Eighth International Conference on Architectural Support for Programming Languages and Operating Systems, pages 115–126, October 1998.
7. Mowry, T. Tolerating Latency Through Software-Controlled Data Prefetching. Ph.D. thesis, Stanford University, 1994.
8. Mowry, T., Lam, M., and Gupta, A. Design and Evaluation of a Compiler Algorithm for Prefetching. In Proceedings of the Fifth International Conference on Architectural Support for Programming Languages and Operating Systems, pages 62–73. Association for Computing Machinery, New York, October 1992.
9. Porterfield, A. Software Methods for Improvement of Cache Performance on Supercomputer Applications. Ph.D. thesis, Rice University, 1989.
10. Santhanam, V. Efficient Explicit Data Prefetching Analysis and Code Generation in a Low-Level Optimizer for Inserting Prefetch Instructions Into Loops of Applications. U.S. Patent number 5,794,053, December 1997.
11. Selvidge, C. Compilation-Based Prefetching for Memory Latency Tolerance. Ph.D. thesis, Massachusetts Institute of Technology, 1992.

15

Performance Potential of Effective Address Prediction of Load Instructions

Pritpal S. Ahuja, Joel Emer, Artur Klauser, and Shubhendu S. Mukherjee

Intel Corporation, Shrewsbury, MA, USA **
pritpa.ahuja@intel.com, joel.emer@intel.com, artur.klauser@intel.com, shubu.mukherjee@intel.com

Abstract. Modern, deeply pipelined, out-of-order, and speculative microprocessors are still plagued by the latency of load instructions. This latency is dominated by the latencies to resolve the source operands of the load, to compute its effective address, and to fetch the load's data from caches or the main memory. This chapter examines the performance potential of hiding a load's data fetch latency using effective address prediction . By predicting the effective address of a load early in the pipeline, we can initiate the cache access early, thereby improving performance.

The current generation of effective address predictors for a load instruction is based on either the history or the context of the specific load. In addition, researchers have examined load-load dependence predictors of prefetch cache misses. This chapter examines the performance potential of using a *load-load dependence* predictor to predict effective addresses of load instructions and issue them early in the pipeline. We call this predictor the DEAP predictor.

We show that on average DEAP can improve the accuracy of effective address prediction by 28% over a perfect combination of last address, stride address, and context-based address predictors across our seven benchmarks from the SPEC95 and Olden suites. We find that an ideal hybrid of these four predictors—a predictor that always picks the right predictor for a load—can potentially achieve performance close to that of a Perfect predictor in most cases. We use an oracle-based simulation approach to evaluate our timing results. This method allows us to measure the upper bound of the performance from effective address prediction using a mostly realistic pipeline. However, our timing simulation method does not account for the penalty due to mis-prediction of an effective address and assumes a zero-cycle latency from address prediction resolution to address predictor update.

15.1 Introduction

The latency of load instructions—from fetch to commit—continues to plague modern out-of-order and speculative microprocessor designs. A load's latency is dominated by three components: effective address computation, store-load dependence solution, and data fetch. We define effective address computation latency as the sum of the latency from the time a load is fetched until its source operands are ready and the

** The authors did this work while at Compaq Computer Corporation.

latency to compute the effective address itself. The store-load dependence resolution latency is the latency to determine whether a load depends on a prior uncommitted store. Finally, data fetch latency is the latency to fetch the load's data from caches or the main memory.

Unfortunately, a load's effective address computation and data fetch latencies continue to be major problems in today's microprocessors, even though recent memory disambiguation techniques (e.g., [1, 2]) have largely solved the store-dependence resolution problem. The effective address computation latency remains high because in many programs it takes a long time for a load's source operands to become data-ready. Pointer chasing (via load-load dependence chains) is a classic example of such a code. Data fetch latency continues to be high for two reasons. First, the gap between processor and DRAM performances continues to widen, which causes cache miss latency to appear significantly worse in each generation of processors. Second, the complexity of modern, wide-issue, and out-of-order machines increases both the width and length of result buses from the data caches to the execution units. This, in turn, increases the data fetch latency from L1 SRAM caches. Thus, on modern microprocessors, the load-to-use latency on cache hits has increased to between three and five cycles [4].

This chapter examines the performance potential of hiding a load's data fetch latency, particularly on cache hits on L1 or L2 caches, using effective address prediction. Modern microprocessors, in their quest for higher clock speeds and performance, have become deeply pipelined, with 20 or more pipeline stages (e.g., Intel Willamette [12]). Because of such deep pipelining, we usually have a large number (five or more) of stages from the point where an instruction is renamed until the instruction reaches the execution stage of the pipeline. Such deep pipelining potentially opens up a window of opportunity in which we can predict a load's effective address early in the pipeline, issue the load speculatively, and fetch the data from the data cache. If the prediction is correct, then we can hide a load's data fetch latency, particularly for cache hits. This allows instructions dependent on the load to issue earlier, thereby improving the number of instructions committed per cycle (IPC).

Figure 15.1 shows an example of such a pipeline in which we predict the effective address of loads and issue them via a bypass path to the memory system in the pipeline. In this figure and throughout the rest of the chapter, we assume that the bypass path for loads originates after the register rename stage. This allows a load instruction to fetch its data directly into the correct physical register and not into an intermediate staging buffer.

The performance potential of effective address prediction depends on the prediction accuracy of the effective address predictors—Perfect, LAP, SAP, CAP, and DEAP. The Perfect (and perhaps non-implementable) predictor always predicts the correct effective address for a load. LAP (Last Address Predictor) predicts that a load will use the same effective address that it had used the last time it executed [3, 7]. The SAP (Stride Address Predictor) predicts an effective address by using the load's last address and a stride [8, 9, 10]. CAP (Context-based Address Predictor) predicts effective addresses based on the history of prior addresses encountered by a load [4]. Finally, DEAP (Dependence-based Address Predictor) is an effective address predictor that predicts effective addresses based on dependences between load instructions. DEAP is a variant of Roth et al.'s load-load dependence predictor [5] . However, unlike the Roth et al. work, which used the dependence predictor to prefetch cache misses, we use DEAP to issue loads early in the pipeline by predicting their effective addresses.

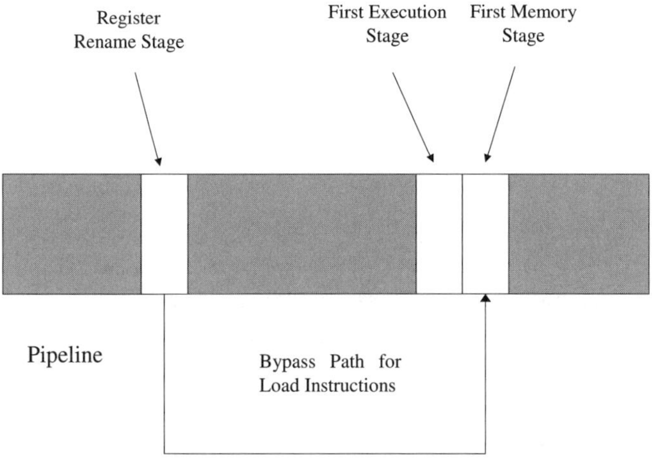

Fig. 15.1. Effective address prediction and load issue via bypass path.

To understand the performance potential of each of these predictors, we use a prediction from a predictor only when it is correct. We do not account for the penalty for a misprediction of an effective address. Additionally, we assume a zero-cycle latency from address resolution to predictor update. Such a method has both advantages and disadvantages. This method allows us to study the performance potential (i.e., the upper bound of performance) of these predictors. This also frees us from worrying about the exact details and performance degradation due to the recovery mechanisms necessary when any of the predictors mispredicts. However, this method also does not account for performance differences due to different recovery costs of the different predictors.

We show that DEAP can improve the accuracy of effective address prediction by 28% over a perfect combination of LAP, SAP, and CAP across our seven benchmarks from the SPEC95 and Olden suites. Specifically, on our three pointer-intensive Olden benchmarks, between 19% and 49% of the dynamic loads' effective addresses are correctly predicted only by DEAP, and not by any other predictor.

We find that one or more of LAP, SAP, CAP, or DEAP predicts the majority of loads accurately. Across our seven benchmarks from the SPEC95 and Olden suites, the four effective address predictors make predictions on 64%–99% of dynamically executed loads. The predictors accurately predict between 73% and 95% of these loads.

Additionally, we find that an ideal hybrid of LAP, SAP, CAP, and DEAP captures most of the performance benefit available from a Perfect predictor. The Perfect predictor can boost performance between 7% and 244% in our seven benchmarks. The ideal hybrid of LAP, SAP, CAP, and DEAP can capture 82% of the Perfect predictor's performance improvement, except for compress. These predictors boost performance because they allow the pipeline to prefetch both L1 cache hits and L2 cache hits. Unfortunately, for compress, these predictors are unable to predict the effective addresses of loads that miss frequently in the L1 data cache but hit in the L2, and account for most of the performance degradation.

We use a method called *oracle simulation* for this study. Ideally, for upper bound studies, we would like to have all information about an instruction at the fetch stage itself. For example, knowing the direction of a branch at the fetch stage would allow us to study the performance benefit from a perfect branch predictor. Unfortunately, in a detailed simulation model of an out-of-order and speculative pipeline, such information is not available at the fetch stage because prior instructions that the branch may depend on may not have executed.

Oracle simulation solves this problem. With oracle simulation, we run two simulations—one that models the detailed out-of-order, multi-stage pipeline and a second one that models a single-stage pipeline. Every time the out-of-order pipe fetches an instruction, the corresponding single-stage pipe executes the instruction completely. Thus, the second pipe has complete information about the instruction. Specifically, for our case, the second pipe can return the effective address of loads when they are at the fetch stage of the first pipe. This helps us implement the Perfect effective address predictor as well as verify if the predictor from other predictors are correct.

The rest of the chapter is organized as follows. Section 15.2 describes our four effective address predictors. Section 15.3 discusses our evaluation methodology. Section 15.4 discusses results. Section 15.5 describes related work. Finally, Section 15.6 presents our conclusions.

15.2 Effective Address Predictors

In this section, we describe the four predictors: LAP, SAP, CAP, and DEAP. We also simulate a Perfect Effective Address Predictor, which always returns the correct effective address of a load instruction. Section 15.3.2 describes how we implement these predictors in our simulator.

15.2.1 LAP: Last Address Predictor

A Last Address Predictor (LAP) [3, 7] predicts that a load will reuse the same effective ffective address that it used the last time it executed. LAP works well for loads that access the same variables repeatedly (e.g., globals). In our evaluation, LAP can accurately predict the effective addresses of almost 35% of the dynamic loads (averaged across our seven benchmarks) on which LAP makes a prediction. For our LAP implementation, we use a direct-mapped, tagged cache indexed by the PC of the load. Each LAP entry contains a tag, the predicted address (i.e., last address), and a two-bit saturating counter. LAP does not make a prediction if the PC does not exist in the tagged cache or until the saturating counter has not reached its maximum count.

15.2.2 SAP: Stride Address Predictor

A Stride Address Predictor (SAP) predicts that the effective address of a load will be a fixed offset (or stride) from the load's effective address it produced the last time it executed. SAP is well suited for array accesses in which a load sequences through different elements of an array. Our SAP implementation accurately predicts

48% of dynamic loads (averaged across our seven benchmarks) on which it makes predictions.

For our SAP implementation, we use a direct-mapped, tagged cache indexed by the PC of the load. Each SAP entry contains a tag, the last address, the predicted stride, the last stride seen, and a confidence counter. The predicted address is the sum of the last address and the predicted stride. The last stride seen is the difference between the last effective address and next-to-last effective address used by the load. SAP changes the predicted stride only if it encounters the same stride twice in a row [9, 10]. SAP makes a prediction only if the PC exists in the tagged cache and if the confidence counter has reached its maximum count.

15.2.3 CAP: Context-Based Address Predictor

A Context-based Address Predictor (CAP) predicts a load's effective address based on the history of prior addresses encountered by the load. Loads often sequence through a fixed pattern of addresses, such as in recursive data structures. CAP works well with such recursive data structures. CAP can also capture some of the effective addresses that are accurately predicted by LAP and SAP. This is because LAP is a degenerate case of CAP with no history. Similarly, CAP can capture a sequence of strided addresses if CAP's history captures the sequence of strided addresses. Nevertheless, SAP is a more compact representation of strided addresses and, therefore, we expect SAP to have a higher accuracy for strided access patterns. For our seven benchmarks, CAP accurately predicts 52% of the loads on which it makes predictions.

In this chapter we use Bekerman et al.'s implementation of a CAP [4]. This implementation of CAP uses two tables, the load buffer (LB) and the link table (LT), as shown in Figure 15.2. The load buffer is a per-static-load table that maintains the recent history of effective addresses of the associated load. The link table is a second-level table that provides the address used for effective address computation. The load buffer is indexed by part of the load's PC. Each load buffer entry contains a tag (the rest of a load's PC bits), a saturating counter, the load's offset as found in the load instruction itself, and the history. The saturating counter serves as a confidence estimator. Thus, CAP will not return a prediction unless the value of the counter is above a certain threshold. The load buffer history bits contain the history of prior base addresses of a load instruction. We update the CAP history as follows: $history = (history << m) XOR(new\_base\_address >> 2)$. That is, the history is shifted left m bits and XORed with the new base address shifted right by two. We shift the new base address by two bits because the lower two bits do not matter except for unaligned accesses.

We index the link table using the history bits of a load buffer entry. Because of this, CAP's history maintains only base addresses, multiple load buffer entries may map into the same link table entry. To avoid destructive aliasing, the link table also contains a tag, which is the history of the load buffer entry itself. The link table contains the link, which is the base address of the predicted load. To obtain the complete effective address, we must add the offset from the load buffer with the link address from the link table. Finally, a link table entry also contains a few pollution-free bits. The pollution-free bits record a few bits of the base address of a probing load. We update the link table entry when two consecutive accesses to the link table have the same pollution-free bits.

Like the other predictors, CAP does not make a prediction if it does not find a matching PC in the load buffer or if there is tag mismatch in the link table.

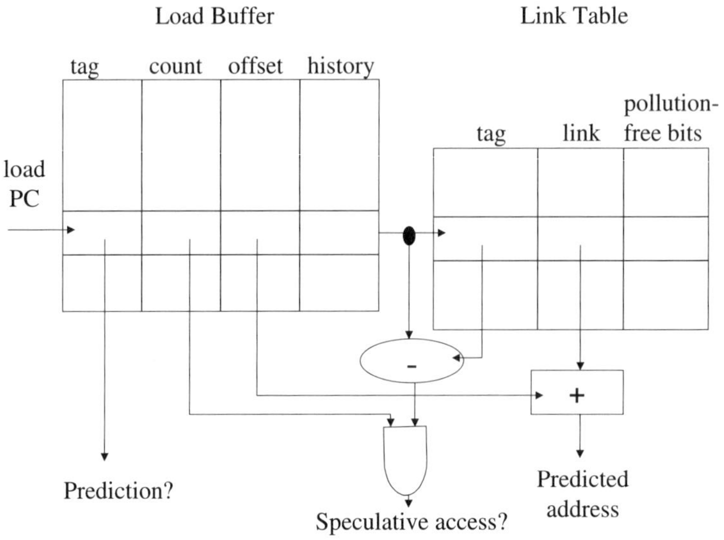

Fig. 15.2. A context address predictor (CAP).

15.2.4 DEAP: Dependence-Based Address Predictor

Our Dependence-based Effective Address Predictor (DEAP) predicts effective addresses based on dependences between load instructions. Two load instructions are dependent if the first one (the producer load) loads a value that is the base address for the second load (the consumer load). DEAP recognizes such dependences and predicts the effective address of the consumer load based on the value loaded by the producer. DEAP is well-suited for predicting effective addresses in pointer-chasing programs, which have such load-load dependence patterns. Of the three Olden benchmarks [11] we examine in this chapter, DEAP can accurately predict 59% of the total number of dynamically executed loads on which it makes predictions.

We have derived DEAP from Roth et al.'s load-load dependence predictor [5], which we refer to as the RMS predictor. [3] The RMS predictor captures dependences between producer and consumer loads. However, the RMS predictor does not always capture the precise effective address of a specific instance of a consumer load. First, we describe the RMS predictor. Then, we show how we derive DEAP from the RMS predictor.

The RMS Predictor

The RMS predictor consists of two tables: the Potential Producer Window (PPW) and the Correlation Table (CT). The PPW maintains a list of the most recently

[3] RMS comes from the first letter of the authors' last names: Roth, Moshovos, and Sohi.

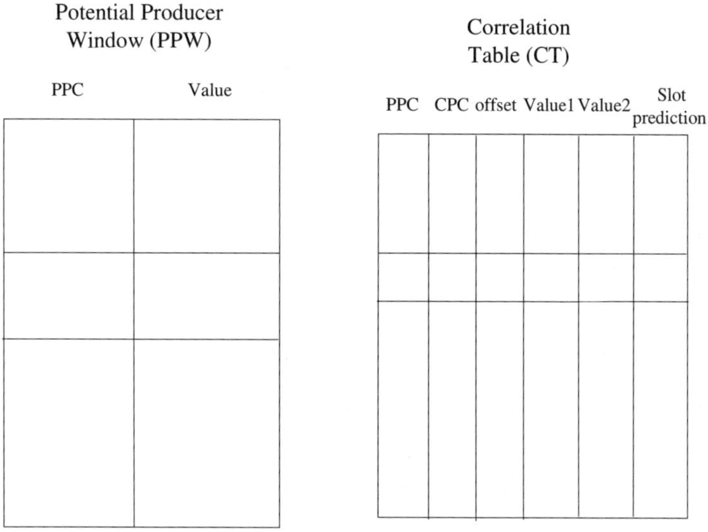

Fig. 15.3. DEAP configuration (PPC = Producer PC, CPC = Consumer PC).

loaded values and their corresponding instructions. Thus, loads in the PPW are loads that can potentially be producer loads. The CT maintains correlations or dependences between producer and consumer loads. As a load completes, we enter its PC and loaded value into the PPW. At the same time, we do an associative search of the PPW to find if a prior load produced this load's base address. If so, then this load is a consumer load of the prior load. This establishes the load-load dependence template that we record in the CT. Subsequently, when the producer load appears again, the RMS predictor will search the CT associatively for a match. If there is a match, the RMS predictor will trigger a prefetch on the value (i.e., base address) loaded by the producer load + offset of the consumer load obtained from the CT.

The RMS predictor works great for prefetching load misses but may not be as precise for effective address prediction in a few cases. Figure 15.4 shows such an example. In this example, the RMS predictor establishes a dependence between PC1 and PC2. However, the real dependence exists between PC1 of the first iteration and PC2 of the second iteration. That is, PC1 of the first iteration loads the base address of PC2 of the second iteration. Unfortunately, if we use the RMS predictor to predict effective addresses, then we would incorrectly predict that the effective address of PC2 in the first iteration is loaded by PC1 from the first iteration. This, however, works well for prefetching load misses-the purpose Roth et al. originally designed the RMS predictor for. This is because Roth et al. trigger a prefetch using the base address (and adding in any necessary offset) loaded by the producer load from PC1 of the first iteration. As long as this prefetch does not cause too much cache pollution, it is irrelevant whether PC2 from the first iteration or second iteration uses the prefetched cache block. However, we do not have this luxury for effective address prediction, which must precisely predict the addresses for PC2 in every iteration.

Deriving DEAP from the RMS Predictor

We construct DEAP by augmenting the RMS predictor with more precise dependence information (Figure 15.3). Like the RMS predictor, DEAP has the PPW and the CT. Like RMS, DEAP's PPW has two fields: PPC and Value. The PPC is the potential producer PC, and Value is the value (a potential base address of a subsequent load) loaded by the potential producer load. Like the RMS predictor, DEAP's CT maintains the PPC (producer PC), CPC (consumer PC), and offset of the consuming load. Unlike the RMS predictor, DEAP's CT has several additional fields. Each entry in DEAP's CT can have one or more Value slots (Value1, Value2, ...) and a slot predictor. Also, unlike the RMS predictor, we force DEAP to have only one entry corresponding to a consumer PC to simplify the implementation of DEAP. We could have had multiple consumer PC entries like the RMS predictor, but that would have made the slot prediction more complicated.

When a load commits, we take three update actions. First, as in the RMS predictor, we enter the load into the PPW. Second, we associatively search the CT with the load's PC for a match on the PPC field of the CT. For every matching entry, we record the value read by the load into the entry. We maintain the Value1, Value2, ... etc. fields as a circular queue, so this newly loaded value will remove the oldest value loaded in every matched CT entry. Third, we associatively search the CT with this load's PC for a match on the CPC field. Since all CPC entries in DEAP are forced to be unique, this consumer load's PC will match only one CT entry. Then, we will search the Value slots in the CT entry for a match. If there is a match, we update the slot predictor to point to this slot in the CT entry.

The DEAP probe is simpler than the update. We probe the CT with a load's PC. If the probe finds a CT entry with a CPC value that matches the load's PC, we examine the slot predictor to obtain the specific slot to use in the prediction. We add the value (i.e., base address) from the predicted slot of the CT entry and the load's offset to predict an effective address for the load. However, DEAP does not make a prediction if there is no matching CPC entry in the CT.

There is another subtle difference between RMS and DEAP. The RMS predictor is probed by producer loads so that the producer loads can trigger the prefetch of the corresponding consumer loads' data. In contrast, the DEAP predictor is probed by consumer loads to obtain their own effective addresses. This enables the pipeline to issue consumer loads early in the pipeline.

15.3 Evaluation Methodology

This section describes Asim-our simulator framework, the machine model we simulated using Asim, and the benchmarks we used for our evaluation.

15.3.1 Asim

Asim is a simulation framework developed by the VSSAD, Alpha Development Group, to rapidly prototype modern out-of-order and speculative microprocessors [16]. Asim is divided into two major components—a front-end instruction feeder

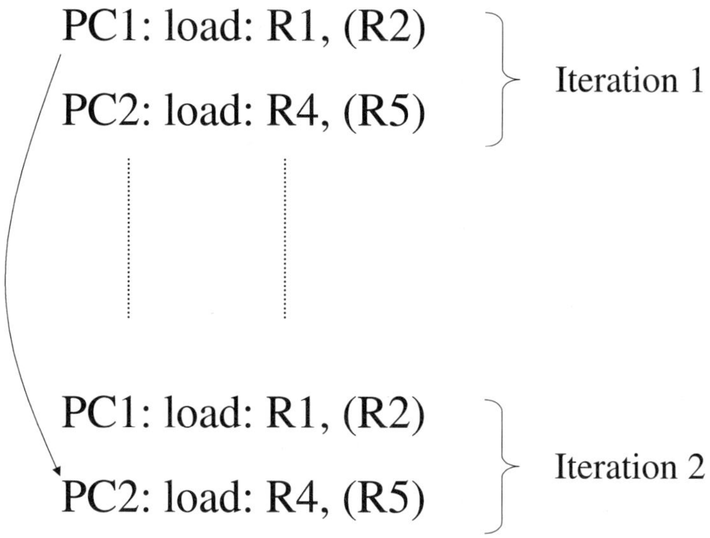

Fig. 15.4. Load-load dependence across iterations.

and a back-end performance model. The front-end feeder fetches, issues, and executes instructions as well as reads and writes memory under the control of the performance model, which can direct the feeder to go down and recover from wrong speculative paths. This level of control allows us to perform detailed simulation of out-of-order and speculative microprocessors. We have structured Asim's performance models as a bundle of modules and buffers. Modules execute algorithms with almost no notion of time, while buffers connect modules and incorporate time in them. For example, a data cache could be a module. A data cache probe would return the data via the result bus, which we model as an output buffer. However, this output buffer from the data cache module will capture both the time to run the data cache probe algorithm in hardware as well as the time on the result bus. Modeling at this level of detail allows us to accurately prototype a modern microprocessor. Asim modules can be used in different contexts. For example, they can work independently (called the Stand-alone model) or within a timing framework (called the Timing model). For example, the data cache module can run by itself and return cache hit or miss rates. At the same time, we can plug in the same data cache module into a Timing model to understand the behavior and timing of the data cache in a real pipeline model. In this chapter, we use both the Stand-alone and Timing models to understand the behavior of the five predictors. The Standalone model gives us the accuracy of our predictors, while the Timing model shows the impact of effective address prediction in a real pipeline.

15.3.2 Oracle Simulation

Oracle simulation allows us to perform upper bound studies of realistic pipelines. For example, in this chapter using oracle simulation, we study the upper bound of the performance of a Perfect effective address predictor with a modern, out-of-order, and speculative pipeline. Our Perfect predictor obtains the correct effective address for an instruction by querying the oracle, which runs simultaneously with the main simulation thread. Then, Perfect sends the predicted loads down a fast path to the memory system in the pipeline (Figure 15.1). The entire pipeline remains unchanged except for the fast path and higher bandwidth to the memory system.

We implement the oracle using Asim's multi-threading support. Normally, in Asim, each benchmark is run in two threads—the Feeder thread and the Timing thread. With oracle simulation, each benchmark is run in three threads-the Feeder thread the Timing thread, and the oracle thread. The Feeder thread feeds instructions to the Timing Thread. The Timing thread corresponds to the conventional detailed pipeline model simulation with out-of-order issue and speculative execution. The oracle thread, however, fetches the same instruction stream as the Timing thread, but executes each instruction immediately upon fetching. [4]

In oracle mode, the simulator keeps track of the relationship between corresponding instructions in the Timing and oracle threads. During the simulation we can find the Oracle thread counterpart to each instruction in the Timing thread. The simulator allows us to query this Oracle Instruction for its input values, computed output values, and internal state, such as branch direction and effective address. This query is possible even before the respective instruction in the Timing thread has issued since the corresponding instruction in the cracle thread has already executed with the correct input values and produced the correct output values. Note that the Oracle thread follows the Timing thread down all paths of execution, including speculative paths. In the case of a misprediction recovery, both the Timing thread and the Oracle thread restore their state to the same point (i.e. the killed instruction) and continue to execute along the correct path. Although other researchers have used the separation of Feeder and Timing threads to model modern out-of-order and speculative processors (e.g., Bechem et al. [17]), we are not aware of any prior work that used Oracle threads for upper bound studies of the nature explored in this chapter.

15.3.3 Simulated Machine Model

Table 15.1 shows the configurations of the four effective address predictors we implemented in Asim. Table 15.2 shows the base processor configuration we use in all our simulations. Figure 15.1 shows how we integrated our predictors with our realistic pipeline model. All the five predictors—Perfect, LAP, SAP, CAP, and DEAP—make predictions right after the register rename stage of the pipeline. However, to study the upper bound of performance available from effective address prediction with a realistic pipeline, we made the following assumptions:

[4] Unfortunately, we cannot run the Timing Thread in the same way - that is, execute an instruction completely on fetch — because we need to accurately model the relative occurrence of instruction-related events. For example, we cannot correctly model the impact of speculation and wrong-path instructions without a detailed pipeline model.

Table 15.1. Effective Address Predictor Configurations.

Predictor	Total Bytes	Configuration
LAP	45 kB	4k-entry, 2-way table
SAP	60 kB	4k-entry, 2-way, 2-delta, strided predictor
CAP	70 kB	4k-entry, 2-way load buffer, 4K entry direct-mapped link table
DEAP	3.8 kB	128-entry, depth=2, fully associative CT; 32-entry, fully associative PPW

Table 15.2. Base processor configuration used in all simulations. Note results are independent of our choice of write-back or write-thru cache.

128 entry instruction queue
128 kB 2-way set-associative L1 instruction cache
128 kB 2-way set-associative L1 write-thru cache
A larger and more powerful 21264-like branch predictor
8 instructions maximum issued per cycle
4 D-Cache Ports (any combinations of load and stores), 2 cycle access
8M Direct Mapped, Write-back, Unified Second Level Cache 12 cycle access

- We probe and update the predictors in the same cycle. Perfect is always correct, so it does not need to be updated. However, we update the other four predictors using the correct effective address available from the oracle. Additionally, DEAP requires producer loads to update the DEAP tables with the value it loaded. We assume that this update happens immediately in the same cycle and not when the producer load commits. In a real implementation, such an update may be delayed and must happen speculatively.
- We allow loads for which the predictor makes a correct prediction to go down a fast path. The fast path is a bypass from the frontend of the pipe (after the rename stage) to the memory access stage of the pipeline. The fast path never stalls, so the fast path must provide 8 load ports (because we can issue up to 8 instructions, and hence 8 loads, per cycle). [5]
- To avoid any unwanted interaction of store-load dependence predictor with our effective address predictors, we use a perfect memory dependence predictor for all our simulations.
- Finally, we have not implemented any recovery mechanism. This allows us to study the upper bound of performance of effective address prediction without having to worry about quirks in individual recovery mechanisms for different predictors.

[5] This increases the total number of load ports in our machine to 12 (4 in the regular path and 8 extra ports on the fast path). However, our experiments, not shown here, reveal that our base machine model (with no fast path) has almost no performance gains with greater than 4 load ports on the seven benchmarks we evaluated in this chapter.

15.3.4 Benchmarks

We use a mix of seven benchmarks in our evaluation—three from SpecInt95, one from SpecFp95, and three from the Olden benchmark suite [11]. The SpecInt95 and SpecFp95 benchmarks are from the SPEC suite (http://www.spec.org), while the Olden benchmarks are pointer-intensive benchmarks from Princeton University. We believe these provide a good mix of benchmarks because they represent programs from widely different application areas. We added Olden to our evaluation because the SPEC benchmarks are not particularly pointer-rich. Table 15.3 summarizes the characteristics of our seven benchmarks. Compress compresses large text files using adaptive Limpel-Ziv coding. Gcc compiles pre-processed source code into optimized SPARC assembly code. M88ksim simulates the Motorola 88100 processor running Dhrystone and a memory test program. Mgrid calculates a 3D potential field. Em3d simulates the propagation of electro-magnetic waves in 3D. Health simulates the Colombian health care system. Finally, Tsp computes an estimate of the best hamiltonian circuit for the traveling-salesman problem. Em3d, health, and tsp use a variety of pointer-based data structures, such as lists, binary trees, and quadtrees. Figure 15.5 shows improvements in IPC over the base results reported in Table /refatable3.

Table 15.3. Benchmark characterization. We skipped between 30 million and 2 billion instructions to reach the interesting point of each benchmark. M = million, K = thousand. Warmup = number of instructions for which we warm up the simulator without collecting statistics. Tot inst = total number of instructions simulated.

Benchmark	Suite	Warmup	Tot Insts	Loads	Stores	Base IPC
compress	SpecInt95	1M	30M	5.8M	1.7M	1.6
gcc	SpecInt95	1M	30M	7.4M	3.3M	2.2
m88ksim	SpecInt95	1M	30M	4.1M	2.0M	2.2
mgrid	SpecInt95	1M	30M	10.8M	2.0M	6.1
em3d	Olden	1M	30M	10.6M	2.0M	1.9
health	Olden	1M	30M	10.0M	4.0M	0.8
tsp	Olden	1M	30M	7.7M	318K	1.5

We compiled all the benchmarks above using the Compaq GEM compiler tuned for the Alpha 21264 processor at peak optimization levels. Also, we skipped between 30 million and 2 billion instructions to get to the interesting part of each benchmark.

15.4 Results

In this section, we discuss our results from the Stand-alone and Timing models. We also perform some sensitivity tests with the effective address predictors.

15.4.1 Stand-alone Model/Results

Asim's Stand-alone models allow us to study the prediction coverage and accuracy of our effective address predictors. Perfect is an ideal effective address predictor,

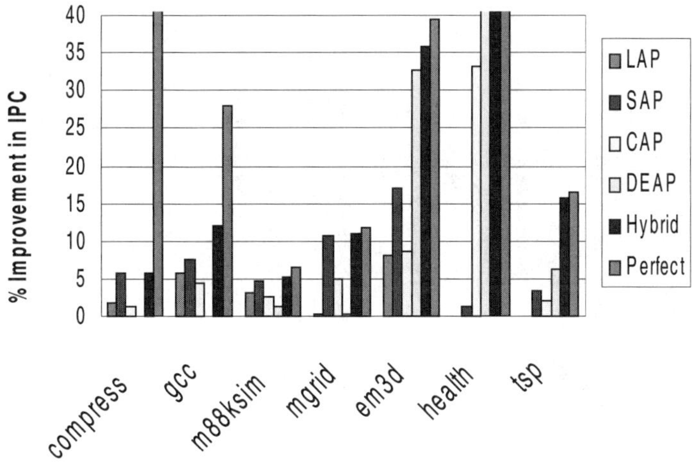

Fig. 15.5. Potential IPC improvement from effective address predictors. The vertical axis is the percent improvement in IPC over the base IPCs reported in Table 15.3. Four bars that are cut off from the top are: compress-Perfect = 60%, health-DEAP = 218%, health-Hybrid = 234%, health-Perfect = 244%.

whose coverage and accuracy is 100% in the Stand-alone model. [6] Figure 15.6 shows the coverage and Figure 15.7 shows the accuracy of the other four predictors—LAP, SAP, CAP, and DEAP. Figure 15.6 shows that a hybrid of the four predictors-LAP, SAP, CAP, and DEAP-could cover (i.e., make a prediction on) a large percentage of dynamically executed loads in our seven benchmarks. Individually, the predictors have widely different coverage. LAP, SAP, CAP, and DEAP cover 39%, 53%, 54%, and 32% of all loads, respectively. However, the hybrid predictor on average covers 85% of loads across the seven benchmarks. Figure 15.7 shows that an ideal hybrid, which can always pick the best predictor for each load, can provide very high prediction accuracy. Like the coverage results, the individual accuracy results vary between 29% and 52% across the predictors. However, an ideal hybrid could correctly predict the effective addresses of 81% of dynamically executed loads on which it makes predictions on.

Table 15.4 explains why the ideal hybrid can predict the effective addresses with such high accuracy. Table 15.4 shows a breakdown of correctly predicted loads for each predictor, and Figure 15.9 shows the corresponding Venn diagram of predictor coverage. For example, the column S shows the percentage of loads that were

[6] Perfect's coverage is, however, not 100% in the Timing model because Perfect does not make a prediction on loads that depend on a recent prior uncommitted store. In contrast, the Stand-alone model simply executes instructions without a pipeline model and, hence, Perfect makes predictions on, and therefore covers, all loads in the Stand-alone model.

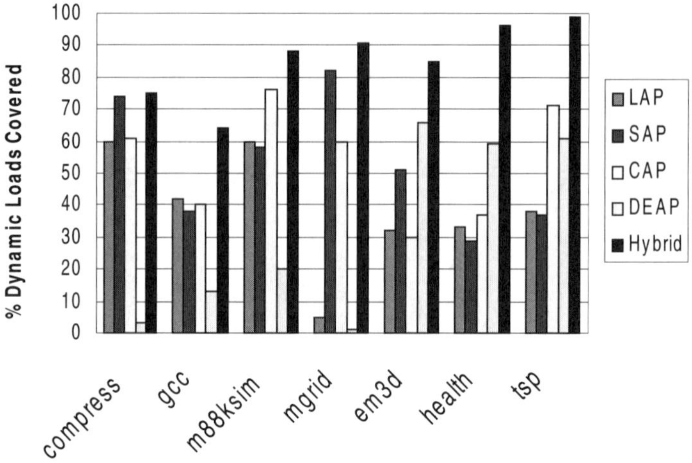

Fig. 15.6. Percentage of dynamic loads covered by all predictors. Hybrid means that at least one predictor tried to predict the effective address of a dynamic load.

correctly predicted only by SAP. Similarly, the SC column shows the percentage of loads that were correctly predicted by both SAP and CAP and not by any other predictor. The S number does not include the SC number. As Table 15.4 shows, SAP, CAP, and DEAP appear to accurately predict different loads. For example, only SAP correctly predicts the effective addresses of 27.9% of the loads in mgrid, while CAP alone correctly predicts 23.8% of the loads in m88ksim. On the other hand, only DEAP accurately predicts between 19% and 49% of the loads in the Olden benchmarks. Thus, an ideal hybrid of these predictors can result in very high prediction accuracy.

15.4.2 Timing Model/Results

Asim's Timing model combined with oracle simulation allows us to study the upper bound of the performance from effective address prediction. As Figure 15.5 shows, the potential performance improvement from effective address prediction varies widely among the benchmarks. The potential performance improvement (as shown by the Perfect predictor) ranges from as low as 7% to as high as 244%. Interestingly, however, the ideal hybrid—the predictor that always picks the correct predictor for each load—performs very close to the Perfect predictor for most benchmarks. Individually, on average, LAP, SAP, CAP, and DEAP result in 3%, 7%, 8%, and 36% performance improvement, respectively. The ideal hybrid results in 44% improvement, while the Perfect predictor performs 58% better. Note that the Perfect predictor makes predictions on all loads except those that are dependent on recent prior stores in flight. Similarly, the other predictors do not make predictions on loads that depend on recent prior stores in flight.

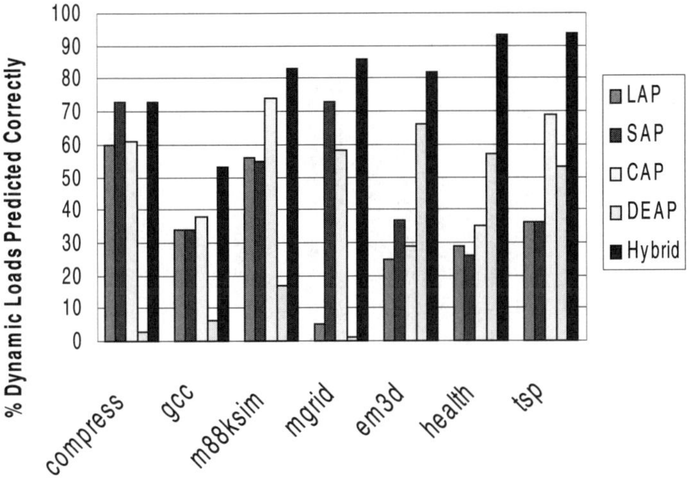

Fig. 15.7. Percentage of dynamic loads predicted by all predictors. Hybrid means that at least one predictor accurately predicted the effective address of a dynamic load.

	L	S	C	D	LS	LC	LD	SC	SD	CD	LSC	LSD	LCD	SCD	LSCD	None
compress	0.0	12.1	0.2	0.3	0.1	0.0	0.0	0.1	0.0	0.0	57.9	0.0	0.0	0.0	2.4	26.8
gcc	1.9	1.7	12.8	2.5	8.1	0.8	0.2	0.9	0.2	0.6	21.3	0.6	0.0	0.1	1.5	46.7
m88ksim	1.4	1.3	23.8	1.3	3.1	0.8	0.2	0.3	0.1	0.3	35.2	1.2	0.0	0.1	13.8	17.2
mgrid	0.0	27.9	12.8	0.1	0.3	0.0	0.0	40.5	0.0	0.2	4.1	0.0	0.0	0.0	0.3	13.8
em3d	0.0	15.5	0.0	27.1	0.1	0.0	2.5	0.1	2.2	10.5	0.2	5.4	4.9	1.5	11.5	18.5
health	0.8	0.7	12.5	49.1	3.1	3.4	0.3	0.1	0.2	1.2	15.5	3.2	0.0	0.1	2.6	7.1
tsp	0.2	0.2	4.9	19.4	3.9	0.2	0.1	0.1	0.1	32.8	30.9	0.4	0.0	0.0	0.4	6.4

Table 15.4. Breakdown of accurately predicted dynamic loads as a percentage of covered loads. L = % loads accurately predicted by LAP alone and no other predictor. S = % loads accurately predicted by SAP alone. C = % loads accurately predicted by CAP alone. D = % loads accurately predicted by DEAP alone. LS = % load accurately predicted by both L and S, but not by L and S individually and not by another predictor either. We define various combinations of L, S, C, D in a similar way. None = no predictor accurately predicted these loads. Figure 15.9 shows a Venn diagram that illustrates the breakdown of accurately predicted loads in this table.

Several interesting results stand out:

- The ideal hybrid performs very well for all benchmarks except compress. This is because none of the predictors can accurately predict a large fraction (25%) of the dynamically executed loads in compress (Figure 15.8). Thus, for the hybrid predictor, only 22% of all loads that miss in the L1 cache go down the fast path. In contrast, the Perfect predictor, which can issue the loads that miss earlier

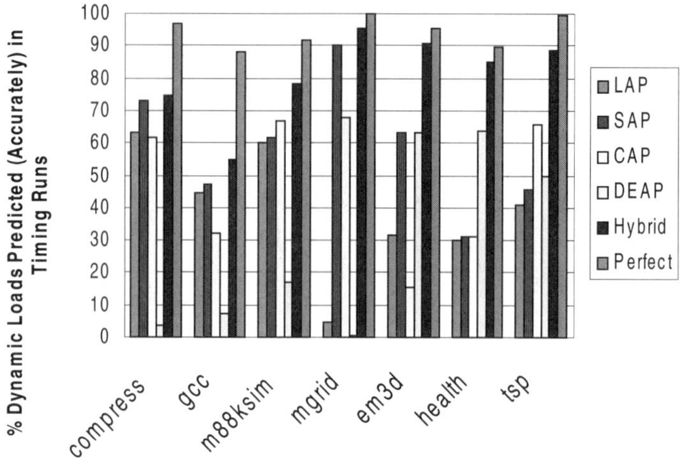

Fig. 15.8. Percentage of dynamic loads predicted accurately in the timing runs.

in the pipe and thereby prefetch the L1 misses (and L2 hits) ahead of time, accurately predicts 97% of the loads.

- DEAP is extremely effective for the Olden benchmarks and provides a performance improvement between 49% and 63%. This is because DEAP can predict loads that are in pointer-chasing codes, such as the Olden benchmarks. This is because of two reasons. Like the RMS predictor, DEAP can prefetch L2 hits that miss in the L1 cache. However, more importantly, unlike the RMS predictor, DEAP helps prefetch L1 hits. This is critical to performance improvement because a large percentage of the predicted loads actually hit in the L1 cache (Figure 15.10).
- Finally, we found that increasing the DEAP size had very little impact on performance of these benchmarks. Increasing the DEAP size by roughly seven times gave a performance improvement of less than 1%.

15.5 Related Work

In this chapter, we draw upon a huge body of prior research on effective address prediction. The predictors LAP, SAP, and CAP are based on work in several papers, such as [4, 7, 8, 9, 10, 13, 15]. Additionally, many papers, such as [3, 4, 15], performed a comparative study of some of the predictors and their hybrids.

We improve upon this prior body of research by evaluating DEAP and understanding its prediction rates and performance. DEAP is a variant of the RMS predictor [5]. However, unlike the RMS predictor, which was used by Roth et al. to prefetch cache misses, we use DEAP to prefetch L1 cache hits and issue loads early

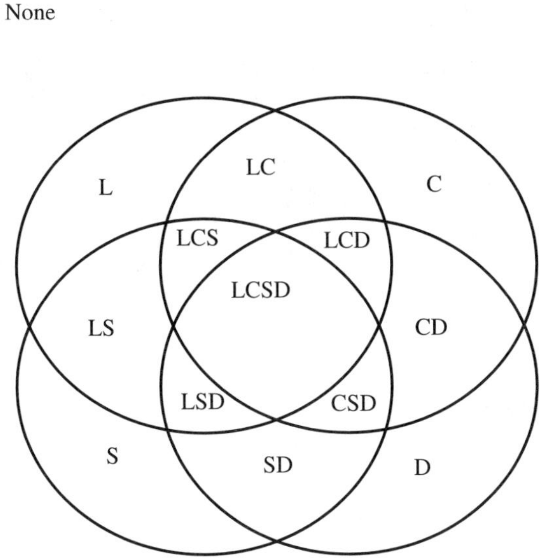

Fig. 15.9. Explanation of columns in Table 15.4. This Venn diagram shows how we break down the accurately predicted loads into different categories.

in the pipeline. We compare DEAP with LAP, SAP, and CAP in terms of their prediction rates and upper bound of performance achievable from these predictors. We also show that on six of our seven benchmarks an ideal hybrid predictor, which picks the correct predictor for each load, can achieve performance close to a Perfect effective address predictor.

Although we focussed on effective address prediction, there are other ways to generate effective addresses earlier in the pipeline. Austin and Sohi [14] proposed overlapping effective address computation with cache access with the help of special circuits and software support. Bekerman et al. [6] proposed tracking certain registers and immediate values to calculate a load's effective address earlier in the pipeline. We believe that a combination of these techniques along with the effective address predictors we studied in this chapter will lead to good effective address prediction rates.

15.6 Conclusion and Future Work

Modern, deeply pipelined, out-of-order, and speculative microprocessors continue to be plagued by the latency of load instructions. This latency is dominated by the

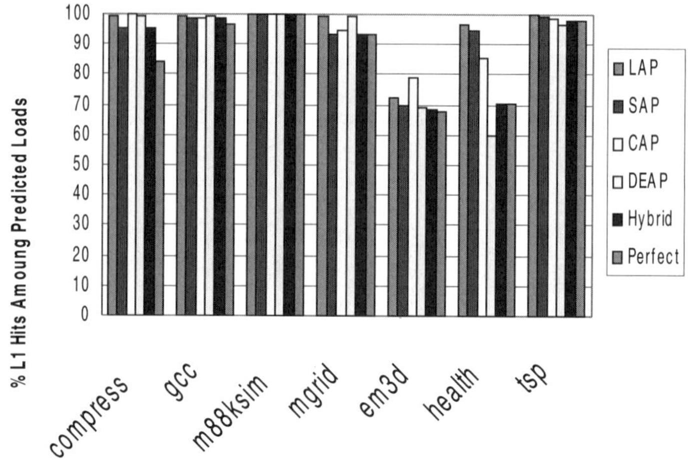

Fig. 15.10. Percentage of loads that hit in L1.

latencies to resolve the source operands of the load, to compute its effective address, and to fetch the load's data from caches or the main memory. This chapter examined the performance potential of hiding a load's data fetch latency using effective address prediction. By predicting the effective address of a load early in the pipeline, we could initiate the cache access early, thereby improving performance.

The current generation of effective address predictors for a load instruction is based on either the history or the context of the specific load. In addition, researchers had examined load-load dependence predictors to prefetch cache misses. This chapter examined the performance potential of using a load-load dependence predictor to predict effective addresses of load instructions and issue them early in the pipeline. We call this predictor the DEAP predictor.

We showed that on average DEAP could improve the accuracy of effective address prediction by 28% over a perfect combination of last address, stride address, and context-based address predictors across our seven benchmarks from the SPEC95 and Olden suites. We found that an ideal hybrid of these four predictors (including DEAP), which always picked the right predictor for a load, could potentially achieve performance close to that of a Perfect predictor in most cases.

We used an oracle-based simulation approach to evaluate our timing results. This method allowed us to measure the upper bound of the performance from effective address prediction using a mostly realistic pipeline. However, our timing simulation method did not account for the penalty due to misprediction of an effective address and assumed a zero-cycle latency from address prediction resolution to address predictor update.

This work can be extended in several ways in future. To accurately reflect pipeline effects, one must model the penalty due to the mis-prediction of the various effective address predictors as well as realistic latencies for address prediction resolution to address predictor update. Also, it will be interesting to understand the combined impact of load-load dependence prediction on cache misses (or prefetching) as well as cache hits (as discussed in this chapter) for long-latency pipelines. An analytical model may help in this effort.

Acknowledgments

We would like to thank Rick Kessler, Geoff Lowney, and Paul Rubinfeld for their valuable feedback on early drafts of this chapter.

References

1. Chrysos G, Emer J (1998) Memory Dependence Prediction Using Store Sets, In: Proceedings of the 25th Annual International Symposium on Computer Architecture (ISCA), June 1998.
2. Moshovos A, Breach SE, Vijaykumar TN, Sohi GS (1997) Dynamic Speculation and Synchronization of Data Dependences, In: Proceedings of the 24th Annual International Symposium on Computer Architecture (ISCA), May 1997.
3. Reinman G, Calder B (1998) Predictive Techniques for Aggressive Load Speculation, In: Proceedings of the 31st Annual International Symposium on Microarchitecture (MICRO), December 1998.
4. Bekerman M, Jourdan S, Ronnen R, Kirshenboim G, Rappoport L, Yoaz A, Weiser U (1999) Correlated Load-Address Predictors, In: Proceedings of the 26th Annual International Symposium on Computer Architecture (ISCA), May 1999.
5. Roth A, Moshovos A, Sohi GS (1998) Dependence Based Prefetching for Linked Data Structures, In: Proceedings of the 8th International Conference on Architectural Support for Programming Languages and Operating Systems (ASPLOS), October 1998.
6. Bekerman M, Yoaz A, Gabbay F, Jourdan S, Kalaev M, Ronen R (2000) Early Load Address Resolution via Register Tracking, In: Proceedings of the 27th Annual International Symposium on Computer Architecture (ISCA), June 2000.
7. Lipasti MH, Wilkerson CB, Shen JP (1996) Value Locality and Load Value Prediction, In: Proceedings of the 17th International Conference on Architectural Support for Programming Languages and Operating Systems, pp. 138–147, October 1996.
8. Chen T-F, Baer J-L (1995) Effective Hardware-Based Data Prefetching for High Performance Processors, IEEE Transactions on Computers, 44(5):609–623, May.
9. Eikermeyer RJ, Vassiliadis S (1993) A Load Instruction Unit for Pipelined Processors, IBM Journal of Research and Development, 37:547–564, July.
10. Sazeides Y, Smith JE (1997) The Predictability of Data Values, In: Proceedings of the 30th International Symposium on Microarchitecture (MICRO), pp. 248-258, December 1997.
11. Carlisle MC and Rogers A (1995) Software Caching and Computation Migration on Olden, In: Proceedings of the Fifth ACM SIGPLAN Symposium on Principles and Practice of Parallel Programming (PPoPP), July 1995.

12. Smith J (2000) Slow Wires, Hot Chips, and Leaky Transistors: New Challenges in the New Millennium, Panel at the International Symposium on Computer Architecture (ISCA), June 2000.
13. Gonzalez J, Gonzalez A (1997) Speculative Execution via Address Prediction and Data Prefetching, In: Proceedings of the 11th International Conference on Supercomputing (ICS), p. 196–203, July 1997.
14. Austin T M, Sohi G S (1995) Zero-cycle Loads: Microarchitecture Support for Reducing Load Latency, In: Proceedings of the 28th Annual International Symposium on Microarchitecture (MICRO), pages 82–92, December 1995.
15. Black B, Mueller B, Postal S, Rakvie R, Tamaphethai N, and Shen JP (1998) Load Execution Latency Reduction, In: Proceedings of the 12th International Conference on Supercomputing (ICS), June 1998.
16. Mukherjee S (2001) The Asim Manual, Confidential Document, Compaq Computer Corporation.
17. Bechem C, Combs J, Utamaphethai N, Black B, Blanton RD, Shen JP (1999) An Integrated Functional Performance Simulator, IEEE Micro 19(3):26–35, May/June.

Part V

Workload Considerations

16

Evaluating Novel Memory System Alternatives for Speculative Multithreaded Computer Systems

AJ KleinOsowski[1] and David J. Lilja[2]

[1] University of Minnesota, Minneapolis, MN, USA ajko@ece.umn.edu
[2] University of Minnesota, Minneapolis, MN, USA lilja@ece.umn.edu

Abstract. This work models and evaluates a new cache structure for scalable multithreaded computer systems. Multithreaded architectures that support the speculative execution of multiple concurrent threads of execution require a special speculative memory buffer to detect and potentially correct dependences at run time. The main question being addressed in this study is whether this speculative memory buffer should be merged with a nonspeculative cache, or kept separate. As a related question, we also evaluate whether the traditional cache structure should be private to each processing element, or whether the cache should be shared among all processing elements. Our results and cost-for-performance analysis show that, on average, the novel hybrid level-1 data cache (which merges a distributed level-1 data cache with the speculative memory buffer) has a 13% slowdown as compared to an ideal shared level-1 cache with separate speculative memory buffers. The distributed level-1 cache with separate speculative memory buffer showed, on average, a 4% speedup compared to an ideal shared level-1 cache with separate speculative memory buffers.

16.1 Introduction

Advances in device physics have taken us from the invention of the transistor, to submicron feature sizes, to the emerging field of nanoscale electronics. Performance benefits of this feature size scaling, however, are reaching a plateau [1]. Since scaling the transistors in computer systems is becoming increasingly difficult, computer architects resort to finding clever ways to compute multiple things at once–thereby making workloads run faster. Explicitly or automatically detecting and exploiting parallelism in modern workloads shows great potential for performance increases in current and next generation computing devices.

Threads of execution within a program are typically loop iterations or multiple paths of a control structure. These threads most often have cross iteration data dependences that are difficult, if not impossible, for the compiler to detect at compile time. Therefore, multithreaded architectures [6, 9, 15, 16, 19] require hardware to support data dependence checking and speculative execution. In many multithreaded architectures, the compiler identifies possible data dependences and then special hardware determines, at run time, whether these data dependences are true dependences or simply false alarms. True data dependences are resolved and enforced with speculative memory buffer hardware. False alarms are treated as regular loads and stores, essentially bypassing the speculative memory buffer.

The main question we propose and evaluate in this study is whether this speculative buffer should be merged with a nonspeculative cache or kept separate. As a related question, we also evaluate whether the traditional cache structure should be private to each processing element or whether the cache should be shared among all the processing elements. Our motivation is to quantitatively evaluate the performance of a novel, hybrid level-1 data cache, which merges a distributed level-1 data cache with the speculative memory buffer.

16.2 Background and Motivation

Several multithreaded architectures have been proposed that support synchronization and communication between threads. In the M-Machine [6], XIMD [19], Elementary Multithreading [9], and Multiscalar approaches [15], data values are speculated and then, if the speculations turn out to be incorrect, the thread that speculated incorrectly is terminated and restarted. This requires each read and write to memory to be checked and validated. Synchronization information and data are passed among thread units via hardware extensions to the register file. In the case of the Multiscalar approach, another piece of hardware, the speculative versioning cache [7], also can be used to enforce data dependences.

In the Superthreaded [16] approach, data dependences are checked and enforced, not speculated. This means that only writes to memory, not reads, need to be buffered. Since fewer addresses need to be checked in the Superthreaded approach as compared to other multithreaded approaches, the bandwidth required for the Superthreaded speculative memory buffer will be lower than the bandwidth required for other multithreaded speculative memory buffers. Furthermore, the Superthreaded speculative memory buffer will need fewer entries than other multithreaded memory buffers, thereby allowing it to be smaller than other multithreaded memory buffers.

In this work, we use the Superthreaded Architecture [16] as a test platform. Previous work on this architecture assumed a shared level-1 data cache and a distributed speculative memory buffer separate from the level-1 data cache. Further evaluation of the shared level-1 data cache led to suspicion that threads would contend and stall while waiting for an available read or write port [17]. The only way to resolve this bottleneck would be to have one or more read and write ports per thread unit. On a large-scale system with eight thread units, assuming two read ports and one write port per thread unit, this would mean the shared level-1 data cache would need 16 read ports and 8 write ports. Having enough ports on a shared level-1 data cache to reduce the bottleneck effect makes the shared level-1 data cache hardware too expensive to be a viable option. Instead, we choose to distribute the level-1 data cache.

Distributing the level-1 data cache immediately raises a red flag: How do we enforce coherence among the caches? Since our compiler conservatively identifies all possible data dependences in a thread's execution path, these shared data items are kept in the speculative memory buffer. Updates to shared data items are passed to downstream threads via the unidirectional communication ring. In this way, cache coherence is already built into the Superthreaded Architecture.

Prior work [2] on the Superthreaded architecture showed high variance in the number of active speculative memory buffer entries among different benchmark program workloads. This variance in speculative memory buffer use means that some programs filled the speculative memory buffer to capacity and other programs used very few of the speculative memory buffer entries. In the Superthreaded approach, if a speculative thread fills its speculative memory buffer, that thread must stall until all parent threads retire and the thread becomes nonspeculative. Once the thread is nonspeculative, it can flush its speculative memory buffer entries to the main shared memory and continue executing. Needless to say, stalls due to a filled speculative memory buffer serialize execution and drastically increase the run time of a benchmark program.

In order to avoid stalls due to a filled speculative memory buffer, we propose a hybrid level-1 data cache (shown in Figure 16.3) that merges the speculative memory buffer with a distributed, nonspeculative data cache. Entries in this hybrid structure can be used as either a traditional cache line, or as a speculative memory buffer entry. In this way, we significantly increase the speculative memory buffer entries available to workloads that need many entries. For workloads that need only a few speculative memory buffer entries, the hybrid entries can be used as traditional cache lines, thereby making use of otherwise unused die space.

The hybrid level-1 data cache does not come without trade-offs. Most notably, in order to avoid overflow in any of the cache rows, the hybrid cache must be able to put an entry in any cache block. This requires a fully-associative lookup when searching the hybrid cache for a block. Also, the coherence mechanism for the Superthreaded Architecture works at the word level. This requires a very small block size of 4 bytes (one word) for the hybrid structure. Our evaluation and the results presented in Section 16.5 will show whether the increased performance of the hybrid level-1 data cache outweighs the implementation trade-offs of this novel structure.

16.3 The Superthreaded Architecture Model

The Superthreaded Architecture [16] was developed to address the unexploited parallelism available in classically hard-to-parallelize general purpose programs. As feature sizes shrink, more transistors become available on computer chip dies. The Superthreaded Architecture makes use of these extra transistors by adding special thread management and memory operation filtering hardware to a standard superscalar core. Multiple copies of the core and special hardware (a so-called thread unit) are then put together on a single die.

Each thread unit is connected to its successor via a unidirectional communication ring. Thread units each have a local register file and local level-1 instruction cache. The cache arrangement of each thread unit is under investigation in this work.

A program begins executing on a single thread unit while all other thread units are idle. When a parallel region is encountered, a special superthreaded instruction wakes up the downstream thread unit and sends this thread unit all the data it needs to begin executing an iteration of the loop. This newly active thread unit soon executes the instructions to wake up its neighbor and send its neighbor data. Each thread wakes up its downstream thread until there are no more idle threads in the system. The youngest thread stores the wake-up instruction and data in a special buffer that holds these instructions until the oldest thread finishes its iteration of the loop and goes back to being idle. At this time, the oldest thread receives the wake-up instruction and data and then becomes the youngest thread in the system. This cycle of wake up-execute-idle-wake up proceeds until all iterations of the parallel region are complete.

16.4 Methodology

In this study, we simulate the functionality and performance of three cache architectures for speculative multithreaded computer systems. To that end, we simulate the access time and power requirements of generic cache architectures of the same sizes, associativities, and port requirements as those used in our functional simulations. We then extrapolate cycle latencies from the access time results (given in nanoseconds) and feed these cycle latencies into our functional simulations to obtain overall performance results.

Each of the three cache architectures we evaluate has its own requirements in terms of associativity and block size. Taking the access time and power requirements of these different cache architectures into consideration in the functional simulations helps us rigorously evaluate which cache architecture alternative is the best in terms of implementation cost and functional performance for the Superthreaded Architecture.

16.4.1 Access Time and Power Requirements Simulation

We use the Cacti [18] simulator to gather access time estimates in nanoseconds and per-access power requirement in nanojoules. Cacti uses an analytical model based on transistor and wire characteristics derived from SPICE [4] simulations. With Cacti, we can vary the block size, number of ports, number of sets, associativity, and fabrication technology parameters.

In this work we assume a target machine fabricated with 0.18 micrometer fabrication technology running at a clock speed of 1 GHz. This means a cache with a 1 nanosecond access time would have a 1 cycle latency. To convert the nanosecond access times from the Cacti simulations to cycle latencies for the performance simulations, we use the formula

$$CacheLatency = ceiling(\frac{AccessTime}{1nanosecond})$$

Per-access power consumption is calculated using an empirical formula built into Cacti. Cacti's power model takes into consideration the technology parameter, the length of the port wires based on the cache size, and the amount of hardware needed to drive varying levels of cache associativity.

16.4.2 Functional Simulation

The three cache architectures that we functionally test and the nomenclature we use to refer to these configurations are:

S (shared): Shared level-1 data cache with distributed, distinct speculative memory buffers;

D (distributed): Distributed level-1 data cache with distinct, distributed speculative memory buffers;

H (hybrid); Distributed, hybrid level-1 data cache that combines the level-1 data cache and the speculative memory buffer.

Figures 16.1, 16.2, and 16.3 pictorially show these three configurations.

Simulations are performed with our execution-driven simulator, Simca [10], which is an extension of the sim-outorder simulator from the SimpleScalar [3] suite. For our baseline performance, we simulate a shared level-1 data cache configuration

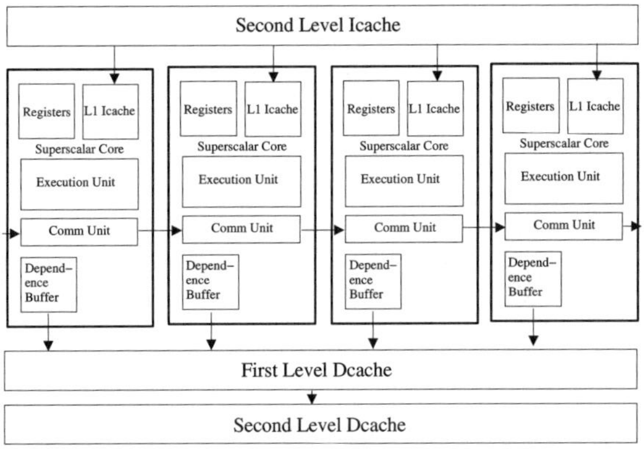

Fig. 16.1. Shared level-1 data cache with distributed, distinct speculative memory buffers.

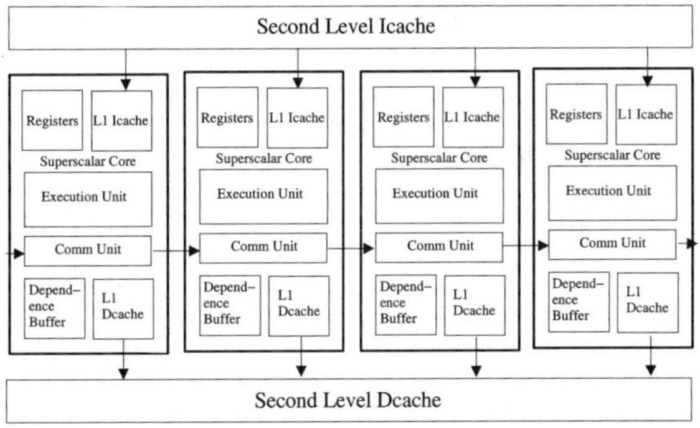

Fig. 16.2. Distributed level-1 data caches with distributed, distinct speculative memory buffers.

with infinite read and write ports, yet for the access time of this cache structure, we use the access time of a structure with two read ports and one write port. This infinite port assumption and overly optimistic access time will make the performance of the shared cache appear better than it could ever achieve on a real system. Thus, these baseline simulations show an upper bound on the performance that can be obtained on this multithreaded architecture.

To compare the performance of the three cache configurations, we run three sets of simulations, each with a different cache size. The cache sizes in the Group 2 simulations are twice as large as the cache sizes in the Group 1 simulations, and the cache sizes in the Group 3 simulations are twice as large as the cache sizes in the Group 2 simulations. Doubling and then quadrupling the cache sizes gives us a good indication of whether the performance trends hold as we scale up the computer system.

We keep the hardware cost of the different configurations within a group approximately equal. For example, for the first set of simulations, we use a 32 kB shared

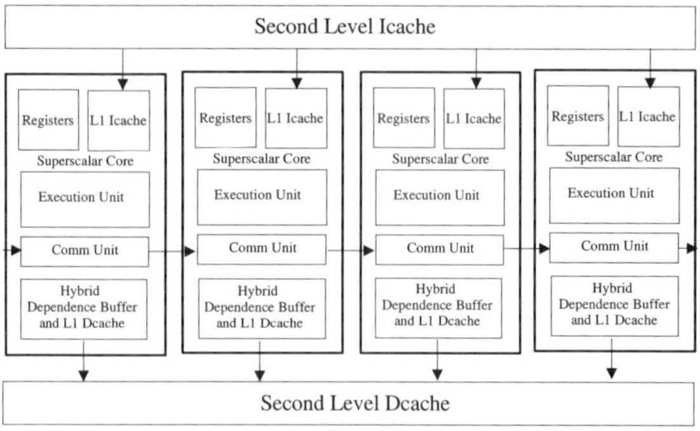

Fig. 16.3. Distributed, hybrid level-1 caches that combine the level-1 data cache and the speculative memory buffer.

cache with four thread units. This 32 kB shared cache is equivalent to four 8 kB distributed caches. For the shared and distributed cache configurations, we use a 128 entry (512 byte) speculative memory buffer. In the case of the hybrid configuration, we do not have the additional hardware cost of the 128 entry speculative memory buffer since the hybrid cache is, in essence, a very large, general purpose, speculative memory buffer. However, the hybrid configuration is fully associative, whereas the shared and distributed configurations are 4-way set-associative. The added overhead of the fully associative cache decoder is approximately equivalent to the missing 512 bytes incurred by the distinct speculative memory buffer, thereby making all three configurations approximately equal in terms of hardware cost.

Table 16.1 summarizes the configuration parameters used for each simulation. The latencies for these structures are determined by the cache access time simulations run with Cacti. These latencies will be stated and discussed in Section 16.5.

As our workload, we use a combination of programs from the SPEC 92, SPEC 95, and SPEC 2000 suites [5, 8], as well as a few standard Unix utilities. To obtain results in a reasonable amount of time, we used reduced reference input files [13] for some benchmarks and truncated the simulation of other benchmarks. Table 16.2 lists our benchmark programs, their origins, their committed instruction counts, and their total number of accesses to the level-1 data cache.

16.5 Results

The following results show the implementation costs and performance of our three alternative cache architectures for multithreaded computer systems.

16.5.1 Power Requirements

Ideal performance of our shared level-1 data cache would require a large number of ports. Therefore, we began our analysis by looking at the power implications of scaling the number of read and write ports on the shared level-1 cache. Part (a) of Figure 16.4 shows these results for a 128 kB cache with 32 bytes per block and 4-way associativity.

Table 16.1. Simulation nomenclature and parameters used for each simulation. All simulations use a 2 MB, 64 bytes/block, 4-way associative level-2 data cache. Simulations are run first with 4 thread units, then with 8 thread units.

Simulation Name	*Parameters*
Group 1	
1D4,8	Distributed level-1 data cache, 8 kB, 32 bytes/block, 4-way associative, 128 entry (512 byte) speculative memory buffer, random replacement policy, 4 or 8 thread units
1S4,8	Shared level-1 data cache, 32 kB for 4 thread units, 64 kB for 8 thread units, 32 bytes/block, 4-way associative, 128 entry (512 byte) speculative memory buffer, random replacement policy, 4 or 8 thread units
1H4,8	Hybrid level-1 data cache, 8 kB, 4 bytes/block, fully associative, random replacement policy
Group 2	
2D4,8	Distributed level-1 data cache, 16 kB, 32 bytes/block, 4-way associative, 128 entry (512 byte) speculative memory buffer, random replacement policy, 4 or 8 thread units
2S4,8	Shared level-1 data cache, 64 kB for 4 thread units, 128 kB for 8 thread units, 32 bytes/block, 4-way associative, 128 entry (512 byte) speculative memory buffer, random replacement policy, 4 or 8 thread units
2H4,8	Hybrid level-1 data cache, 16 kB, 4 bytes/block, fully associative, random replacement policy
Group 3	
3D4,8	Distributed level-1 data cache, 32 kB, 32 bytes/block, 4-way associative, 128 entry (512 byte) speculative memory buffer, random replacement policy, 4 or 8 thread units
3S4,8	Shared level-1 data cache, 128 kB for 4 thread units, 256 kB for 8 thread units, 32 bytes/block, 4-way associative, 128 entry (512 byte) speculative memory buffer, random replacement policy, 4 or 8 thread units
3H4,8	Hybrid level-1 data cache, 32 kB, 4 bytes/block, fully associative, random replacement policy

Table 16.2. Benchmark programs used in this study.

Benchmark	*Source*	*Instructions Simulated (in millions)*	*Level-1 Data Cache Accesses (in millions)*
Alvinn	SPEC FP 1992	94.3	35.8
Cmp	Standard Unix Utility	5.8	1.6
Compress	SPEC INT 1995	1.9	0.6
Ear	SPEC FP 1992	1020.2	282.7
Hydro2d	SPEC FP 1992	33.4	8.6
M88k	SPEC INT 1995	1063.2	305.7
Mcf	SPEC INT 2000	1619.3	720.2
Wc	Standard Unix Utility	6.0	2.0

In Figure 16.4, Part (a), we see that the plot of the per-access power requirement follows a quadratic curve. This result confirms our assumption that adding enough ports (two read ports and one write port per thread) to the shared level-1 data cache to avoid contention would make the shared structure unrealistically expensive (in terms of power) to implement.

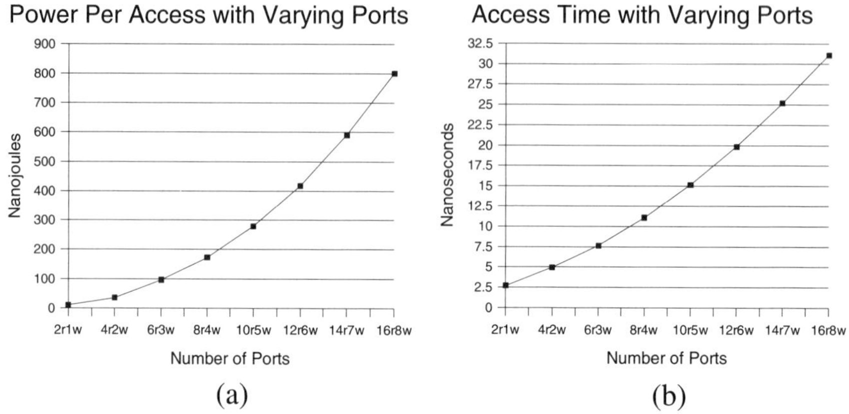

Fig. 16.4. Part (a): Power per access for shared 128 kB level-1 data cache with a varying number of read and write ports. Part (b): Access time for 128 kB level-1 data cache with a varying number of read and write ports.

Table 16.3 shows the per-access power requirement of the different configurations studied in the performance analysis simulations. From these results, we see that the distributed level-1 cache with the distinct memory buffer has the lowest per-access power requirement across all three groups of simulations. We also see that the shared level-1 cache has an exorbitant per-access power requirement. In the case of the Group 3 simulations, the per-access power requirement of the shared level-1 cache configuration is 3051% higher than the per-access power requirement of the distributed level-1 cache configuration. In all groups of simulations, the per-access power requirement of the hybrid cache configuration fell somewhere between the per-access power requirement of the distributed and shared level-1 cache configurations.

Since the per-access power requirement of the shared level-1 cache configuration in Table 16.3 was so high compared to the power requirement of the distributed and hybrid cache configurations, we proceeded to look at how that power requirement scaled down if we reduced the number of ports on the shared cache. Table 16.4 compares the results of 2 read ports and 1 write port per thread, the ideal performance case, to the ideal power case where we have only 2 read ports and 1 write port, regardless of the number of threads. Wilson and Olukotun [17] concluded that the best performance per implementation cost occurred with two cache ports. Therefore, in Table 16.4 we also include a column showing the per-access power requirement of a compromise case with 4 read ports and 2 write ports, regardless of the number of threads.

In the ideal power case, where all cache structures have 2 read ports and 1 write port, we see that the power use of the shared level-1 cache configuration is the lowest in all simulations by at least 35%. However, when we look at the compromise case, we see that the distributed level-1 cache once again has the lowest power requirement in all but one simulation. Even in the eight thread Group 1 simulations, where the shared level-1 cache configuration used less power than the distributed level-1 configuration, the power savings were only 20% of the distributed level-1 configuration.

16.5.2 Access Time Requirements

The analysis of the access time results very closely parallels the analysis of the power requirement results. We see in Part (b) of Figure 16.4 that when we scale up the number of ports for the shared level-1 cache configuration to the point where we have 2 read ports and 1 write port per thread, the access time increases quadratically. At the high end of this curve, we see an access time of 31.15 nanoseconds. Assuming a 1 GHz target machine, this equates to a level-1 cache latency of 32 cycles. Most commercial processors have a 1 or 2 cycle latency for their level-1 data cache. By direct comparison, we see that implementing a shared level-1 data cache with enough ports to avoid contention would actually slow overall performance.

In Table 16.3, we see the access times of the various configurations used in the performance analysis. These access times are converted into cycle latencies (assuming a 1 GHz target machine) and then fed as parameters to our performance simulations. We use the shared level-1 cache configuration as our baseline for our performance simulation. Therefore, we use the best access times possible for the shared level-1 data cache. These best access times occur with 2 read ports and 1 write port. Table 16.5 shows how the shared level-1 data cache access time varies when we scale up the number of ports.

16.5.3 Performance Results

The performance results in Figures 16.5 and 16.6 show that the distributed configuration has, on average, a 4% speedup compared to the ideal shared configuration. The hybrid configuration has, on average, a 13% slowdown compared to the ideal shared configuration.

The distributed configuration was faster than the ideal shared configuration in 39 of the 48 simulations. The worst performance of the distributed configuration was for the Group 1, four thread simulation of Hydro2d with a 3.24% slowdown as compared to the ideal shared configuration. The best performance for the distributed configuration was the Group 3, eight thread simulation of compress with a 15.37% speedup. Overall, the Group 1, four thread simulations of the distributed configuration showed minimal slowdown while all other simulations (except for the Group 2, eight thread simulation of mcf) showed positive speedup.

The hybrid configuration was slower than the ideal shared configuration in all 48 simulations. The best performance of the hybrid configuration was the Group 1, eight thread simulation of alvinn with a 0.22% slowdown. Overall, alvinn had only modest slowdown for the hybrid configuration with an average slowdown of 2.03%. Most other simulations (35 of the 48), however, had a greater than 10% slowdown.

16.6 Conclusion

In this work, we set out to study whether the speculative memory buffer should be merged with a nonspeculative cache or kept separate. As a related question, we

Table 16.3. Power per access and access time for configurations used in the performance analysis.

Config	*MB pwr(nJ)*	*L1 pwr(nJ)*	*Total pwr(nJ)*	*MB Acc(ns)*	*L1 Acc(ns)*
1d4	4*1.61=**6.44**	4*3.88=**15.52**	**21.96**	**1.95**	**1.24**
1s4	4*1.61=**6.44**	**58.99**	**65.43**	**1.95**	**1.70**
1h4	4*11.93=**47.72**	**0.00**	**47.72**	**2.48**	**2.48**
1d8	8*1.61=**12.88**	8*3.88=**31.04**	**43.92**	**1.95**	**1.24**
1s8	8*1.61=**12.88**	**463.06**	**475.94**	**1.95**	**2.05**
1h8	8*11.93=**95.44**	**0.00**	**95.44**	**2.48**	**2.48**
2d4	4*1.61=**6.44**	4*4.37=**17.48**	**23.92**	**1.95**	**1.43**
2s4	4*1.61=**6.44**	**101.67**	**108.11**	**1.95**	**2.05**
2h4	4*21.0=**84.00**	**0.00**	**84.00**	**3.24**	**3.24**
2d8	8*1.61=**12.88**	8*4.37=**34.96**	**47.84**	**1.95**	**1.43**
2s8	8*1.61=**12.88**	**800.86**	**813.74**	**1.95**	**2.69**
2h8	8*21.0=**168.00**	**0.00**	**168.00**	**3.24**	**3.24**
3d4	4*1.61=**6.44**	4*5.17=**20.68**	**27.12**	**1.95**	**1.70**
3s4	4*1.61=**6.44**	**172.85**	**179.29**	**1.95**	**2.69**
3h4	4*39.11=**156.44**	**0.00**	**156.44**	**4.80**	**4.80**
3d8	8*1.61=**12.88**	8*5.17=**41.36**	**54.24**	**1.95**	**1.70**
3s8	8*1.61=**12.88**	**1642.02**	**1654.90**	**1.95**	**3.27**
3h8	8*39.11=**312.88**	**0.00**	**312.88**	**4.80**	**4.80**

also evaluated whether the traditional cache structure should be private to each processing element or whether the cache should be shared among all processing elements.

The shared cache is an attractive option since it can amortize the die space necessary for the cache across the thread units which will allow for a very large cache. However, since this large cache will be far away from the thread units, the access time will be high due to the long port wires between the cache and the thread units. Also, multiple thread units will contend for access to the cache during each cycle, inducing stalls.

The distributed cache could be an alternative to the shared cache since the small distributed cache is local to each thread, thereby eliminating port contention and long port wires. However, the distributed caches must be small since we have multiple copies of the cache. The small cache will not be able to hold many cache lines and therefore may have frequent misses.

Both the shared and distributed caches have the speculative memory buffer in a small, separate structure. If this structure overflows, threads are halted and parallel execution becomes serial. The hybrid cache eliminates the overflow problem by allowing every line in the cache to act as a speculative memory buffer entry. The trade-off for the hybrid cache is that the hybrid cache must be fully associative in order to allow a cache block to be placed anywhere in the cache. As the hybrid cache scales in size, its access time becomes large due to the fully associative nature of this structure. Also, the block size of the hybrid cache must be very small (4 bytes) in order to work with existing coherence policies.

Since the performance of the hybrid configuration was worse than that of the ideal shared configuration in all simulations, our results show that we did not have

Table 16.4. Power per access with shared level-1 configurations with varying numbers of ports.

Configuration	*8r4w, 16r8w Ports* *Ideal Performance* *Total Power(nJ)*	*2r1w Ports* *Ideal Power* *Total Power(nJ)*	*4r2w Ports* *Compromise* *Total Power(nJ)*
1d4	21.96	21.96	21.96
1s4	65.43	11.61	22.04
1h4	47.72	47.72	47.72
1d8	43.92	43.92	43.92
1s8	475.94	19.87	35.08
1h8	95.44	95.44	95.44
2d4	23.92	23.92	23.92
2s4	108.11	13.43	28.64
2h4	84.00	84.00	84.00
2d8	47.84	47.84	47.84
2s8	813.74	23.19	48.01
2h8	168.00	168.00	168.00
3d4	27.12	27.12	27.12
3s4	179.29	16.75	41.57
3h4	156.44	156.44	156.44
3d8	54.24	54.24	54.24
3s8	1654.90	34.27	87.62
3h8	312.88	312.88	312.88

enough instances of memory buffer overflow to outweigh the increased access time of the hybrid configuration. This means we are better off with a distinct speculative memory buffer in its own small structure. This small structure may overflow at times; however, the fast access time of this small structure will make up for the performance loss the few times it overflows. A general purpose level-1 data cache should be used in conjunction with this special hardware structure.

Our results show that distributing the level-1 data cache over the thread units improves performance over the large shared level-1 configuration in most cases. In the cases where there is a slowdown, the slowdown is very modest. Implementing a shared level-1 data cache with a large number of read and write ports would be unrealistically expensive in terms of die size and power consumption. Therefore, since our distributed level-1 data cache has a much lower power consumption and much faster access time, multithreaded computer systems should make use of small, per-thread level-1 data caches and separate, small, specialized structures for handling cross-iteration thread dependences.

Acknowledgments

This work was supported in part by National Science Foundation grants EIA-9971666 and CCR-9900605, by a University of Minnesota-IBM Shared Research Project equipment grant, and by the Minnesota Supercomputing Institute. Many

Table 16.5. Access time with shared level-1 configurations with varying numbers of ports.

Configuration	*8r4w, 16r8w Ports Ideal Performance L1 Access(ns)*	*2r1w Ports Ideal Power L1 Access(ns)*	*4r2w Ports Compromise L1 Access(ns)*
1d4	1.24	1.24	1.24
1s4	5.35	1.70	2.61
1h4	2.48	2.48	2.48
1d8	1.24	1.24	1.24
1s8	19.39	2.05	3.38
1h8	2.48	2.48	2.48
2d4	1.43	1.43	1.43
2s4	7.16	2.05	3.38
2h4	3.24	3.24	3.24
2d8	1.43	1.43	1.43
2s8	31.15	2.69	4.95
2h8	3.24	3.24	3.24
3d4	1.70	1.70	1.70
3s4	11.08	2.69	4.95
3h4	4.80	4.80	4.80
3d8	1.70	1.70	1.70
3s8	45.38	3.27	6.27
3h8	4.80	4.80	4.80

thanks to the attendees of the Workshop for Memory Performance issues (ISCA 2001) for their helpful feedback on the preliminary version [12] of this work. Thanks as well to Chris Johnson [11] and Chuck Li [14] for their work on the VHDL and Verilog implementations of the memory structures examined in this work.

References

1. Vikas Agarwal, M.S. Hrishikesh, Stephen W. Keckler, and Doug Burger. Clock rate versus IPC: The end of the road for conventional microarchitectures. In *International Symposium on Computer Architecture (ISCA)*, June 2000.
2. Christoffer Amlo. The Superthreaded multiprocessor: The instruction set architecture and the parallel execution manager. Master's thesis, University of Minnesota, Department of Electrical and Computer Engineering, Minneapolis, Minnesota, September 1999. Also available as ARCTiC Lab technical report number ARCTiC-99-08.
3. Todd Austin, Eric Larson, and Dan Ernst. Simplescalar: An infrastructure for computer system modeling. *IEEE Computer*, 35(2):59–67, February 2002.
4. W. Banzhaf. *Computer-Aided Circuit Analysis Using SPICE*. Prentice Hall, Englewood-Cliffs, NJ, 1989.
5. Standard Performance Evaluation Corporation. SPEC benchmark suites. Various benchmark suites available. Details available at http://www.spec.org.

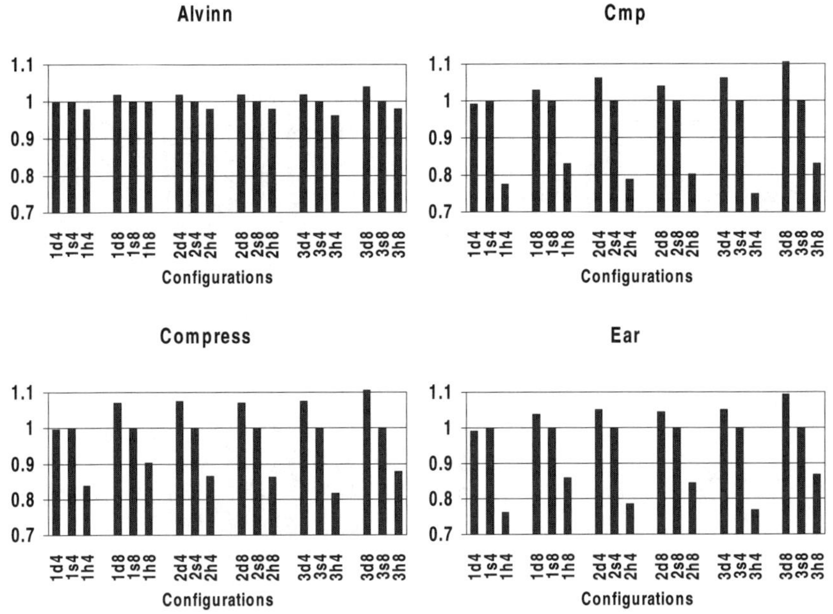

Fig. 16.5. Performance results for Alvinn, Cmp, Compress and Ear. Run time is normalized per group to the run time of the shared configuration.

6. Marco Fillo, Stephen W. Keckler, William J. Dally, Nicholas P. Carter, Andrew Chang, Yevgeny Gurevich, and Whay S. Lee. The M-Machine multicomputer. In *International Symposium on Microarchitecture (MICRO)*, November 1995.
7. Sridhar Gopal, T.N. Vijaykumar, James E. Smith, and Gurindar S. Sohi. Speculative versioning cache. In *International Symposium on High-Performance Computer Architecture (HPCA)*, 1998.
8. John L. Henning. SPEC CPU 2000: Measuring CPU performance in the new millennium. *IEEE Computer*, 33(7):28–35, July 2000.
9. Hiroaki Hirata, Kozo Kimura, Satoshi Nagamine, Yoshiyuki Mochizuki, Akio Nishimura, Yoshimori Nakase, and Teiji Nishizawa. An elementary processor architecture with simultaneous instruction issuing from multiple threads. In *International Symposium on Computer Architecture (ISCA)*, May 1992.
10. Jian Huang and David J. Lilja. An efficient strategy for developing a simulator for a novel concurrent multithreaded processor architecture. In *International Symposium on Modeling, Analysis, and Simulation of Computer and Telecommunication Systems*, July 1998.
11. Chris Johnson. Superthreaded multi-processor: Hardware design of the memory buffer unit. Master's thesis, University of Minnesota, Department of Electrical and Computer Engineering, Minneapolis, Minnesota, October 1999.
12. AJ KleinOsowski and David J. Lilja. Performance analysis of a novel cache architecture for speculative multithreaded computer systems. In *Workshop on*

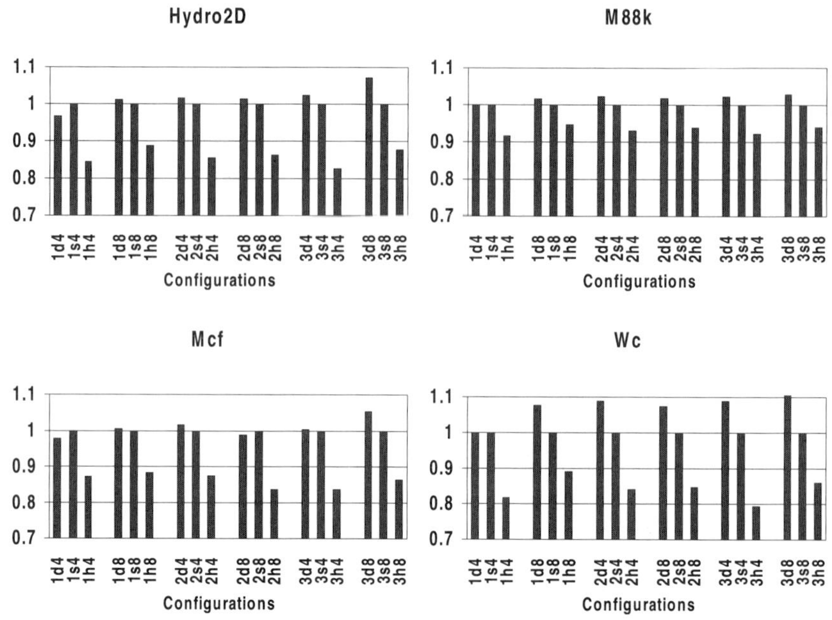

Fig. 16.6. Performance results for Hydro2d, M88k, Mcf and Wc. Run time is normalized per group to the run time of the shared configuration.

Memory Performance Issues, International Symposium on Computer Architecture (ISCA), July 2001.

13. AJ KleinOsowski and David J. Lilja. MinneSPEC: A new SPEC benchmark workload for simulation-based computer architecture research. *Computer Architecture Letters*, 1, June 2002.
14. Chun-Tao Li. Memory buffer implementation in the Superthreaded architecture. Master's thesis, University of Minnesota, Department of Electrical and Computer Engineering, Minneapolis, Minnesota, August 2001.
15. Gurindar S. Sohi, Scott E. Breach, and T.N. Vijaykumar. Multiscalar processors. In *International Symposium on Computer Architecture (ISCA)*, June 1995.
16. Jenn-Yuan Tsai, Jian Huang, Christoffer Amlo, David J. Lilja, and Pen-Chung Yew. The Superthreaded processor architecture. *IEEE Transactions on Computers*, 48(9):881–902, 1999.
17. Kenneth M. Wilson and Kunle Olukotun. High bandwidth on-chip cache design. *IEEE Transactions on Computers*, 50(4):292–307, 2001.
18. Steven J.E. Wilton and Norman P. Jouppi. Cacti: An enhanced cache access and cycle time model. *IEEE Journal of Solid-State Circuits*, 31(5):677–688, 1996.
19. Andrew Wolfe and John P. Shen. A variable instruction stream extension to the VLIW architecture. In *International Conference on Architectural Support for Programming Languages and Operating Systems (ASPLOS)*, April 1991.

17

Evaluation of Large L3 Caches Using TPC-H Trace Samples

Jaeheon Jeong[1], Ramendra Sahoo[2], Krishnan Sugavanam[2], Ashwini Nanda[2], and Michel Dubois[3]

[1] IBM, Research Triangle Park, NC, USA jjeong@us.ibm.com
[2] IBM Research, Yorktown Heights, NY, USA ashwini@us.ibm.com
[3] Department of EE-Systems, University of Southern California, Los Angeles, CA, USA dubois@paris.usc.edu

Abstract. In this chapter we evaluate the miss rates of four L3 cache architectures for small-scale multiprocessors. Eight processors are partitioned into 1, 2, 4, or 8 clusters with 8, 4, 2, or 1 processors, respectively. Each cluster has a large L3 cache, and the aggregate amount of L3 cache in each of the four architectures varies between 64 MB and 1 GB. The target of our evaluations is decision support systems. We use bus trace samples obtained during the execution of a 100 GB TPC-H on an 8-way multiprocessor. These 12 time samples were taken at one hour intervals during the first day of execution of TPC-H. Each sample contains 64 M bus references.

We first show the distribution of bus references across samples and across processors in the same sample. The major problem with time samples is the cold start misses at the beginning of each sample. We show the cache warm-up rate for all cluster architectures and cache sizes. Unfortunately, systems with aggregate L3 cache sizes above 128 MB are never completely warm with our samples of size 64 million. Thus we evaluate cache architectures under three conditions: cold cache at the beginning of each sample, warm sets only, and stitched trace. We classify misses to understand their cause. Observations are similar across all three simulation types. We also show that the 12 time samples exhibit similar behavior.

One of the major observations using the twelve 64 M reference trace samples is the large number of interprocessor and IO coherence misses.

17.1 Introduction

The design of large-scale servers must be optimized for commercial workloads and Web-based applications. Unfortunately, the state of the art in evaluation techniques has not kept up with the increasing complexity of enterprise servers and their workloads. These servers are high-end, shared-memory multiprocessor systems with large memory hierarchies. Techniques to understand and evaluate such memory hierarchies are sorely needed, and current approaches are inadequate.

Traditionally, processors and memory systems have been designed and evaluated using scientific workloads such as the SPEC benchmark suite. Recently, complete system simulation tools such as Simics [7] and SimOs [10] have enabled the evaluation of OLTP (On-Line-Transaction Processing) and DSS (Decision Support System) applications. The conclusion of these studies is that OLTP and DSS workloads behave very differently from scientific workloads [1].

Unfortunately, the validity of current evaluation approaches using complete system simulation is questionable, especially for the evaluation of complex memory systems with large caches. Cache sizes are driven upwards by the ever-growing size and complexity of commercial workloads. The memory behavior of such large cache hierarchies cannot be evaluated correctly using untuned workloads with drastically reduced sizes and that are often obtained with an artificially simplified setup.

Trace-driven simulation is a common approach to evaluate memory systems. Unfortunately, storing and uploading full traces for full-size commercial workloads is practically impossible because of the sheer size of the trace. To address this problem, several techniques for sampling traces and for utilizing trace samples have been proposed [4, 6, 9, 12].

For this study, we have collected and evaluated time samples obtained from an actual multiprocessor machine running TPC-H [11], a decision support system, for several days. With the samples, we first analyze the effects of cold-start bias and the number of references needed to warm up very large caches of up to 1 GB. We then evaluate various L3 cache architectures for multiprocessor architectures.

The work reported in this chapter is part of an on going collaboration between IBM and U.S.C. to exploit the resources of the IBM Watson Server Performance Laboratory to evaluate the memory behavior of high-end (enterprise) servers for large commercial applications. MemorIES [8], developed by IBM, was originally designed to emulate memory hierarchies in real time and is plugged into the system bus of an IBM RS/6000 S7A SMP system running DB2 under AIX. This system can run database workloads with up to 1 TB of database data.

To enable the tracing work, we have configured MemorIES to store all the bus transactions it captures in the board's memory. The content of the memory is uploaded periodically to disk to form trace samples of bus activity.

17.2 TPC-H Traces

17.2.1 Tracing Environment

The IBM Memory Instrumentation and Emulation System (MemorIES) was designed to evaluate trade-offs for future memory system designs in multiprocessor servers. The MemorIES tool is capable of emulating single caches or multiple caches in real time with no slowdown in execution speed [8].

Figure 17.1 shows the block diagram of MemorIES. MemorIES uses seven field programmable gate arrays (FPGAs) and 1 GB of SDRAM memory to implement the cache tag and state tables. The address filter filters out unrelated bus transactions (e.g., retries) and groups the transactions based on bus IDs. The master controller implements global event counters and orchestrates the operation of MemorIES. The current board design can emulate up to four nodes with shared caches. Each emulated shared cache node is implemented using one Altera 10K250 FPGA and four 64 MB SDRAM DIMMs. The four nodes run in lock-step mode and share the cache states among nodes to maintain cache coherence.

MemorIES sits on the bus of a conventional SMP and passively monitors all the bus transactions, as shown in Figure 17.2. The host machine is an IBM RS/6000 S7A SMP server, a bus-based shared-memory multiprocessor. The server configuration consists of eight Northstar processors running at 262 MHz and a number of IO

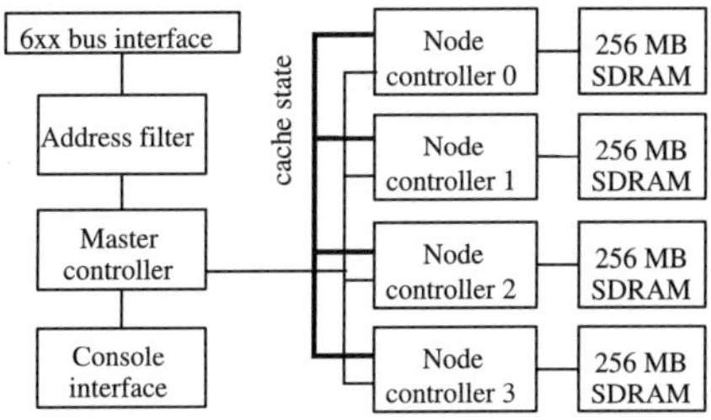

Fig. 17.1. Block diagram of MemorIES.

processors connected to the 6xx bus operating at 88 MHz. Each processor has a private 8 MB 4-way L2 cache. The cache block size is 128 bytes. Currently the size of the main memory is 24 GB.

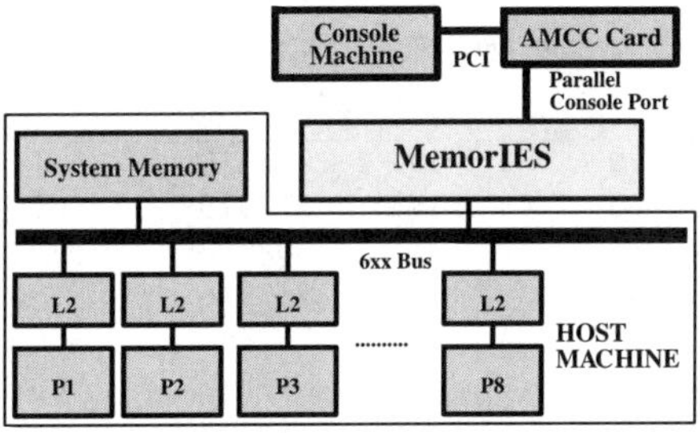

Fig. 17.2. Operating environment of MemorIES.

The board can emulate several SMP nodes, each having a shared cache, by keeping the state information on lines that would be shared in the caches of the emulated SMPs. The tool can be programmed through its console software and/or by reconfiguring the on-board FPGAs.

In each configuration, the board captures all the memory references on the 6xx bus of the host system and maintains cache tag and state information for the emulated shared cache(s). The parameters that can be evaluated include cache capacity, line size, associativity, number of caches, cache protocols, and replacement algorithms. Various cache statistics such as hit ratio, read/write ratio, effect of I/O on hit ratio, and amount of cache-to-cache interventions, to name a few, are collected using counters in the emulation board.

Currently, a standard 100 GB TPC-H benchmark runs on top of DB2 under AIX. The database setup is based on a popular benchmarking environment. The TPC-H benchmark consists of a lengthy execution, often read-only queries accessing a large portion (up to 85%) of the database. Its execution is a throughput run and takes three days on the server.

To use MemorIES as a tracing tool, we had to reprogram the FPGA controllers. Instead of emulating target caches, MemorIES has been reprogrammed to capture bus transactions in real time and to store them into its SDRAM. Later on, as the on-board memory fills up, the trace is uploaded to a disk. With its 1GB of SDRAM,

MemorIES can collect up to 128 M bus references without any interruption since each record occupies 8 bytes.

With this scheme, both time and set sampling are possible. We have opted for time sampling. Both the length of samples and interval between samples are programmable. Currently, the minimum interval between two consecutive samples of 128 M references is around two hours and is primarily limited by the low speed of the IO driver on the console PC.

17.2.2 Trace Samples

Although MemorIES can store up to 128 M references per sample, the size of each sample collected for this study is 64 M references. Currently, it takes about one hour to dump to disk a sample of 64 M references or 512 MB. Our trace consists of 12 samples with roughly one hour between samples and its overall size is 6 GB. The trace samples were taken during the first day of a three-day execution of a 100 GB TPC-H.

Table 17.1. Breakdown of references in the first sample in each processor.

PID	read	read-excl	clean	ikill	write/inv	write/cln	upgrade	wr/flush
0	3944601	221999	0	192	295218	5677	1629223	67102
1	4001991	217725	64	160	270918	5096	1685160	64724
2	4175661	208862	0	96	303913	5267	1742245	65406
3	3908973	213590	0	0	286916	5430	1610544	66424
4	4101762	209785	64	128	254847	5080	1640377	66063
5	3932938	217326	0	64	314963	5100	1580184	65686
6	4166149	192101	0	0	248305	4533	1821616	65143
7	3851738	200694	0	288	225611	4758	1654915	64449
IO	978887	0	0	0	12	0	0	16232121

Table 17.2.2 shows the reference counts of every processor and for every transaction type in the first trace sample. It shows that the variance of the reference count among processors (excluding IO processors) is very small. The references by IO processors are dominated by write/flush. We found similar distributions in the rest of the samples.

Table 17.2.2 shows the reference counts of eight transaction types in each of the 12 trace samples. We focus on the following classes of bus transactions: reads, writes (read-excl, write/inv), upgrades, and write/flushes (essentially due to IO write). In the 12 samples, processor reads and writes (including upgrades) contribute to around 44% and 21% of all bus transactions, respectively.

An amazing 35% of all bus transactions are due to IO writes. IO writes are caused by input to memory. On each IO write, the data block is transmitted on the bus and the processor write-back caches are invalidated to maintain coherence with IO. This input data will most likely be needed by some processor(s) at a later time, causing a bus miss transaction. This effect is not critical when caches are small enough so that they cannot retain the data between the time of an IO transaction and the time of the processor access. But the write/flushes due to IO may be quite costly in the context of very large caches that are able to retain data blocks for large periods of time. We also found some noticeable variations in some reference

Table 17.2. Reference count per transaction type in the 12 trace samples.

PID	read	read-excl	clean	ikill	write/inv	write/cln	upgrade	wr/flush
1	33062700	1682082	128	928	2200703	40941	13364264	16757118
2	29574629	1446244	0	2272	2677942	43781	10059975	23304021
3	28717853	1335718	0	0	2835185	35304	10637496	23547308
4	27727985	1405457	6432	6720	2900043	54407	8734182	26273638
5	25799000	1774029	0	0	3067320	51339	9517591	26899585
6	28760710	4021657	96	96	6077446	44147	6367359	21837353
7	29087095	1959379	0	608	2953071	57934	7265500	25785277
8	28830726	1929086	0	160	2866096	59072	7312608	26111116
9	26092006	1970931	96	320	3206843	57642	7186243	28594783
10	26899985	1768684	72	66	3279821	50629	7148337	27961270
11	36070868	1079535	0	0	2009423	96048	10462970	17390020
12	36516311	1108966	50560	51936	2159616	145164	10631200	16445111
Avg	44.35%	2.66%	0.01%	0.01%	4.50%	0.09%	13.50%	34.88%

counts across trace samples. For instance, notice the wide variation in the number of upgrades among samples.

17.3 Evaluation Methodology

We have used the 12 trace samples to evaluate memory system architectures with very large caches. In this section, we briefly describe the methodology used in our trace-driven simulations.

17.3.1 Target L3 Cache Architectures

We focus on the evaluation of various L3 caches for future high-end servers using the 12 samples. One interesting design option is to share L3 caches among a number of processors. Given that our traces are obtained from an 8-way multiprocessor, we consider four clustering schemes such that a cache is shared by 1, 2, 4, or 8 processors, corresponding to systems with 8, 4, 2, or 1 clusters, respectively.

For a fair comparison of these four clustering schemes, we compare them for the same aggregate (total) amount of L3 cache, varying from 64 MB to 1 GB. Throughout this evaluation, the cache block size is 128 bytes, caches are 4-way set-associative, and the LRU replacement policy is used. We adopt the MESI coherence protocol implemented on an IBM RS/6000 server.

17.3.2 Miss Classification

To evaluate the performance of L3 cache architectures with the trace samples, we use the miss rate as a metric. We decompose misses into the following four categories: cold misses, coherence misses, replacement misses, and upgrade misses. To do this, we first check whether a missing block in a cache was previously referenced inside the cluster. If not, the miss is a cold miss. Otherwise, we check whether the missing block was last invalidated in the cache. If it was, the miss is a coherence miss. Otherwise, the miss is due to replacement.

Independently of the classification above, whenever an upgrade request misses in the L3 caches, we classify the miss as an upgrade miss. Upgrade misses do not occur in L3 caches when cache inclusion between the processors' L2 caches and the L3 caches is maintained. With our bus traces, however, we cannot maintain L2/L3 inclusion, and upgrade misses can occur in the L3 cache. Therefore, strictly speaking, the simulation results presented in this work can be considered correct if L2/L3 inclusion is not maintained. However, we have not observed any significant effect caused by non-inclusion. As we will see, upgrade misses are relatively very few as compared to other misses.

To understand the cold-start bias better, cold misses are further decomposed into cold-cold misses and warm-cold misses. A cold-cold miss occurs on a cold miss such that an empty cache blockframe is allocated, whereas a warm-cold miss occurs on a cold miss such that a warm blockframe is allocated. Thus warm-cold misses happen in sets that have been filled, whereas cold-cold misses happen in sets that have not been completely filled. It is important to make this distinction. Cold-cold misses are really unknown references [13]. They could be any kind of miss or even a hit in the full trace. By contrast, warm-cold misses are sure misses. They miss in the full trace, although they might be any kind of miss.

17.4 Simulation Results

We first evaluate the cache cold-start effect for each sample and then we classify L3 cache misses for various cache sizes and memory system architectures.

17.4.1 Cache Warm-up

Cache Blockframe Warm-up Rates

Figure 17.3(a) shows the average fraction of warm blockframes as a function of the reference number across all 12 samples for two clustering schemes. We simulate each trace sample starting with empty caches. A blockframe is deemed warm after a block has been allocated to it for the first time. For every number of references, we calculate the average number of warm blockframes across all samples. In each graph, we vary the aggregate cache size from 64 MB to 1 GB. From the graphs, we see that caches larger than 128 MB are never completely warm with 64 M references. This implies that, for cache sizes greater than 128 MB, no references are left for trace-driven simulation after caches are warm.

The graphs also indicate that more references are required to warm up the cache as the caches are shared by more processors. This is mainly due to sharing effects among processors in each cluster.

Cache Set Warm-up Rate

Figure 17.3(b) shows the warm-up rate of cache sets. A cache set is deemed warm once all its blockframes have been accessed at least once. The graphs indicate that the cache set warm-up rate is much lower than the cache blockframe warm-up rate for large caches. This implies that cold blockframes are spread among many cache sets.

If, in the trace-driven simulation of very large L3 caches, we only use the references to warm cache sets, the evaluation will be naturally biased to a (relatively) small number of hot cache sets. Thus,this approach is debatable since a good set-sampling strategy might produce a more usable trace.

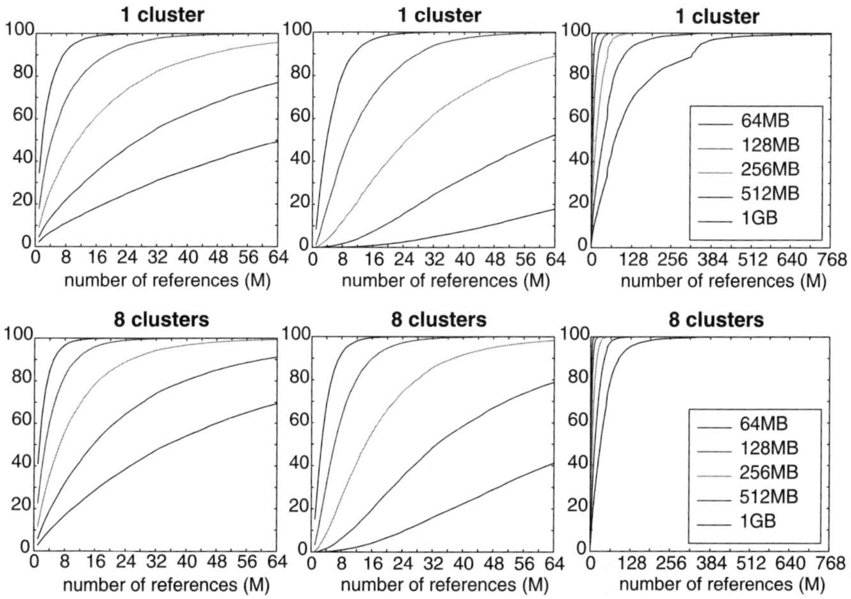

(a) blockframe (%) (b) set (%) (c) blockframe-stitched (%)

Fig. 17.3. L3 cache warm-up rate.

Stitched Trace

Figure 17.3(c) shows the warm-up rate of cache blockframes with the stitched trace made of the 12 samples connected together as if there was no gap between them. The total number of references is 768 M. The results indicate that 1 G references will be required to warm up the L3 cache hierarchy in the worst case, which is the 1 GB shared cache in a one-cluster system. The curves also indicate that the 100 GB TPC-H benchmark touches enough memory addresses to utilize 1 GB of L3 cache.

17.4.2 L3 Cache Miss Rate Classification

Cold Caches

In this section, we analyze the components of the miss rate assuming empty L3 caches at the beginning of each sample. To calculate the miss rate, we apply each trace sample to empty caches and then we sum up all the misses and legitimate memory references measured during the simulation of every sample. Figure 17.4 shows the miss rate in the four different clustering schemes.

Consider first the miss rate in the 8-cluster system with a total of 64 MB L3 cache, or 8 MB of L3 cache per processor. The simulated system comprises 8 processors, and each processor has an 8 MB L2 cache and an 8 MB L3 private cache. Clearly, if inclusion was maintained, all accesses to the L3 caches should miss. From the graph, we see that the miss rate is in fact around 90%. The 10% difference indicates the effect on L3 cache miss rate of not maintaining L2/L3 inclusion.

Figure 17.4 shows that a large fraction of misses are due to coherence activity in systems with more than a single cluster. Coherence misses are decomposed into five classes, depending on the type of bus access that caused the invalidation (rdx, write, upgrade, IO, and misc). Upgrades are, by far, the main cause of coherence misses in systems with more than one cluster. Note that coherence misses due to upgrades are different from upgrade misses. Upgrade misses are misses for upgrade references, whatever the cause of the misses. Coherence misses due to upgrades are misses for non-upgrade references, but the cause of the miss is invalidation by a prior upgrade reference.

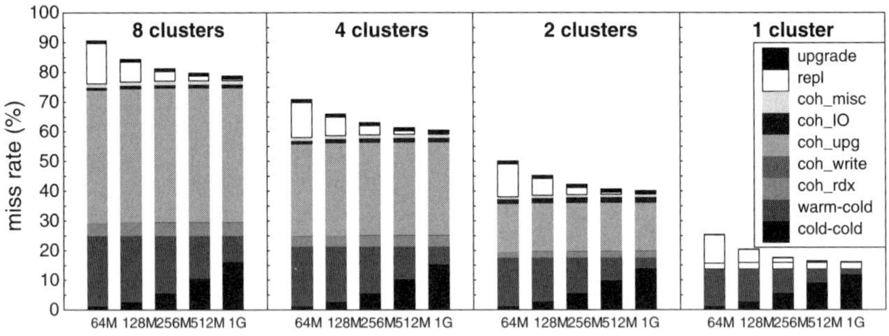

Fig. 17.4. Miss rate classification with cold caches.

Another important source of misses in all systems is the cache cold start. Cold misses are decomposed into cold-cold misses and warm-cold misses as defined before. As the cache size increases to 1 GB, replacement misses almost vanish and cold-cold misses dominate the cold miss rate. In reality, this large portion of cold-cold misses might be cache hits or other kinds of misses if the caches were warm at the beginning of the samples.

As the caches are shared by more processors, the number of warm-cold misses slowly decreases, mainly because of the prefetching effect among processors. Coherence misses are also greatly reduced because there are less chances to invalidate copies in other caches. In the one-cluster system, coherence misses are completely eliminated except for the coherence misses due to IO writes. Finally, the number of upgrade misses is practically insignificant in all cases.

In summary, we observe the following from the miss rate with cold start.

- Coherence misses constitute a large portion of misses except for the one-cluster system and are mainly due to invalidations propagated by upgrades. This is because upgrades are not filtered by L3 caches, whereas other memory references are mostly filtered. When the caches are fully shared, coherence misses are completely removed except for the coherence misses due to IO writes.

-The very large size of the coherence component means that the major way to improve the performance of systems with more than one cluster is to cut the number of coherence misses.

- As the cache size increases, cold-cold misses become a dominant part of the cold miss component, and the large number of cold-cold misses in very large L3 caches shows that the error due to cold start is significant for those systems, especially for the single cluster system, in which interprocessor coherence misses have been eliminated.

Warm Cache Sets Only

To try to eliminate some of the error due to cold-cold misses, we now count misses and memory references only for the cache sets that are filled.

Figure 17.5 shows the average miss rate for memory references to warm cache sets only. One way to judge the validity of this evaluation approach is to see how the cold miss rate changes with different cache sizes in each clustering scheme since all cold misses are warm-cold misses and thus their number should, in theory, be independent of the cache size. From the graphs, we see that the cold miss rates are roughly constant across different cache sizes for a given clustering of caches, especially for systems with little cache sharing. As more processors share a cache, the impact of cold misses tends to decrease slightly with the cache size.

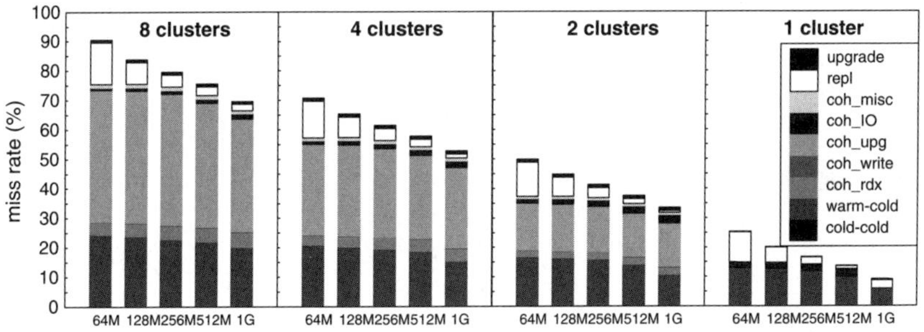

Fig. 17.5. Miss rate classification for warm cache sets only.

Tracking warm sets only can remove the cold-start bias but, as mentioned before, the evaluation of the miss rate is still biased because many sets are not included in the evaluation, especially in the case of larger caches.

Stitched Trace

Figure 17.6 shows the miss rate for the stitched trace assuming that caches are empty at the beginning of the trace. With this trace, the number of cold misses is independent of the cache size, and the number of cold-cold misses is negligible. The fraction of replacement misses is significantly higher in this approach, which indicates that there is significant reuse of data across references separated by hours of execution.

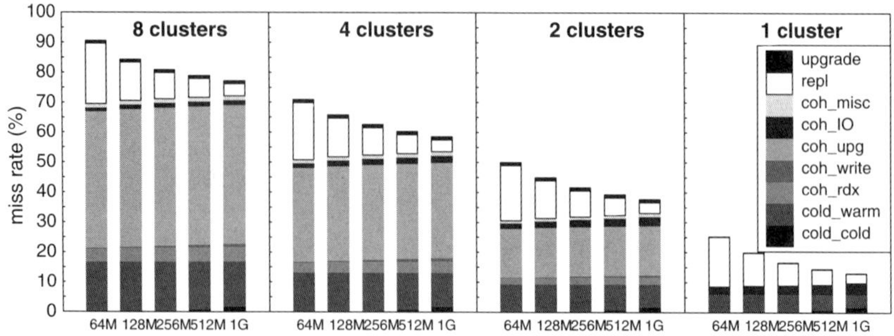

Fig. 17.6. Miss rate for the stitched trace with cold start.

Variations Across Samples

Figure 17.7 shows the variation of the miss rate classification across the 12 trace samples for the four different clustering schemes and for cold caches at the beginning of each sample. We see that the miss rate profile across samples is consistent across all cache sizes and clustering schemes. One exception is sample 6, which seems to be an outlier, both from Table 17.2.2 and Figure 17.7. However, even if we remove sample 6 from the evaluations, the observations made in this chapter are not significantly altered.

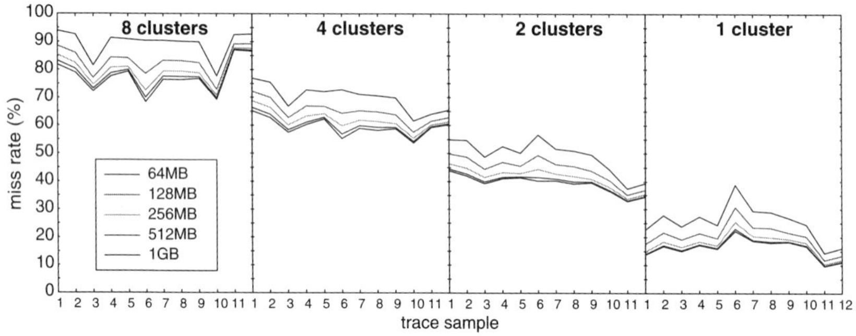

Fig. 17.7. Variation of miss rate across the 12 trace samples.

17.4.3 A Closer Look at Coherence Misses

In the previous section, we found that coherence misses make up more than 50% of the total number of misses in the 8-cluster system. This is a somewhat unexpected result given that TPC-H is mainly composed of read-only queries. In this section, we first explore the source of coherence misses by measuring the distribution of misses across the address space. Since the address space is very large, we measure statistics at the granularity of an 8 KB page. Second, we examine the impact of coherence activities on replacement misses since reducing replacement misses is one of the key objectives in the design of L3 caches. In this section, our experiments are based on the stitched trace with cold caches at the beginning of the trace.

Distribution of Coherence Misses in Address Space

We examined the distribution of reads, writes, upgrades, and coherence misses in the physical memory address space. The number of coherence misses is measured in an 8-cluster system with 8 MB L3 caches.

We observe a strong peak at the bottom of the address space. This peak covers two consecutive pages and includes 37% of all reads, 31% of all upgrades, and 52% of all coherence misses, while the remaining references are widely spread across a large spectrum of memory addresses. At the peak, the number of cold misses, replacement misses and references by IO is negligible. Eight groups of blocks dominate the activity in these two pages. Each group is made of five consecutive 128 byte cache blocks and the groups show similar access patterns. Moreover, there is one strong peak inside each group, and these peaks have almost equal magnitude. At the peak, 85% of all reads missing in the cache are due to upgrade invalidations, and each upgrade invalidates roughly three shared copies on average.

From the distribution in the address space, we cannot exactly pinpoint the source of this activity. However, the data strongly indicate that the peak comes from kernel-level interprocessor communication (e.g., locks or producer-consumer type communication) since the peaks are extremely narrow in the address space and appear at the bottom of the address space.

Figure 17.8 shows the miss rate of the stitched trace excluding the references to the two pages with very high miss and coherence activity. Misses are classified into four classes. By ignoring the references to the pages causing the peak of activity, the cold miss rate goes from 17% to 25% and the replacement miss rate goes from 21% to 30% in the 8-cluster system with 8 MB L3 caches. However, misses are still mostly due to coherence activity.

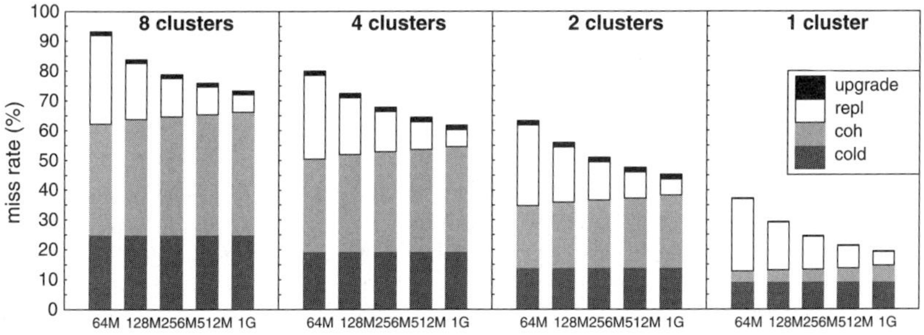

Fig. 17.8. Miss rate of the stitched trace excluding reference peaks.

Coherence vs. Replacement Misses

So far, we have classified a miss as a replacement miss if the block was last replaced in the cache. However, a large number of these replacement misses are unavoidable, even if the cache sizes were infinite, because they would become coherence misses instead [5].

In this section, we count as coherence misses all replacement misses such that they would have been coherence misses if the caches were infinite and no replacement ever occurred. We now classify a miss as a replacement miss only if

1. The block was last replaced in the cache, and
2. No other processor or IO device executed a store to the same block between the replacement and the miss.

The rationale for case 2 is that the miss is unavoidable if a remote store occurs on the block due to coherence and so we consider it as a coherence miss. The net result of this classification is that the effects of interprocessor and IO coherence are far more pronounced than what was suggested in previous figures.

Table 17.4.3 shows the fraction of replacement misses that would become coherence misses in systems with infinite caches. The table shows that the fraction goes up as the cache size increases and that the rate of increase is faster as more processors share a cache. In the case of a cache shared by all 8 processors, the coherence activity is purely due to IO. This trend indicates that efforts to cut down on replacement misses such as cache replacement algorithms may not be very rewarding and that IO plays a critical role in shared cache performance.

Table 17.3. Fraction of replacement misses classified as coherence misses (%).

clusters	64 MB	128 MB	256 MB	512 MB	1 GB
1	18.50	25.41	35.40	46.71	56.09
2	23.95	28.86	36.52	45.76	55.04
4	24.35	28.16	33.10	39.73	48.15
8	20.43	24.05	28.12	31.30	36.20

17.5 Related Work

Work related to this chapter falls into two categories: trace sampling and evaluation of commercial workloads.

Puzak [9] introduced trace stripping and set sampling. Trace stripping is based on a filter cache, and the references that miss in the filter cache are collected to accurately evaluate cache miss rates. Puzak also showed that trace sampling using one-tenth of cache sets leads to a reliable miss rate estimation.

Wang and Baer [12] extended Puzak's techniques using filter caches and proposed methods to evaluate miss count, write-back count, and invalidation count. Their method keeps in the trace all writes on clean blocks in addition to the references that miss in the filter cache.

Chame and Dubois [4] proposed processor sampling techniques based on cache inclusion for large-scale multiprocessor systems. They examined whether cache inclusion can be maintained for different set-mapping functions and showed that the traces of references to a small number of sets can be expanded for a larger number of sets if caches are evaluated using stack algorithms.

Kessler et al. [6] compared a variety of trace sampling techniques based on set sampling and time sampling under the 10% sampling rule and for a multiprogrammed workload. They showed that the cold-start bias is the main reason behind the inaccuracy of time sampling and that set sampling outperforms time sampling. In another paper [12], the same authors evaluate various techniques to correct for the cold-start misses in each time sample. They try approaches similar to ours (cold caches at the beginning of each sample, warm set only, and stitched trace) in addition to using an analytical model. Unfortunately, they do not find a reliable approach to offset the effect of cold-cold misses (unknown references). In our traces, we separate cold-cold misses (which may miss or hit in the full trace) from warm-cold misses (which miss for sure in the full trace but might be any kind of miss).

Barroso et al. [1] studied the evaluation of commercial workloads using SimOS. They addressed the difficulty of evaluating commercial workloads and presented results for TPC-D, whose behavior resembles the behavior of TPC-H. Due to their simulation approach, the database was scaled down to 500 MB. They found that the numbers of cold misses, coherence misses, and replacement misses are comparable in the context of systems with 2 MB board-level caches.

In [2, 3], a system based on Alpha 21364 and a single-chip multiprocessor were evaluated for OLTP workloads using SimOS. It is shown that chip-level integration can take advantage of lower memory access overhead and enhances the performance of OLTP benchmarks.

17.6 Conclusion

In this work, we have programmed the IBM MemorIES to take time samples of a 100 GB TPC-H run on a multiprocessor. Twelve time samples of 64 MB references each were collected during the first day of execution of TPC-H. Our TPC-H bus trace is mainly composed of reads, writes, upgrades and IO writes. Each of these access types makes up around 44%, 7%, 14%, and 35% of all references, respectively.

The trace samples have been used to evaluate various clustering schemes for L3 caches in a system with 8 processors. The trace samples with 64 M references are not enough to warm up L3 cache systems with an aggregate amount of cache larger than 128 MB. Consequently, the evaluations based on cold caches, warm blockframes, and warm cache sets fail to yield a totally credible miss rate due to the cold-start effect. The stitched trace with 768 M references eliminates most of the transient effects, except that accuracy is compromised by the fact that there are huge gaps in the trace.

One of the major observation using the twelve 64 M reference trace samples is the dominance of interprocessor and IO coherence misses. Efforts spent on improved replacement policies will be futile until the number of coherence misses can be brought down. In systems with one cluster, we must first bring down the number of misses due to IO coherence. To do that, we might consider updating the shared cache instead of invalidating it on an IO write on the bus. In a system with more than one cluster, we must first bring down the number of misses due to upgrade invalidations. In systems with more than one cluster, 50% of these coherence misses are concentrated in a very narrow band of the physical address space. This observation is useful to optimize the performance of database applications or the operating system.

At this point, we cannot verify the accuracy of the samples since we do not have the actual miss rates for the entire run. The accuracy of time sampling is affected by two factors: the cold-start effect in each sample and the sampling rate. To improve the sampling rate, we simply have to take more time samples. MemorIES allows us to solve the cold-start effect by applying a new technique, which we call *cache snapshots*. Since MemorIES can emulate target cache systems in real time, we can use the time between samples to emulate a set of caches with different architectures and fill these caches up before the next sample is taken so that we have the content of these caches at the beginning of each sample. The content of these emulated caches is dumped with the sample at the end of each time sample. By playing with cache inclusion properties [5], the content of these few emulated caches can be used to restore the state of many different cache configurations at the beginning of each sample, thus eliminating the cold-start effect. In this framework, a trace collection experiment consists of several phases, repeated for each time sample: a phase, in which we emulate the target caches to get the snapshots, the trace sample collection phase, and the trace dump phase in which the snapshots and the trace samples are dumped to disk.

Given that the tracing tool can collect up to 128 M references per trace sample, saving the cache snapshots can be extremely useful and cost-effective. The snapshot of a 1 GB cache occupies only 32 MB out of the 1 GB SDRAM available in MemorIES, which leaves enough RAM on the board to collect up to 124 M references per trace sample. We have developed the FPGA programs to take cache snapshots and are currently collecting traces with snapshots. However, the results presented in this chapter do not include snapshots. Once we have the trace with the cache snapshots, we will be able to firm up the conclusions of this work.

Acknowledgments

Michel Dubois and Jaeheon Jeong were funded by NSF grant No. MIP-9223812, NSF Grant No. CCR-0105761, and an IBM Faculty Partnership Award.

References

1. Barroso L, Gharachorloo K, Bugnion E (1998) Memory System Characterization of Commercial Workloads. In: Proceedings of the 25th ACM International Symposium on Computer Architecture.
2. Barroso L, Gharachorloo K, Nowatzyk A, Verghese B (2000) Impact of Chip-Level Integration on Performance of OLTP Workloads. In: Proceedings of the 6th International Symposium on High-Performance Computer Architecture.
3. Barroso L, Gharachorloo K, McNamara R, Nowatzyk A, Qadeer S, Sano B, Smith S, Stets R, Verghese B (2000) Piranha: A Scalable Architecture Based on Single-Chip Multiprocessing. In: Proceedings of the 27th International Symposium on Computer Architecture.
4. Chame J, Dubois M (1993) Cache Inclusion and Processor Sampling in Multiprocessor Simulations. In: Proceedings of ACM Sigmetrics, pp. 36–47.
5. Dubois M, Skeppstedt J, Stenstrom P (1995) Essential Misses and Memory Traffic in Coherence Protocols. Journal of Parallel and Distributed Computing 29(2):108–125.
6. Kessler R, Hill M, Wood D (1994) A Comparison of Trace-Sampling Techniques for Multi-Megabyte Caches. IEEE Transactions on Computers 43(6):664–675.

7. Magnusson P et al. (1998) SimICS/sun4m: A Virtual Workstation. In: Proceedings of the 1998 USENIX Annual Technical Conference, pp. 119–130.
8. Nanda A, Mak K, Sugavanam K, Sahoo R, Soundararajan B, Smith T (2000) MemorIES: A Programmable, Real-Time Hardware Emulation Tool for Multiprocessor Server Design. In: Proceedings of the Ninth International Conference on Architectural Support for Programming Languages and Operating Systems.
9. Puzak T (1985) Analysis of Cache Replacement-Algorithms. Ph.D. Dissertation, University of Massachusetts, Amherst, MA.
10. Rosenblaum M, Herrod S, Witchel E, Gupta A (1995) Complete Computer System Simulation: The SimOS Approach. IEEE Parallel and Distributed Technology 3(4):34–43.
11. Transaction Processing Performance Council (1999) TPC Benchmark H Standard Specification. Transaction Processing Performance Council. http://tpc.org.
12. Wang W, Baer J (1991) Efficient Trace-Driven Simulation Methods for Cache Performance Analysis. ACM Transactions on Computer Systems 9(3):222–241.
13. Wood D, Hill M, Kessler R (1990) A Model for Estimating Trace-Sample Miss Ratios. In: Proceedings of the ACM Sigmetrics Conference on Measurement and Modeling of Computer Systems.

18

Exploiting Intelligent Memory for Database Workloads

Pedro Trancoso[1] and Josep Torrellas[2]

[1] Department of Computer Science, University of Cyprus, Cyprus
pedro@ucy.ac.cy
[2] Department of Computer Science, University of Illinois at Urbana-Champaign, Urbana, IL, USA, torrella@cs.uiuc.edu

Abstract. The increased transistor integration on a single chip has allowed for emerging technologies such as the merging of memory and logic. These chips, known as Intelligent Memory, offer increased bandwidth and reduced latency from computation to memory.

In this work, we focus on exploiting the features of a proposed Intelligent Memory chip, FlexRAM, for database workloads. To achieve this goal, we developed FlexDB, a simple DBMS prototype that includes modified parallel algorithms, an efficient data redistribution algorithm, and simple mathematical models for query optimization.

We tested FlexDB using three queries from the TPC-H benchmark on a simulated system configured with FlexRAM chips including up to 64 processing elements and a total memory size large enough to fit the whole database. Compared to a single processor system, the speedup values for a single FlexRAM chip system range from 4 to 92. These results scale when we add more FlexRAM chips to the system. Compared to a shared-memory multiprocessor, we observe that for two out of the three queries our approach achieves a speedup between 4 and an order of magnitude. This leads us to conclude that commercial workloads may benefit significantly from the use of Intelligent Memory chips such as FlexRAM.

18.1 Introduction

The increasing number of transistors available on a chip creates the conditions for innovative chip configurations [6]. One option is to merge memory and logic on the same chip. This emerging technology, known as Intelligent Memory, can be applied to produce chips that contain both memory and processing elements. The benefits of such an architecture are obvious. By pushing computation close to memory, we achieve higher bandwidth and lower latency.

The main contribution of this chapter is to investigate the potentials of Intelligent Memory architectures for general-purpose applications such as databases. In

Part of this work was developed while P. Trancoso was with Intercollege, Limassol, Cyprus.

order to achieve this goal, we present a prototype of a simple DBMS system, called FlexDB, that exploits the features of FlexRAM, an Intelligent Memory chip, for database workloads. We propose changes to the existing parallel algorithms to map them to the new architecture, a data redistribution algorithm for data to be moved efficiently within the chip, and simple mathematical models used to choose between the algorithms. Another major contribution is the study of the design space of the FlexRAM chip and the comparison of its performance with traditional multiprocessor systems for database workloads.

We tested FlexDB on a simulated system configured with FlexRAM chips having up to 64 processing elements and a total memory size large enough to fit the whole database. The workload chosen is composed of three queries from the TPC-H benchmark. Compared to a single-processor configuration, the speedup values for a FlexRAM system range from 4 to 92, depending on the query. These results scale almost linearly when we increase the number of FlexRAM chips in the system. Compared to a shared-memory multiprocessor configuration, we observe that, while there is a performance degradation for one query, for the other two our approach achieves a speedup between 4 and an order of magnitude. This leads us to conclude that commercial workloads may benefit significantly from the use of Intelligent Memory chips such as FlexRAM.

This work is presented as follows. In Section 18.2 we discuss the related work. In Section 18.3 we present a detailed description of the FlexRAM architecture. In Section 18.4 we describe the FlexDB prototype. The experimental setup and results are presented in Section 18.5 and Section 18.6, respectively. Finally, in Section 18.7 we discuss the conclusions reached from this work.

18.2 Related Work

Intelligent Memory has recently become a research topic for several projects. Notice that the industry's interest in this technology is shown by the proposal of several new products [20, 26, 27]. According to their role, Intelligent Memory chips may be classified into three main categories: specialized processors (e.g. C-RAM [10] and Imagine [25]), main chip in the system (e.g. IRAM [22], Raw [34], and Smart Memories [19]), and as part of the memory chips of the system (e.g. Active Pages [21], DIVA [13], and FlexRAM [15]).

The systems built around the chips from the last category are general purpose and usually include a general-purpose processor and both conventional and Intelligent Memory chips. The different architectures have in common the fact that they contain several processors and a certain amount of memory per processor. FlexRAM, though, has a unique design, as it contains a hierarchy of processing elements: the chip is divided into multiple blocks containing processing elements and private memory and a memory processor that is able to access any memory location on the chip. In this work, we were interested in exploiting this flexibility for database workloads.

The interest in focusing on database workloads is justified by the fact that recent studies identify memory accesses as the major performance bottleneck for modern systems [2, 3, 31, 32]. Also, most of the suggested Intelligent Memory architectures are evaluated using only scientific workloads.

Previous work on exploring Intelligent Memory for database applications includes the IDISK [16] and the Active Disks [1] projects. Both projects propose to embed these chips in the disk controller board attached to each disk. Our objectives are different, as we intend to study general-purpose systems.

Barroso et al. [4] present a study for database workloads using an advanced chip multiprocessor architecture called Piranha. Due to its fast link to memory, Piranha has characteristics similar to FlexRAM. The main difference is that FlexRAM includes many simple processing elements instead of a few powerful ones. We will show that this design option has considerable benefits for some queries.

Alternatively, software solutions have been proposed to reduce the memory access bottleneck [5, 24, 28, 32]. These studies focus on a better utilization of the cache. In addition to the memory latency reduction achieved by these approaches, FlexRAM offers increased bandwidth and a higher degree of parallelism for the application.

18.3 FlexRAM

In this section, we summarize the characteristics of FlexRAM in order to understand the choices made when designing the FlexDB database system. A more detailed presentation of this architecture may be found in [15].

The design of this Intelligent Memory chip considers the following objectives: extracting high-memory bandwidth, running legacy codes efficiently, minimizing memory cost increase, and being general purpose.

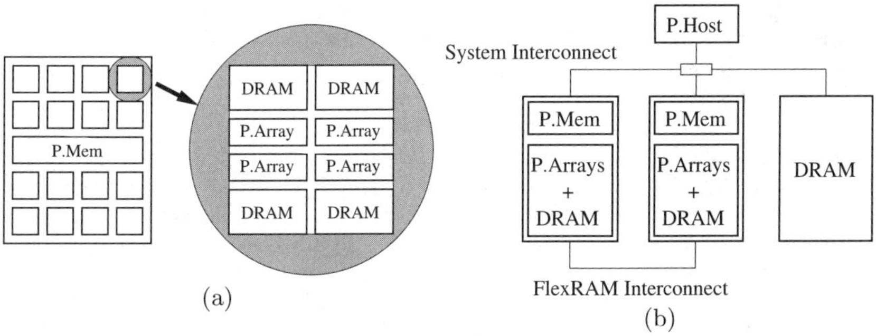

Fig. 18.1. FlexRAM: (a) Internal layout and basic block; and (b) complete system.

Figure 18.1(a) shows on the left the layout of the FlexRAM chip. Each chip contains a main processing unit known as the *P.Mem* and several *Basic Blocks*. Each Basic Block, shown on the right side of the same figure, contains four subblocks, each one with a portion of DRAM and a processing element known as the *P.Array*. The chip's internal communication links are limited to the *Notify* and *Global Buses*, which are used for P.Mem transactions. The communication between P.Array elements is limited to the corresponding neighbors in order to avoid complexity and higher cost as well as to allow for scalability.

Notice that there are significant differences between P.Mem and P.Arrays. In particular, P.Mem processors include a private cache, more functional units, and more load store units. In addition, P.Mem processors are able to access any memory location within the chip and any memory location of another chip when using the

FlexRAM Interconnect. An example of a system configured with FlexRAM and regular DRAM chips is shown in Figure 18.1(b).

To execute an operation in a certain computation unit, this operation has to be set up and started by the unit immediately above it in the hierarchy. This means that the P.Host sets up and starts the operation for the P.Mems and the P.Mems set up and start the operation for the P.Arrays. To know when an operation has finished, the higher-level unit polls on a certain memory location/ which is updated by the lower-level unit.

18.4 FlexDB

To exploit the characteristics of this architecture, we developed a simple prototype of a DBMS called FlexDB. FlexDB is composed of two major components: Algorithms and Optimizer.

18.4.1 Algorithms

In this section, we will discuss the techniques we used to map the existing parallel algorithms into the FlexRAM architecture. A detailed survey by Graefe [11] includes the description of several parallel algorithms.

Data Repartition. As in this architecture P.Array communication is limited, we cannot use the traditional repartitioning algorithms where each computation node analyzes its data and ships them directly to the destination node [9]. Instead, we use the ability of each P.Array to communicate with its neighbors, in order to build a *software virtual ring* within the memory chip. Basically, in this algorithm, each node scans its own data and sends it to its "right" or "left" neighbor, depending on whether the destination is further to the "right" or "left," respectively. This process is repeated until all the data arrive at their final destination. We implement this algorithm in two steps: *data separation* and *data move*. In the first step, *data separation*, each P.Array reads its local data and separates them into four different bins: *Left* if they need to be sent to another P.Array in the same chip and to its left; *Right* if they need to be sent to another P.Array in the same chip and to its right; *Local* if this is the correct destination; and *Remote* if the data need to be sent to a P.Array in another chip. In the second step, *data move*, which is depicted in Figure 18.2, each P.Array reads the *Left* bin from its right neighbor and the *Right* bin from its left neighbor and distributes the data in its own bins accordingly. Notice that while the P.Arrays are repartitioning the data that need to be moved within the chip, the P.Mems are repartitioning the data that need to move across chips. These two operations are executed in parallel. Finally, a disadvantage of this ring communication being implemented in software is the memory overhead for the repartitioning bins.

Scan. In this work, we implemented two scan algorithms: *Sequential Scan* and *Index Scan*. *Sequential Scan* is fully parallel and therefore will always run in the P.Arrays. No data repartitioning is required as long as the input data are balanced among all the nodes. *Index Scan* can also be parallelized as long as each P.Array contains a partial index structure that covers all the tuples in its local memory. The creation of this index may be done offline.

Join. In this work, we will consider two different join algorithms: *Index Join* and *Hash Join*. The parallel versions of these algorithms require either global memory

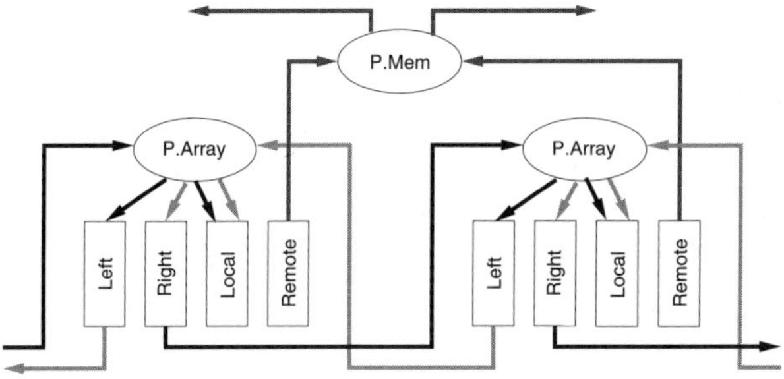

Fig. 18.2. Data move step of the data repartition algorithm.

access, replication, or data repartition. To execute *Index Join* in the P.Arrays, it is required to replicate all tuples from the first table. We will consider this case only if the benefit of the parallel execution is larger than the replication overhead (size and time). In this case, each P.Array checks the whole first table against the index to the local portion of the second table. If the replication overhead is too large, this operation can be performed in parallel by the P.Mems. In this version, each P.Mem checks the local portion of the first table against the index to the whole second table.

Hash Join also has two versions. If we want to execute this algorithm in the P.Arrays, we need to use a version of the parallel hash join algorithm similar to the one used for Shared-Nothing architectures. This algorithm is executed in two steps: data repartition and hash join on the partitioned data. For the first step, we use the repartitioning algorithm as described at the beginning of this section, while for the second step we use a regular hash join in each P.Array. If the data repartitioning is too costly, we can use a version of this algorithm that runs on the P.Mems. In this case, we revert to a Shared-Everything algorithm where each P.Mem cooperates in building a global hash table for the second table. Each P.Mem inserts in that hash table all the tuples local to its chip. Then, each P.Mem reads the local tuples of the first table and uses them to probe the global hash table to find a match.

Sort. In this work, we use the *quicksort* [17] algorithm. To execute this algorithm in parallel, we need to start by using the data partitioning algorithm previously described to perform a range partitioning of the data. Then we use quicksort on each P.Array.

Group. Grouping is a trivial operation when performed after sorting. It requires only to check if consecutive tuples belong to the same group or not, and this can be performed by the P.Arrays. Notice that in some cases the group might extend to more than one P.Array. Consequently, the P.Array needs to check its neighbors to do that grouping.

Aggregate. This operation is performed in a hierarchical way. First each P.Array applies the aggregate function to its local tuples and produces a single value. Then each P.Mem collects all the values from each local memory block and produces a single value for the whole chip. Finally the P.Host collects all the values from each chip and produces the result value.

18.4.2 Optimizer

Query optimization is a complex problem. This problem becomes more difficult to solve when the objective is a parallel query execution plan. In our case, we add more complexity to the problem by having different versions of the same algorithm, depending on which processing element it executes. If data do not need to be repartitioned, the operation is executed on the P.Arrays. Otherwise, the optimizer needs to evaluate the cost/benefit of using the P.Arrays as opposed to using the P.Mems, which offer a smaller degree of parallelism but require no data repartitioning.

In our implementation, we used a 2-step parallel query optimizer, as suggested for the XPRS system [30]: first we use the information of the best serial query execution plan for the ordering of the operations and then we select the algorithm for each operation based on our simple mathematical cost models.

These simple models account for memory accesses and computation operations for the FlexRAM architecture. The number of memory accesses was obtained by analyzing the set of instructions necessary for the algorithm to operate correctly. These models are very simple and do not account for effects such as caching. We assume a uniform distribution of data which also means that when data need to be repartitioned, the probability that a data element is in the correct place is $\frac{1}{N}$ if N is the total number of possible destinations. To understand these models, we describe below the cost model for the Hash Join on the P.Array processors (*HJa*). For this description, we assume that c is the number of FlexRAM chips in the system, n is the number of P.Arrays per FlexRAM chip, and a and b are the total number of tuples for tables A and B respectively. Because write operations to data within and across the chip have different latencies, we use Wr and Wr^*, respectively.

HJa. As was previously described, this algorithm is composed of two steps: data repartition and join. Each of these is further divided into two phases: data separation and data move for the data repartition, and build and probe for the join. The data separation step requires each P.Array to read its local data for both tables ($\frac{a+b}{n \times c}$). For the data move step each P.Array will read the neighboring *Left* and *Right* bins multiple times. Notice that due to the uniform data distribution the *Local* portion of the data will be $\frac{1}{n \times c}$ of the original, the *Remote* portion will be $\frac{n \times c - n}{n \times c}$ of the original, and the *Left* and *Right* portions will each be $\frac{n-1}{2 \times n \times c}$ of the original. Because both P.Array and P.Mem operate in parallel during the data move step, the cost will be the larger of the two. After the data are repartitioned, each P.Array operates independently on its local data. First it builds the hash table ($\frac{b}{n \times c}$ data elements) and finally it uses the data from the other table ($\frac{a}{n \times c}$ data elements) to probe the hash table and find matching tuples. We consider the *join factor* (*jf*) as the ratio between the product of the size of the two input tables and the size of the result table. The cost model for this algorithm can be expressed as presented in Figure 18.3.

18.4.3 Validation

To validate the prototype system designed for this work, we compared the execution for both the FlexDB system and PostgreSQL [23, 29], an open-source database system. The workload used is composed of queries 1, 3, 9, 20, and 21 from the Wisconsin Benchmark [8]. These queries include all the basic operations: sequential and index scans, join, aggregate, and group. Three sets of different data sizes were used ranging from the original size (650 kB) up to twenty times larger (13 MB). The execution was performed on a PC equipped with an AMD Athlon 1.1 GHz processor

$$Cost(HJa) = DataSeparation + DataMove + Build + Probe$$

$$DataSeparation = \frac{a+b}{n \times c} \times (Rd + Hash + Compare + Wr)$$

$$DataMove(P.Array) = \frac{n^{n+1} - n \times (n-1)^n - 1}{n \times c^2} \times (a+b) \times$$
$$(Rd + Hash + Compare + Wr)$$

$$DataMove(P.Mem) = \frac{c-1}{c^2} \times (a+b) \times (Rd + Hash + Wr^*)$$

$$DataMove = \max(DataMove(P.Array), DataMove(P.Mem))$$

$$Build = \frac{b}{n \times c} \times (Rd + Hash + Wr)$$

$$Probe = \frac{a}{n \times c} \times (Rd + Hash + Compare) + \frac{a}{n \times c} \times \frac{b}{n \times c} \times jf \times Wr$$

Fig. 18.3. Cost model for P.Array Hash Join.

with 128 MB RAM, running Red Hat Linux 7.1. The measurements of the execution cycles were done using the processor's performance counters.

The results obtained were very satisfactory. Although the absolute execution time is different for the two systems, as the data size is increased, the execution time for both systems scales in the same way. For four out of five queries, the drift in the scaling between the two systems is on average 5%. In absolute values, on average, a query running on FlexDB executes 25 times faster than a query executing on PostgreSQL. An exception to these results occurs for the query that uses the index scan algorithm, which executes 400 times faster in FlexDB. We attribute this result to the difference between the implementation of the two algorithms as one handles data resident on disk and the other memory-resident data.

18.5 Experimental Setup

18.5.1 Hardware

In this work, we simulate a system architecture similar to what was shown in Figure 18.1-b. The simulation environment is a MINT-based [33] execution-driven simulator that is able to model dynamic superscalar processors [18]. In this environment, for each processing element we have a thread of execution.

The system is configured with a main processor, the P.Host, and one or more FlexRAM chips, each one including one P.Mem and several P.Array processors. In the baseline system configuration, the FlexRAM chip contains 8 basic blocks composed of 4 P.Array processors and each one with its own 4 MB DRAM memory.

The details of the different computation elements are summarized in Table 18.1. In addition, the memory latency of this system for a row buffer miss is 88 cycles from the P.Host and 14 cycles from the P.Mem. For a row buffer hit, the latencies are 82 cycles from the P.Host and 8 cycles from the P.Mem. The system bus modeled supports split transactions and is 16 B wide.

We model traditional systems, for both single processor and shared-memory multiprocessor configurations, using the same simulation setup but by having only the

Table 18.1. Parameters used in the simulation for the FlexRAM system.

	P.Host	P.Mem	P.Array
Freq	800 MHz	800 MHz	800 MHz
Issue Width Issue Width	out-of-order 6-issue	in-order 2-issue	in-order single-issue
Func. Units	3Int, 3FP, 2Ld/St	2Int, 1FP, 1Ld/St	1Int, 1FP, 1Ld/St
Pending Ld/St	8/16	4/8	1/1
Branch Penalty	4 clk	2 clk	1 clk
L1 Data Cache	write-through, 32-Kbyte, 4-way, 32-byte line, 1-clk hit	write-back, 8-Kbyte, 2-way, 32-byte line, 1-clk hit	---
L2 Data Cache	write-back, 256-Kbyte, 4-way, 64-byte line, 8-clk hit	---	---

P.Host processors active. The number of P.Host processors determines the number of processors in the traditional system setup.

Since our current simulator supports only a single-chip configuration, we emulate systems with multiple chips by loading only a fraction of the total data into the simulated chip's memory area. Notice that this simple emulation is valid because there is no operation where two processing units in distinct chips request in parallel an update to the same data element. Therefore, there are no coherency problems.

Notice that although the clock frequency value for the FlexRAM chip may seem too aggressive (800 MHz), previous works have reported that it is possible to integrate DRAM and on-chip logic that is as fast as logic-only chips by having a small penalty of 10% in the density compared to memory-only chips [14, 20].

18.5.2 Database System and Application

The database system used in this work is the FlexDB prototype as described in Section 18.4. To obtain the serial query execution plans, we use PostgreSQL version 6.5 [23].

For this work, we studied three different queries from the standard TPC-H [7] Decision Support Benchmark. This benchmark represents a complex business analysis application for an industry that manages, sells, and distributes products worldwide. For this work we selected a query that operates on a single table (Q6), a query that operates on two tables (Q12), and a query that operates on three tables (Q3).

In this study, we consider the database to be memory-resident. This fact does not seem to be a limitation because of the developments in hiding IO latency as described by Barroso et al. [3]. Therefore, for the 128 MB memory capacity, we used a database size of 100 MB for both Q6 and Q12. Due to Q3's longer running time and memory overhead for the data repartition operations, we scaled down the data size to 50 MB for that query only.

18.6 Experimental Results

In Table 18.2, we present the execution cycles for single-processor execution (P.Host) for each query, broken down into three categories: *Busy*, which accounts for the useful instructions; *Memory*, which accounts for the waiting of memory requests; and *Hazard*, which accounts for stalls in the pipeline due to hazards.

Table 18.2. Single-processor execution cycles.

	Busy	Memory	Hazard	Total
Q3	646592	4199033	1163759	6009384
Q6	984737	6002951	1710669	8698357
Q12	1167544	7575693	2654610	11397847

The values in the table are to be used as a reference for the results presented in the following sections.

18.6.1 Intra-Chip Parallelism

One of the objectives of this work is to evaluate the design space for the FlexRAM chip, in particular the most appropriate configuration in terms of the number of P.Array processors per chip, for database workloads.

In Figure 18.4 we present the speedup for the FlexRAM approach compared to the single-processor configuration. We show the speedup values for the three queries (Q3, Q6, and Q12) for FlexRAM with 8, 16, 32, and 64 P.Arrays per chip. In addition, we present the average speedup for each configuration.

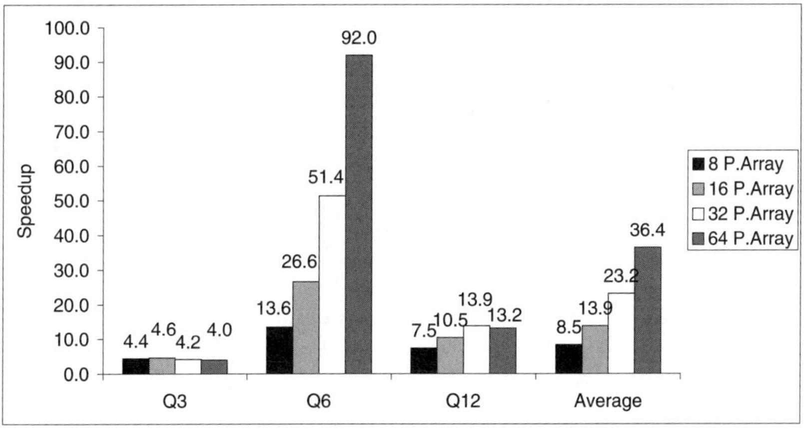

Fig. 18.4. Speedup for different FlexRAM configurations: 8, 16, 32, and 64 P.Arrays.

The query that shows the largest speedup values is Q6. These values, which range from 13.6 for the 8 P.Array configuration to 92.0 for the 64 P.Array configuration, are larger than the linear speedup, considering the number of P.Array processors. We attribute this to the higher memory bandwidth and lower memory latency for the P.Array processors when compared to a traditional system configuration.

For the other two queries the speedup values are smaller. For Q12 we observe speedup values ranging from 7.5 to 13.9, while for Q3 the speedup values range from 4.0 to 4.6. Notice that for both queries the larger speedup values are not achieved for the configurations with the largest number of P.Array processors. Consequently, the benefit of increasing the number of P.Array processors does not seem to be as relevant for these two queries. We identify three factors that inhibit larger speedup values. First, the data repartitioning becomes a bottleneck. Second, the restricted amount of data input for operations at a higher level of the query plan reduces the amount of potential parallelism. Third, for some operations the data are skewed, creating load imbalance.

We performed a detailed analysis of the execution for query Q12 and we observed a large amount of load imbalance. This load imbalance occurs for the data partition operation of one of the tables in the join (*Orders*). We may conclude that configurations with a large number of P.Array processors have a larger probability of generating data skew and load imbalance and the data exchange operations become more costly.

Regarding the system's configuration, although the average speedup for the three queries achieves its highest value of 36.4 for a FlexRAM chip configuration with 64 P.Array processors, the configuration that presents the best balance seems to be the one with 32 P.Array processors.

Overall, the results show that the FlexRAM/FlexDB approach has a large potential, in particular for simple queries such as Q6. In addition to the smaller latency and larger bandwidth, the large number of simple processing elements available in the FlexRAM chip seems to be a major advantage. The moderate results obtained for the more complex queries show that not only must the applications be carefully partitioned but also that the limited connectivity between the P.Array processors seems to be one limitation of this architecture.

18.6.2 Inter-Chip Parallelism

In addition to the parallelism obtained from the P.Array processors in a chip, we need to explore the cases where the system contains multiple FlexRAM chips. In Figure 18.5(a) we present the speedup values for two of the three queries (Q6 and Q12) for system configurations with one, two, and four FlexRAM chips, with 32 P.Array processors each. Due to its complexity and running time, we do not present the results for query Q3.

These results show again that query Q6 scales well—almost linearly. Query Q12 also improves its performance but at a smaller rate. The limitations presented in the previous section also apply to this case. One important fact that can be observed from these results is that the speedup values for the queries are larger for a system with 2 FlexRAM chips of 32 P.Array processors each compared to a single FlexRAM chip with 64 P.Array processors (see Figure 18.4). One reason for these results is the fact that each P.Array handles less data during data repartitioning, as part of it is remote and handled in parallel by the P.Mems.

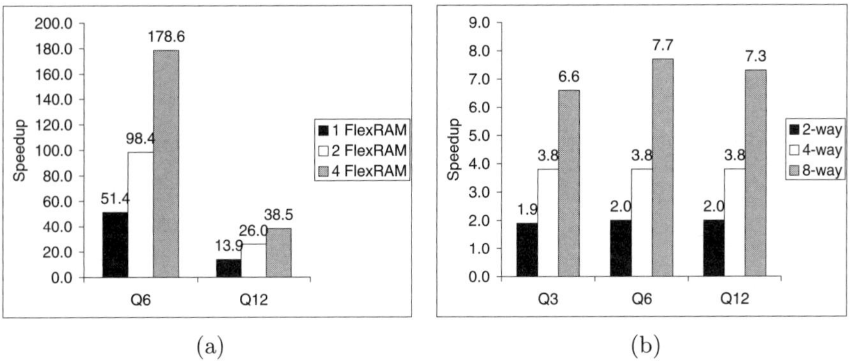

Fig. 18.5. Speedup for different system configurations: (a) 1, 2, and 4 FlexRAM chips; and (b) 2-way, 4-way, and 8-way shared-memory multiprocessors.

18.6.3 Traditional Systems

In this section, we present a comparison between our approach and a traditional shared-memory multiprocessor. In Figure 18.5(b) we show the speedup values for the three queries when executing on 2-way, 4-way, and 8-way shared-memory multiprocessors. From the results, we can observe that the speedup values increase almost linearly with the increasing number of processors in the system. This linear increase occurs for all queries. Consequently, we may conclude that this system configuration adapts better to the limitations previously described (data repartition bottleneck, restricted data at higher-level operations, data skew, and load imbalance). The fact that this type of application scales well for shared-memory configurations has already been previously reported by Barroso et al. [4].

One objective of this work is to compare the speedup achieved by a traditional shared-memory system with the one achieved by a system configured with FlexRAM chips. In reality, we are comparing the performance of two different approaches: a small number of powerful processors versus a large number of simple processors. In order to achieve this goal, we need to find system configurations of similar price and compare their performances. As we do not have any pricing information on the FlexRAM chip, we will use the die area as an estimate of the cost. According to the FlexRAM designers [15], each P.Mem processor occupies 12 mm^2 and each P.Array occupies 1.5 mm^2, using 0.18-micron technology. Consequently, for our baseline FlexRAM configuration, the processing area overhead of the chip (1 P.Mem and 32 P.Arrays) accounts for $60mm^2$. Therefore, we may argue that a comparable shared-memory system is a 5-way system configured with 5 P.Mem processors. Notice that with this same area we are not able to build a shared-memory system using P.Host processors, as their area is much larger. For example, the AMD Athlon XP Palomino core requires 128 mm^2 in 0.18-micron technology [12]. While this analysis ignores the increased cost of production of an Intelligent Memory chip and the fact that a large chip may have a worse yield, the results presented in Figure 18.4 show that, for two out of the three queries, the FlexRAM system achieves speedup values even larger than the 8-way shared-memory configuration. In particular, the speedup values for the single FlexRAM system are 1.9 to 6.7 times the ones achieved for an

8-way shared-memory system and 3.7 to 13.5 times the ones achieved for a 4-way shared-memory system. The only query that does not achieve higher speedup values is Q3.

In conclusion, although a traditional shared-memory multiprocessor system may achieve near linear speedup, which is beneficial for complex queries and when data are skewed, a FlexRAM configuration can, in most cases, achieve a higher speedup. For simpler queries, the speedup reaches an order of magnitude.

18.7 Conclusion and Future Work

In this work, we focused on exploiting the features of a proposed Intelligent Memory chip, FlexRAM, for database workloads. This chip has the advantage of containing a memory processor that can access any location in the memory and several small processing units that are only able to access their local memory blocks.

In this chapter, we presented a simple prototype DBMS called FlexDB that was designed to exploit the features of FlexRAM. FlexDB contains modified parallel database algorithms that map to the new architecture and an efficient data redistribution algorithm. In addition, we developed simple mathematical models to choose between the algorithms for the different processing elements.

We tested FlexDB using three queries from the TPC-H benchmark on a system configured with FlexRAM chips with up to 64 processing elements and a total memory size large enough to fit the whole database. Compared to a single-processor system, the speedup values were between 4 and 92. These results also scaled well for configurations with an increasing number of FlexRAM chips. While comparing the speedup values of the FlexRAM system to a shared-memory multiprocessor, we observed that for two out of the three queries our approach achieves a speedup between 4 and an order of magnitude. This leads us to conclude that although FlexRAM has limited connectivity between the processing elements, the high degree of parallelism, high bandwidth, and low latency offered by FlexRAM result in large speedup values compared to traditional approaches.

We are currently studying ways to further improve the performance of our system. In particular, we need to study the problems with data skew and load balancing for complex queries. In addition, we are exploiting the area of extending the connectivity between the P.Array elements.

Acknowledgments

We would like to thank the graduate students from the I-ACOMA group for their help with the installation and use of the FlexRAM simulator. For this work, P. Trancoso was partially sponsored, through a Visiting Scholar grant, by the I-ACOMA group, Computer Science Department, University of Illinois at Urbana-Champaign.

References

1. M. Acharya, M. Uysal, and J. Saltz. Active Disks: Programming Model, Algorithms and Evaluation. In *Proceedings of ASPLOS VIII*, pages 81–91, 1998.

2. A. Ailamaki, D. DeWitt, M. Hill, and D. Wood. DBMSs on a modern processor: where does time go? In *Proceedings of the 25th VLDB Conference*, pages 266–277, 1999.
3. L. Barroso, K. Gharachorloo, and E. Bugnion. Memory System Characterization of Commercial Workloads. In *Proceedings of the 25th International Symposium on Computer Architecture*, pages 3–14, 1998.
4. L. Barroso, K. Gharachorloo, R. McNamara, A. Nowatzyk, S. Qadeer, B. Sano, S. Smith, R. Stets, and B. Verghese. Piranha: A Scalable Architecture Based on Single-Chip Multiprocessing. In *Proceedings of the 27th International Symposium on Computer Architecture*, pages 282–293, 2000.
5. P. Boncz, S. Manegold, and M. Kersten. Database Architecture Optimized for the new Bottleneck: Memory Access. In *Proceedings of the 25th VLDB Conference*, pages 54–65, 1999.
6. D. Burger and J. Goodman. Guest Editors' Introduction: Billion-Transistor Architectures. *IEEE Computer Magazine*, 30(9):46–49, September 1997.
7. Transaction Processing Performance Council. TPC Benchmark^{TM} H (Decision Support), Standard Specification, June 1999.
8. D. DeWitt. The Wisconsin Benchmark: Past, Present, and Future. In J. Gray, editor, *The Benchmark Handbook*. Morgan Kaufmann Publishers, San Mateo, CA, 1991.
9. D. DeWitt, R. Gerber, G. Graefe, M. Heytens, K. Kumar, and M. Muralikrishna. GAMMA: A High Performance Dataflow Database Machine. In *Proceedings of the VLDB Conference*, pages 228–237, 1986.
10. D. Elliot, W. Snelgrove, and M. Stumm. Computational Ram: A Memory-SIMD Hybrid and its Application to DSP. In *Proceedings of the Custom Integrated Circuits Conference*, pages 30.6.1–30.6.4, 1992.
11. G. Graefe. Query Evaluation Techniques for Large Databases. *ACM Computing Surveys*, 25(2):73–170, June 1993.
12. Tom's Hardware Guide. A New Kind of Fast: AMD Athlon XP 2200+. http://www6.tomshardware.com/cpu/02q2/020610/thoroughbred-07.html.
13. M. Hall, P. Kogge, J. Koller, P. Diniz, J. Chame, J. Draper, J. LaCoss, J. Granacki, J. Brockman, A. Srivastava, W. Athas, V. Freeh, J. Shin, and J. Park. Mapping Irregular Applications to DIVA, a PIM-based Data-Intensive Architecture. In *Proceedings of Supercomputing 1999*, 1999.
14. S. Iyer and H. Kalter. Embedded DRAM Technology: Opportunities and Challenges. *IEEE Spectrum*, pages 56–64, April 1999.
15. Y. Kang, W. Huang, S.-M. Yoo, D. Keen, Z. Ge, V. Lam, P. Pattnaik, and J. Torrellas. FlexRAM: Toward an Advanced Intelligent Memory System. In *Proceedings of the 1999 International Conference on Computer Design*, pages 192–201, 1999.
16. K. Keeton, D. Patterson, and J. Hellerstein. A Case for Intelligent Disks (IDISKs). *SIGMOD Record*, 27(3):42–53, August 1998.
17. D. Knuth. *Sorting and Searching*, volume III of *The Art of Computer Programming*. Addison-Wesley, Reading, MA, 1973.
18. V. Krishnan and J. Torrellas. An Execution-Driven Framework for Fast and Accurate Simulation of Superscalar Processors. In *Proceedings of the Parallel Architecture and Compilation Techniques*, 1998.
19. K. Mai, T. Paaske, N. Jayasena, R. Ho, and M. Horowitz. Smart Memories: A Modular Reconfigurable Architecture. In *Proceedings of the 27th International Symposium on Computer Architecture*, pages 161–171, 2000.
20. IBM Microelectronics. Blue Logic SA-27E ASIC. *News and Ideas of IBM Microelectronics*, February 1999.

21. M. Oskin, F. Chong, and T. Sherwood. Active Pages: A Computation Model for Intelligent Memory. In *Proceedings of the 1998 International Symposium on Computer Architecture*, pages 192–203, 1998.
22. D. Patterson, T. Anderson, N. Cardwell, R. Fromm, K. Keeton, C. Kozyrakis, R. Thomas, and K. Yelick. A Case for Intelligent DRAM. *IEEE Micro*, 17(2):33–44, March/April 1997.
23. PostgreSQL. http://www.postgresql.org.
24. J. Rao and K.A. Ross. Cache Conscious Indexing for Decision-Support in Main Memory. In *Proceedings of the VLDB Conference*, pages 78–89, 1999.
25. S. Rixner, W. Dally, U. Kapasi, U. Khailany, A. Lopez-Lagunas, P. Matterson, and J. Owens. A Bandwidth-Efficient Architecture for Media Processing. In *Proceedings of the 31st Symposium on Microarchitecture*, pages 3–13, 1998.
26. Samsung. Embedded DRAM. http://www.usa.samsungsemi.com/products/asic/embedde dram.htm.
27. Mitsubishi Semiconductors. eRAM. http://www.mitsubishichips.com/eram/eram.html.
28. A. Shatdal, C. Kant, and J.F. Naughton. Cache Conscious Algorithms for Relational Query Processing. In *Proceedings of the 20th VLDB Conference*, pages 510–521, 1994.
29. M. Stonebraker. The Design of the POSTGRES Storage System. In *Proceedings of the VLDB Conference*, pages 289–300, 1987.
30. M. Stonebraker, P. Aoki, and M. Seltzer. The Design of XPRS. In *Proceedings of the VLDB Conference*, pages 318–330, 1988.
31. P. Trancoso, J-L. Larriba-Pey, Z. Zhang, and J. Torrellas. The Memory Performance of DSS Commercial Workloads in Shared-Memory Multiprocessors. In *Proceedings of the Third International Symposium on High-Performance Computer Archithecture*, 1997.
32. P. Trancoso and J. Torrellas. Cache Optimization for Memory-Resident Decision Support Commercial Workloads. In *Proceedings of the 1999 International Conference on Computer Design*, pages 546–555, 1999.
33. J. Veenstra and R. Fowler. MINT: A Front End for Efficient Simulation of Shared-Memory Multiprocessors. In *Proceedings of MASCOTS'94*, pages 201–207, 1994.
34. E. Waingold, M. Taylor, D. Srikrishna, V. Sarkar, W. Lee, V. Lee, J. Kim, M. Frank, P. Finch, R. Barua, J. Babb, S. Amarasinghe, and A. Agarwal. Baring it all to Software: Raw Machines. *IEEE Computer*, 30(9):86–93, September 1997.

Author Index

Subject Index